# CliffsNotes®

# Praxis II Elementary Education (0011/5011, 0012, 0014/5014) with CD-ROM

## 2ND EDITION

*by*
*Jocelyn L. Paris, M.Ed.*
*and Judy L. Paris, M.Ed.*

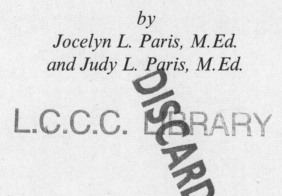

WILEY

John Wiley & Sons, Inc.

*CliffsNotes*® Praxis II Elementary Education (0011/5011, 0012, 0014/5014) with CD-ROM, 2ⁿᵈ Edition

Published by:
**John Wiley & Sons, Inc.**
111 River Street
Hoboken, NJ 07030-5774
www.wiley.com

Copyright © 2012 John Wiley & Sons, Inc., Hoboken, NJ

Published by John Wiley & Sons, Inc., Hoboken, NJ
Published simultaneously in Canada

Library of Congress Control Number: 2012936851
ISBN: 978-1-118-10439-2 (pbk)
ISBN: 978-1-118-23721-2; 978-1-118-22394-9; 978-1-118-26219-1 (ebk)

Printed in the United States of America

10 9 8 7 6 5 4 3 2 1

For general information on our other products and services or to obtain technical support, please contact our Customer Care Department within the U.S. at (877) 762-2974, outside the U.S. at (317) 572-3993, or fax (317) 572-4002.

John Wiley & Sons, Inc., also publishes its books in a variety of electronic formats and by print-on-demand. Not all content that is available in standard print versions of this book may appear or be packaged in all book formats. If you have purchased a version of this book that did not include media that is referenced by or accompanies a standard print version, you may request this media by visiting http://booksupport.wiley.com. For more information about Wiley products, visit us at www.wiley.com.

Updates to this book are available on the Downloads tab at this site: http://www.wiley.com/WileyCDA/WileyTitle/productcd-11181043390.html. If a Downloads tab does not appear at this link, there are no updates at this time.

# About the Authors

**Jocelyn** has had a colorful and enriching life centered on teaching. She graduated with a B.A. from the University of Arizona and obtained her Master's in Elementary Education at Northern Arizona University. She has taught preschool through high school age students ranging in all abilities from severe to profound mentally retarded to deaf to gifted to emotionally and behaviorally challenged. Jocelyn has taught in a multitude of settings as well: public school, charter school, residential school for the deaf and blind, private school, and Montessori school. She also is author of *Idioms*, published by Butte Publications, Inc. Jocelyn loves to coach sports and has coached basketball, volleyball, and soccer for elementary through high school varsity teams. One of her true passions lies with Camp Abilities, a fundamentally appropriate sports camp for the Visually Impaired. She has been involved in these camps for the past six years in Arizona, New York, and Alaska.

For more than 35 years, **Judy** has been professionally involved in the field of education as a teacher, a special education director, a superintendent, a consultant, an author, and a mentor and currently serves as adjunct faculty at several universities. She holds degrees and certifications in special education, early childhood education, elementary education, and educational leadership/administration. She has presented a paper at Oxford and was named Teacher of the Year. Although retired from public education, she currently creates plays for young children, develops college courses and exams, teaches in summer enrichment camps, conducts professional development workshops, and writes educational materials. It is because of her desire for all children to be allowed to learn through discovery, to be offered a variety of educational opportunities, and to experience the world around that has led to her newest endeavor of developing a children's museum for her community.

*Authors' Acknowledgments*

To Chip for always being in my back pocket; to Mabel for greeting me each day with a smile and kisses; to Haley for PB&J sammies; to Justin and Andrea for keeping me updated on the weather; to Gram and Gramp for coupons and jokes; to Mom and Dad for supporting and loving me; and to my students for keeping me young, making me old, listening to my stories, educating me, laughing at my jokes, and renewing my faith in the future. — Jocelyn L. Paris

To the most amazing educator I know, who awakes each day to instill knowledge in our youth, who yearns for a beautiful tomorrow, who strives to support the unfortunate, and who will make an enormous difference to future generations.... my Jocelyn. —Judy L. Paris

*Editorial*

**Acquisition Editor:** Greg Tubach

**Project Editors:** Kelly Dobbs Henthorne and Suzanne Snyder

**Copy Editor:** Lynn Northrup

**Technical Editors:** Jane Burstein, Carol Klages, Sandra McCune, Suzanne Snyder, Mary Jane Sterling, Agnes Yard, and Michael Yard

*Composition*

**Proofreader:** Jacqueline Brownstein

John Wiley & Sons, Inc., Composition Services

# Table of Contents

# PART IV: PRACTICE TESTS WITH ANSWER EXPLANATIONS

# Introduction

Although teaching is a rewarding profession, it can be difficult. Consistent reevaluation of teaching methods and ever-changing social attitudes toward education are always affecting the education profession. Examinees who have made it this far know that teaching requires a consistent increase in knowledge of the field. The Praxis exam is just one way to ensure that teachers have the core subject knowledge necessary to be teaching as well as the knowledge (curriculum, instruction, and assessment) needed in this profession. Individuals strive to become the best teachers possible, so studying for the Praxis exams is an important step. All good teachers prepare and do their homework!

As a Praxis II examinee, pat yourself on the back, as you have chosen an excellent study guide that will help you prepare for the Praxis II exam. It will also be useful in your elementary classroom for years to come as a resource for quick study of basic core knowledge. Taking the Praxis II exams should be the final stage toward the acquisition of teaching certification/license, so ensuring success by careful study is a positive move in an education career. The elementary Praxis II exams are focused on broad content knowledge, instructional theories, strategies and methods, as well as a general understanding of elementary students.

Effective educators utilize content knowledge and apply principles to classroom structure, behavior management, curriculum design, and assessments. Educators should seek current information on policies, research, and strategies. Joining professional organizations, reading research studies, taking university courses, attending professional development trainings, and subscribing to professional journals will help educators be more able to improve student programs.

Children in elementary schools possess individual strengths and specific needs. It is the educator's role to address both in an appropriate manner so that all children may learn and develop into capable citizens. Teachers must be creative, flexible, and confident as they work in educational settings, providing activities to students who possess a wide range of abilities. Working with elementary students can be stimulating yet demanding.

## Getting Started

Whether you are a recent college graduate or an experienced teacher, taking the Praxis II exam meets certain state certification requirements. The final score on the exam will reflect what has been gained from teacher preparation courses and from utilizing current teaching practices in the classroom. To prepare for the actual exam, examinees may also want to review college texts, conduct Internet research, or visit the library.

The practice tests offered in this guide provide information about the format and types of questions on the Praxis II elementary education exams. The content and questions in the practice tests and on the actual exams may differ in both substance and difficulty. After completing a practice test in this guide, examinees may use the answers and detailed explanations for further study on specific topics.

## Format of the Exam

Each Praxis II exam identified in this guide is designed to help individuals evaluate general content knowledge regarding the teaching of elementary students. The practice tests are a reflection of the actual exams. Each of the elementary practice tests included here is slightly different in composition. Two of the practice tests are comprised of a set of *multiple-choice questions,* although the number of questions varies. One test includes *essay exercises* that require more detailed narrative answers. All of the test questions are based on instructional situations, issues surrounding curriculum or assessment, or broad content knowledge pertinent to the education of elementary students.

Three general topics are related to the Praxis II elementary education exams described in this study guide, and each has an accompanying practice test. The specific code numbers and titles are listed here:

Elementary Education: Curriculum, Instruction, and Assessment (0011–written test, 5011–computerized test)

Elementary Education: Content Area Exercises (0012)

Elementary Education: Content Knowledge (0014–written test, 5014–computerized test)

# Multiple-Choice Questions

The multiple-choice questions found on the Praxis exams are designed to assess an individual's knowledge of the subject material taught at the elementary level. The multiple-choice questions are factually written, so examinees should think carefully when making final answer selections.

Multiple-choice questions include a **stem** (statement) and four answer choices, the correct answer being the **key.** The stem may be written in one of these formats: *question, statement, fill-in-the-blank, LEAST/EXCEPT choices, Roman numerals, or graphs/tables/reading passages*. The four answer choices that follow the stem are identified by letter selections "A," "B," "C," and "D." The three **distractors** may be related to the correct answer, but select only the best possible answer.

In both the practice test and the actual exam, some of the multiple-choice questions may be based on a scenario that resembles an actual classroom situation. Examinees should read the brief excerpt and think about how the posed questions should be answered in reference to only the information provided. Consider what an educator should do if placed in this particular circumstance.

# Multiple-Choice Format and Strategy

The exam questions reflect the *best practices* used in elementary education. To answer discrete multiple-choice questions correctly, strong reading skills are necessary. Reading with care to understand the basic premise of the question while remaining confident in the knowledge of the area tested is essential.

Prior to answering questions on the practice test or actual exam, read and then reread each question. Think about the selection before looking at the list of answer options. Check to see whether the choice selected is one of the four listed, which makes finding the best answer an easier task. If the information in the question is unknown, look at all of the options and use the process of elimination to remove any choices that seem impossible or not probable. That will help in selecting a correct answer from fewer choices.

The types of multiple-choice formats are as follows:

## Fill-in-the-Blank or Complete the Statement

This type of question offers information through a partial sentence that must be completed using one of the posed options. Select the best option to complete the sentence, using facts and data about elementary education.

## Question/Statement or Which of the Following . . .

This type of question poses a short question or delivers a statement that must be answered by selecting one of the four options provided. The most frequently used question type on multiple-choice exams is the question that begins with "Which of the following . . . ." To answer these, read the question carefully and think about all the options, choosing the one that BEST suits the question.

# LEAST/NOT/EXCEPT

This type of question requires the selection of an answer that is incorrect, or least likely to be correct. These questions place a negative slant on the outcome of the answer, so be careful when selecting the appropriate response. These questions require an examinee to decide which of the three options are correct answers, and then to eliminate those in order to determine the incorrect answer. One strategy to use is to restate the question in a positive way so the three correct answers may be selected, thereby leaving the fourth choice as the answer to be used.

For example:

> *Which of the following is NOT included on . . .*
>
> *Which is the LEAST likely . . .*
>
> *All of the following are true EXCEPT . . .*
>
> *Which choice is NOT a component of . . .*

The multiple-choice questions termed with "LEAST," "NOT," or "EXCEPT" are included on the Praxis II elementary education exams, but samples are **not** included in this guide on the practice tests, so examinees will study only the correct information in preparing for the Praxis II elementary education exam. These questions on the actual exam can be tricky, so use caution.

## Roman Numerals

This type of question format offers selections where more than one answer is included in the four choices. Examinees must read a list of several correct answers that are identified by Roman numerals. The examinee must choose the one final answer that includes all of the correct answers.

## Graphs/Tables/Reading Passages

In this type of question, examinees must first review additional materials, such as a graph, or they must read a selection prior to considering the exam question and selecting an answer. Once examinees study this additional information, they must carefully consider the question posed and the answers offered.

# Essay Writing 101

An essay is defined as a short piece of writing on a specific topic or subject. In an essay, the writer must present views clearly, concisely, and succinctly. The essay should contain an introduction, body, and conclusion as well as have well-supported opinions.

Essays should be well thought out in argument and content. The content provided must be supported by specific details with a clearly defined purpose. There are specific steps to use when writing an essay.

- *Analysis*—Clearly define the aims of the essay, include reasons, and give evidence or facts.
- *Main Point*—Pinpoint the main points and add supporting details.
- *Outline*—Sketch out the essay, jot down key points, and map out the structure of the arguments.
- *Introduction*—Grab the reader's attention, set up the issue, and lead into the argument. In a short essay (fewer than 1,000 words), after grabbing the reader's attention, begin describing a specific, concrete situation.
- *Body*—Focus on the argument or information in detail and present clear ideas and opinions.
- *Conclusion*—Use wrap-up sentences to conclude the essay. Restate or summarize the main point(s) in a fresh and rephrased manner in order to leave the reader with a memorable impression.

# Constructed-Response Questions

An essay exercise poses a complex problem related to elementary education in which the examinee must develop a written answer. Each of the essay questions presented relates to one of the four main subject areas, or it may pertain to the integrated subjects. The questions focus on instructional approaches, methods or strategies, solving problems, achieving goals, outlining curriculum, or addressing assessment.

Answers must be written in an exam answer booklet provided at the testing center. The essay answers will be scored using a predetermined, standardized grading rubric. Because the questions are not known prior to the exam, examinees must be careful to pace their writing while attending to the responses with all the necessary information.

Several strategies helpful to examinees for essay questions on the Praxis II elementary education exam follow:

- Read the question to be answered prior to reading the rest of the information given.
- Take notes while reading the essay question to help with forming an answer.
- Outline the ideas and content that are important to writing an essay answer.
- Think about the necessary details and focus on the accuracy of the answer.
- Develop a clear and concise narrative response specific to the situation.
- Review your response to be sure you answered all points.

It is very important for examinees to write clear, concise, complete answers and watch for questions that have more than one component, requiring multiple responses. If an essay answer is written in too simple a format, the answer may not receive full credit. The Praxis II elementary education exam that includes essay questions in this study guide is Elementary Education: Content Area Exercises (0012).

# Time Frame

The amount of time allowed for taking each Praxis II elementary education exam is based on the specific format of the individual exam. For the three Praxis II elementary education exams listed, examinees are allotted 2 hours to answer between 110 and 120 multiple-choice questions and 2 hours to answer 4 essay questions.

The specific exams, the number of questions, the format, and the time limits are as follows:

| Curriculum, Instruction, and Assessment (0011/5011) | 110 MC Questions | 2 hours |
| Content Area Exercises (0012) | 4 Essay Questions | 2 hours |
| Content Knowledge (0014/5014) | 120 MC Questions | 2 hours |

Examinees should practice pacing themselves prior to taking the actual exam. They should consider the time needed when taking the practice test. When taking the actual Praxis II elementary education exam, examinees need time to read each question, to consider each answer, and to review all of the final possible selections before submitting the exam for a score. When writing an essay answer, examinees need time to read the question, consider the formation of a narrative answer, take the time to write the answer, and then review the answer prior to submission.

When faced with multiple-choice questions, examinees must consider all of the possibilities and select the most appropriate response. If an examinee is unsure of the correct response for a multiple-choice question, an answer to the question should still be made as there is no penalty for guessing exam answers. On the essay questions, examinees should make every attempt to develop a thorough and thoughtful response in a narrative format.

# Content of the Exam

Each of the specific Praxis II elementary education exams identified in this guide are comprised of content categories, and the actual exams assess an examinee's understanding of the concepts and the applications of the concepts related to these specific content categories.

This general list outlines the broad exam topics, the number of questions, and the percentage of the final score that is dedicated to that content section for each exam.

## Elementary Education: Curriculum, Instruction, and Assessment (0011/5011)

| | | |
|---|---|---|
| Reading and Language Arts Curriculum, Instruction, and Assessment | 38 | 35% |
| Mathematics Curriculum, Instruction, and Assessment | 22 | 20% |
| Science Curriculum, Instruction, and Assessment | 11 | 10% |
| Social Studies Curriculum, Instruction, and Assessment | 11 | 10% |
| Arts and Physical Education Curriculum, Instruction, and Assessment | 11 | 10% |
| General Information About Curriculum, Instruction, and Assessment | 17 | 15% |

## Elementary Education: Content Area Exercises (0012)

| | | |
|---|---|---|
| Reading/Language Arts | 1 | 25% |
| Mathematics | 1 | 25% |
| Science or Social Studies | 1 | 25% |
| Interdisciplinary Instruction | 1 | 25% |

## Elementary Education: Content Knowledge (0014/5014)

| | | |
|---|---|---|
| Language Arts | 30 | 25% |
| Mathematics | 30 | 25% |
| Social Studies | 30 | 25% |
| Science | 30 | 25% |

# Note to Examinees

The content of these two examinations (0011/5011 and 0014/5014) remains the same, so studying should not differ. However, the method of test taking will differ, so examinees need to consider their personal test-taking skills regarding a paper-delivered (handwritten) exam or a computer-delivered exam.

Examinees may prepare for all three of these Praxis II elementary education exams, 0011/5011, 0012, and 0014/5014, by using the content provided in this study guide. The book contains one practice test for each of the three Praxis II elementary education exams and the attached CD contains two practice tests for each exam (one from the current book and one that appears only on the CD).

Since the content of these three Praxis II elementary education exams is so closely related, examinees would benefit from studying all of the sections of this study guide prior to taking any of the three Praxis II elementary education exams: 0011/5011, 0012, or 0014/5014.

# Frequently Asked Questions

Examinees generally have questions prior to taking a Praxis II elementary education exam, and the following questions are presented as those most commonly posed. However, if an examinee needs further assistance, check the Educational Testing Service at www.ets.org/praxis or call 1-800-772-9476.

**Q.  What are the Praxis II elementary education exams about?**

**A.**  The Praxis II elementary education exams have been developed by the Educational Testing Service (ETS) to measure an individual's knowledge in specific topic areas related to elementary education. These topics include general education content and practices that measure the knowledge of prospective teachers. Many states require these examinations in order to complete the certification or licensure process for professional practice. Some professional organizations also may require the completion of one or more Praxis exams for membership.

**Q.  How should an examinee register for a Praxis II exam?**

**A.**  Most individuals find that registering online is quick and easy. Contact the Educational Testing Service on their website or at the telephone number listed previously. Registration may be completed any time prior to taking the test, but it is recommended that registration be completed 1–3 months ahead of the testing date.

**Q.  What if an examinee misses the registration period for the preferred test date?**

**A.**  Late registration is allowed, but there may be a fee added for late registration. Examinees should hurry to be situated for the correct exam and obtain a seat at the test location. Check specific information about late registration on the ETS website.

**Q.  Can the registration date be changed if needed?**

**A.**  Contact ETS as soon as possible if a conflict or problem arises with confirmed registration dates. ETS should be able to help with scheduling issues or changes to the existing registration, but remember, a fee may be incurred.

**Q.  Which states require the Praxis II elementary education exams for certification?**

**A.**  Some states use certification tests developed by the state or by a separate testing company, and these states do not require the use of the Praxis II elementary education exams. Contact the specific Department of Education to find out which exams are required in each state of interest. Ask about the scores considered as passing, since acceptable scores differ among states. If an examinee has already taken the exam in one state and is moving to another state, the individual should ask whether the current score will be accepted. Most states will allow the transfer of a score as long as it meets the required passing score in that state and the score is recent.

On the ETS website (www.ets.org/praxis/states) examinees may access specific requirements by clicking on the name of that state. However, it is highly recommended to speak with someone at the state department of education, because regulations sometimes change before websites are updated.

**Q.  How does an examinee know which exam should be taken?**

**A.**  States mandating Praxis II elementary education exams for certification or licensure differ on the type of exam required. Research these requirements by contacting the Department of Education in the particular state. The teacher certification office should have the information needed to select the correct exam or combination of exams.

**Q.  What is considered a passing score for teacher certification?**

**A.**  The teacher certification office at the Department of Education in each state should provide the score considered acceptable for passing. Contact this office in the specific state to find out which score is adequate for teacher certification.

**Q.** **When can examinees expect to receive the scores?**

**A.** ETS attempts a quick return of scores, so expect the scores to be delivered in four to six weeks, pending no major holidays. A list of dates is available on the ETS website, as well as an informational guide to interpret the score received.

**Q.** **Are accommodations permissible for an individual with a disability or primary language concerns?**

**A.** Yes. Individuals may apply for nonstandard exam accommodations if they have a disability according to the Americans with Disabilities Act qualifying requirements or if a test-taker has a documented health need. Information on accommodations is available online on the ETS website. Accommodations for examinees whose primary language is not English should check online for current information about eligibility and documentation.

**Q.** **What should examinees plan to bring to the exam site on the date of the test?**

**A.** Examinees need to bring the following:

- Identification that includes name, a photo, and signature
- A second form of identification that includes the same information (optional but recommended)
- Proof of registration
- Several sharpened #2 pencils and an eraser
- Ink pens for essay answers (some exams)
- Watch (optional but recommended)
- Extra clothing (optional but recommended, as room temperatures may vary)

**Q.** **How can examinees best prepare to take a Praxis II elementary education exam?**

**A.** Using this study guide should help improve the chances of passing a Praxis II elementary education exam. Understanding the exam format, taking the practice tests, and reviewing the contents of the study guide should reinforce an examinee's base of knowledge.

# Using This Study Guide

*CliffsNotes Praxis II: Elementary Education* includes several supports to help guide examinees:

- **Overview Curriculum, Instruction, and Assessment Section (0011/5011):** This section includes information that supports all subject areas of elementary education. This section outlines learning theories and guidelines for developing curriculum, preparing lessons, managing the classroom, and implementing assessments.
- **Curriculum, Instruction, and Assessment Information (0011/5011):** This section pertains to the specific subject areas covered in the exam (0011/5011): language arts, mathematics, science, social studies, and arts and physical education.
- **Overview Content Area Exercises (0012):** This section includes examples of exam questions for the four major subjects found on the exam (0012).
- **Overview Content Knowledge Information (0014/5014):** This comprehensive section for each subject area should be used to study the specific content categories described in the exam (0014/5014).
- **Final Thoughts and Tips:** A review of the test-taking strategies is provided with tips for test preparation to aid in achieving exam success.
- **Practice Tests:** A sample full-length written test is provided for each of the three separate topics in elementary education. These tests are offered as a guide regarding the content and format of the actual Praxis II elementary education exam. An added study tool to the practice tests are the answers with detailed justifications for each correct answer.
- **CD-Rom Practice Tests:** A sample full-length computer-based test is provided for each of the three separate topics.

# CURRICULUM, INSTRUCTION, AND ASSESSMENT (0011/5011)

# Chapter 1
# Overview Curriculum, Instruction, and Assessment (0011/5011)

The Praxis II exam (0011/5011) covers a broad-based set of materials related to the common subjects taught at the elementary education level. In a multiple-choice format, this two-hour exam includes 110 questions centered on language arts, mathematics, science, social studies, fine arts, and physical education. The questions are related to curriculum planning, instructional design, and the assessment of students.

The breakdown of the content categories for the Curriculum, Instruction, and Assessment exam is as follows:

| Reading and Language Arts | 38 Questions | 35% |
|---|---|---|
| Mathematics | 22 Questions | 20% |
| Science | 11 Questions | 10% |
| Social Studies | 11 Questions | 10% |
| Arts and Physical Education | 11 Questions | 10% |
| General Information | 17 Questions | 15% |

The materials included in this section pertain primarily to the general information of curriculum, instruction, and assessment, but this information may also be applied directly to specific elementary topics or subject areas (science, math, language arts, social studies, and integrated subjects). Examinees may also want to study the content-specific section for each of four main subject areas in this guide in Chapters 8–12.

Examinees should be knowledgeable in all subject areas, as well as with the general aspects of the educational process. Review of previously learned concepts, an understanding of educational practices, and the ability to apply those concepts and practices will enable the examinee to acquire a satisfactory score on the Praxis II.

Remember that to enhance the academic process, educators should do the following:

- Acknowledge the theories of development and learning, incorporating them into a personal philosophy.
- Gain knowledge about the core subjects at the elementary level.
- Design and plan effective instruction that encompasses all learners.
- Encourage students to be active participants in creating the learning environment, activities, and experiences.
- Promote learning opportunities that allow students to interact with adults and work cooperatively with others.
- Utilize multiple instructional strategies and a variety of methods.
- Provide adequate materials and developmentally appropriate activities and experiences.
- Instill the use of critical thinking skills, problem-solving skills, and decision-making skills in daily activities.
- Manage behaviors through positive situations, modeling, and training.

Curriculum, instruction, and assessment are the critical elements of educational programming in all subject areas.

Curriculum is *what* is taught.

Instruction is *how* it is taught.

Assessment examines *whether* it was taught and *how well* it was learned.

## Knowledge and Understanding of Human Development

In order to adequately and effectively educate children, teachers must be knowledgeable about the stages and theories related to human development. There are long-standing thoughts about human development and contemporary ideas focused on current research and observation. Educators should review the content of these concepts about human development to better understand how children evolve in the early stages. This review will aid teachers in creating a positive classroom environment and incorporating the theories of learning into instructional delivery.

Study the following theories that relate to human development. There are other human development theories, but these are the most commonly known. Search for others through college texts, online, or by using library resources.

## Constructivism—Piaget

A popular early theory of human development, **constructivism** implies that learning evolves and becomes more complex and more complete over time as individuals build upon prior knowledge, which is often based on previous experiences. Jean Piaget was instrumental in describing that children develop by constructing or building knowledge based on what is already known. He believed that disequilibrium, equilibrium, and assimilation (and sometimes accommodation) are steps in the process of constructing knowledge.

The two principles of this theory are as follows:

1. Learning is an individualized process and individuals may learn different things from the same experience.
2. Learners must be active in the learning process in order for them to gain from the experience.

## Socio-Cultural or Social Development—Vygotsky

This theory was defined by the Russian psychologist Lev Vygotsky, who based it on the idea that when children have assistance with learning, they can do more collaboratively than by themselves. He thought that the development of higher order functions (such as cognitive skills and communication abilities) in an individual stem from social interactions. Vygotsky described the **zone of proximal development** as the difference between what a child can do on his or her own and what that child can do with assistance, whether it is from an adult or a peer. Growth of the individual is also affected by the culture of those with whom the child interacts. Vygotsky believed that children who interact and work with others perceive things differently, and this collaboration facilitates movement into this zone where certain learning processes occur.

## Ecological Model—Bronfenbrenner

Urie Bronfenbrenner believed that the child is at the center of an integrated system that functions interactively within itself and may be diagrammed using four concentric circles. He identified those circles using the following names and definitions:

- **Microsystem:** Includes the child, the environment, and those people or entities with whom the child directly interacts, such as the family, the school, and the neighborhood.
- **Mesosystem:** Pertains to the interactions of the individuals who surround the child as they work with each other in the child's environment but not directly affecting the child.
- **Exosystem:** Comprises the broader community in which the child lives, which may include the extended family, friends of the family, and social services in the community (physician, firefighter, and so on).
- **Macrosystem:** Entails the attitudes, ideologies (laws, values), and customs of the culture in which the child lives.

## Hierarchy of Needs—Maslow

Abraham Maslow created a hierarchy in which one may observe the more sophisticated needs of an individual at the top levels of the hierarchy. He believed that basic needs (the bottom level) must be met for a child to grow and develop; the most basic needs being those that are physiological (air, food, water, rest, shelter). As those basic needs are met, a child may advance up the five steps of the various levels to the top level, where the child develops into his or her own potential and becomes the best he or she can be. If all the needs on this hierarchy are met, the child will have the ability to seek knowledge, learn, and develop appropriately.

The following outlines the hierarchy from bottom level (I) to top level (V):

- Level I: Basic needs; exploration, manipulation, and physiological needs
- Level II: Security, protection, and safety
- Level III: Closeness and love
- Level IV: Esteem and self-esteem
- Level V: Self-actualization

## Psychosocial Theory—Erikson

Erik Erikson identified **eight stages** of human development related to personality, each thought to influence the next stage in the developmental process. He believed that personality is a critical component of development in early childhood and continues to develop even after an individual reaches the age of five years. The stages of his theory are thought to be present at birth (innate) and emerge according to an individual's upbringing and experiences. An individual proceeds through the stages due to a crisis that unfolds and is resolved. However, an individual may continue to have later experiences that alter certain stages and affect personality traits.

The eight stages are:

1. Trust vs. Mistrust
2. Autonomy vs. Shame and doubt
3. Initiative vs. Guilt
4. Industry vs. Inferiority
5. Identity vs. Role confusion
6. Intimacy vs. Isolation
7. Generativity vs. Stagnation
8. Integrity vs. Despair

## Domains of Learning

Five specific areas of development are referred to as the early **domains of learning.** Educators generally address these domains in the early childhood years to ensure that a student is developing appropriately across all sectors. These five learning domains affect one another as a child develops, and instruction should support these domains, providing the child with a strong foundation of learning concepts and skills.

The five domains, which are briefly summarized in this section, include the following:

1. Cognitive domain
2. Language/Communication domain
3. Physical domain
4. Social-Emotional domain
5. Self-help/Adaptive behavior domain

### Cognitive Domain

The **cognitive domain** is the most critical of the five domains because it is comprised of mental skills that are essential for the development of all other domains throughout an individual's lifetime. This domain focuses on the primary mental skills such as thinking and reasoning. Other mental skills include remembering, problem solving, decision making, naming, recognizing, making generalizations, understanding cause-and-effect relationships, and analyzing perceptions. The theorists who most closely concentrated their philosophy on this domain include Skinner, who developed the operant behavior theory; and Piaget, who is known for the constructivist or cognitive development theory.

## Language/Communication Domain

Communication and language are essential in life. This domain is another critical domain of development. **Language**, the systematic use of sounds, signs, or written symbols for the purpose of communication or expression, must become meaningful to children, and they must acquire skills using language structures, pattern combinations, gestures, facial expressions, early literacy, and expressive and receptive language in order to develop in this area. The skills of this domain are acquired based on a child's environment and experiences. Early literacy development is a child's first introduction to reading and writing. Children must be exposed to activities that stimulate their oral language and listening skill development in order for them to acquire reading and writing skills later.

## Physical Domain

The physical (motor) domain is the first area to develop after birth as children begin moving even in the womb. Because children interact with their environment in very physical ways, they continue to collect large amounts of data throughout their lives. The physical domain includes these more specific areas: gross motor (large muscles); fine motor (small muscles); sensory-integration (tactile, vestibular, and proprioception); and perceptual (coordination of muscles and movement). The theories formed by Gesell, Piaget, Ayres, and Kephart apply to the physical domain of learning.

## Social-Emotional Domain

Emotions are an expression of feelings that reflect needs and desires. If an individual's basic needs are met, a bond forms with the caregiver, which permits other social relationships to emerge and more complex emotions to evolve. Children gain social skills through many interactive experiences in their daily lives. This strengthens their personal perception of self-esteem, self-confidence, and self-competence.

Other factors influence the proper development of the social-emotional domain. The cognitive and language domains both affect and are affected by the development of the social-emotional domain. The establishment of an effective and age-appropriate environment is also a critical component during a child's developmental stages.

Theories related to the social-emotional domain include the humanism theory (Maslow), operant behavior theory (Skinner), psychosocial theory (Erikson), social learning theory (Bandura), and multiple intelligences theory (Gardner).

## Self-Help/Adaptive Behavior Domain

Adaptive behaviors, self-help, or personal skills necessary throughout a lifetime are generally acquired during daily routines in early development primarily influenced by parental involvement. Adaptive behaviors are based on the child's age and level of development, as well as the cultural mores of the family (preferences, beliefs, and values). When children master the adaptive domain competencies, they strengthen their self-esteem and develop a sense of independence.

# Pedagogy/Learning Theories

Educational pedagogy is the academic or scholarly influence on the act of learning. Theories are the foundation of educational principles and help to define educational practices and instructional delivery models. Understanding how individuals learn aids educators in their development of unit and lesson plans so they can address all learners.

Numerous theories are related to learning, but only a few broad-based learning theories have been selected for description in this section. Examinees most likely studied many pedagogical aspects of education and instruction in their coursework. It is not important whether an individual agrees with all the possible theories, but rather that the individual understands and can apply those approaches that are most appropriate for the students being served.

Educators should evaluate their personal philosophy about how children learn. This individual philosophy is generally based on existing learning theories. Learning theories can be the guidelines on how to deliver instruction to students. Educators know that not every theory works for or relates to every student and his or her needs. Students are uniquely individual, so the approaches used to address their learning needs should be based on researched information.

# Cognitive

Based on the work of Piaget and the concepts related to Gestalt psychology, the cognitive theory reflects the internal mental processes that are used to acquire knowledge. These processes include such areas as problem solving, memory, and language. This theory describes how people understand, analyze, and solve problems.

Cognitive theorists believe that students acquire new information and gain new skills based on prior knowledge. Instruction under this theory must be delivered at the appropriate level or stage of student development and should be guided in the environment so students can develop an application of learned skills. Motivational activities will enhance and encourage learning. Instructional application of this theory includes learning styles, metacognition, peer tutoring, scaffolded instruction, and behavioral temperaments.

# Behavioral

The behavioral theory describes a systematic approach to learning and instruction and is based on the work of B.F. Skinner and the concept of stimulus-response. He believed that learning is a function of the changes in behaviors and the responses to these events. The primary components of this theory emphasize the effectiveness of explicit teaching and direct instruction. It also incorporates the "ABC" model of instruction ("A" = antecedent or stimulus; "B" = target behavior or response; "C" = consequences or reinforcement). The focus is on measurable learning behaviors that can be observed and documented.

# Developmental

This theory emphasizes the natural progression of growth, focusing on the sequence of the developmental stages of cognitive abilities. In this approach, the key concept to learning suggests that a level of maturity or *readiness* must be reached; when children mature, they naturally begin to learn.

# Psychodynamic

This pedagogical approach is based on the premise that human behavior and human relationships are shaped by conscious and unconscious influences. It has been determined that an individual's personality and his or her reactions to situations are the result of interactions in the mind, genetic constitution, emotions, and the environment. These factors affect a person's behavior and mental state. Therefore, the psychodynamic theory is the study of human behavior based on motivation and the functional significance of emotions created through the research of Brucke, Jung, and Freud.

# Social Learning

The social learning theory was constructed by Albert Bandura, who discovered that children learn from others through observations, from imitation, and through modeling. This theory encompasses attention, memory, and motivation. According to this social learning approach, educators would be wise to model and demonstrate learning activities and key concepts, so children may observe others and the situation in order to learn what they need to do.

# Ecological

This theory focuses on family background, family culture, and the social experiences that impact a student's development and future academic success. Individuals develop within their personal environments, facing various situations and interactions with other individuals and the setting. These influences from the home, the school, and the community affect how much the student will achieve, and his or her academic success is related to these past and present experiences.

# Eclectic

This approach to learning promotes the combination of various pedagogical practices to better meet the academic needs of students. Professionals may select components from the different theoretical approaches to design instruction in a more individualized manner. Some approaches work better for certain types of students in different environments and for various age groups. This approach offers the educator a more theoretical basis for developing a personal philosophy as well as the ability to change the approach based on the evolving needs of students.

# Multiple Intelligences

Howard Gardner introduced this theory of multiple intelligences, each specifically named and each comprised of distinguishing features. This theory has an impact on the instructional presentation delivered in classrooms because individuals possess a range of intelligences, which include not only academic aspects, but other talents and skills. Gardner believed that individuals possess all of the intelligences, yet some of the intelligences are evident at a higher and more noticeable level. He emphasized that educators should teach students to the entire set of intelligences in order to address the needs and capabilities of all individuals. This theory offers a method for diverse instruction.

The nine intelligences are defined as follows:

- **Verbal**—This intelligence strand focuses on the ability to express oneself orally or in writing; the individual may possess the ability to master other languages. The most emphasized intelligence in classrooms, verbal intelligence includes instruction through lecture and textbooks.
- **Logical**—The intelligence of logic, reasoning, and problem solving, logical intelligence promotes sequential and orderly instruction and structured environments. Instruction conforms to teacher-directed activities.
- **Visual**—This intelligence enables individuals to use spatial reasoning (use of charts, maps, illustrations, puzzles, and so on) to grasp ideas and solutions to problems prior to explaining them or applying them.
- **Musical**—This intelligence is the ability to use patterns, sounds, and rhythms to make sense of the environment. Musical intelligence is not a sole auditory intelligence and includes the study and instruction of mathematics.
- **Intrapersonal**—This intelligence focuses on the affective reasoning, which includes feelings, values, and attitudes and promotes meaningful learning.
- **Interpersonal**—This area supports interactions with other individuals in the learning process, such as cooperative groups and interactive whole-group instruction, in order to make more sense of the information.
- **Kinesthetic**—Interacting with the physical environment defines this area of intelligence, and it encourages activities that utilize fine and gross motor skills, such as learning centers, science experiments, drama-based lessons, and hands-on learning experiences.
- **Naturalist**—This intelligence includes skills such as classification and categorization, which are used in the fields of biology, anatomy, zoology, and geology.
- **Existential**—A broad-based intelligence, the existential intelligence encompasses aesthetics, philosophy, and religion and permits students to understand their relationship to the world with skills such as summarization and synthesizing.

# Learning Styles

Learning styles are the different approaches or diverse ways of learning. Some educators do not believe there are different styles of learning while others believe that because individuals are unique, discovering a student's learning style is key to academic success.

According to Neil Fleming, a common and widely used category of learners is defined. Under his definition of the VAK or VARK Model-(Neuro-linguistics) there are three types of learners:

- **Auditory:** These individuals learn by listening. They are able to interpret meaning by listening to voice, pitch, tone, and inflection of the presenter. These students can learn best through lectures, discussions, presentations, and listening to others.
- **Visual:** These individuals learn by watching or seeing. It helps these students to see the presenter's facial expressions and body language, as well as the content of a lesson. They can gain the most from information in books, videos, handouts, diagrams, whiteboard, and by taking notes.
- **Tactile/kinesthetic:** These individuals learn by doing, touching, and moving. They gain the most from instruction when it is delivered in an interactive, hands-on approach where they may be active and explore the content.

Theories of learning styles include the following:

- VAKOG—Visual, auditory, kinesthetic, olfactory, gustatory (Bandler-Grinder); this theory is based upon how the human mind processes information.
- Left-right cerebral, left-right limbic brain dominance (Herrmann)
- Physical, psychological, sociological, emotional, environmental (Dunn and Dunn)
- Concrete random and sequential, abstract random and sequential (Gregorc-Butler)
- 4-MAT system that includes "if, why, how, what"
- Experiential Learning Theory Model (Kolb)
- Democratic Education Model (Sudbury)
- VAK or VARK Model — Neuro-linguistics (Fleming)

# Curriculum

**Curriculum** is a designed plan for learning that requires purposeful preparation by the teacher who will organize and manage the learning situation, impart the core content knowledge, and promote the development of skills expected for the learners. Planning, effectiveness, and addressing learner differences all affect the quality of the curriculum. Curriculum is also a process that includes the knowledge that is to be transmitted to the students and the outcomes or products to be assessed.

Learning is planned and guided at various levels within and around the school and classroom. Specifying in advance what is intended to be attained and achieved, as well as how these goals will be met, is all part of curriculum. A school as a whole and teachers as individuals need to determine the following when developing a curriculum:

What educational purposes are being worked toward?

What types of learning and experiences will help attain these purposes?

How can these methods and experiences be organized effectively?

How should these experiences be assessed and how is the end result measured?

Curriculum helps provide a framework for learning, a structural foundation for concepts and information. It should be a guide to what concepts to teach but it should also be flexible, reflect the real world, unify student learning, and build on prior knowledge.

Curriculum is influenced by several factors, and these must be considered when planning and implementing it at an elementary level. These factors include societal values, content standards, accountability systems, research studies, community expectations, culture and language of learners, and the diversity of learning styles.

# Components

The framework of curriculum is set according to individual states by the standards that are presented for each grade level. These standards encompass the knowledge and skills desired for learners and therefore guides the implementation of the curriculum.

Every curriculum is designed with a set of **critical components**. These include:

- Vision statement/introduction
- Goals and objectives
- Content expectations/standards
- Grouping and pacing plans
- Pedagogy/teaching practices
- Instructional strategies/learning activities
- Products and materials
- Assessment
- Resources/technology use
- Extension activities
- Differentiated instruction techniques
- Closure and follow-up

# Purpose

A curriculum reflects the values, needs, and desires a school and community hold for students. It should enable each learner to reach his or her potential and the highest level of achievement possible. The curriculum should allow individuals to flourish using their own talents and abilities. It must deliver a sense of enthusiasm and motivation for learning, promote physical and emotional well-being, and address various beliefs and cultures. It should enable individuals to gain skills (making informed choices and decisions, thinking independently, communicating with others) necessary to lead a productive and contributing life.

A curriculum should meet the needs of the learners and provide the following:

- Varied opportunities to gain core knowledge
- Assorted activities to apply the learned knowledge
- Methods to integrate the various subjects and disciplines
- Strategies for addressing diverse learners
- Activities that are motivating and challenging
- Assessments that promote continued learning

# Design

A curriculum plan is usually created in a chart format and encompasses a range of academic goals, instructional objectives, specific skills, and so on. It is organized according to the successive levels at which each is taught. The instructional plan can be established when the teacher considers the content of the subject, the levels of the students, and the curriculum goals. The teacher designs the plan and develops the educational activities that are meaningful to the students to enhance their success.

**Scope and sequence** is a vital design component of the curriculum. It is essential to the whole school plan as well as the planning by individual teachers in developing learning sequences. The scope and sequence is an outline of the topics and skills to be taught at each grade level. **Scope** includes those decisions about what information and activities are significant and manageable. Consideration of **sequence** includes critical decisions about what is necessary to include for the sequential development of skills and the acquisition of key concepts of the content.

## Instructional Objectives

The purpose of an **instructional objective** is to provide an understanding of the desired learning outcomes. The objective should be consistent with the overall broad-based goals set for the curriculum or individual subject area. Objectives help identify what an educator intends for the learner to know at the end of the unit or lesson. Each objective should be stated in realistic, measurable, precise terms and include three components: 1) targeted audience; 2) the behavior that is expected of the learner; and 3) the conditions under which the learner must demonstrate knowledge.

## Implementing Standards

Under the No Child Left Behind Act (NCLB) of 2001, schools are required by federal law to demonstrate standards-based instruction in their educational programs. National organizations have developed standards they believe are critical to the effective learning of all children across the country. Each state has now established a set of standards for the subject areas taught at each grade level.

When educators use and apply standards, they should ensure that the standards are

- Rigorous, manageable, and developmentally appropriate.
- Focused on the academic subjects and core curriculum.
- Leveled so students may complete work and perform in diverse ways.
- Written clearly for all parties to understand.

## Integrated Curriculum

An **integrated or interdisciplinary curriculum** is one that builds upon knowledge across various subjects. It allows learners to explore a common theme that incorporates more than one area of study. Teachers may present more meaningful experiences and link concepts in unique and creative ways. Students may pursue the study of a specific topic that provides learning activities related to mathematics, art, social studies, science, language arts, music, and other subjects. This supports skill development and knowledge acquisition by linking subjects in a more authentic manner.

An integrated curriculum includes a combination of topics and subjects, varied resources, thematic units, flexible schedules, variations in assessments, and a multitude of instructional activities that link concepts. This integrated curriculum approach has been determined to improve academic achievement, instill motivation and interest, and promote lifelong learning for students.

## Types of Planning

Teachers plan in different ways and according to the requirements set forth by their state, their district, and their school. Some teachers must provide comprehensive, detailed unit and lesson plans that align with the school curriculum, the district competencies, and the state standards. Some teachers may be able to provide general plans with broad objectives and abbreviated activities. Either way, educators must become efficient and effective planners in order to meet the goals of the institution and the goals for the learner. Three types of planning are used:

- **Long-range planning** includes those plans necessary for the year, the semester, the quarter, or the month. Teachers must be aware of the expectations and competencies established in the district and incorporate the standards in these plans, predicting where the students should be by the end of the selected time period. In long-range planning, the plans are generally broken into units or themes, and teachers must also consider the standardized testing needs that will arise.
- **Daily planning** comprises the regular everyday plans used in the classroom. For elementary teachers, this means covering the standards and objectives outlined in the unit plan for all subjects. It may require that the teacher create plans for certain electives (art, physical education, music, and so on) or develop an integrated instructional approach.
- **Individual planning** is necessary when teachers are faced with diverse student needs, such as students who are gifted or talented, or those placed in special education. Special accommodations or curriculum modifications may be necessary for all of these students, and teachers must make plans for including these students in the general education plans.

# Materials

Curriculum materials are educational resources (selected according to the subject, content, and grade level) that provide students with instructional experiences and activities to meet curriculum objectives and learner goals. Curriculum materials are essential to instruction and meeting the academic needs of all students. Curriculum materials appear in many forms. They may be made commercially, created by the teacher or the student, found on the Internet, or located in libraries, museums, or other community institutions.

Materials should be provided for all curricular areas taught, and whenever possible, cross over multiple subjects for integration of topics and content. Several points should be considered when teachers select curriculum materials:

- Examine the instructional situation to determine the best use and type of materials.
- Choose materials that are appropriate for both the learners and the subject or topic area.
- Keep materials in working order, safe, and easy to handle or manage.
- Make materials accessible to all learners and keep them in close proximity to the classroom.
- Train learners on the guidelines for the use of the materials and their safe return to specific locations.

Examples of curriculum materials include games, posters, collections, models, transparencies, kits, textbooks, computer programs, manipulatives, art supplies, music materials, video or sound recordings, puppets, and educational toys.

# Environments

Creating a viable environment conducive to active learning takes planning and preparation. When done well, it is a preventive strategy. A positive classroom climate fosters student achievement, and teachers should collaborate with their students to adopt a code of conduct, create classroom procedures, and improve room arrangements.

# Instruction

Effective classroom instruction depends on planning, which is a systematic and organized way to address subject materials by developing lessons and activities for the learners. Designing instruction supports the teacher in the classroom and helps the teacher visualize the whole picture related to a topic. Educators must know themselves, their personal philosophy, their individual teaching style, and the learners in order to plan the appropriate instruction.

Three purposes for the process of instructional design are as follows:

1. Identifies the outcomes of the instruction for the learners
2. Guides the development of content through a scope and sequence
3. Establishes the assessment plan to gauge instructional effectiveness

The process of designing and preparing for instruction includes the following:

1. Define the instructional goals (general statements of expectations and outcomes).
2. Perform an instructional analysis (identification of the learning steps to reach goals).
3. Distinguish present knowledge, skill, and behavior levels of students (the focus of instruction).
4. Identify performance objectives (specific statements of learner outcomes).
5. Choose instructional methods (strategies and techniques to impart knowledge and content based on objectives and outcomes).
6. Gather instructional materials (based on methodologies and learners but may be changed as instruction occurs).
7. Conduct formative evaluation (ongoing assessment to alter instruction based on learner needs).
8. Conduct summative evaluation (at the end of instruction to verify effectiveness of teaching and how well learner achieved objectives).

Research studies collaboratively identify the fundamentals of effective instruction as

- High expectations for learners.
- Active engagement of students.
- Thematic unit instruction.
- Interactive cross-age tutors.
- Cooperative learning activities.
- Teacher effectiveness.

# Principles

A **principle** is a fundamental truth or proposition that serves as the foundation for a system of beliefs. In education, principles provide framework for teaching. The aim of education is to enable students to be productive in the world, to engage in lifelong learning, and to be self-directed, which is carried out by a structured, stimulating, and effective principle-driven curriculum. After the aims and goals of curriculum have been outlined and explicitly defined, concrete principles for attaining the objectives should be constructed. Some basic curricula principles include the following:

- The subject matter of the curriculum should be directly related to real life; students will learn the skills needed for the modern world (useful skills, habits, talents, attitudes, values, and knowledge) through active participation.
- Lessons should be varied and take into account all learning styles as well as recognize different abilities and skills.
- Social demands and psychological traits will affect learning.
- Vocational training is beneficial to students as well and should be addressed within the curriculum.
- Knowledge is gleaned through experiences and activities, not merely through storage of facts; a marriage of experiences and information is essential to learner success.
- Arrangement of information taught should follow developmental phases.

Principles often vary from district to district, school to school, and teacher to teacher, but all serve the same basic purpose. And, even though they are varied, they can each be traced back to a similar basis. Some basic principles of curriculum design include the following:

- *Basic Concepts*—Focusing on the big idea and limiting the number of new concepts introduced in a single lesson may assist the learner in understanding and comprehension. Focusing on the fundamentals before moving into more complex and specialized concepts will help establish a solid learning base; relevant prior knowledge is needed to build upon.
- *Communication*—Using simple terms to first teach the basic, initial concepts will allow learners to focus on more advanced concepts. Utilizing clear and concise models will help solidify information.
- *Mediated Scaffolding*—Providing sufficient guided practice with new concepts then moving into individual practice will help learners cement concepts in their minds. Teaching a limited number of new concepts each day could help learners focus on the basic tasks and assist in memorization and application of the concepts learned. Self-study is essential to mastery of a skill or concept but needs to be appropriately directed, monitored, and assessed.
- *Integration*—Once learners reliably and consistently demonstrate base concept knowledge, introducing superlative and comparative concepts will help develop higher-order skills and knowledge. Materials presented in logical order are easier to learn and remember as well as concepts that draw knowledge from more than one subject area.
- *Review*—Allowing ample opportunity for learners to demonstrate understanding and comprehension in a myriad of ways will increase the ability to remember and recall the concept in diverse circumstances.

These principles help shape and form curriculums as well as help determine teaching methods. While each teacher has his or her own unique style, most adhere to these principles in some form or another.

# General Models of Instruction

The type of model selected for instruction should be based on the learners, the content to be delivered, and the teacher's abilities. The following are some of the models known, and each may have select variations. Specific models, which are more commonly used, are further defined in this section.

| Model | Creator | Benefits | Limitations |
|---|---|---|---|
| Brain-based | Brooks | • Allows natural flow of learning according to function of the brain<br>• Promotes environment, content lessons, and student involvement as factors of learning | • Takes time to manage and implement for diverse learners<br>• Teachers should be familiar with brain research and human development, including stages of learning |
| Cognitive-constructivist | Piaget | • Stimulates critical thinking and problem-solving skills<br>• Allows independent learning<br>• Promotes child-centered, active learning activities<br>• Bases new knowledge on students' previous experiences | • Requires teacher to be knowledgeable about subject material and provide proper modeling |
| Cooperative learning | Johnson | • Integrates multiple intelligences and learning style theories<br>• Focuses on social and academic goals<br>• Adapts to any content or subject<br>• Improves academic achievement | • Difficult for some types of students<br>• Additional time needed for planning and monitoring<br>• May need to instruct on social skills |
| Conceptual-expository learning | Ausubel | • Helps when presenting abstract concepts<br>• Emphasizes deductive reasoning<br>• Instills higher level of thinking | • Teacher directed<br>• Concepts may be too advanced for learners |
| Delineator approach | Gregorc | • Teaches students using both concrete and abstract perceptual qualities<br>• Helps students learn to create sequential order | • Some students may have difficulty with concrete level |
| Direct instruction | Hunter | • Improves academic achievement<br>• Supports learners with varied needs<br>• Enhances structure for sequential learners | • Some teachers may not follow the steps carefully or review information or monitor students accurately |
| Discovery learning | Bruner | • Improves learners' interest/motivation<br>• Promotes inductive reasoning, intuitive thinking, and critical thinking skills<br>• Allows students to be actively and independently engaged | • May not offer benefits to lower- or higher-level learners<br>• Questions have an effect on achievement |
| Inquiry learning to implement (inductive) | Taba | • Inspires motivation and meaning for learners<br>• Develops problem-solving and critical thinking skills<br>• Encourages use of scientific methods<br>• Acknowledges that learning requires interaction between the learner and the data | • Takes more time than most models to implement<br>• Limited effect on academic achievement<br>• Some students have problems with the step of application of information |
| Mastery learning ("all children can learn") | Bloom | • Allows individual time for acquiring knowledge<br>• Continues process after assessment<br>• Implements remediation as needed | • Students may feel intimidated or overwhelmed by repeated concepts<br>• Students may be at uniquely different levels of learning<br>• Requires time and patience of teacher and ability to monitor all students effectively |
| Multiple intelligences | Gardner | • Addresses the various types of intelligences<br>• Allows students to be successful in all lessons | • Requires time for teacher to identify strengths of individuals |
| Traditional learning approach | | • Follows standardized scope and sequence in textbook, written assignments, and exams<br>• Sets milestones and accomplishments<br>• Establishes grading rubric | • Does not address individual styles or specific teaching style<br>• Promotes artificial learning of information and concepts<br>• Teacher-directed without much active learner involvement |

## Cooperative Learning

The Cooperative Learning Model can be utilized with any subject. It is a common instructional model that integrates theories and focuses on academic goals, improving academic achievement.

Johnson and Johnson identified five elements in this approach:

- **Positive interdependence**—Students understand that success is linked to other students and their success, knowing that each must contribute effort for the entire group to be successful.
- **Promotive interaction**—Students support one another by sharing resources, encouraging one another's efforts and contributions, solving problems together, and checking for understanding.
- **Accountability**—Students realize that each member in the group is responsible for learning the material so the group may achieve the final goal.
- **Interaction**—Students know that interpersonal skills must be used to be successful, which include utilizing effective communication, addressing problem solving, instilling decision making, building rapport, promoting compromise, and providing cooperation.
- **Group processing**—The group assesses their ability to function and addresses the acquisition of knowledge, which may include on-task behaviors, goals met, cooperative efforts, and feedback on data.

## Direct Instruction—Madeline Hunter

Hunter's model includes instructional sequence steps (essential elements of instruction) for any subject area and any grade level. Her model focuses on direct instruction, a systematic instructional method requiring the educator to have a grasp of the subject at a level of mastery. It places instructional theory into practice.

Direct instruction is the technique used when the teacher very specifically provides support for curricular topics. Use of this approach demonstrates instruction that proceeds in steps to accommodate students' understanding of the information and materials, with the primary outcome being successful participation of students as active learners. Review of previous concepts and monitoring of student learning are important components in this approach.

| Hunter's Essential Elements of Instruction | |
|---|---|
| Standards/expectations/objectives | Identifies what students will be able to do as a result of this lesson |
| Anticipatory set | Prepares students for the upcoming lesson with an opening activity—the "hook" |
| Instruction | Outlines what the teacher must do to present the lesson—deliver concepts, provide information, instill knowledge, or develop skills<br>• Input<br>• Modeling<br>• Check for understanding |
| Guided practice | Explains how the teacher helps students to do the work of new tasks |
| Closure | Describes how the teacher helps students to summarize new information and gain skills |
| Independent practice | Imposes opportunities to practice new learning tasks or apply skills |

## Explicit Instruction

Explicit instruction is a well-developed and systematically designed instructional approach used for all elementary school content areas: reading, mathematics, language arts, social studies, sciences, physical education, and the fine arts. Explicit instruction is synonymous with direct instruction (Madeline Hunter Model), which is based on the behavioral theory (Stimulus-Response method).

This approach promotes the use of materials and activities that give students structure and support during the learning process with a focus on the academic tasks to be learned. Each step toward goal attainment is taught to students and includes modeling, positive feedback, and practice opportunities. The environment must accommodate learning and be organized so students may work toward predetermined skills. The teacher is in control of the lessons, the environment, and the materials, while allowing proper time for instruction, student practice, and performance. Students are provided feedback and are expected to gain mastery before moving to the next skill level.

## Bloom's Taxonomy

Benjamin Bloom and John Carroll created the Mastery Teaching Model in 1971 with a focus on defining objectives in terms of measurable outcomes. They recommended that after instruction occurs, students should be assessed, and the areas of concern readdressed. They believed this process had a positive effect on student achievement and developing a student's self-concept. Bloom then designed a taxonomy for categorizing learning structures in educational settings, which incorporated specific questions to achieve the various levels. Bloom's Taxonomy is a well-known process used in elementary education programs to guide instruction.

| Levels | Skills | Verbs | Questions |
|---|---|---|---|
| Knowledge (find out) (remember) | • Observe and recall information<br>• Know dates, events, places<br>• Know major ideas/concepts<br>• Remember previous material | Define<br>List<br>Show<br>Describe<br>Label<br>Collect<br>Observe<br>Identify<br>Name<br>Match<br>Locate<br>Listen | Who?<br>What?<br>When?<br>Where? |
| Comprehension (understand) | • Understand information<br>• Interpret facts<br>• Contrast and compare<br>• Grasp the meaning of material<br>• Explain and summarize<br>• Predict outcomes and effects or trends | Discuss<br>Define<br>Restate<br>Explain<br>Report<br>Review<br>Predict<br>Estimate<br>Express<br>Give<br>Chart<br>Summarize<br>Associate | Why?<br>How? |
| Application (use) | • Use information<br>• Use methods, concepts, theories in new situations<br>• Apply rules, laws, methods, theories<br>• Solve problems using appropriate techniques | Apply<br>Demonstrate<br>Classify<br>Illustrate<br>Compute<br>Solve<br>Use<br>Examine<br>Employ<br>Modify<br>Relate<br>Interpret | Application of?<br>How to use? |

| Levels | Skills | Verbs | Questions |
|---|---|---|---|
| Analysis (take apart) | • Recognize patterns<br>• Organize parts<br>• Understands implications<br>• Identify components<br>• Conclude and clarify | Analyze<br>Explain<br>Order<br>Distinguish<br>Connect<br>Sort<br>Arrange<br>Test<br>Divide<br>Criticize<br>Infer<br>Calculate<br>Compare | Diagram?<br>Explain?<br>How?<br>What? |
| Synthesis (create new) | • Arrange things in a new way<br>• Generalize from given facts<br>• Relate knowledge from various areas<br>• Predict and draw conclusions | Compile<br>Produce<br>Combine<br>Collect<br>Create<br>Manage<br>Design<br>Assemble<br>Invent<br>Develop<br>Compose<br>Formulate | What if? |
| Evaluation (judge) | • Assess the validity and value of ideas/theories<br>• Make choices based upon reasoning and valid arguments<br>• Verify the value of data and evidence<br>• Recognize bias and subjectivity | Evaluate<br>Contrast<br>Value<br>Debate<br>Measure<br>Support<br>Decide<br>Rank<br>Justify<br>Convince<br>Criticize<br>Select | Why?<br>Why not? |

# Differentiated Instruction

**Differentiated instruction** (DI) is an educational strategy used to ensure that all students will acquire information and learn regardless of individual abilities, strengths, interests, and needs. DI incorporates student-centered instruction and a variety of strategies to achieve outcomes for all learners. Using the approach of DI focuses on the various learning styles of all students to ensure that instruction is appropriate for individuals during educational activities, class tasks, student groupings, and assessment.

When using DI, educators vary the content offered, the process of presentation, and the product that is the end result of the instruction. Instruction may be delivered using various learning formats: whole class, small groups, and individuals. Acquiring the skills of using DI takes time and practice, as it is a learned skill. Effectively and efficiently being able to address various learners, plan for the appropriate instructional practices, monitor the goals and outcomes, utilize consistent assessment of instruction, and implement proper delivery is considered mastery of this strategy.

## Guided Instruction

This approach to instruction is a combination of the teacher-centered and student-centered approaches, which allows the teacher to balance these approaches based on the students' needs. Teachers can guide the direction of the instruction, facilitating the learning process while students are then provided with time for practice and application of what is learned.

# Instructional Formats

Instructional formats, which describe the manner in which instruction is delivered, vary according to the type of students (gifted, delayed, tactile learner, and so on), to the needs of the student (needs glasses, auditory device, preferential seating, and so on), the teacher preferences, and the subjects or content to be presented. These formats may include the use of motivational acts, modeling, drill and practice, demonstration, corrective feedback, and reinforcements. These formats may be used with either individual students or small groups of students.

The formats that are most often used include the following:

- **Co-teaching**—Two teachers actively share the teaching of all students.
- **Peer tutoring**—Educators employ strategies that include same-age and cross-age peers to tutor other students.
- **Collaboration**—Teachers with diverse expertise work together to enhance the education of students.
- **Cooperative learning**—Educators implement classroom situations that promote learning among students through cooperation, not competition.

# Methods/Strategies

**Strategies** are the skills or techniques used to assist a student in accessing learning through the curriculum. The strategies and methods selected for the classroom must support the learners and their needs, while encouraging independence, generalization of skills, and application of knowledge. Most strategies are backed by empirical research. This empirical evidence suggests that all students benefit from quality strategies implemented daily. Some strategies work with certain groups of individuals, and some are better for particular subject areas. Educators must ensure that the strategies are well designed and selected based on the emphasis of the learners' needs and abilities so knowledge will be transferred and applied. Educators should seek research-based methods and strategies that demonstrate proven effectiveness for elementary-age students. The principles to consider when choosing a strategy include evidence of structured instruction, opportunities for practice, comprehensiveness, and whether it fosters independence.

## Developmentally Appropriate Practices

Utilizing developmentally appropriate practices is to consider the level at which a student is presently functioning when creating curriculum, addressing standards, designing the environment, and developing instructional activities. Classroom teachers who follow the concept of developmentally appropriate practices take into account the various stages of human development and sequentially follow the ability levels of the students in order to progressively develop skills at a higher level. The activities and practices evolve according to student developmental levels.

The purpose of using developmentally appropriate practices is to meet the needs of all learners in a suitable environment in the best possible manner. Educators must consider the age of the students, ability and skill levels, interests, cultural backgrounds, and social behaviors when creating curriculum activities and then build upon these various events to enhance learning according to each student's developmental stage.

Sometimes state standards are not at the appropriate level to impose developmentally appropriate practices, so the educator must work at establishing suitable activities and addressing the instructional needs of the students. In order to create an environment that promotes developmentally appropriate practices, teachers should integrate the standards into the curriculum, provide adequate materials and equipment, participate in ongoing training, and use effective communication with parents.

## Integration Strategies

There are many strategies available to integrate subjects across the curriculum as well as many reasons why this practice is so beneficial to students. Strategic integration is an instructional design component that combines essential information in ways that result in new and more complex knowledge. The strategic integration of curriculum content encourages students to learn how to use and apply specific knowledge beyond the classroom. Characteristics of the proper integration of strategies include the following:

- Design offers opportunities to integrate several big ideas.
- Content learned must be applicable to multiple contexts.
- Complex concepts and facts should be integrated once mastered.

## Scaffolded Instruction

**Scaffolding** is a teaching strategy that provides a temporary support or some guidance to the learner who may not be ready to perform a task independently. Scaffolded instruction may be organized into the format of a series of steps, leveled tasks, certain materials, and personal support during the initial learning period of a new concept in order to reduce the task complexity by structuring it into manageable chunks, which increases success and completion. It allows a student to have the necessary support in the beginning, and then gradually decrease the teacher's participation as the individual becomes more competent. It then ends with independent practice as the student masters the various steps and skills. The degree of scaffolding changes with the abilities of the learner, the goals of the instruction, and the complexities of the task. Gradual and planned removal of the scaffolds occurs as the learner becomes more competent in task completion. The purpose of scaffolded instruction is to allow all students to become successful in independent activities.

**Scaffolded Instruction**

**Apply**

↑

**Practice**

↑

**Model**

↑

**Teach**

Two types of scaffolded instruction are **verbal** and **procedural.**

In **verbal instruction,** the teacher uses prompting, questioning, and further explanations to encourage students to move into higher functioning levels. Examples: paraphrasing, think-alouds, content reinforcement, modeling, and appropriate speech patterns.

In **procedural instruction,** specific instructional techniques such as the following may be used:

- Instructional frameworks include the specific teaching, modeling, and practicing of the skill as well as setting expectations for independent application.
- One-on-one teaching and modeling involves working directly with the student to meet needs.
- Small group instruction helps a less experienced or less able student when one who is more experienced practices or models a newly learned skill.
- Grouping or partnering is designed so teachers place students who are more experienced in a topic with those who are less experienced.

## Cooperative Learning

**Cooperative learning** is a strategy that engages groups of students of different levels of ability, using a variety of activities and materials, to study and improve their comprehension of a particular topic or subject. This technique assists students with learning activities in a student-centered environment to keep them actively involved in the work. Students must utilize social skills and teamwork such as positive interdependence, individual accountability, interactions with others, and equal participation.

Research demonstrates that the cooperative learning technique promotes student understanding and academic achievement, increases attention and retention, and aids in developing communication skills, while it promotes social skills and self-esteem. Students realize they may gain from the experience and involvement of others, be more responsible for their own learning, and celebrate the accomplishments of a group effort.

Cooperative learning includes different situations with students:

**Grouping Model**

**Independent Work**

↑

**Partners**

↑

**Triads**

↑

**Small Group**

↑

**Whole Class**

Following are examples of pairing strategies:

- **Think-Pair-Share**—The teacher poses a question or topic to the students and allows them time to think before discussion; partners talk about the question or topic and then share their answers and discussions with the class.
- **Round Robin Recall**—Students are divided into small groups and each member must recall all they know about a topic or subject presented in a set amount of time.

## Questioning Strategies

An important skill that teachers should develop is the technique of appropriately asking a question and waiting for an answer. When referring to Bloom's Taxonomy, questions to students may begin at the **knowledge** level and proceed to the higher order of thinking skills at the **evaluation** level to better assess student gains. At the first level, the questions are based on the information just learned, while at the final level, questions are based on critical thinking and application of content. For example, questions at each level may be as follows:

Knowledge: Define the . . .

Application: How would you use the . . . ?

Evaluation: Decide which method . . . and compare . . .

## Task Analysis

Using the method of **task analysis** helps a student learn a specific skill by breaking down the assignment or activity into sequential steps. The student learns each step of the task as he or she moves toward the preferred level of skill achievement.

Task analysis is conducted to accomplish the following:

- Determine instructional goals and objectives.
- Describe and define specifically the tasks the learner will perform.
- Outline the knowledge type needed for a task (declarative, procedural, or structural).
- Aid in selecting the appropriate learning outcomes in order to promote instructional development.
- Order, prioritize, and rank tasks.
- Establish instructional methods, strategies, and activities that foster learning.
- Determine appropriate learning environments.
- Create assessments and evaluations.

## Content Enhancements

**Content enhancement** is a research-based instructional approach designed to be used in order to meet both individual and group needs while maintaining the integrity of the content taught. It allows curriculum content to be presented in an understandable and easy-to-learn manner. Content enhancement routines focus on actively engaging students with the content being taught. This approach allows teachers to use various techniques that enhance more complex information in the curriculum so students may remember and utilize it more efficiently. Types of content enhancements include guided notes, graphic organizers, and mnemonic strategies.

## Graphic Organizers

**Graphic organizers** are effective instructional tools that help organize information in a more concrete manner. They provide a visual, holistic representation of facts and concepts, depict the relationship of facts within an organized framework, and relate new information to prior knowledge. Graphic organizers may be used before instructional activities to activate prior knowledge and to encourage student prediction. They can be used during instruction to help students process and reorganize information. After instruction, graphic organizers help summarize learning, support the organization of ideas, provide a structure for review, and assess the degree of student understanding. Types of graphic organizers include concept maps, sequence chains, story maps, main idea tables, flowcharts, matrixes, and Venn diagrams.

## Wait Time

Adequate processing time, known as **wait time,** is the amount of time that occurs between the moment a task is presented or a question is asked and when the learner is asked to respond. Research shows that when teachers provide a pause period between a question and student response, students tend to reply with more thoughtful answers as they have time to process the request. Often, students are given only a few seconds to answer a question posed by the teacher, and it results in brief responses or no answers at all.

The amount of response (wait) time will vary based on students' ages and cognitive levels, as well as the complexity of the task, topic, or question. If a task or topic is considerably new, the amount of time allocated to think and formulate a response should be greater than that provided for a task that is more familiar. Some studies showed that at the elementary level, a decrease in achievement was attributed to waiting too long for responses to low-level questions.

## Peer Tutoring

**Peer tutoring** is an effective strategy when properly used under the guidance of a teacher. To begin the process of peer tutoring, the teacher selects a student who demonstrates mastery and competencies in a particular subject or topic. That student is paired with a student who needs assistance in order to gain mastery or to access content knowledge. The students work together periodically so the student needing assistance can learn from the peer modeling and then practice the observed skills.

## Student Responses

Students who are actively engaged in learning achieve greater success. Interactive learning activities keep students involved in the learning activities, encourage them to be more responsible for their learning efforts, and provide them with adequate practice of skills necessary to move to another level of learning. Educators should attempt to elicit student responses several times per minute to check for understanding and on-task behaviors. Some methods include question/answer periods, student writings, and activities.

## Instructional Pacing

**Pacing** is the rate at which the instruction is delivered through presentations and in response solicitations. Pacing may be influenced by variables such as the complexity of a task, the newness of a task, and the range of student differences. Research suggests that instruction should be presented at a brisk and consistent pace, because the benefits include

- More information may be provided.
- Learners are more engaged in the activity.
- Behavior problems are limited.

## Feedback for Correct and Incorrect Responses

Studies and educational best practices suggest that immediate feedback from the teacher to the student should be provided in the classroom for both correct and incorrect responses. Corrective feedback should be instructional and not accommodating. The feedback delivered to reinforce correct responses should be consistent and specific. Feedback should be subtle yet built in as part of the regular learning process. It should not interfere with the timing of the next question, the content delivery, or personal interactions; otherwise, learners may suffer from learning disruptions and have problems with memory and recall.

## Terms

Terms related to instruction include the following:

- **Ability grouping**—Placing students together according to performance and academic achievement levels
- **Accommodation**—Adjustment that does not change the curriculum, but enables a student to participate in educational activities he or she might not otherwise be able to do
- **Active student response**—Measure of the engagement of a student in tasks and activities
- **Adaptation**—Change made to the environment or curriculum
- **Chained response**—Breaking down a task into smaller component parts so a person may complete the task, starting with the first step in the sequence and performing each component progressively until the task is final
- **Chaining**—Technique in which student performance is reinforced so the student will continue to perform more complex tasks in the sequence
- **Choral responding**—Oral response of students (in unison) to a question or problem presented by the teacher
- **Chunking**—Strategy that helps a student learn, remember, and organize large amounts of information
- **Cloze procedure**—Use of semantic and syntactic clues that aid in completing a sentence
- **Concept generalization**—Ability of a student to demonstrate content knowledge by applying the information to other settings without prompts from the teacher
- **Contingent teaching**—Strategy for helping a student and eventually fading out the support as the student gains mastery of the skill or task
- **Cooperative learning**—Students are divided into groups to work together to complete a task, participate in an activity, or create a project

- **Corrective feedback**—Aids students in understanding correct and incorrect responses while informing them of their progress

- **Cues and prompts**— Used for teaching, guiding, or supporting a learner while participating and being actively engaged in an activity; may include verbal cues, physical prompts, verbal prompts, shadowing, modeling, hand-over-hand, brailling, and coactive movements

- **Demonstration**—Student observes the teacher or another student completing a task and then makes the attempt at task completion

- **Drill and practice**—Use of consistent repetition and rehearsal

- **Facilitated groups**—Students engage in active learning with lessons designed and overseen by the teacher but managed by the students

- **Fluency building**—Measure that encourages practice of skills to improve the accuracy and rate of use

- **Generalization**—Ability to use skills learned across various settings

- **Guided practice**—Providing opportunities to gain knowledge by offering cues, prompts, or added sequential information

- **Learning centers**—Specific areas or activities that enhance the curricular content and allow independent or small group instruction

- **Mnemonics**—Enhances memory through key words, acronyms, or acrostics

- **Modeling**—Helps make connections between the material to be learned and the process to learn it by acting out sequences so students may imitate the task

- **Naturalistic teaching**—Procedures that involve activities interesting to students with naturally occurring consequences

- **Prompting**—Technique in which a visual, auditory, or tactile cue is presented to facilitate the completion of a task or to perform a behavior

- **Reinforcement**—Provision of a positive contact or object in order to strengthen the possibility that the student will make a similar response to a similar situation in the future

- **Remediation**—Program technique to teach students to reach competency through training and education

- **Repetition**—Continual work on a specific skill or content concept to help build rote memory skills

- **Response cards**—Method that allows all students to answer simultaneously by using signs, cards, or items held up to demonstrate responses

- **Skill drill**—Repetition and practice of new skills until the learner performs without cues and prompts

- **Strategic instruction**—Planned, sequential instruction to show similarities and differences between acquired and new knowledge

- **Systematic feedback**—Providing positive reinforcement and confirmation to improve learning

- **Time trial**—Procedure that improves the fluency of new skills through time limits

- **Universal design**—Concept that everything in the environment, in learning, and in products, should be accessible to everyone

# Motivation

**Motivation** is a critical component in the academic success of students as it allows them to attain goals and reach accomplishments. Motivation is the reason students engage in certain behaviors, which may be to satisfy their basic needs, complete projects, or participate in activities. Educators should naturally want to motivate students and include using methods of motivation in their daily and unit plans, which include interesting lessons, varying the materials, and utilizing unique activities.

Students need to feel motivated to learn and achieve. To assist students in becoming motivated, teachers should develop healthy, trusting relationships and positive rapport with students. Students who are motivated become actively involved in the educational process and are more responsible for their individual achievements. They gain self-confidence and pride in their work, which instills enthusiasm for academics. Various rewards and strategies, both extrinsic and intrinsic, may be used to improve motivation in classrooms for diverse learners.

## Extrinsic Motivators

**Extrinsic motivators** are those that come from outside the individual; these may be small tangible items (money, prizes, stickers), grades, special privileges, or verbal/written praise. The motivating factor is an external reward that can provide the satisfaction that the completion of the task or activity itself may not provide to the student. Some students need to have something for their efforts, and some students need an extrinsic motivator only for a short period of time, until they feel capable and satisfied with their own efforts. Educators should determine through observation, trial and error, or evaluation which students need this support.

## Intrinsic Motivators

**Intrinsic motivators** are those that come from within the individual; students do not need to receive anything for their efforts as they have their own drive or internal need to be successful. Intrinsic motivators may include the feeling of satisfaction, accomplishment, or enjoyment. Many students are intrinsically motivated to learn for the pure joy of it, and they complete work, tasks, and projects or activities because they want to succeed and master a subject. Teachers may capitalize on this form of motivation in students by including a sense of curiosity and excitement in the lessons they deliver.

# Classroom Management

Effective classroom organization and structure are essential to maximizing student academic success. This management determines the learning environment, the teacher's attitude and behaviors, and the impact on students, their achievement, and behaviors. Positive classroom management creates an environment that allows students to flourish. The basic classroom management components include

- An appropriate curriculum.
- Motivating instruction and enticing activities.
- Responsible and engaged students.
- A teacher who models a positive attitude toward education.

To create an appropriate educational environment for students, teachers must plan and implement the proper design and structure for the classroom, create efficient procedures, plan appropriate lessons, maintain order, use effective communication strategies, manage varying situations, consider proper behavior management strategies, and meet the diverse needs of all learners. A positive environment with effective management, in which students understand the expectations, will result in increased instructional time, reinforcement of the learning process, promotion of desired behaviors, and improvement of student-teacher relationships.

Teachers should use proactive strategies that model and teach students to effectively self-manage their behaviors and encourage them to be actively engaged in their own learning process. Students should be involved in creating the instructional environment, which will stimulate their interest in education, thereby promoting lifelong learning. Effective classroom management includes some of these strategies and procedures:

- Use appropriate lessons and materials.
- Minimize interruptions and transitions.
- Vary tasks, assignments, and activities.
- Utilize positive and effective communication.
- Remove visual and auditory distractions.
- Allow adequate time for learning.
- Give directions in a concise, repetitive manner.
- Help students organize work and work area.

- Use modeling and demonstration for new tasks.
- Implement effective transition periods.
- Supply appropriate materials with easy access.
- Establish special areas for enrichment.
- Provide feedback and rewards for desired behavior.
- Support students when they make mistakes.
- Reflect a positive attitude for learning.
- Monitor progress and maintain accountability.
- Be clear about expectations.
- Listen to the learners.

There are three recognized styles of classroom management:

- **Authoritarian**—A method that is restrictive and punitive, with the main focus on maintaining order instead of emphasizing instruction and educational activities
- **Authoritative**—A type of management that encourages students to become independent under an effective management program, using guidelines, expectations, and verbal support appropriate for the learners
- **Permissive**—A style that promotes independence of learners, but offers them limited support for academic skills or managing their behaviors

# Interventions

**Interventions** are the steps teachers take to address student needs when situations arise that imply the student is having difficulty either managing personal behavior or completing academic tasks. Deciding when and how to intervene is an essential classroom management skill.

If a student is having behavior issues, the teacher should attempt various interventions suitable to the student, the grade level, and the situation for a reasonable amount of time. If the problems are not resolved, then seeking the assistance of the school social worker, the psychologist, a peer teacher, or the student assistance team should be considered. Teachers should attempt to address issues with students prior to seeking assistance from others, but knowing the resources available is also important.

For students who have problems with academic tasks, setting up structured study times, accessing additional help (such as a tutor), finding more one-to-one time with the student, or contacting the student's family for help should be typical interventions. However, if these are not successful, it may be necessary for the teacher to work with the school assistance team to begin the process of evaluation to determine specific academic needs.

# Behavior Management

The classroom environment influences behaviors, and behaviors have a significant impact on learning. In order to maintain effective classroom management, student behaviors must be adequate, whether controlled by the teacher or self-regulated by the student. Classroom management and response to behaviors are a reflection of the teacher's attitudes about teaching and the students, as well as reflective of teaching style.

Behavior management requires an understanding of human development and the knowledge about the availability and training in a designed program that integrates the needs of individuals into the environment. Setting standard guidelines and establishing expectations for students' behaviors in a classroom help to establish a foundation for learning. A system of rewards and consequences helps manage the typical behaviors demonstrated in elementary classrooms.

General strategies of behavior management techniques include the following:

- Create a comfortable and safe environment.
- Involve students in creating rules and procedures.
- Develop expectations and model appropriate behaviors.
- Use immediate feedback and provide consistent reinforcements.

## Behavior and Classroom Management Models

Maintaining behaviors is primary to creating an effective learning environment that is reflective of proper classroom management. Establishing rapport, getting to know the learners, and being respectful and trusting helps both the learners and the teacher. Many models of behavior intervention may be used with elementary-age students. Some educators combine models and individualize their approach to address behaviors.

| Theorist | Approach | Definition | Concepts |
|---|---|---|---|
| Glasser | Glasser Model | When an individual makes good choices, good behavior results. | Implement consequences for good and bad behavior.<br>Establish class-wide discipline. |
| Kounin | With-It-Ness | Teacher is able to manage the learners, because the teacher is "with it" and alert to the group. | Address off-task behaviors.<br>Instill motivation.<br>Use effective instructional pace. |
| Kyle, Kagan, and Scott | Kyle, Kagan, and Scott Approach | Utilizes win-win discipline and three pillars:<br>a. no adversaries<br>b. shared responsibility<br>c. long-term learned behavior | Identify disruptive behaviors and create structures.<br>Incorporate win-win solutions for preventive results. |
| Canter | Canter Model | Educator is in charge of the class and manages learners. | State expectations clearly and concisely.<br>Remain calm, but firm.<br>Insist on desired behaviors. |
| Jones | Fred Jones Model | Learner motivation and desired behaviors are stressed. | Use nonverbal actions to prevent undesirable behaviors.<br>Identify classroom structure and rules immediately. |
| Skinner | Neo-Skinnerian Model | The desired behaviors can be obtained by shaping and modeling. | Shape behaviors by implementing consequences and rewards.<br>Remain consistent. |

## Terms

Behavior management terms include the following:

- **Antecedent**—Stimulus used in behavior management and behavior modification that occurs prior to the behavior and establishes the reason for the behavior
- **Behavior intervention**—Strategies or actions used to extinguish, change, or redirect an inappropriate behavior
- **Consequence**—Stimulus that follows a behavior action used in behavior management or behavior modification to increase or decrease the behavior
- **Contingency contract**—Written agreement between the student and the teacher that outlines the expected performance and the reinforcers to be used
- **Modeling**—Imitation used to set in place the desired behaviors
- **Negative reinforcement**—Strategy used in behavior modification in which the student is motivated to use a desired behavior in order to avoid a negative consequence
- **Positive reinforcement**—Strategy used in behavior modification in which the student is motivated to use a desired behavior because of a reward to be obtained

- **Response generalization**—Application of a learned behavior or skill to another setting
- **Target behavior**—Behavior most often to be extinguished or changed, although it may be that a positive behavior should be used in other school situations

# Cultural and Linguistic Diversity

Tremendous growth has occurred in the United States during the first decade of the twenty-first century. The numbers of English language learners (ELLs) entering public schools has created a demand for programs of specific language instruction. It is a challenge for the schools to design and implement these programs as well as for the educators who strive to instruct all students in the core curriculum and ensure that academic achievement is successful.

Since the 1960s, there has been a shift in immigration patterns from non-European countries. The number of English language learners entering public schools has increased in the past 25 years. Hispanic enrollment increased 48 percent and Asian-American enrollment increased 85 percent between 1980 and 1990. More than 3.5 million students whose primary language was not English attended school in the United States in the year 2000. It is estimated that between the late 1990s and 2010 English language learners have increased by more than 50 percent.

Language and culture are two factors that influence how children learn. There are a growing number of students whose first language is not English. Across the nation, achievement data research shows that ELL students score behind their same-aged peers in most subject areas. Many educators are concerned about how ELL students will meet state standards. A general approach available to schools is the Response to Intervention model (RTI) that focuses on screening students to determine who needs assistance in academics. Once selected, students proceed through a tiered level of interventions to support their progress in the general curriculum.

To aid ELL students in their learning, teachers should remember to

- Use spoken and written language patterns and structures that are above the learner's abilities.
- Repeat key words, phrases, and concepts.
- Slow the speech rate and clearly articulate sounds.
- Avoid using difficult words and unnecessary vocabulary.
- Simplify instructional materials.

Accountability measures have required that states include English language proficiency standards and tests. Districts must establish a philosophy about ELL instruction in order to adopt the most appropriate instructional model. Research shows that effective models include the integration of language, literacy and academic content, cooperative learning periods, professional development programs, parent support, and the monitoring and assessment of outcomes.

Several specific models are considered effective:

- **English immersion:** Instruction is delivered completely in English in a simplified manner so students may learn English while gaining content of academic subjects.
- **English as a second language:** Similar to immersion, it also included supports to individuals in their native language. Students may be grouped according to one language or several different languages and may attend classes for a period to work on English or all day to receive instruction in both English and the core subjects.
- **Transitional bilingual education:** Students are grouped by their native language and receive instruction for some subjects in the native language while also spending time on developing English skills.
- **Two-way bilingual education:** Students receive instruction from team teachers in two languages so they may become proficient in both languages (also called dual-immersion or dual-language education).

In addition to the numerous languages represented in elementary populations, classes appear to be more culturally diverse than in previous decades. Research on the various cultural groups resulted in generalizations about how these groups interact and communicate. Due to the range of diversity in schools, educators must exercise cultural sensitivity to and cultural awareness of their students. A way to promote this is to create an attitude or environment of cultural appreciation. Children's literature can provide valuable classroom resources that support multicultural education.

# Enrichment

Enrichment is a technique used for extending a lesson or unit for those students who are capable of participating in more instruction or gaining additional information. This list offers suggested strategies to aid elementary education teachers in planning instruction that addresses enrichment. These strategies are often used with students who are considered gifted or talented:

- Self-paced instruction
- Compacting or telescoping curriculum
- Mentoring programs
- Tiered lessons
- Summer programs
- Additional special focus courses
- Ability grouping
- Advanced placement courses
- Extracurricular programs
- Skipping grade levels

# Assessment

A major factor in identifying student success in any academic area is the evaluation of learning. **Assessment** is part of the educational process in which a teacher may gather, examine, and share information about the skills, abilities, and achievements of individual students. The teacher may use this information to set new goals for learning, create expectations, and determine future outcomes.

The primary purpose of assessment is to evaluate student achievement, make decisions pertaining to instruction, and review instructional programs. An assessment helps gather data that allows students to understand their own learning process and aids the teacher in designing activities and selecting strategies appropriate for the students. Whether using daily informal assessment techniques or standardized testing, the results provide valuable information.

There are two general types of instructional assessments:

- **Formative assessment** is the collection of data through ongoing daily lessons or units of study in order to analyze student achievement and assist students in the ongoing learning process.
- **Summative assessment** is the collection of data at a specific completion point in the learning process in order to identify student needs and make decisions or alterations that support student learning. This type of evaluation is most often used at the end of a unit of study to analyze a particular concept or skill or at the end of a grading period to measure progress in a subject area.

## Formal Assessment

A broad category under this topic is **formal assessment.** Formal assessments are systematic evaluations with strict procedures for administration and scoring. These assessments are often used to comply with requirements and issues of accountability, report cards or progress reports, and curriculum effectiveness. Often referred to as standardized tests, they are used to:

- Provide information on student progress.
- Deliver information on the placement of students.
- Help in planning educational activities for all students.

- Improve instruction for individuals and groups.
- Evaluate programs and classrooms.
- Meet the accountability requirements.

Standardized testing has a set of uniform procedures for administration and scoring, and these procedures must be followed to ensure that valid and reliable testing conditions are present. Standardized testing includes a set of norms, compares students to others at the same age, and evaluates for knowledge of concepts and information. Standardized assessments include achievement tests, aptitude tests, competency evaluations, and performance examinations.

**High-stakes testing** is used to comply with the accountability requirements under the education reform structure and the No Child Left Behind mandate. These tests measure how well schools are educating youth by assessing student achievement levels. Since this is such a new process with very little research on the effect of the tests or the procedures for administration, professionals are unsure of the type of information best gathered through high-stakes testing or how to use the information. The topic of high-stakes testing is a current educational issue that is under debate.

| Pros | Cons |
| --- | --- |
| Instills higher expectations | Promotes rote memory instead of more complex cognitive skills |
| Focuses on instruction in specific subject/content area | Focuses the instruction on the content that is on the test |
| Improves student performance in testing | Lacks funds and guidelines for remediation of learners |
| Identifies under-performing schools and educators | Discriminates against culturally and linguistically diverse groups |

# Informal Assessment

Informal educational assessments are periodic evaluations that help professionals gather pertinent information about a student in the natural environment. These informal measures may be used to support a more formal or standardized assessment or for continued and ongoing progress evaluations. Informal assessments do not follow a specific set of norms and are open to teacher, professional, or parent interpretation. They may include anecdotal records, running records, portfolio assessments, and dynamic assessments.

# Interpretation of Data

Instructional decisions are often made based on the information gathered through an assessment. Assessment data helps to identify student achievement during instructional periods. The data may be collected informally on a daily basis, gathered at the end of an instructional unit, collected throughout the studies, or gathered periodically when using more formal testing. The use of data information helps the teacher adjust instruction for students, supporting the learning process for all individuals. Knowledge of test terms, procedures, statistics, and scoring will help educators understand outcomes related to student tests as well as how to deliver information to other professionals in meetings or parents at conferences.

# Procedures

Appropriate assessment procedures are necessary to obtain valid, reliable, and accurate data about students and instruction. The assessment must have a clearly stated purpose and be closely related to the outcomes being sought. It is best when the assessment is ongoing so the information may be used to change the subject content or alter the instruction or situation for the learner to better meet needs. The assessment tools must be appropriate for the student in order to gather relevant academic information.

Education reform has focused on accountability through assessment; how this occurs continues to be a debated issue. Teachers must be knowledgeable about the assessment process and the various techniques, as well as the options that are available for use in their classrooms. Standardized tests, district tests, and high-stakes state tests are best administered in a child's primary language, free from racial or cultural bias.

# Types of Assessment Strategies

Assessment in the classroom should not always be separated from the instruction. Creating an environment in which daily instruction and assessment are integrated provides regular and effective information to the teacher. Many different strategies may be implemented to meet the assessment needs of particular situations, and these can be described according to two different categories: **authentic** and **traditional** assessment. Authentic assessments are those that are considered alternatives to traditional examinations. Traditional assessments are reflected by "paper and pencil" tasks.

Examples of authentic assessments include the following:

- **Performance tasks**—Require that students complete a problem or project, which includes an explanation for the answer and addresses a particular skill
- **Observation**—A simple method of assessment to identify the performance of students completing various activities and tasks, using anecdotal records and checklists for recording documentation
- **Journal writing**—Written reflections that allow teachers to informally gauge student learning through their thinking processes, formation of ideas, and development of skills in creative and factual writing
- **Portfolios**—A collection of completed student work selected by the student and the teacher to demonstrate strengths, progress, and skills

Examples of traditional types of assessments include the following:

| Quizzes | Essay questions |
|---|---|
| Chapter tests | Formal assessments |
| True/false questions | Multiple choice questions |
| Fill-in-the-blank questions | Matching |

# Terms

Types of measurement tools that may be utilized include the following:

- **Achievement test**—Formal tool used to measure student proficiency in a subject area already learned
- **Alternative assessment**—Informal tool that provides more options to students who apply knowledge and use learned skills to solve realistic problems and complete projects related to real-life situations
- **Anecdotal record**—Informal measurement based on an observation of student work or performance
- **Aptitude test**—Formal measure of standardized or norm-referenced tests that evaluate student ability to acquire skills or gain knowledge
- **Authentic assessment**—Method that is less concrete and more subjective to determine a student's understanding and performance of specific criteria (write a story, create a project, give a presentation)
- **Criterion-referenced test**—Formal measure that evaluates a student on certain subject area information by answering specific questions, while not comparing one student to another
- **Curriculum-based measure**—Measure that helps determine student progress and performance based on the lessons presented in the curriculum, so a teacher may better assist the student
- **Diagnostic assessment**—Method to collect information about a student to use in assessment throughout the period of instruction
- **Direct daily measurement**—Classroom form of daily assessment of a student's performance on the skills that are taught each day; may be used to modify instruction for particular students as needed
- **Dynamic assessment**—Tool that determines a student's ability to learn in a certain situation rather than documenting what the student has actually learned
- **Ecological-based assessment**—Informal observation of a student interacting with the environment during a regular schedule

- **Intelligence test (IQ test)**—Norm-referenced test used to measure cognitive behaviors in order to assess student learning abilities or intellectual capacity

- **Norm-referenced test**—Formal standardized evaluation used to compare a student to other peers in the same age group; aids in developing curriculum options

- **Observation**—Method in which a teacher or other professional watches a student in different settings to obtain information regarding performance and behaviors

- **Performance-based assessment**—Informal measure used to assess a student's ability to complete a task that is specific to a topic or subject area

- **Portfolio assessment**—Informal method of gathering information and samples of completed work over a period of time (art, projects, reports); useful for tracking progress of a particular student

- **Rubric**—A set standard rating scale used to determine performance abilities on a single task

- **Standards-based assessment**—Formal evaluation such as a criterion-referenced or norm-referenced test that measures student progress toward meeting goals or standards previously established

# General Topics

Teaching involves more than just providing new concepts and content to students. Teaching requires that educators be actively involved in their careers by enrolling in memberships of organizations, seeking training opportunities, working with parents, and collaborating with peers. Teachers should be reflective practitioners who continue to improve professionally by assessing their knowledge, evaluating their instructional abilities, and using creative new ideas and techniques to address learners' needs.

# Professional Development

Education reform over the past several years has focused on professional teacher training to enhance student academic success. Teacher preparation is an ongoing process as standards are refined, high-stakes tests are promoted, technology advances, and students evolve. Educators must be realistic in their abilities to utilize state standards, manage accountability factors, and deliver consistent curriculum activities.

Teachers play a key role in the development of students, and in order to be effective, teachers must also develop their own professional repertoire. Teachers need time to work with colleagues both for training and planning. Educators should avoid isolation; they should support a shared vision and be involved in team efforts.

# Teaching Styles

Educators often develop a style of teaching early in their careers, which is based on their beliefs about teaching, their personal preferences, and their abilities. Some educators believe they should use a teaching style that is teacher-centered, acting as the information authority. Other professionals prefer a student-centered approach, acting as a facilitator of learning. Individual teachers cultivate a preferred teaching style, but they may mix elements of various styles to create something quite unique yet effective.

According to Grasha (1994, 1996), teaching styles can be described in five ways:

| Teaching Style | Description |
| --- | --- |
| Expert | Possesses knowledge of subject and challenges students' competence and skill development in the content |
| Formal authority | Prefers standard and acceptable procedures; clear expectations and structure but often rigid and inflexible |
| Personal model (demonstrator) | Leads by example; models, guides, and directs students; considers various learning styles |
| Facilitator | Promotes independence, initiative, and responsibility; consults, supports, and encourages students |
| Delegator | Encourages autonomy in learners and is available as a consultative resource |

# Collaboration

Working with other teachers and professionals enhances your career as an educator, but these relationships are built on trust and respect, which must be earned and reciprocated. Involving the community in the classroom is another way to collaborate with other adults who have interests in promoting education. Include community mentors and experts and use the community as a resource for culturally and linguistically diverse students. The collaboration of education, recreation, and health services all enhance the well-being of students.

In schools where teachers work collaboratively, students can sense coherency and consistency of expectations, which can lead to improved behavior and achievement. For teachers, collaborations can lead to collegiality, which can help break the isolation of the classroom and offer daily satisfactions. It is one method that helps teachers and administrators avoid end-of-year burnout and can usually stimulate enthusiasm. Working closely together on matters of curriculum and instruction allows teachers and other staff to feel better equipped for classroom work. Frequently, professional relationships are forged that are able to withstand differences in viewpoints and occasional conflict.

Teacher collaboration also helps avoid the "sink-or-swim," trial-and-error mode that new teachers typically face. It helps bring experienced and beginning teachers together to reinforce competence and confidence.

Teacher teamwork makes the complex tasks involved in curriculum and in education more manageable as well as stimulates new ideas and promotes coherence in a school's curriculum and instruction. Together, in a team situation, teachers have the organizational skills and resources to try innovations that would otherwise exhaust the skill, resources, and energy of a single teacher.

Schools can benefit from teacher collaboration in a variety of ways:

- Through formal and informal training sessions, study groups, and conversations about teaching, teachers and administrators get the opportunity to develop together.
- Teachers are better prepared to support one another's strengths and accommodate weaknesses. By working together, teachers are able to reduce individual planning time and at the same time increase the cache of ideas and materials.
- Schools will be better prepared and organized to examine new ideas, methods, and materials. Through collaboration the faculty becomes adaptable and self-reliant.

# Technology

Technology has impacted education and classroom activities in multiple ways, as it changes students' experiences and the educational environment. Technology provides increased access and refined practices in such areas as communication, research, and record keeping. It offers visual and auditory input, such as access to historical archives and artifacts, research on collections from other libraries or scientists, photographs and visual images, and virtual tours of museums.

The field of technology has skyrocketed in the last decade, encompassing every aspect of our daily lives. Computers and computer-related studies have grown immensely within the educational setting. Most Americans use the Internet, computers, or cellular technology to conduct everyday activities. Technology is a common and motivating tool for teachers to use in order to help students learn how to solve complex problems as well as develop higher order thinking, creativity, and research skills.

Both technology-enhanced education and technology-delivered education have evolved greatly over the last few years. There are multiple positive aspects that technology can provide for the classroom and for the learner. Some can include:

- Provides prompt feedback
- Involves multiple disciplines
- Respects diverse learning styles

- Encourages communication between students and teachers
- Promotes cooperation between peers
- Emphasizes time on-task
- Offers active learning techniques
- Supplies a vast network of information
- Bridges abstract and concrete thinking

There are many types of technology available for classroom use. A wide variety of tasks and lessons can be created based upon technology. The key for educators is to be fluent in the various forms of technology in order to provide quality education. Some technology that can be used in the classroom includes:

| | |
|---|---|
| Cellphones | Keyboarding |
| Class blog or wikis | Mobile devices |
| Class website | Podcasts |
| Classroom PCs | Projectors |
| Computers | Publishing applications |
| Digital cameras | SMART technologies (boards) |
| Drawing and illustration applications | Tool-based applications |
| DVDs | Video camera |
| Educational software | Video streaming |
| Interactive whiteboards | WebQuests |
| Internet | Wireless microphones |

There are four main categories for the application of technology within the classroom:

- **Media for Inquiry**—Data modeling, online databases, spreadsheets, hypertext, online microscopes, and online observatories
- **Media for Communication**—E-mail, blogs, word processing, face-to-face conferencing, simulations, tutorials, and social networks
- **Media for Construction**—Robotics, control systems, and computer-aided design
- **Media for Expression**—Animation software, music composition software, design and illustration applications, video software, and interactive video

Students can learn *from* technology in which the technology serves as a tutor or helps to build the learner's base knowledge and foundation. Or students can learn *with* technology in which the technology serves as a tool to help foster higher ordered thinking, creativity, and problem-solving skills. Integrating technology into the classroom is an essential component to a successful student.

# Parents

Professionals are encouraged to include parents and families as partners in the educational process and to involve them in the classroom and other school activities. Educators should acknowledge the role that parents play in a child's life and gain parental support through positive actions and responses. Teachers should create an alliance with parents and work together to guide and enhance the student's education.

This parent-teacher partnership is a meaningful component to education programs. Research shows that actively involved parents can have a positive influence on their child's performance at school, resulting in a higher, more successful academic level. Parents may provide continued support to their child and offer resources to the class, which adds opportunities for unique learning situations.

Communication with parents is necessary for developing a positive partnership and may include class newsletters or websites, parent-teacher conferences, handwritten or e-mailed messages, telephone calls, home visits, and specific homework activities.

| Working with and Supporting Parents | |
|---|---|
| **Researcher** | **Description** |
| Popkin "Active parenting" | Parents must establish leadership roles in the family, so they can effectively train, support, and encourage their children, teaching them to make proper choices and use appropriate behaviors. |
| Dinkmeyer/McCay "Step approach" | Parents should implement a system of goals, giving choices, setting limits, utilizing logical consequences, using I-messages, practicing reflective listening, and teaching values. |
| Baker | Parental involvement programs and training help to improve relationships and support, which enhance learning. |
| McCormack-Larkin | Ongoing communication with parents is a critical element in successful school achievement. |

# Chapter 2
# Reading/Language Arts Curriculum, Instruction, and Assessment (0011/5011)

The reading and language arts portion of the Praxis II exam (0011/5011) assesses an examinee's overall knowledge and application of information regarding curriculum, instruction, and assessment, specifically in reading, grammar, writing, and speaking. In this section of the study guide, examinees will find content specific to these topics and the more general elementary practices will be found in Chapter 1.

The 0011/5011 exam measures how well an examinee knows how to develop and deliver instruction based on reading and language arts content knowledge. This exam utilizes examples of elementary school situations in a multiple-choice question format. This section of the study guide includes the information necessary for the examinee to clearly utilize the content of 0014/5014 in the implementation of curriculum and instruction and the use of assessments in reading and language arts instruction.

The acquisition of language begins even before birth and emerges more completely through a series of developmental stages in early childhood. Educators must build upon a child's experiences and knowledge of the language in order for the student to achieve success in school. Learning to read and understanding how to use the components of language is a difficult area to master.

Reading and language arts are two critical components in a student's education. The subject of language arts is comprised of the areas that include reading, spelling, and composition that aim at developing reading and writing skills. This includes comprehension and written and oral language skills most often taught at the elementary level and continuing through high school.

Reading achievement is the single most essential skill for success in school, as all subjects require that individuals be able to read to gain information. Three factors can predict reading achievement:

1. The ability to recognize and name letters of the alphabet
2. Basic general knowledge about print
3. The awareness of phonemes

The National Institute for Literacy and the Center for Education Statistics suggests that more than 40 million adults are functionally illiterate and that students at the elementary-school level still lack basic skills. Gaining these skills requires strong oral language ability and an understanding of the use of language. Learning reading skills is not a natural process supported only by literacy-rich environments and the acquisition of certain skills through practice. It is much more.

Reading is the act of finding meaning from print. It is a multifaceted process that requires motivation and skills in word recognition, comprehension, and fluency. Children learn to read when their teacher is knowledgeable about language development and skilled in the reading process, as well as focused on the appropriate instruction and strategies. Research shows that the most important variable in a reading program is the teacher's knowledge and possession of skills to execute a comprehensive program. For children to succeed, educators must be careful diagnosticians and focus on individual skills as they approach instruction.

Reading and the use of language arts skills is a basic necessity in our society. Students need these skills to function on a daily basis as children and then later as adults. Establishing a rigorous program and teaching reading and language arts with fidelity will ensure that students gain the proper skills. Implementing an integrated curriculum based on national and state standards for reading and language arts that includes developmentally appropriate activities, as well as motivational and meaningful tasks, will help all students gain skills to the best of their individual abilities.

# Standards Overview

More than ten years ago, the International Reading Association (IRA) together with the National Council of Teachers of English (NCTE) published 12 standards for the area of English Language Arts. The purpose of the standards is to provide an outline that ensures that all students are proficient language users in school, in the community, and in their work. These standards, developed through work by educators, parents, researchers, and others, delineate the language skills necessary for students to become productive citizens, who appreciate and contribute to the culture and society, who pursue a life full of personal goals directed at their own interests, and who continue to communicate and learn in the world around them.

Children need appropriate opportunities, an array of experiences, proper materials, and adequate resources to acquire language skills. These standards, set forth by the IRA and the NCTE, should help educators in the development of curriculum and instruction to encourage students to use emerging literacy abilities. These standards are general broad statements so teachers may continue to be innovative in their teaching and use a variety of instructional strategies for their diverse students.

Following is a summary list of the standards, and examinees should notice that the concepts are interrelated. Students will:

1. Read a variety of print and nonprint texts to develop an understanding of texts and the world; to gain new information; to respond to personal and societal needs.

2. Read a wide range of literature in several genres from different periods to expand their understanding of the various dimensions of the human experience.

3. Apply strategies to comprehend, interpret, and evaluate texts in the process of learning to appreciate various uses and pleasures gained from text. This draws on prior experience, knowledge of word skills, and text features.

4. Modify the use of spoken, written, and visual language in utilizing more effective communications applied to various audiences and purposes.

5. Implement strategies for writing and use a variety of writing process elements to learn how to deliver a purposeful message to different audiences.

6. Use and apply knowledge of language structure, grammar, techniques, and genre to compose print and nonprint texts.

7. Perform research and evaluate and synthesize data to communicate findings that align with the purpose and suit the audience.

8. Use technology-related sources and other resources to collect and interpret information and to create and communicate knowledge.

9. Develop an understanding of and respect for diversity in language across cultures, ethnic groups, geographic regions, and social roles.

10. Use their first language to develop competency in the English language arts and to gain access to the curriculum.

11. Participate as knowledgeable members of a variety of literacy communities.

12. Use spoken, written, and visual language to accomplish personal purposes.

# Curriculum and Instruction

Language arts integrates the areas and skills related to reading, spelling, writing, and grammar. In elementary school, students learn the basic components and structures of these individual areas and practice the skills in order to apply them across the curriculum to other academic subjects. The curriculum focuses on content defined as grade-appropriate and aligns state as well as district standards and requirements into the plan.

Researchers believe there are certain types of knowledge and specific skills necessary for students to become successful in learning how to read and write. Educators should be familiar with the developmental stages of language acquisition, as well as promote the use of oral language and vocabulary. Children must have speaking and listening skills prior to gaining reading and writing skills. Three skills that are critical to learning to read and write include the following:

- Print knowledge—Understanding of print letters, words, and books
- Emergent writing—Using print in meaningful ways
- Linguistic awareness—Comprehending language use

Reading and writing foundations are built upon a student's previous knowledge as well as increasing and improving their language with experiences that include listening, thinking, and speaking opportunities. Creating letter-sound relationships is a part of the stories that children may read and the content they write. During the instructional process these should be tied to meaning. The use of big books, trade books, class books, and other sources rich in rhyme, rhythm, and repetition engages young children and should be used daily in the classroom.

## Language Acquisition

Language awareness is the ability to understand the sound structure of language. It is the process by which individuals learn to perceive, produce, and use words to communicate and understand. It is an oral language and listening skill that is essential to learning how to read and write. Language acquisition, which includes syntax, phonetics, and vocabulary, is a phenomenal undertaking for an individual because it depends on the background, experiences, and exposure at a very young age.

Children begin to develop language skills as infants. Babies can listen to sounds, imitate what they hear, and begin to use common words, finally putting together a string of two to four words that have meaning. Children's vocabularies grow as they develop and socialize. By the time they begin preschool, most are able to speak in sentences, tell stories, share feelings, and have conversations.

Children acquire language in natural settings during typical experiences, but not without the guidance and models of adults and older children. They must learn from adults how language is used effectively in the world. Children must hear how language is used and separated into different parts in order to acquire the basic skills.

Examples of linguistic awareness (the understanding of how words and language work) include the following:

- Developing vocabulary
- Recognizing rhyming words
- Matching words by sounds
- Understanding syllables
- Printing letters and words
- Writing messages and stories

Here are some examples of activities to aid children in gaining language acquisition:

- Play games with sounds.
- Use clapping to emphasize syllable breaks.
- Sing songs with rhymes and rhythms.
- Recite poems with alliterative passages.
- Read stories with predictable sound patterns.
- Utilize jokes and silly riddles for verbal play.
- Use pictures in books to encourage oral language.

# Print Awareness and Knowledge

Early literacy skills lead to reading and writing readiness and encompass the development of print awareness and knowledge. Children as young as 2 years old can gain knowledge about print and realize that those symbols have meaning, a concept which motivates their interest in words and ultimately in learning to read and write. Encouraging an interest in reading is a primary factor in developing future reading skills.

**Print knowledge** is the understanding that printed letters and words have meaning. Children realize that letters become words, words become sentences, and sentences have meaning. Print knowledge includes the awareness that books are used for a purpose.

Examples of print knowledge skills include an understanding that:

Print has meaning.

Print and pictures are different.

Print has different purposes.

Books have rules (title and author listed, how it opens, and so on).

Grammar is involved with printed words.

Activities that help young children gain awareness and knowledge of print include the following:

Pointing out letters and respective sounds

Reading single words and explaining them

Singing the alphabet

Reading signs while driving or shopping

Reading stories aloud

Using big books for group readings

Talking about stories

Practicing language experience stories

Using traditional songs and rhymes

Providing a special area for children to look at reading materials independently

Using environmental print in the classroom

Playing alphabet and word games

To learn skills for reading, students must first learn that print has meaning. This occurs at different ages and stages depending on a student's previous experiences with print. After students are taught the process of print awareness, they are more ready to become successful readers, and the following skills of reading emerge:

- Being aware that sounds are represented in printed words, which is **phonemic awareness**
- Identifying words in print, which is vocabulary development or **word recognition**
- Decoding the sounds of familiar and unfamiliar words, which is the use of **phonics**
- Constructing an understanding from the words, which is **comprehension**
- Coordinating the words and meaning so reading becomes automatic, which is **fluency**

# Reading

Children learn to read and write from the many opportunities available in the home and at school on a daily and regular basis. When parents read aloud and use reading and writing in the home, children become aware of the importance and gain skills indirectly. When teachers promote vocabulary and allow children to interact with books and writing materials, children become interested in learning more. Children need experiences with reading and writing, so they may draw upon this previous knowledge to apply it to word meanings, cues, and language structures in their academic work.

The purpose of teaching reading is to help students

- Gain information from text.
- Improve communications.
- Increase pleasure.

Developing **decoding skills** is the process of understanding that letters in text represent the sounds (phonemes) in speech. In order to learn how to decode words, a student must understand that letters in text represent the phonemes in speech. Phoneme awareness is a necessary prerequisite for developing decoding skills in an alphabetic writing system. Some students have difficulty developing decoding skills as they lack phonological processing skills, while others may not have received adequate instruction in the domains that are essential for acquiring decoding skills (print concepts, letter knowledge, understanding of the alphabetic principle). Students require ample opportunities to practice as well as real-world situation practice to become fluent and automatic in word recognition. Using an across-the-curriculum approach to teaching reading seems to provide a strong collective opportunity for students to acquire and practice needed skills.

Creating a curriculum that focuses on reading and integrates other subject areas can be a challenge for educators. Educators must be cognizant of the scope and sequence established for the school curriculum as well as the standards set at the state level and requirements at the district level. A reading program requires that teachers use a variety of strategies and methods and base their instruction on conducting individual diagnostics on all students. Curriculum development for reading and language arts should include instruction in phonemic awareness, phonics, spelling, reading fluency, grammar, writing, and reading comprehension strategies. A curriculum is a guide and not a substitute for a well-trained and effective teacher.

The National Research Council recommends that instead of simply developing a program that focuses on phonics instruction and whole-language instruction, educators should integrate their approach and utilize appropriate activities and materials. They should include instruction in alphabetic principle (understanding that word sounds are linked to certain letters and patterns), phonemic awareness, vocabulary, fluency, and comprehension in a comprehensive approach to learning to read.

## Reading Levels

Teachers spend a lot of time building literacy skills with students at all levels. This is often a challenge due to the vast array of needs found within one classroom. Differentiating reading assignments and instruction by utilizing the various levels can help teachers meet the diverse needs of learners. Research studies indicate that grouping students according to their reading abilities can be instrumental in improving their skills.

Assessment of student reading abilities will help provide details on specific skills and can offer prescriptive approaches to improve specific areas. Screening tools and diagnostic instruments aid in grouping students based on their abilities. Students may be grouped in a three-tiered system that consists of 1) below-level learners (struggling readers); 2) on-level learners (general readers); and 3) independent learners (advanced readers).

When time is scheduled every day for skill development, the teacher may provide direct instruction to students so they will be better able to grasp skills that are lacking. Ongoing diagnostics aid the teacher in regrouping students as skills are mastered, although research suggests that teachers should leave students in their groups for extended periods in order to ensure attainment and build confidence in their reading.

## Reading Approaches

There are several leading perspectives about the instruction of reading at the elementary level. These approaches have proven to be effective for different types of learners, yet each may suggest that there needs to be more variety for the learner rather than using only one approach. Combining approaches, or selecting core principles from several approaches, is recommended, since classes vary from year to year and needs are diverse.

**Whole language** is an approach based in both research and practice. Studies include the psycholinguistic and social nature of the process of reading, how individuals may learn concepts and express ideas, how reading and writing are interrelated within the structures of language, and the basics of literacy. This approach coincides with the constructivist theory of learning. The approach promotes the use of students' language knowledge and their experiences to increase and improve their reading abilities. Key concepts of the **whole language approach** include the following:

- **Meaningful context:** Reading materials are based on content and information that has meaning for the student and the age group.
- **Acceptance of all learners:** Teachers work with students to create the environment and the instructional activities.
- **Flexible structure:** Ample time is allowed for students to be engaged in meaningful projects and lessons in which they are responsible for their own learning.
- **Supportive classroom:** Teachers expect students to cooperate and interact to enhance their own learning.
- **Integrated approach:** Other subject areas are combined into thematic units and lessons.
- **Focused expectations:** Teachers provide whole texts and encourage reading and writing at a higher level.
- **Context skill development:** As students read and write, teachers interject skills in spelling, grammar, reading, and writing.
- **Collaboration and scaffolding:** Teachers provide ongoing support to students and work together to meet learner needs.
- **Authentic assessments:** Regular diagnostics based on individual student work are integrated across the curriculum.

**Phonics instruction** is an approach that evolved around the same time period as the whole language approach. One method of reading instruction, it promotes the relationships between the sounds in spoken language (phonemes) and the letters that represent the sounds when written (graphemes) for word recognition. Systematic, explicit phonics is considered an effective method because the instruction includes sets of letter-sound relationships that are organized into sequences, and the directions for the instruction are precise and clear. This method of instruction may be used either separately or in combination with other methods. Key points of the **phonics instruction approach** include the following:

- Explicit instruction in phonemic awareness and functional phonics is necessary.
- Phonics instruction may be best suited to use in context.
- Children learn phonics when they address reading and writing activities.

Terms related to phonics instruction include the following:

- **Analogy-based phonics:** A strategy that helps students use parts of words they have learned to attack words that are unfamiliar to them.
- **Analytic phonics:** A method that enables students to analyze letter-sound relationships from learned words to unfamiliar words while not pronouncing any sounds in isolation.
- **Embedded phonics:** A type of explicit instruction for using letter-sound relationships during the reading of connected text as a way to help students sight-read new words.
- **Intrinsic phonics:** A type of instruction taught gradually to students using context during meaningful reading periods.
- **Onset-rime phonics:** The instruction of separating onsets and rimes (both different components of words) in words so students may read them and then blend the parts together into the word.
- **Phonics and spelling:** A method of teaching students to segment words into phonemes and create words by writing the letters for the phonemes.
- **Synthetic phonics:** A method of teaching students to convert letters or combinations of letters into sound sequences and then blend the sounds to form words.

There are various ways to promote phonics in the classroom. Using student names, reciting nursery rhymes, playing sound games, reading poems, and singing songs, while also reading alphabet books, discussing words and sounds, making word banks, and pointing out consonants and vowels are just a few examples of ways to instill phonics.

Using the **basal reading approach (whole word),** students are often taught through a series or predeveloped program that includes readers, manuals, workbooks, flashcards, and tests. There have been some programs with adjustments to this approach as publishers are considering the stages of reading when designing their series. Due to the emphasis on emergent literacy, programs have been moved down to the kindergarten and even the preschool level and include a preprimer, a primer, and a first reader. Basal programs can be either **meaning-emphasis** or **code-emphasis** programs, and developers often recommend that teachers use a direct approach to reading.

In the **literature-based reading approach,** children's literature and trade books are utilized in a leveled format. The readers are selected through a specific criteria based on reading stages or grade levels. Using this approach helps students become interested and motivated to read and to be able to select various types of literature. Components include the following:

- The teacher reads aloud to the class.
- Students participate in oral reading periods.
- Shared reading activities are provided.
- Sustained silent reading blocks are included.

The **linguistic approach** focuses on the mastery of words rather than using isolated sounds. The materials that teachers use in this approach generally lack pictures so students will not be distracted from the reading; however, this limits oral language development.

The **language experience approach** integrates the development of reading skills with listening, speaking, and writing. Students dictate stories to the teacher, which become the basis for the students' first reading experiences. In the language experience approach, it is assumed that writing is a secondary system derived from oral language, while whole language looks at writing and reading as structurally related.

The **individualized reading approach** is a less structured approach to reading in which students are allowed to choose the reading selections and work at their own rates for improving reading skills and comprehension. The educator facilitates the program by completing diagnostics, meeting with students individually to listen to their oral reading, and evaluating their comprehension. This approach may be complicated for some learners who lack motivation and basic reading skills.

# Literature

Literature is one area of language arts that is important to skill development and other subject areas. The study of literature allows students to make comparisons and connections to self, to others, to the environment, and to the world.

Literature study provides students with the

Exposure to a variety of genres.

Understanding of cultural diversity.

Appreciation for a variety of literature.

Identification of major components: perspectives, themes, main ideas, dialogues, characters, and outcomes.

Application of skills and content to other subject areas.

Desire to continue to enjoy good literature for a lifetime.

Because students gain insight into such areas as cultures, historical periods, ideas, and values from reading literature, these readings may be influential on their development and their writings later. Reading various types of literary works allows students to learn to analyze and interpret the messages delivered by the author.

Students should be taught the components and types of literature available, as investigating literature will continue throughout their school career and hopefully throughout their lifetimes. They need to know the genre, the content, the structure, and the language of the text, and use their prior knowledge to glean the appropriate information from the context of the passage or story. Merging new information with prior knowledge will help build upon their skills.

In using literature to improve skills, the selection of genre and specific content should be based on one of three student reading abilities:

1. **Independent level:** Student reads, comprehends, and can make responses without assistance.
2. **Instructional level:** Student reads to comprehend with assistance and may need pre-reading help such as an introduction to characters, new vocabulary, or asking questions.
3. **Frustration level:** Student is unable to read and comprehend even with assistance.

There is a wide variety of genres available in the study of literature, and these may be utilized at all grade levels and integrated with other subject areas.

- Autobiographies
- Biographies
- Epics
- Fables
- Fairy tales
- Fantasy
- Folk tales
- Historical fiction
- Indian legends
- Mystery
- Myths
- Novels
- Plays
- Poetry
- Science fiction
- Short stories
- Tall tales

A **narrative** is a piece of literature that tells a story and incorporates the elements of sequential events, time, characters, and plot to deliver a description to the reader. It may be fictional or nonfictional and in the format of a poem, a song, a story, and so on. Using narratives in the classroom not only improves a student's reading skills, but moves the student toward developing and improving writing skills. Narratives include new vocabulary, descriptive words and phrases, and realistic views of people and the environment. Educators can incorporate reading narratives with writing in journals, creating personal stories, improving oral and written vocabulary, and comparing format to other types of literature.

Another type of literature important in language arts instruction is poetry. **Poetry instruction** should focus on an understanding of literal and figurative meanings of words, and the definitions and uses of metaphors, similes, and patterns of language. Studying the structural elements of poetry such as assonance, alliteration, rhyme, and rhythm will also guide students to improve word knowledge and the use of language.

# Writing

The nature of writing, as well as the expectations of writing, have undergone tremendous changes in the past century and a half. Many of these changes have occurred due to advances in technology (software, computers, networks, and so on). These developments affect not only the way writers write, but also the way readers are able to access written text. Writing continues to be a huge part of students' lives outside of the classroom as evident with such activities as e-mailing, texting, blogging, making websites, keeping a journal, and creating a project.

Writing is a tool for thinking. As people write they must think of the subject matter, the concepts they wish to convey, the ideas they wish to express, the tone they seek to set forth, and the purpose for which they write. Writing generates ideas and is a medium for thought. Different purposes for writing can yield different ideas and help solve problems, construct questions, revamp old ideas, and expand underdeveloped concepts.

Writing goes hand in hand with reading. These are often taught simultaneously with increased skill development as children mature. Both are necessary for all content areas. Learning to write involves a complex cognitive process and can be very difficult for the many diverse learners in a classroom. Readers expect written documents to conform to certain expectations: grammatically correct, appropriate spelling, usage and syntax coordination, and style according to the genre of writing. Therefore, reading and writing are symbiotic skills for which students must learn formulas and structures. Writers become better readers, and readers become better writers.

Students learn to write by writing, and students need instruction on how to write, as well as knowledge about the structures of writing. Writing should be practiced in both real-world and classroom situations to solidify the process. Students need to be familiar with the assorted purposes of different writings and should be able to employ processes and strategies in a variety of situations.

There are many ways to incorporate writing into the classroom. Each technique must keep in mind the purpose for which the writing occurs; a note to a brother is vastly different in tone and structure than a business report. Teachers can incorporate the different types of purpose into many of the techniques used to teach writing. A common way to teach writing is often through a writing workshop to teach the stages of writing and help children master form, structure, and production process (outline, draft, revisions, publication).

Teachers may also draw on process-based writing instruction and the six-traits approach to writing. In process-based instruction, teachers may scaffold instruction to meet the diversity of learners as they

- Model the trait or strategy.
- Use guided practice with the trait or strategy.
- Allow individual practice of the trait or strategy.
- Promote application of the trait or strategy.

In the **six-traits approach,** the key components aid learners of all abilities to access and use good writing. It breaks the difficult process of writing into six smaller processes:

- **Ideas**—The message that presents the purpose, includes the theme, the main idea, and the details to engage the reader and deliver understanding
- **Organization**—The construction of the piece into the proper format, using a beginning, a middle, and an end to pursue the purpose
- **Voice**—The personal and unique style of the writer that provides the reader with a connection to and an interest in the piece
- **Word choice**—The use of words, phrases, and language selected by the writer to create the appropriate meaning
- **Sentence fluency**—The manner in which the writer composes the sentences and paragraphs to give a flow to the piece that is rhythmic and easy to read
- **Conventions**—The grammar, spelling, punctuation, and word use that is considered when the piece is edited to support its meaning and purpose

# Emergent Writing

Young children are playful with writing when given the opportunity to use the proper materials (paper, pencils, and so on). Setting up centers in the classroom will help to instill a desire to write for a purpose. When writing activities are attached to a meaningful purpose, children become more interested and develop skills that lead to success with writing. Younger children should begin using writing instruments to draw and scribble. They must develop their fine motor skills in order to have proper control for more formal written assignments. Materials and activities should be age-appropriate and easily accessible.

Once a child has mastered the stage of scribbling, he or she will move to one-letter spelling and then writing a few words. This leads a child into talking as he or she works, experimenting with the sounds of language. The child may write his or her name or the name of a pet, use simple phrases, and move toward constructing invented spelling of words.

Examples of emergent writing include the following:

> Scribbling
>
> Drawing
>
> Copying
>
> Printing letters
>
> Inventing spelling
>
> Composing messages

# Spelling

Spelling is the formation of words from letters according to set principles of a language. Research has shown that spelling is a developmental process with five complex stages, and instruction in spelling is essential to the developmental process. More than one stage may be present in a sample writing by an individual student. These stages include the following:

1. **Pre-communicative**—Uses symbols from the alphabet but no knowledge of letter-sound correspondence
2. **Semi-phonetic**—Begins to understand letter-sound correspondence
3. **Phonetic**—Uses a letter or group of letters for every speech sound heard and may not conform to the more conventional spelling
4. **Transitional**—Understands the conventional alternative for sounds and the structure of words
5. **Correct**—Knows the orthographic system and the basic rules, making generalizations

Spelling can be described using three of the most common categories:

1. **Regular spelling** is considered the regular spelling manner for words in which the pronunciation can be predicted based on the spelling because the spelling reflects one or more typical patterns. These patterns are useful in reading selections in which there are unfamiliar words.
2. **Irregular spelling** is considered those words that do not follow the regularly established patterns of spelling and therefore, the spelling for these words must be memorized.
3. **Invented spelling** is a student's attempt to use his or her personal judgment to guess how a word is spelled. It may be a step for some students in the process of learning to spell and reaching the final stage of **correct spelling,** where they apply spelling principles appropriately. Even students who are receiving standard spelling instruction may continue to use invented spelling for a couple of years.

When teachers are knowledgeable about the developmental stages in the spelling process, they are more apt to create an appropriate plan for instruction. It is recommended that students learn phonetic relationships and sound-spelling correspondences and be able to adjust the principles and rules of spelling as they move through the stages. At each stage, teachers should instruct students in different strategies on how to approach spelling. Students should learn about alphabet knowledge, letter-sound correspondences, left-to-right directionality, word families, spelling patterns, phonics, word structures, irregular spellings, and manipulating or building words.

Spelling and pronunciation comply with certain patterns in the English language even though they may not always have letter-by-letter or sound-to-sound correspondence. Instructional strategies aid students in learning to decode unfamiliar words. Strategies for spelling should include a focus on learning the rules and guidelines for using word roots, prefixes, suffixes, endings, vowels, and syllable construction.

There are several ways to promote spelling in the classroom, aside from the formal or standard spelling instruction. Some professionals believe that providing students with meaningful and frequent writing assignments will help them improve their spelling skills, as they may apply what they have learned through the stages to their written work. During these writings, teachers should be aware of their focus on correctness, as it may inhibit student growth in this area. Students who are continually corrected regarding their writing tend to shut down and then not produce the writing that they are perhaps capable of producing/handling. Teachers must be aware that some students have creative writing abilities or thoughts that are ready for paper before they have learned all the principles of formal writing (grammar, spelling, etc.). Teachers must know the developmental stages of writing and at times accept work for the content with no corrections or limited corrections. Teachers may use games, puzzles, and alphabetizing words to promote spelling skills. Using words from various sources to enhance spelling practice, such as words from student writing assignments or from a list of high frequency words, is also beneficial.

# Grammar

Grammar is the structure of language, and all languages follow grammatical principles and patterns. Knowledge of grammar (syntactic context) and word meanings (semantic context) supports an individual's ability to identify and recall words. Grammar is important because it makes it possible for communication to occur about language usage and structure, and it enables us to talk about how sentences are built, why certain words are utilized, and how words are grouped. Understanding grammar makes sentences and paragraphs clear, interesting, and precise.

Grammar involves the type of words and the different word groups in a language, as well as the process of how to contrive sentences and paragraphs that deliver a message that is understandable to a reader. There are three important grammatical cues or signals:

1. Word endings (indicate nouns, verbs, adjectives, adverbs)
2. Function words (such as articles, determiners, prepositions, auxiliary verbs, conjunctions)
3. Word order/usage (for example, subject, verb, direct object)

An individual's knowledge of word endings, function words, and word order helps the reader realize the different meanings possible in a sentence.

Instruction in grammar is an essential component of a reading and language arts program, as students need an understanding of grammar in order to build upon their reading skills and improve their writing skills. Research suggests that learning grammar may best be accomplished in the context of reading, writing, and speaking. A strong recommendation for grammar instruction is that it is best provided as one of the elements of literature instruction. Students may explore the details of sentence structures and designs in poetry and other narratives, a strategy which is a more authentic and meaningful way to teach grammar.

Teaching grammar is essential to providing students with the needed skills for becoming competent and advanced readers and writers. There are a variety of theories and various research studies about how to effectively teach grammar. In general, most emphasize the idea that spending less time explaining and more time actually practicing skills is the most effective way to teach grammar. Other key concepts for teaching grammar include the following:

Furnish ample exposure to the structure/concept in use even before the concept is taught (read or listen to language that incorporates the grammar skill).

Teach patterns so that students may look for and recognize such patterns in daily language.

Utilize metalinguistic language and grammatical jargon to help students comprehend language and have vocabulary to discuss language.

Present one variable of grammar at a time in order to cement foundations for further grammatical concepts.

Systematically review and practice grammatical concepts to master skills.

Scaffold and progress through the stages of practice: guided, paired, and independent.

Be open to spontaneously instruct grammatical structure when it naturally arises in communication.

Pre-assess, assess during, and post-assess grammatical competency in student writing exercises.

# Comprehension Skills

Comprehension is the ability to understand text or the written word. There are both literal meanings and inferential meanings (text-based and knowledge-based). Comprehension requires that students actively participate in the reading process. They should be encouraged to use their previous knowledge and experience and connect to the text in order to gain understanding.

Comprehension instruction can be part of an educator's language arts program, built into both pre-reading and post-reading activities. Comprehension instruction requires explicit instruction for some students, especially those who possess fewer skills or lesser abilities. Assessing comprehension skills in an ongoing manner will aid the teacher in refining or adjusting instruction and will support students in the acquisition of skills.

Three essential types of connected text are important for student comprehension: expository, narrative, and procedural. In order to comprehend text fully, students need skills focused on the following:

- **Typographic signals:** Interpreting the use of grammar and symbols such as question marks, exclamation marks or capitalization
- **Descriptions:** Interpreting the author's use of descriptive words and phrases such as adjectives, adverbs, idioms, metaphors, and hyperbole
- **Referent words:** The use of adverbs and pronouns that refer to nouns, subjects, and verbs
- **Cohesive ties:** Words used to connect text, such as "anyway" or "nevertheless"
- **Elliptical sentences:** Text in which words may be omitted by the author and the reader must infer meaning
- **Inferences:** Readers must interpret meaning as inferences are needed in simple text and text-based or knowledge-based materials

Teaching explicit techniques helps instill effective comprehension skills. Using explicit instruction includes the following:

- **Direct instruction/explanation**—Teacher describes why a strategy helps and how and when to apply it.
- **Modeling**—Teacher demonstrates how to use and apply the strategy.
- **Guided practice**—Teacher assists students in how to learn the strategy and then when to apply it.
- **Application**—Teachers support the students in practicing the strategy until they are independent in its use.

# Instructional Strategies

There are numerous **instructional strategies** used for reading and language arts; some are commercially designed and some are teacher constructed. Most include components of the critical core skills that students need to improve their skills and experience success in school. Some of the strategies come from instructional programs that are philosophically formatted, and educators must identify the programs and strategies best suited to their personal style and individual students.

Some key strategies to use include the following:

**Monitoring comprehension**—Teach children to self-monitor so that they understand when they comprehend what they are reading and when they do not. In a self-monitoring situation, students will have pre-established strategies (ones that have been taught to them) to use to help resolve problems in comprehension as they arise.

**Graphic organizers**—Can help illustrate concepts and relationships between concepts. Graphic organizers help readers focus on concepts and their relation to other concepts, a skill that leads to comprehension and under-standing of the text being read. They help students write summaries about what they read in a well-organized and clear manner. Graphic organizers are also called maps, webs, charts, graphs, clusters, frames, and semantic orga-nizers. Types of graphic organizers include concept maps, sequence chains, story maps, main idea tables, flow-charts, matrixes, and Venn diagrams.

**Question and answer**—Questions are essential as they provide a purpose for reading; focus on specific concepts; promote self-monitoring of comprehension and concept relating; and encourage active thinking as the student reads. Question and answer also teaches the students to think about how they glean knowledge from the text: explicitly, implicitly, or from personal experience. The four types of questions are:

1. Think and search—Answers require the student to recall information and search through the text to find the answer as the answer is found in more than one area of the text.
2. Right there—The answer is found in one place in the text, and there is only one correct answer.
3. On your own—Questions arise from the student's own experiences and background knowledge, and answers are dependent upon each individual student.
4. Author and you—Students use prior experience and knowledge and relate it to knowledge gained from the text. Answers are often a mix of individual experience and text information.

**Structure**—Students learn to recognize the various parts of a story or text; categories of content (character, set-ting, event, theme, conflict, climax, resolution, and so on) are used to improve comprehension.

**Metacognition**—Thinking about thinking allows students to monitor understanding, to clarify the purpose for reading a text, to adjust reading speed, and to exercise control over their own reading. When students think about their own thinking, it allows them to use self-monitoring strategies such as identifying where the difficulty occurs, realizing what the difficulty is, restating the difficulty in their own terms, reviewing the text for help, and using past experiences to bring about understanding.

**Reading aloud**—Research stresses that opportunities for reading aloud have a profound effect on children and their success in reading as well as their overall academic achievement in school. Reading aloud helps promote language acquisition, improves oral vocabulary and usage, and increases reading comprehension skills. There appears to be a direct correlation between the amount of time spent reading aloud in homes and the education of the mother. Reading aloud is a significant contributing factor to a child's interest in reading and is one of the most critically important activities for parents and caregivers to be involved in with the children because it pre-pares them to become successful readers.

**Cooperative learning**—Students work together as partners or in small groups on clear and specific tasks. Students often help each other learn strategies for comprehension as well as encourage cooperative interaction as a peer. Cooperative learning is a good model of real-world situations that students will encounter in future employment situations.

## Building Vocabulary

Vocabulary refers to the words a student needs to know in order to communicate effectively as well as the words needed to read and write effectively. Educators continually work on increasing students' oral vocabulary, which improves not only their reading and writing abilities, but also their verbal communication skills. Using strategies that help students determine the meanings of unfamiliar words and instilling a curiosity for exploring word meanings and use of these words adds to reading comprehension and writing ability.

The teacher's use of language is an essential and key component for the student's vocabulary development. The teacher's use of sophisticated and higher level vocabulary (which is explained as needed) helps vocabulary growth, stimulation, and word consciousness in students. Teachers can accomplish sophisticated vocabulary usage by adding unique words or phrases during daily tasks (for example, the child who feeds the classroom animals is called the "zoologist" or the student who informs the class of the date is the "chronologist"). Use of sophisticated synonyms is an easy way to infuse upper-level vocabulary into the classroom (for example, instead of using "a lot," use "plethora" or "cornucopia"; when walking in a line, ask students to line up "parallel" to the wall instead of "next to"; when discussing a solution to a problem, use words like "resolve" or "rectify").

Another strategy to increase vocabulary is to teach children how words are made, the different components of words (roots, suffixes, prefixes). This will allow students to recognize patterns in words and encourage students to reach solutions on the word's meaning. Vocabulary is not merely knowing a high volume of words, but knowing how to use them appropriately. A deep knowledge of the word's usage, classification, and history can be critical to vocabulary development.

**Word consciousness** is awareness of words and their meanings as well as interest in their usage. Vocabulary growth is highly related to unstructured contexts such as oral communication and casual reading. Using a higher level of vocabulary within the classroom encourages not only motivation in students, but vocabulary competency as well. Teachers who use sophisticated vocabulary and correlate it to students' prior knowledge or experience are ensuring that students receive effective and powerful instruction.

## Phonemic Awareness

Skills of phonemic awareness are those necessary to recognize that spoken words consist of certain patterns and sequences of individual sounds. Phonemic awareness helps an individual to recognize that two words start and end the same, to blend sounds together, to know letters by sight and sound, and to gain sound patterns in language.

A strong correlation exists between phonemic awareness and future reading success. Research indicates that successful independent readers have an excellent grasp of phonemic awareness, which results in proficient decoding skills. This decoding skill development may come at an earlier rate for those who have phonemic awareness than for those who are not aware of phonemes. Poor readers generally exhibit a lack of phonemic awareness.

It is recommended that phonemic awareness instruction be accomplished in a natural and authentic manner. Teachers should use playful, and interesting ways to teach young children to be aware of the sounds (phonemes) in spoken words. They may use music and songs, poetry and rhymes, or games and puzzles to instill a desire to learn and use words.

There are five levels of phonological awareness, from simple to complex:

1. Rhyming and alliteration
2. Sentence segmentation
3. Syllable blending and segmentation
4. Onset rime, blending, and segmentation
5. Phoneme blending and segmenting words into phonemes

## Phoneme Instruction

A **phoneme** is the smallest phonetic unit in a language and possesses a distinct meaning and speech sound. A phoneme helps to distinguish one word from another word.

All words have phonemes, and most words have more than one. Helping students understand phonemes assists them in becoming successful readers. Several different strategies promote an understanding of phonemes so that students may apply this knowledge to developing reading skills.

- **Phoneme addition**—Making new words by adding a phoneme to a word. (For example, add /t/ to *rain*, which is *train*.)
- **Phoneme blending**—Providing a sequence of spoken phonemes and then forming a word. (For example, /s/ /i/ /t/ is *sit*.)

- **Phoneme categorization**—Identifying words that do not belong in a set. (For example, *ton, tea, sit, tug; sit* does not belong as it does not start with a /t/.)

- **Phoneme deletion**—Identifying the word that remains when a phoneme is removed from an existing word. (For example, remove /c/ from *crock* and it leaves *rock*.)

- **Phoneme identity**—Recognizing the same sounds in a variety of words. (For example, the same sound in *sit, sat, sin, son* is /s/.)

- **Phoneme isolation**—Recognizing separate sounds in words. (For example, the first and last sounds in *top* are /t/ and /p/.)

- **Phoneme segmentation**—Breaking a word into separate sounds and counting them. (For example, three sounds in *pig* are /p/ /i/ /g/.)

- **Phoneme substitution**—Changing one phoneme for another to make a new word. (For example, in *bed*, change the phoneme /d/ to /t/ to make *bet*.)

## Instructional Approaches

The following instructional approaches are used across the curriculum at the elementary level in all subject areas. These may be more fully described in Chapter 1 along with other approaches that may be helpful to reading and language arts instruction.

## Direct Instruction

This approach teaches children complex skills and strategies through the introduction of specific principles. Concepts may be separated into smaller components that are taught in steps until the students fully understand the skills. Students are allowed to practice the skills to mastery and then exhibit their ability to generalize or apply the skills to other venues and subject areas. This approach is most useful in teaching reading and language arts skills because it requires students to proceed with a series of steps before completely understanding and using any of the specific processes.

## Inquiry-Based Instruction

This method may be used to integrate subject areas of the curriculum. Inquiry-based instruction presents situations for students to solve and is most effective in science and math instruction. Inquiry-based instruction is useful in advancing reading skills, language development, and writing abilities because students can link their previous experiences and knowledge to the activity and ask questions as they investigate it. Students may communicate their findings through journal writing, oral presentations, and written reports.

## Cooperative Learning

A successful teaching strategy, cooperative learning incorporates a variety of learning activities across the curriculum. It is used with small teams of students who are generally grouped by the teacher in either a homogeneous or heterogeneous manner. Team members aid one another in advancing in the subject area and mastering skills. Its pertinence to reading and language arts comes in the rich oral language, writing, and reading that occur as students proceed through the process. Particularly helpful in reading and writing instruction is grouping students of varying levels of abilities, so that peer mentoring is included in the activity.

# Assessment

Proficiency in reading demonstrates the ability to read text in an automatic and fluent manner. Many children do not read well and have difficulties decoding words, recognizing words, and gaining meaning from the words in context. Analyzing students' progress is essential to help them to become more skilled in reading and language arts.

Steps in monitoring student achievement in reading and language arts may be identified in three stages:

1. **Pre-reading**—Prior to the instruction of new skills, check for independence, use of vocabulary, and the application of background information to discover the areas that may need further attention. This stage is often completed by administering a screening tool.

2. **Reading**—As students are involved in the learning process and working on gaining and practicing skills, teachers can monitor skill development through ongoing classroom assessments. This stage is often completed by administering authentic and/or informal evaluation measures.

3. **Post-reading**—After a certain set of skills have been taught and students have been exposed to practice and application opportunities, teachers will want to identify the acceptable level for the mastery of skills and then focus on addressing problematic areas. This stage can be followed by the use of modified instruction and future planning.

Following are some types of assessment tools commonly used in elementary education in the area of reading and language arts. These tools may also be utilized in other subject areas:

- **Standardized reading test**—Often conducted by a classroom teacher, these standard reading tests evaluate word recognition, vocabulary, and comprehension; however, they do not have direct relevance to improving instruction. Generally computer-scored, with imposed time limits, these norm-referenced tests can offer an overview of student achievement in reading and language arts.

- **Portfolios**—Portfolios are a collection of samples of student work in one or more areas that demonstrate student achievement. They are useful in monitoring student writing progress and are excellent tools to use for parent-teacher conferences to demonstrate progress and skill attainment.

- **Profile**—A profile differs from a portfolio in that it does not include samples of work, but rather is a collection of ratings or descriptions about the student and his or her work. It provides information about what a student knows, what the student can do in various areas, and what skills have already been mastered.

- **Performance task**—A performance task delivers beneficial information to the teacher, particularly for writing tasks and checking language arts skills such as grammar and spelling. A task, a problem, or a question is presented and requires students to construct responses using strategies, organizing data, formulating and generalizing, and justifying answers through their writings.

- **Anecdotal records**—These descriptions of meaningful student events observed by the teacher are collected as notes. The teacher then interprets the information in order to modify and adjust instruction for individual students. These records are particularly useful to educators in observing reading and writing skills during actual class time for future academic planning.

- **Teacher-made test**—This evaluation is specifically designed by the teacher in a variety of formats for a select group of students; it is neither commercially produced nor standardized.

# Terminology

The topics of reading and language arts are extensive. There is a broad array of philosophies about how to teach students in these areas, and there are multiple programs that could be used for instruction in classrooms. How an educator proceeds with instruction reflects a composite of his or her education background, work experiences, personal teaching beliefs and style, state standards, district requirements, and diversity of students.

The examinee should be familiar with the following terms:

- **Alphabetic principle:** The concept that written language is comprised of letters that represent sounds in spoken words

- **Blend:** A sequence of consonants before or after a vowel in a given syllable (tr, sh)

- **Comprehension strategy:** Specific techniques that promote reading comprehension such as predicting or gaining word meanings from context

- **Decoding:** An ability to sound out new words or to interpret a word from print to speech through the skill of sound-symbol correspondence
- **Morpheme:** The smallest unit of language that has meaning and may be a part of a word (syllable, prefix, or suffix) or an entire word
- **Onset and rime:** Parts of words in the spoken language smaller than syllables; an onset is the initial consonant sound of a syllable such as in *track* (tr-); a rime is the portion of the syllable with the vowel and the remainder of the word such as in *track* (-ack)
- **Oral language:** Development of spoken language system that includes vocabulary, listening skills, and grammar ability
- **Orthographic knowledge:** Comprehending that sounds in language are represented by printed or written symbols
- **Peer response and edit:** A process for students to share feedback with one another on their writing
- **Phoneme:** The smallest unit of sound that may change the meaning of spoken words; there are about 41 to 44 phonemes in the English language
- **Phonemic awareness:** Blending sounds in a word in order to say the word, which is a critical component of reading
- **Phonics:** Promotes understanding of alphabetic principles and the relationship between phonemes and graphemes
- **Phonological awareness:** Understanding that sounds are related to written words
- **Print awareness:** Knowing the basic concepts about written words, such as symbols have meaning, print organization, reading left to right, and separating words by spaces
- **Shared writing:** A cooperative effort between students and the teacher to compose a written piece by providing thoughts, ideas, and content
- **Word attack:** Reading strategies that help a learner read written words
- **Word roots:** Words from other languages that are the origin of English words
- **Writing aloud:** A strategy in which the teacher shares his or her thoughts as he or she composes a written piece with students, which is a modeled writing technique

# Chapter 3
# Mathematics Curriculum, Instruction, and Assessment (0011/5011)

Our world is full of mathematical situations. The expectations for individuals in today's society to know, understand, and apply math is beyond that of times past. People face math problems daily when making store purchases, using measurements in cooking, applying time concepts, and using spatial organization to move furniture. They must apply and use math when they create spreadsheets, balance a checkbook, select insurance, and pursue numerous other tasks in school, at home, and at work.

Students need to develop math competence in order to function in the world. Since they are exposed to math on a daily basis they must be aware of its importance. Although individuals have different interests and abilities when it comes to the subject of math, educators should be prepared to teach the basic concepts and help students understand how to apply and generalize this knowledge. To help them retain a positive attitude and feel competent in their math knowledge, educators should engage students in successful and meaningful opportunities to study and use mathematics.

Mathematics education begins in preschool and continues through adulthood, even beyond the academic rigor and structure. The world is changing rapidly, and math is an essential skill that is necessary for individuals to master. Implementing a well-balanced curriculum that includes the national standards for mathematics and activities that are exciting, developmentally appropriate, and realistic will aid students in learning the value of math and pursuing further study of this subject. In addition, multidisciplinary and integrated approaches need to be utilized to further increase mathematics concept knowledge and application.

Students may easily see the connection of math in their current lives beginning as early as elementary school if educators implement meaningful activities and connect children's lives to the use of mathematics. Later, when students begin to make career choices, they may be interested in jobs related to this subject, such as being a mathematician, a statistician, an engineer, a teacher, a scientist, or an actuary.

There are six principles set forth for school mathematics by the National Council for Teachers of Mathematics (NCTM) that address primary topics of math:

1. **Equity**—Focuses on expectations and supports for students
2. **Curriculum**—Emphasizes appropriate activities and concepts aligned with standards and articulated by grades
3. **Teaching**—Encourages educators to be knowledgeable about math concepts and principles so they may engage the learners
4. **Learning**—Encourages students to gain math understanding and build upon prior knowledge
5. **Assessment**—Evaluates the learners and the programs that are instrumental in mathematics education
6. **Technology**—Impacts math in numerous ways and should influence what and how mathematical topics are taught

The NCTM adheres to 10 core beliefs related to mathematics education in school programs. These beliefs emphasize the improvement of these programs, promote competence in math, and suggest how to utilize it in today's world. They are summarized here:

1. Students should be challenged in mathematics instruction to meet their needs in the future.
2. Qualified teachers, knowledgeable about math and children, should deliver the mathematics instruction.
3. Mathematics curriculum should focus on the primary standards and concepts through all grade levels.
4. Students in elementary school must be able to utilize and apply number, algebra, geometry, measurement, and statistics concepts.
5. The classroom environment and learning activities should be related to mathematics content; teachers should focus on mathematical thinking and reasoning.

6. Mathematics understanding is broadened when it is meaningful to students and integrated with other subject area concepts.

7. Technology is a critical component to mathematics instruction and should regularly include the use of computers and calculators.

8. Students may require alternative approaches to learning math concepts, using math strategies, and understanding the different algorithms.

9. Assessments should be incorporated with and related to the mathematical content.

10. The learning of mathematics and the development of math programs must be channeled by ongoing research.

The NCTM has created a broad band of standards that are available for review. These standards provide educators with an overall view of the needs of students in this academic subject area. An overview and a brief outline of the standards for elementary school aged students, in grades pre-K to 6, are included below.

# Standards Overview, Grades Pre-K to 6

The general academic standards for mathematics instruction detail a comprehensive series of goals that students should acquire in grades pre-K through 12, although this guide emphasizes those in grades pre-K to 6. These standards illustrate the mathematic knowledge, skills, concepts, understanding, and application that students should learn. The mathematical content in the first five standards includes numbers and operations, algebra, geometry, measurement, data analysis, and probability. The mathematical content in the second set of five standards includes the processes of problem solving, reasoning and proof, communication, connections, and representation. These 10 standards represent the basic skills and concepts necessary to individuals as they live and work in the world.

# Standards Pre-K to 6

Included here are the 10 general standard strands and the primary objectives related to the strands. More detailed information on the standards is available through national mathematics organizations.

1. **Numbers and Operations**

   Understand numbers, ways of representing numbers, relationships among numbers, and number systems.

   Understand meanings of operations and how they relate to one another.

   Compute fluently and make reasonable estimates.

2. **Algebra**

   Understand patterns, relations, and functions.

   Represent and analyze mathematical situations and structures using algebraic symbols.

   Use mathematical models to represent and understand quantitative relationships.

   Analyze change in various contexts.

3. **Geometry**

   Analyze characteristics and properties of two- and three-dimensional geometric shapes and develop mathematical arguments about geometric relationships.

   Specify locations and describe spatial relationships using coordinate geometry and other representations systems.

   Apply transformations and use symmetry to analyze mathematical situations.

   Use visualization, spatial reasoning, and geometric modeling to solve problems.

4. **Measurement**

   Understand measurable attributes of objects and the units, systems, and processes of measurement.

   Apply appropriate techniques, tools, and formulas to determine measurements.

5. **Data Analysis and Probability**

   Formulate questions that can be addressed with data and collect, organize, and display relevant data to answer them.

   Select and use appropriate statistical methods to analyze data.

   Develop and evaluate inferences and predictions that are based on data.

   Understand and apply basic concepts of probability.

6. **Problem Solving**

   Build new mathematical knowledge through problem solving.

   Solve problems that arise in mathematics and other contexts.

   Apply and adapt a variety of appropriate strategies to solve problems.

   Monitor and reflect on the process of mathematical problem solving.

7. **Reasoning and Proof**

   Recognize reasoning and proof as fundamental aspects of mathematics.

   Make and investigate mathematical conjectures.

   Develop and evaluate mathematical arguments.

   Select and use various types of reasoning and methods of proof.

8. **Communications**

   Organize and consolidate mathematical thinking through communication.

   Communicate mathematical thinking coherently and clearly to peers, teachers, and others.

   Analyze and evaluate the mathematical thinking and strategies of others.

   Use the language of mathematics to express mathematical ideas precisely.

9. **Connections**

   Recognize and use connections among mathematical ideas.

   Understand how mathematical ideas interconnect and build upon one another to produce a coherent whole.

   Recognize and apply mathematics in contexts outside of mathematics.

10. **Representations**

    Create and use representations to organize, record, and communicate mathematical ideas.

    Select, apply, and translate among mathematical representations to solve problems.

    Use representations to model and interpret physical, social, and mathematical phenomena.

The mathematics portion of the Praxis II exam (0011/5011) assesses an examinee's overall knowledge and application of the information regarding curriculum, instruction, and assessment—specifically number concepts, four mathematical operations, number properties, problem solving, geometric concepts, measurement, probability and statistics, and the use of technology. In this section of the study guide, examinees will find content specific to these math topics. The more general elementary practices are found in Chapter 1.

The 0011/5011 exam measures how well an examinee knows how to develop and deliver instruction based on mathematics content knowledge. This exam utilizes examples of elementary situations through multiple-choice questions. This section of the study guide includes the information necessary for the examinee to be able to clearly demonstrate the core mathematics content knowledge covered under Chapter 10 in the implementation of curriculum and instruction and the use of assessments in mathematics education.

# Curriculum

The primary goal in teaching mathematics is for students to understand that math makes sense in their lives. Because math is regularly used by individuals and the concepts are applicable to a variety of situations, the instruction should focus on the meaningful aspects of using mathematics. Learning math is like building with blocks; each one adds support to the next block and is important to the previous block. Without the general mathematics foundations (basic math skills), more complex mathematics structures (complicated math concepts) cannot be attained.

# Number Sense

Number sense is an individual's basic understanding of numbers and operations and how to apply this knowledge to solve dilemmas and make decisions about mathematical problems and concepts. This area of math, according to research, develops gradually by experimenting with numbers—visualizing them, using them, and understanding their relationships.

At the elementary level, the curriculum will focus on numerical relationships, writing numbers, and recognizing numbers. Students will move from basic counting techniques and concepts to understanding the size and relationships of numbers. They will be able to learn place values and operations once they have gained number sense.

It is important to provide children with opportunities to "play" with numbers and develop activities that allow them to count numbers, and make adjustments to their groups of numbers. Manipulatives such as blocks, counters, buttons, wood craft sticks, and other small objects that can create a larger group will aid young children in learning to count to 3 place numbers and group similar items in small groups of 10.

When students understand number relationships, they build a foundation of basic concepts or mastery. Basic facts mean the addends and the factors in addition and multiplication problems that are less than 10. In subtraction and division it means that the facts relate to addition and multiplication and both parts equal less than 10.

Understanding basic facts can be categorized by grade levels. This means that the knowledge and concepts are mastered and solutions may be recalled quickly by the learners:

| | |
|---|---|
| Kindergarten | Number recognition and rote counting to 20 or beyond |
| First grade | Addition and subtraction without manipulatives or using fingers |
| Second grade | Addition and subtraction usage on worksheets and timed tests |
| Third grade | Multiplication and beginning division |
| Fourth and fifth grades | Refined mastery of multiplication and division |
| Sixth grade | Review and practice previous math facts and begin statistics, problem solving, and geometrical concepts |

## Counting Objects

Children learn to count at a very young age, even before they enter school. In order to do so, they must have the vocabulary to count (names of numbers) and the ability to sequence the numbers. In the early grades, educators can play games, sing songs, and read children's literature that include the numbers, their sequential order, and the counting activities to enhance a child's automatic knowledge of numbers and how to count. After children can count with ease, an educator should challenge students with such strategies as counting on and counting back. **Counting on** means to recite or list numbers in order or to name numbers one by one to determine the total of a whole group. **Counting back** means to recite the numbers from larger to smaller as if subtracting one number from another. Using mathematics tools such as number lines and counters allows students to conceptually and procedurally practice these skills.

## Comparing and Classifying Objects or Sets

Once elementary students develop number sense, they gain the idea that numbers have relationships to one another. Concepts in number sense such as *more* or *less* demonstrate a basic relationship between numbers. Since students know these concepts from their basic numbers, the idea may be applied to learning more about sets.

Children need opportunities to practice using these skills. Manipulatives can be used to construct sets to compare and classify. Activities with manipulatives such as *make sets of more/less/same* or *find sets with the same amount* will provide practice in visualizing the concept of comparing and classifying sets.

## Exploring Sets

Students should be exposed to the various types of sets that exist, not just related to mathematics. Students should apply their knowledge of math sets to daily life, such as identifying groups of animals, fruits, colors, or books. They can learn how these sets might be arranged according to specific numbers, such as a set of 6 hippos live in one cage and a set of 4 hippos live in the other; therefore the zoo has a total of 10 hippos. Set models may be used to help students visualize the organization of sets. These may be drawings or objects within a perimeter or border.

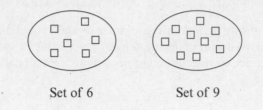

Set of 6          Set of 9

## Number Patterns

When students have gained skills in counting, they can move forward in their knowledge of numbers by learning to recognize number patterns and relationships. Patterns exist throughout the world in our daily lives. Learning to recognize patterns and their purpose through mathematics instills a skill that will be used again and again.

Four types of number relationships exist in the set of 1–10:

1. **Spatial**—Recognizing sets of objects in number patterns and figuring out how many exist without counting.
2. **One and two more, one and two less**—Comprehending the relationship of one number's position to another number's position (3 is one more than 2 or 5 is two less than 7).
3. **Anchors of 5 and 10**—Discovering how combinations of the numbers 1 to 10 are related to 5 and 10.
4. **Part-part-whole**—Establishing that two parts constitute a whole (2 and 2 make the whole of 4).

Three types of number activities help in the study of number relationships from 10–20:

1. **Pre-place value**—Connecting the ideas of sets (a set of 5 buttons and a set of 3 buttons equal a set of 8).
2. **More and less**—Promoting the understanding of numbers 10–20 (use of sets of 10 can help children understand that a set of 10 counters and 15 more are 25).
3. **Doubling and near-doubling**—Learning larger numbers (more than 10) may be easier if students understand that doubles make another larger number (the double of 5 is 10, the double of 8 is 16), while near-doubling is a double and one more (17 is the double of 8 and one more).

# Base-Ten Numeration Systems

Students enrolled in grades Pre-K through 2 must develop a solid understanding of the base-ten numeration system. They need to recognize that the word "ten" represents a single entity (1 ten) and/or ten separate units (10 ones). They should learn that these representations are interchangeable because they have the same value. The use of developmentally appropriate concrete materials such as manipulatives as well as calculators will support students in learning these concepts.

## Place Value

Students learn place value over a period of time as they proceed through the grade levels. It is outlined as:

| | |
|---|---|
| Kindergarten | Counting to 100 |
| First and second grades | Working with units and tens, learning place value strategies |
| Third and fourth grades | Using place value in hundreds and thousands |
| Fifth grade | Beginning work with decimals |
| Sixth grade | Comparing and ordering decimals as well as operations with decimals |

Students must have the skills of counting and grouping in order to understand and use place values. Using manipulatives is highly effective in gaining an understanding of place value in young children. It provides the students with visual and kinesthetic access to count a group of items. Not all children will learn place value concepts at the same time.

## Estimation

Estimation skills may be developed when students are more experienced with mental computation and number sense. They also need to understand and use invented strategies, since those require the ability to manage numbers. In the beginning, the opportunities provided to students to learn estimation should be simple, flexible number activities instead of rigid algorithms, because these will help students understand computational fluency and develop computational estimation skills. The instructional goal in estimation is for students to learn how to approximate an answer appropriate to a given situation they are presented with, such as planning a trip, purchasing an item, or figuring the tip on a restaurant bill.

Estimation is an important life skill that is used daily by most adults. The instruction of estimation should include different types of manipulatives (such as base-ten models or 100s charts) and various estimation strategies (such as front-end addition and subtraction, front-end multiplication and division, rounding addition and subtraction, and rounding multiplication and division). It is an important skill to use in measurements and figuring quantities of objects, so it should be taught using situations that reflect or pertain to real-life situations. Estimation indicates that an exact number is not necessary. Teaching students to use such terms as "about," "a little less than," "a bit more than," "close to," and "between" will help them understand the concept and acquire the skills of estimation.

## Reading and Writing Numbers

Mathematics appears to be primarily about numbers, but it is important for students to learn to connect saying numbers and writing numbers. This helps them learn the **word form** (number written with words), the **expanded form** of numbers (the sum of the place values), and the **standard form** (how to write the digits).

To instruct students in the area of reading and writing numbers, have them practice saying different combinations of numbers such as those with decimal placements, three digits, and equations. Have students write out the words for different digit patterns of numbers or read the number words and write the digits. Reading and writing of numbers requires practice and regular usage. Incorporating reading and writing skills into an integrated curriculum with math will boost skill development in many specific areas and provide students with motivation, excitement, and interest in math.

## Expanding Numbers

After students have an understanding of number relationships, they will begin to use larger numbers. Teachers can help extend the number relationships that students know by helping them count by 10s. The use of a **tens frame** as a tool to count in relationships to 100 is very beneficial. Students can use these frames to represent various numbers and develop this skill of expanding numbers. This will support skills in learning to estimate, compare, and compute.

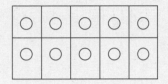

Tens Frame

# Mathematical Operations

The four basic mathematical operations—addition, subtraction, multiplication, and division—are the focus of the elementary mathematics education curriculum beginning in about the first grade. However, students must have a solid foundation of number recognition, counting, and number relationships up through 20 before instruction begins on these mathematical operations. Story problems and manipulatives are recommended methods for instructing students on the meanings and functions of the operations.

## Addition and Subtraction

Students must use addition and subtraction operations in a variety of ways in order to master the concepts. Using interesting and different strategies to entice students into learning the basic math operations of addition and subtraction will provide the foundation they need to complete other operations (multiplication and division), mathematical actions, and solve problems.

Following are some addition strategies with which students should be familiar:

- **One-More-Than and Two-More-Than Facts**—Requires that the student count from a specified number. For example, 2-more-than 6, count on 7, 8.
- **Zero Facts**—Students must learn not to count on when using zero and that zero does not add another number, but holds a place. In addition a number added to zero is that same number. For example, $5 + 0 = 6$ is incorrect; $5 + 0 = 5$ is correct.
- **Doubles**—Ten of the basic facts are doubles. For example, $2 + 2 = 4$, $3 + 3 = 6$.
- **Near-Doubles**—Concept of doubles plus one, in which learners round the smallest addend and then add one more. For example, $3 + 4 = 7$, but thought of as $3 + 3 = 6 + 1 = 7$.
- **Make-Ten Facts**—When one of the addends is 8 or 9, then part of the other addend is added to make 10, and the remaining number is added for the total. For example, $9 + 4 = 13$. The learner takes 1 from the 4 and adds to the 9 to make 10, which leaves 3, and that is then added to 10 to equal 13.

Other addition strategies include adding single digits, adding tens and hundreds, and adding two-digit numbers.

Following are some subtraction strategies with which students should be familiar:

- **Subtraction as Think-Addition**—Focuses and builds upon the part-part-whole relationship. For example, $4 - x = 2$: count 4 manipulatives, cover 2, so how many are left?
- **Subtraction Facts with Sums to 10**—Basic addition facts must first be mastered, as learners must use fact families to learn subtraction facts. For example, $3 + 2 = 5$, $5 - 2 = 3$.
- **Sums Greater than 10**—Builds upon the relationship of addition and subtraction up to 10 and back down to 10 or the extension of the think-addition method.

Other subtraction strategies include subtracting single digits, subtracting tens and hundreds, subtracting two-digit numbers, and subtracting by counting up.

**Story problems** engage students more than simple computation problems, as they are interesting and realistic. Frequent opportunities should be included for solving story problems using a combination of methods that help students through the progression of direct modeling and invented strategies. As students develop various strategies for addition and subtraction, the traditional algorithm should be discussed as the final development in the operation.

Use these sequential steps to teach students to attack the solution of a word problem:

1. Understand what the problem is asking.
2. Determine the essential information.
3. Make a plan to solve the problem.
4. Follow the plan.
5. Check the answer to be sure it makes sense.

## Whole-Number Computation

Whole-number computation is based on place value concepts and the understanding of mathematical operations. Students should be permitted to invent strategies for addition and subtraction problems without having to use specific algorithms. Invented strategies differ from the traditional algorithms because they focus on the number, not just a digit within the number. Use of invented strategies seems to provide benefits over using traditional algorithms, such as enhancing base-ten instruction and ensuring that students can explain their work.

Before inventing strategies, students should use math tools such as counters in direct modeling activities. Students will also benefit from guided activities to share how they solved the problems. Depending on learning styles, some students will then be able to mentally solve the problems and some will be better at expressing the problems in written form. The teacher should be supportive and allow time to use the strategies so students retain skills in whole-number computation.

## Multiplication and Division

Multiplication and division are the more complex operations using the basic facts. However, in order to learn these principles, an individual must first master the concepts of addition and subtraction.

Following are some multiplication strategies with which students should be familiar:

- **Doubles**—Equivalent to doubles in addition problems. For example, $2 \cdot 5 = 10$, $5 + 5 = 10$.
- **Fives Facts**—Builds on the counting-by-5 concept. For example, 5, 10, 15, 20, and so on.
- **Zeros and Ones**—Generalizations that when one factor in multiplication is zero then the answer is 0, and when one factor in multiplication is 1, the answer is the other factor. For example, $0 \cdot 8 = 0$ and $4 \cdot 1 = 4$.
- **Nifty Nines**—The multiples of 9 and students use the pattern. For example, $4 \cdot 9 = 36$ $(3 + 6 = 9)$, $9 \cdot 9 = 81$ $(8 + 1 = 9)$.

Other multiplication strategies include complete number, compensation, multiples of 10 and 100, and two-digit multipliers.

How well students master division facts and operations will depend on how well they mastered multiplication facts and operations. Division represents the recall of a multiplication problem. Students should be made aware of this relationship through class discussion and practice using these concepts.

Use of **fact families** can aid in the explanation and concept development for young children. For example:

$4 \cdot 5 = 20$

$5 \cdot 4 = 20$

$20 \div 4 = 5$

$20 \div 5 = 4$

# Concepts of Number Theory

Number theory is related to the properties of numbers in general. This includes the properties and the use of integers. There are several subcategories of number theory, which are established by the methods used and the types of investigations done. Individuals who work in this field of mathematics are considered **number theorists.**

The specific fields of number theory have historical value and include the following:

- **Analytic number theory**—Includes solutions of calculus and complex analysis (also squares, cubes, integers, primes)
- **Algebraic number theory**—Describes the study of the concept of numbers expanded to algebraic equations
- **Geometry of numbers**—Pertains to basic geometric concepts
- **Combinatorial number theory**—Defines the use of algebraic and analytic methods
- **Computational number theory**—Focuses on the study of algorithms pertinent to number theory
- **Greek number theory**—Refers to integer solutions to linear indeterminate equations (beginning in third century)
- **Classical Indian number theory**—Explains solutions to equations involving fractions, integers, and so on
- **Islamic number theory**—Promotes algorithms and classifications of numbers determined (beginning in ninth century)
- **Early European number theory**—Refers to the discovery of solutions to problems previously unsolved (sixteenth to eighteenth centuries)
- **Beginnings of modern number theory**—Refers to the organization of the current systematic number formulas (nineteenth century)
- **Prime number theory**—Relates to the study of the distribution of prime numbers

## Factors

Factors are related to the operation of multiplication. There are generally two different factors used in a multiplication problem. One demonstrates how many sets or parts and the other represents the size of each set or part. Specifically, the factors are termed the multiplier and the multiplicand and may be used in the instruction of multiplication so children understand the difference between the two numbers. For example, factors of 36 include 1 and 36, 2 and 18, 3 and 12, 4 and 9, and 6 ($6 \cdot 6$).

## Multiples

A multiple of a number is the product of that number multiplied by any other whole number. When computing with fractions, students may need to use the method of finding a common denominator, which can also be described as finding *the multiples of* . Multiples are used to make fraction operations easier to solve. Some students have difficulty determining the multiples so they may rewrite the equation in the simpler form. They must have a good grasp of addition and multiplication as well as division skills to figure the multiples. Practice and use of manipulatives will aid in the instruction of finding common denominators or the multiples of them. For example, multiples of 7 are 7, 14, 21, 28, 35, 42, 49, 56, 63, 70, 77, 84, 91, 98, 105, and so on.

# Variables

Variables are symbols used in problems that represent a set of numbers or objects. Elementary students need to understand that variables are numbers used in operations that may be manipulated. There are three different uses of variables:

- **Specific unknown**—Represents a place holder for a number
- **Pattern generalizer**—Illustrates rules or regularities in our number system
- **Varying quantities**—Changes value within problems

In teaching about variables, sometimes drawings are helpful to illustrate the idea for young elementary students. With older students, equations help promote the concept of variable usage.

# Remainders

Remainders occur in division problems that do not result in simple whole numbers. Before teaching remainders, students must be fluent in the division process at the concrete, representational, and abstract levels as well as have a firm grasp of place value concepts. The concrete level teaches two authentic and naturally occurring division situations:

1. **Measurement ("separating into equal groups")**—This situation requires that division be utilized in order to separate a set of objects into groups that are comprised of a specific number of objects in each for the purpose of being able to determine how many groups one can make.
2. **Partial ("sharing")**—This situation requires division in order to "share" or split a total set of objects equally between a specified number of individuals and determine how many objects each individual gets.

Students should also be instructed that remainders can be used in different ways depending on the context of the problem:

- A leftover quantity
- Partitioned into fractions
- Discarded
- Used to round up
- Rounded to approximation
- Expressed as a decimal

The use of base-ten materials can be highly beneficial when teaching remainders. These types of materials are extremely useful when tackling division problems with larger value amounts (three-digit dividends) as they help reinforce place value.

# Odd and Even

The concept of odd and even numbers is one that is often overlooked in elementary math instruction. The concept, although it appears simple, is actually a difficult abstract concept for the elementary school mind to grasp at times. The idea is not simply to teach that an even number is 2, 4, 6, 8, and so on or that an odd number is 1, 3, 5, 7, and so on. It is necessary to provide an understanding of the meaning of even and odd. Even numbers can be divided into two equal parts, but the reason needs to be explained and ingrained in students' minds. Then they may use this knowledge in other mathematical situations. It is clear to adults that odd numbers cannot be divided into equal parts as there is one more left over (extra). The recommended methods of teaching the concept of even and odd numbers is through oral story problems with discussions and activities followed by the use of manipulatives.

# Rational Numbers

Rational numbers are parts of a whole, expressed as a fraction, a decimal, or a percentage. Rational numbers are used in daily life so they are important for students to learn.

**Fractions** can be a difficult concept for students to master. In order to learn this math concept, it is recommended that positive initial experiences with fractions be implemented. Students should move from a concrete to a symbolic phase very slowly, only after understanding the concrete level. Adequate and appropriate manipulatives should be used when teaching fractions.

There are three types of manipulatives that might be used to teach fractions:

- **Region/area**—These help students to visualize fraction problems where the surface area may be divided into smaller parts. (For example, a 1,500-acre parcel of land may be visualized using patterns, blocks, geoboards, or grids.)
- **Length**—These may model a fraction situation in which dividing a line may be necessary. Use of fraction strips, number lines, and Cuisenaire rods will all help with these relationships.
- **Set**—These are related to a group of objects considered whole, and dividing a set creates fractional parts. Use of beans, small counters, and toys are useful.

In teaching fractions, students need to understand the difference between the number at the top (numerator) and the number at the bottom (denominator). The **numerator** is the counting number that describes how many parts in the whole. The **denominator** describes the counting in terms of the total number of parts that makes the whole. Introducing the appropriate terms will allow students to speak in a mathematical language, which will help solidify the concepts being taught.

As the part-to-whole relationship is emphasized students develop their fraction number sense ability. In addition to counting the parts of a whole, students need to understand the concept that the more equal-sized parts in the whole, the smaller those parts will be. They may be familiar with larger numbers being bigger, but that does not hold true for fractions. For example, the fraction $\frac{1}{6}$ is not larger than $\frac{1}{3}$, even though 6 is larger than 3.

For teaching young children to compute with fractions, Van de Walle recommends these strategies:

- Use simple contextual tasks so students understand the meaning of the task when it is structured in a story problem.
- Connect the meaning of fraction computation with whole-number computation.
- Use estimation and informal methods to develop strategies.
- Explore each of the operations using manipulatives instead of standard algorithms.

To instruct fractions using the four mathematical operations:

**Addition and subtraction:** Apply the common denominator method; understanding that the numerator shows the number of parts and the denominator denotes the type of the part.

**Multiplication:** Indicate that the denominator is a divisor that allows the student to find the parts of the other factor.

**Division:** Apply the lowest-common-denominator method or the invert-and-multiply algorithm.

**Decimals** are related to fractions and are important to study as they comprise our monetary system and the system of scientific measures. Students should have a solid grasp of fractions before beginning the study of decimals and understand that these are related and are not separate concepts. Manipulatives, such as a place-value chart or base-ten blocks, help in defining this relationship.

**Percents** are linked to decimals and fractions and should be taught once students understand both decimals and fractions. Percent should not be taught separately in the overall concept. Percents are based on a comparison to 100. A percent symbolizes a fraction that has a common denominator of 100 and is indicated by the % sign. Fractions and percents can be two different ways of writing the same thing. The goal of comparing fractions and percents is to help learners figure out how to recognize equivalences between common fractions and percents.

Example of fraction, decimal, and percent relationship:

$$\frac{1}{2} = 0.50 = 50\%$$

# Problem Solving

According to the NCTM, instructional programs from grades pre-K through 12 should enable all students to

- Build new mathematical knowledge through problem solving.
- Solve problems that arise in mathematics and in other contexts.
- Apply and adapt a variety of appropriate strategies to solve problems.
- Monitor and reflect on the process of mathematical problem solving.

Problem solving does not just relate to mathematics. Through math education, students can learn much about developing problem-solving skills. Everyone should learn to problem solve, and mathematics education can lead students from the concrete solutions to the abstract solutions, indirectly teaching them a life skill.

Several strategies are particularly helpful in the study of mathematics:

- **Task analysis:** Helps students move to a desired level of skill attainment by learning a specific skill through a series of sequential steps.
- **Guided practice:** Used at the conclusion of a lesson or period, allows the students to ask questions about the concepts and algorithmic procedures. This time ensures that students have gained skills in the topic presented.
- **Closure activity:** Utilizing a math game, a question/answer period, or a problem-solving worksheet, it gives students the added time to summarize what they have learned about math and which algorithms they must remember and practice before the next lesson.
- **Homework:** Provides an added form of practice for the day's math concepts and reinforces the skills and mastery of the operations.
- **Writing:** Used for students to express themselves about what they do in math and explain their mathematical thinking. This can be completed by using student logs, expository writing, and student journals.
- **Cooperative learning:** Instills social skills; helps students develop long-term retention, increase cognitive skills, and improve their ability to communicate while helping one another with math concepts and activities as they work together in assigned groups.

# Geometric Concepts

In elementary school, geometry appears to be a hands-on, exciting area of mathematics. Geometry requires manipulatives, puzzles, and drawings to gain skills in geometric reasoning and spatial relationships. According to the van Hiele theory, there are five levels of learning geometry that are sequential, requiring that students learn each one at their own developmental level, with the final level being at the college level:

0. **Visualization**—Identify shapes and their names according to their visual characteristics and then categorize them.
1. **Analysis**—Learn the classifications of shapes and their similar properties.

2. **Informal deduction**—Learn the properties of shapes and their relationships.
3. **Deduction**—Understand the theorems and axioms of shapes.
4. **Rigor**—Understand axiom systems.

# Measurement

There are many different types of measurements. Measurement knowledge is an essential skill and the concept of measurement is complex. The attributes of measurement include length, weight, time, degree, volume/capacity, and area. To develop conceptual knowledge of measurements, students must

- Understand the attributes to be measured.
- Realize the comparison of the attribute is a measure.
- Acknowledge the types and use of measurement tools.

Kindergarten students begin learning the concepts of measurement by comparing items to find which is longer or which is heavier. They may use their hands or bodies to compare objects that must be measured. As students move through the grades, the concepts of measurement become more complicated and students learn to measure angles, areas, and volumes. On this journey, both informal units of measurement (hand, strips of paper) and standard units of measurement (yards, cups) are learned and utilized. Estimation is another concept used in mastering the measurement concept. Students may guess (estimate) at the size or volume of an object and then use the proper tool of measurement to check their estimation. Students may use various informal units of measure before learning to use the more standard and formal units of measure.

## Length

The first attribute learned in measurement is found by figuring out how long an item is or comparing how long two or more items are, by using manipulatives like a rope, a string, or strips of paper to do the measuring. As the student progresses, the instruments used to measure length become more sophisticated: ruler, tape measure, altimeter (height), caliper, GPS, surveyor's wheel, odometer, ultrasound, and so on.

## Weight

This concept of measurement compares the mass of one object to another. Students may use their hands in the early stages to feel the difference between objects and whether one is heavier or larger than another one. As students increase their skills in measuring mass, the instruments used become more complex and exact: scale, balance, mass spectrometer, loadometer, weighbridge, and so on.

## Volume/Capacity

Measuring volume and capacity relates to three-dimensional objects and figures. Students may use containers to check the amount, such as cups, boxes, and bowls. Upon mastery of the simpler instruments of volume measurement, students may move onto tools such as a graduated cylinder, beaker, flask, pipette, tape measure, and rulers.

## Area

This is a difficult measurement concept to learn, as it is a complex visual task. Learners may use shaped objects to compare measurements of an area. Being proficient with measuring area requires that students learn and possibly memorize the various area formulas associated with geometrical shapes. Often these formulas require that students have a firm grasp of not only multiplication and division of whole numbers, but also fractions and decimals.

## Angles

In fourth or fifth grade, students learn to measure angles through an introduction to the protractor. Instructing students on how to use a protractor will help them understand angle measurement. The measurement of angles depends on the concept of 360°. The concept of the angle is crucial in the geometric world because it is the basis for many operations. It is also critical in trigonometry because the measurement of angles is the basis of that field. Students will need to become well versed in angles so that they have a sound foundation as they advance in mathematical levels.

## Time

Measuring time indicates the duration of when something begins or stops and is actually based on the movement of the Earth. A year is the measurement of how long it takes the Earth to orbit the sun and a day is how long it takes the Earth to complete one full rotation on its axis. Time is used daily in order to determine schedules, appointments, durations, and so on, so it is imperative that students become fluent in telling time. Informal measures may identify the amount of time, while standard measures provide the actual telling of time.

Learning to tell time begins in first grade and the student should show mastery in the fourth or fifth grade, although many students may need until the seventh or eighth grade to master this skill. Students should first learn to tell time by the hour, then by the half-hour, and then by minutes. Activities that may help students learn to tell time include the following:

- Count the days of school using a calendar or timeline.
- Select children's literature that refers to telling time.
- Sequence events that are meaningful to students.
- Construct simple analog or digital clocks for use by students.
- Conduct research about the history of clocks and other timepieces.
- Play games related to the tools of time and the telling of time.
- Use graphs and charts to indicate specific events and periods of time.

## Temperature

Temperature is the degree or intensity of heat present in the human body, an object, or in an environment, and is generally measured by a comparative scale shown by a thermometer. When instructing about temperature, students should learn about the various types of scales used and how they compare to one another. Students should also learn about the three types of temperature scales: Fahrenheit, Celsius, and Kelvin. The concept of absolute zero is introduced in the later years when students understand the concepts of molecules and atoms. Activities that may aid in the comprehension of this form of measurement include the following:

- Schedule a daily time period for weather reports.
- Define the terms of weather, the seasons, and related careers.
- Use tools associated with weather, such as a thermometer or a windsock.
- Allow students to conduct experiments using hot, warm, cold, and cool items.
- Use charts and graphs to measure the weather over a period of time.

## Money

Money concepts include the following:

**Earning** provides students with a sense of independence/recognition, an understanding of financial structures, instills work ethics/habits, and provides knowledge about how money, time, and work are related.

**Spending** helps students understand the difference between their desires and needs, and gives them opportunities to make decisions and be responsible.

**Borrowing** shows students responsibility for paying back what is owed, learning to appreciate what is earned, the consequences of using anothers' money, and how credit systems and interest work.

**Saving** instills the ideas of how to get what you want, how to plan for the future, how spending and earning are related, and how the banking systems function.

When teaching students about money, include problems related to the properties of mathematics (addition, subtraction, multiplication, and division), fractions, percentages, estimates, and decimals, as well as the concepts of earning, spending, saving, and borrowing. Activities that may support the instruction of money concepts include the following:

- Use real coins in the classroom to do estimations and values.
- Invite a coin collector to explain the various types of coins.
- Discuss the history and current use of money and monetary systems.
- Establish a store or center that pertains to the exchange of money.
- Encourage the class to save or collect money for a donation to a charity.
- Use charts and graphs to depict the value of coins.
- Take field trips to banks, stores, financial institutions, a mint, and museums.
- Describe the use of credit cards, checking accounts, and savings accounts.

## Probability and Statistics

Data analysis, statistics, and probability exist in our daily lives and can be meaningful when used in certain situations. Students must have opportunities to explore and experiences to practice these real-world applications. Instruction in probability and statistics should include common situations and involve the student in using reflection, guessing at chances, gathering data, and interpreting results without the structured rules and algorithms common to this particular math. Students should participate in discussion activities about the data and the results to make the process more valuable.

Situations of probability and statistics are much like conducting experiments, and this would be an excellent topic for integrated studies with science. Developing these concept skills can be a motivational challenge for students and it increases their use of intuitive skills, critical thinking skills, and problem-solving skills. Include the following when completing tasks on probability and statistics:

**Data analysis**—This involves creating the questions that will be answered when the data is collected and includes discussion, collaborative group work, and brainstorming methods.

**Manipulatives**—Used in data analysis, these tools can help with sorting, grouping, or classifying sets of objects. Both unstructured (have different attributes with various possibilities) manipulatives and structured (possess a set number of attributes) manipulatives help develop the skill of classification.

**Graphing data**—Once students have learned how to collect data, instruction should provide opportunities to learn how to represent the information. Often graphs are used to demonstrate and compare information. Examples of graphs include bar graphs, pictographs, tally charts, pie charts, and line graphs.

**Interpretation of data**—Students learn how to describe the results of the data that is graphed or charted.

## Calculators and Computers

Calculators and computers are commonly used technology that can support the subject of math. Some educators believe that calculator instruction and usage affects a youngster's ability in a negative way because it decreases paper and pencil tasks, lessens development of logical reasoning, and prevents the child from discovering basic mathematical concepts. Others believe that using a calculator can have beneficial effects once the basic facts and math operations are mastered. Computers are becoming more prevalent in all subject areas and can provide extension activities to existing math lessons. Many mathematics disciplines have commercial computer programs that coincide with the existing curriculum and aid the teacher in the remediation or enrichment of learners.

Activities to practice using a calculator include the following:

- Have students enter meaningful numbers that they can retrieve from memory and try different mathematical operations. For example, enter their age and then add 3 years or enter their age and subtract 5 years.
- Ask students to figure out a bill from a restaurant. Bring in some menus and have the students imagine a meal they want to order. Have them enter numbers on the calculator to figure the entrée, the beverage, and the dessert, and, if developmentally appropriate, figure the tax and tip.
- Have students compare ad prices from grocery stores. They can compare the prices across several stores to make decisions on the best selection. Older students can also use multiple operations, memory function, and percentages.

Activities to practice using a computer include the following:

- Create a spreadsheet about chores and figure allowance over a period of a week or a month.
- Design a chart to use for Sudoku math games.
- Extend the study of geometry by using a drawing program with three-dimensional capability.

## Classroom Management

Educators will find that when math is exciting, challenging, and meaningful, students are more engaged and behavior issues are limited. Aside from students who may not understand concepts and therefore act out, or those who are identified as having learning problems, most students should be capable of mastering mathematics at some level. Making math fun for students will be a challenge for the teacher, but well worth the effort. Using games, manipulatives, and stories will intrigue students and keep them actively involved in the lessons. The mathematical environment created in a classroom will enhance the development of students, who can invent mathematics strategies they will use throughout their lives.

## Manipulatives

Manipulatives are one kind of physical tool that may be used to model mathematical concepts. Considered "hands-on" learning, manipulatives are often used at the elementary level so students can participate more readily in pursuing their understanding of math concepts. Manipulatives are concrete materials used to help students think about math concepts and reflect on solving problems rather than simply finding an answer. They may be commercially made or constructed from household objects, such as wood craft sticks, buttons, dice, and beans.

Manipulatives should not replace a student's ability to apply concepts, and must be used in developmentally appropriate and meaningful ways to be effective. Children should be allowed to maneuver the manipulatives as they need in order to understand the concept, rather than be shown how to use them, requiring that they copy a model from the teacher. This stifles the learning that may be gained through the use of these materials. Keeping manipulatives easily accessible and in good condition helps learners. Manipulatives can be regularly used for a temporary period until the student can move from the concrete to the abstract and apply the mathematical principles learned.

## Content-Specific Pedagogy

Pedagogy is more fully described in Chapter 1. Here are a few of the specific approaches and terms related to mathematics education:

- **Constructivism:** Individuals construct their own knowledge based on previous knowledge.
- **Conceptual knowledge:** Consists of knowledge that is understood; logical relationships and ideas.
- **Models of mathematical concepts:** Use of objects, pictures, or drawings that represents a concept and promotes the relationship of the concept.

- **Multiple intelligences:** Specifically logical-mathematical reasoning involves problem solving that promotes sequential and orderly instruction within a structured environment.
- **Procedural knowledge:** Understanding the rules, procedures, routines, and tasks of mathematics.
- **Problem-based approach:** Student-centered, which helps learners create meaning from mathematics.

# Assessment

As with other assessments in elementary subject areas, the purpose is to monitor student progress, make instructional decisions, evaluate student achievement, and evaluate the program. It is recommended that in mathematics, educators integrate the assessments with the instruction.

In 1995, the NCTM established six standards for assessments related to mathematics. These state that assessments should do the following:

1. Reflect the mathematics that all students need to know and be able to do.
2. Enhance mathematics learning.
3. Promote equity.
4. Be an open process.
5. Promote valid inferences about mathematics learning.
6. Be a coherent process.

In mathematics, the assessments should focus on the mathematical concepts and procedures, the mathematical processes, and the student's disposition to math. Effective assessments and evaluation strategies will allow the students an opportunity to demonstrate their skills and to obtain immediate feedback about how they are performing. Valuable to students and the teacher are assessments that require students to recall and perform the mathematical concepts and operations they have learned. These may be conducted daily, weekly, or at the end of units, because the progress will be critical to ongoing instruction. Assessment is further explained in Chapter 1.

Following are assessment types useful in mathematics education:

- Observation
- Anecdotal notes
- Performance assessment
- Alternate assessments
- Portfolios

# Chapter 4
# Social Studies Curriculum, Instruction, and Assessment (0011/5011)

The National Council for Social Studies (NCSS) states, "the primary purpose of social studies is to help young people develop the ability to make informed and reasoned decisions for the public good as citizens of a culturally diverse, democratic society in an interdependent world." They strongly promote "citizenship education" through social studies in order to preserve the democratic way of life. The NCSS believes that when students understand the basic concepts of social studies—the historical events, the functions of government, and the practice of economics—they can become independent, informed citizens and as adults manage their lives efficiently in a changing society.

The NCSS convened a task force in 1989 to develop the taxonomy of social studies thinking skills. They organized these skills from simple to complex critical thinking skills, which resulted in the following categories being the essential outcomes for students of social studies education:

- Classify information
- Interpret information
- Analyze information
- Summarize information
- Synthesize information
- Evaluate information

The social studies portion of the Praxis II 0011/5011 elementary education exam assesses an examinee's knowledge on teaching strategies and activities related to curriculum components, social organizations, human behavior, social structures, history, geography, government, classroom management, and content-specific pedagogy. In this section of the study guide, examinees will find information specific to social studies topics related to curriculum, instruction, and assessment. The more general elementary practices are found in Chapter 1. Use both of these sections as well as the content knowledge section in Chapter 11, to study for this exam.

A portion of the 0011/5011 exam evaluates how proficiently an examinee understands how to promote learning based on social studies content knowledge. The exam utilizes examples of classroom situations through multiple-choice questions so the examinee may select answers based on knowledge of curriculum, the methods and strategies of instruction, and the assessment of students. This section of the study guide includes the information necessary for the examinee to clearly utilize the content of 0011 in the implementation of curriculum and instruction and the use of assessments in the following areas:

- Curriculum components
- Social organizations and human behavior
- Social structures
- History
- Geography
- Government
- Classroom management
- Content-specific pedagogy

Being familiar with standards is the first essential step a teacher should take in developing curriculum and activities that promote effective and valuable instruction. Instructional activities should be designed to meet student needs while also addressing the required standards as well as assessing the skills to be mastered in social studies.

# Curriculum Components

Basic elements of instruction and development of the curriculum are found in Chapter 1. It includes curriculum components such as scope and sequence, appropriate materials, technology, and learner objectives. This information is used in all elementary subject areas and can be adapted and modified for social studies. The content in this portion of the study guide is more specific to the social studies topics found on the Praxis II 0011/5011 exam.

Curriculum should be carefully designed for the specific grade level and aligned with state and national standards. The content of the social studies curriculum should be integrated with other social sciences as well as other academic subjects and the fine arts. The scope of the curriculum should establish parameters of the topics covered and the material should be sequenced logically with discussions, projects, and authentic activities available to solidify concept acquisition and skill mastery. The social studies curriculum should be enhanced using a wide variety of instructional resources, as these are more interesting for the student and will support universal design in classrooms.

# Social Organizations

This section focuses on social organizations, citizenship, and human behavior in society such as that related to an individual, a family, or a community. **Social organization** of a group encompasses how people interact, the systems of kinship utilized, marriage and family patterns, ranking systems (authority positions), division of tasks, and allocation of goods and knowledge. This type of order system provides organization of culture and society so that new members have a basis for the patterns and arrangement of relationships within the group.

Social organizations have arisen because human beings are social creatures who mostly prefer to live in groups. Because a society demands that individuals interact with others, there must be systems set in place that allow for procreation of life, production of goods and services, decision making, creating meaning and purpose in life (culture, religion, language), and orderly organization of citizens. There are three major forms of organizations in modern societies. These are bureaucracy or formal organizations, markets, and informal social networks.

There is a wide array of social organizations found within societies. Some of these include the following:

- **Families**—Provides for the needs of adults and children but organized in different forms
- **Political**—Meets the needs of citizens as a whole by making collective decisions for the greater good
- **Economic**—Meets the needs of both consumers and producers by providing material goods and services
- **Aesthetic**—Meets the artistic needs of people
- **Recreational**—Meets the physical and recreational needs of people
- **Educational**—Assists in the socialization process and in the transmission of culture as well as information
- **Religious**—Meets the spiritual needs of people

Within a society there is the role of the social contract in order to maintain social cohesion and interdependence. The **social contract** is the agreement about the fundamentals of life that every individual is entitled to and relies upon. It is the set of understandings with which every person in the group agrees or subscribes to. There can be different expectations and understandings within each social organization: rules in games, ethics in business, manners in social situations, and laws of order.

A few key terms useful in the study of social organizations are as follows:

- **Caste system:** A social organization in which society is broken into classes, often based on family lineage, divine law, socioeconomic stature, and sometimes skin color
- **Feudalism:** Developed in Europe in the eighth century; lords ruled over parcels of land; vassals worked for the lords and received protection from the lords; peasants made up the brute labor force, working for the vassals; a social system based on military authority
- **Matriarchy:** Social organization in which the female is the family head and title is traced through the female lineage

- **Meritocracy:** Social organization in which the power is held by those with superior intellect
- **Patriarchy:** Social organization in which the male is the family head and title is traced through the male lineage
- **Separatism:** Social organization that imparts separate facilities and sometimes separate laws/policies for certain groups within society (examples include minorities, gender, socioeconomic class)

A few ideas to teaching social structure include the following:

- Research class systems across the world.
- Discuss tribal structures.
- Analyze historical societies that were successful (Greek, Roman, Mayan, Aztec, and so on).
- Investigate family structure in the United States versus another culture.
- Examine the various "roles" of gender in modern society compared to the past.

# Citizenship

The Center for Civic Education (www.civiced.org) has proposed standards for Civics and Government to implement in school programs. They suggest that teachers provide students with information about the following:

- The definition and structure of government and an explanation of its function
- The basic premises and values of American democracy
- The role of the U.S. Constitution
- The relationship of the U.S. to other nations
- The roles and responsibilities of U.S. citizens

Teachers should include activities for the practice of being a good citizen (citizenship) and not just conduct readings from social studies texts. Books present facts, but may not provide opportunities for students to observe and apply what they have learned to become strong citizens. Educators should also provide activities to engage students in learning about civics and the government as well as practice citizenship skills.

Ways to encourage citizenship include the following:

- Conduct school service projects.
- Develop a class newsletter.
- Establish a classroom management system.
- Encourage individual service projects for the school or community.
- Read about and discuss public issues.
- Visit local government agencies and speak with government officials.
- Join in local community service groups and community activities or services.
- Participate in elections and practice voting.
- Work on school councils or government.
- Be involved in community groups that represent citizenship, such as the Scouts or the YMCA.
- Use participatory writing activities.
- Create a logo, motto, or rules for a class or school.
- Promote involvement in school-based decisions and resolving problems.

Understanding the values, principles, and beliefs of a democratic government and practicing the positive aspects of each is what creates a citizen of the United States. Different perspectives on citizenship education affect the delivery of instruction. Educators have personal and varying viewpoints, sometimes in combination, which may lead them directly toward teaching citizenship in various ways. Two models of instruction are debated in current citizenship education: **transmission** and **transformation.**

Transmission is the learning of government function and following the rules as set forth. The two perspectives are:

1. **Legalistic**—Focuses on following the laws explicitly and acknowledging the rights and responsibilities of citizens
2. **Assimilationist**—Promotes the values of society

Transformation is the analysis of information, the formation of opinions, and the actions taken. The two perspectives are:

1. **Critical thinking**—Encourages open-minded thoughts, views, values, and questions authority
2. **Cultural pluralism**—Provides students with a range of values and ideals and provides information about diversity and other governments

# Anthropology, Sociology, and Psychology

The social sciences have become part of the general social studies curriculum and include anthropology, sociology, psychology, economics, and political science; and most recently, global education, environmental education, and current events. Knowledge of these areas helps students understand their world and how they should function within it. Each of the social sciences is defined by the content knowledge and its individual processes.

**Anthropology** is the study of the cultural traits and the physical characteristics of people. The focus of its content should be on archaeology and prehistory, human evolution, defining culture, comparing different cultures, and identifying cultural changes. Elementary studies focus on the cultural aspects of anthropology and should include daily living, economic systems, social classes, housing, political structures, the arts, religion, and recreation.

Key points to remember in the study of people are as follows:

- Avoid stereotypical content.
- Specify historical periods.
- Use a variety of resources.
- Include diverse information.

Methods and activities to pursue anthropological study include the following:

- Simulate research and archaeology activities.
- Visit museums.
- Conduct library research.
- Study artifacts.
- Utilize online content and other media services.
- Focus on native cultures.
- Identify examples of cultural conflicts.
- Engage in storytelling.

**Sociology** and **psychology** together comprise the study of humans, society, behavior, and relationships. These subject areas provide opportunities for students to investigate their personal identities, compare their families, study peoples' interactions, share experiences about others, and research institutional influences and relationships.

**Sociology** content includes information about institutions, primary and secondary groups, social changes, communication, social problems, and relationships within and among groups of people. Activities should

- Focus on group membership.
- Involve community studies.
- Identify social problems.
- Investigate communication.

**Psychology** content includes individual differences, perceptions, and behaviors. Some activities that specifically relate to this topic are to

- Observe people.
- Identify and compare groups of people.
- Research human emotions.
- Study human development.

Methods and activities that will stimulate the study of sociology and psychology include the following:

- Read biographies.
- Write autobiographies.
- Use photographs and pictorial histories.
- Create family trees.
- Conduct surveys and interviews.
- Identify roles and responsibilities.
- Establish rules of behavior and interactions.
- Study social tensions and issues of history.
- Visit the community to learn about social organizations.

# Social Structures

Social structure allows most daily tasks and activities to be performed with some efficiency. It is the way in which society organizes expected relationships; it gives order and structure by association, institutions, and groups. Because structure is defined as an ordered arrangement of parts, it can be said that social structure is the way the units of a society or group relate to one another or are arranged. Like the parts of a body, each part of the social structure operates to create a unified coordination of the whole.

The movement of people, the import and export of goods, and the use of mass communication have all played an integral part in shaping the world. It is natural that people must interact, and they do so through movement, travel, trade, information flow, and political events. People live unevenly in many different parts of the world and use transportation, industrialization, technology, and economic systems to function within their villages and in the larger society. They live in a global community and must function in a global economy. Social structures, interactions of the parts, enable all these systems to operate as a larger unit, i.e., society or the world.

Social structures are created from the interrelationships among and organization of human beings. Human beings are often organized by certain common and shared objectives and aims. Social structures are comprised of information regarding communication, transportation, industrialization, technology, and economics. Social organizations play a huge role in social structures, as the structure is concerned with the types of groups or organizations created within society. Social organization is an arrangement of parts (people) and exists on the coordination of social relationships, whereas social structure encompasses the positions and rules found within social relationships.

Since social structures are a connectedness of parts, societies are able to function in a harmonious manner. The following are the basic foundations of social structure:

Goals—Humans have diverse needs, attitudes, and interests. However, common pursuit of a goal often develops a strong interrelationship between the individual parts.

Roles/Status—socially defined positions in a society or group are bestowed upon individual members. Each position has roles that must be completed. Individuals receive status and roles through customs, traditions, or societal conventions. Social structure ensures that every member of society is allocated a particular role and status. These roles are combined in order to build the social structure.

**Norms**—These are the approved ways individuals must behave in society. Norms work to define the roles of individuals, which in turn help to make the society stable and sustainable. Each social organization also has its own set of norms and the members within the organization have individual norms.

Students need to be educated about how the relationships of these primary social structures affect the management of a society. Teaching students the complex concepts of social structure can seem a bit overwhelming. However, there are some activities that may help enhance this topic. They include the following:

- Take field trips to community entities and businesses.
- Study various cultures and societies to compare the different socially defined roles.
- Use various types of technology to create representations of social structures.
- Use case studies to examine status and roles within the family unit.
- Study economic systems (household, school clubs, local government).
- Build skills in area of communication (speeches, presentations).

# Economics

Under this topic of social studies, students are expected to acquire basic economic knowledge and to perform economic analysis. Children's development of concept knowledge and their understanding of economic factors move to the more complex and the more abstract as they mature. They do not develop economic reasoning or abstract knowledge for all concepts at the same time.

Both skills and content are important to the development of economic reasoning. Learning how to use reason regarding economic issues is important because the analytic approach to economics differs from approaches used for other related subjects such as history and civics. Economic analysis helps students examine many questions in history, politics, business, and international relations.

The key skills students must develop include the ability to

- Describe economic problems, alternatives, benefits, and costs.
- Examine economic situations.
- Identify the consequences of changes in economic policies.
- Analyze economic evidence.
- Compare benefits and costs.

Students should be able to

- Understand basic economic concepts and key issues.
- Recite economic facts about the United States (unemployment, inflation, and so on).
- Explain historical events from an economic perspective.
- Use economic reasoning to evaluate policy proposals for contemporary issues (unemployment and pollution).
- Trace historical economic patterns.
- Compare economic systems in the world.
- Identify issues related to economics.
- Study economic policies and current status.
- Make decisions and realize that decisions affect self as well as others.
- Understand that not all trade is volunteer and that choices have future impact.

Activities that help in the study of economics include the following:

- Create classroom societies that reflect real-life situations in which students can develop rules and laws, establish a government, and plan the economic system.
- Study the market and seek information on products, compare prices, and analyze advertising.
- Work at an individual level to prepare personal budgets, show ways to economize, and select necessary goods and services based on the budget.
- Establish workforce education in which students learn about careers, gain knowledge about the requirements and responsibilities of contemporary jobs, conduct career research, make career choices, hold career days/fairs, and allow career shadowing.

# History, Geography, and Government

This section includes information about the history, geography, and government of states, regions, the United States, and the world. United States history incorporates the knowledge of the chronological development of the United States (such as colonization, expansion, formation of government, wars and reconstruction, industrialization, and political changes) as well as major themes found throughout U.S. history (political processes; racial, ethnic, and gender struggles; the roles of the United States in the world; economic transformations; and various struggles and achievements). World history is the cumulative study of important themes and cultural comparisons across time and geography. Geography is considered the study of places that includes physical characteristics, geopolitical information, demographics, and economic information.

## United States and World History

Students are very capable of learning history and related concepts if the instruction is clear, appropriate, and meaningful. Learning about the history of the world, the United States, a specific state, a community, a school, or a family all help students learn their place within the world. Teachers need to help create an understanding of historical events as well as develop students' ability to apply historical thinking in the viewing of the human record. Analysis and study of maps as well as graphs related to the past, present, and future are vital to understanding historical concepts. There is a vast array of topics to cover, so educators need to refer to both state and national standards for their specific grade level. To aid students at every level, educators may use the following:

- Developmentally appropriate concepts
- Contextual support
- Multiple-lesson formats
- Cooperative learning activities
- Critical thinking activities
- Discovery-based learning opportunities
- Motivational hands-on activities
- Inquiry-based learning projects
- Assignments where the students are historians
- Variety of resources

Some lesson ideas include the following:

- Research various stereotypes in order to trace the process of change for various groups or minorities.
- Link literature to historical studies (Star-Spangled Banner, Common Sense, Uncle Tom's Cabin, and so on); analyze historical documents (Articles of Confederation, the Constitution, Gettysburg Address, and so on).
- Explore history through electronic field trips and research; this can be a great alternative when actual field trips are not possible (Colonial Williamsburg, the Smithsonian, Liberty Bell, 13 original colonies, and so on).
- Research notable historical figures to help guide students in the knowledge of historical developments.

- Reconstruct historical events throughout the world using dioramas, oral presentations, songs, or plays.
- Write firsthand accounts from certain eras in history.

# Political Science

The primary educational component of social studies that helps to produce a reliable citizen is the knowledge of civics and government. **Civics** is the study of people and their relationships with government and other people in their county. The Center for Civic Education promotes instruction of the basic values of American democracy. **Government** is the study of the legal and political institutions in the world as well as political systems and ideologies of the various countries.

In this content area, students should learn the following:

- What a government is and how it functions
- How rules are made and enforced
- How rules affect family, community, local, state, national, and international places
- Why government is necessary and how power and authority is utilized
- The democratic values and beliefs of civic life

Educators should teach the basic structures of political science and the rights and responsibilities of its citizens. They must help students understand that this nation is comprised of groups of different ethnicity, race, religion, class, language, gender, or national origin, and it is because of these factors that the United States has a diverse population. They need to know that the set ideals of a nation have not always been fair or achieved.

To plan effective instruction in political science, educators should become familiar with the national content and state academic standards. Classroom activities and learning opportunities may then be developed and designed to address the proposed skills. Consider students with a wide range of abilities and acknowledge cultural diversity in all activities. Include discussions on controversial issues and decision making to encourage thoughtful consideration of values topics.

Students should learn the components of decision making that support governmental studies and citizenship education:

- How to identify and define a problem
- How to identify and define values
- How to predict consequences or outcomes
- How to reach decisions
- How to justify decisions
- How decisions can be altered

An example of a curriculum plan focus in political science studies for specific grades includes the following:

- K–second—Families, schools
- Third—Cities
- Fourth—State
- Fifth—Federal government
- Sixth—Ancient and foreign governments

# Citizenship

Educators should want students to become good citizens who are informed voters, who promote positive values, and who perform community service. They should understand the democratic ideals and realize that they have not always been practiced.

Citizenship education should teach students

- How government works, so they can follow rules.
- Ways to change society for the better.
- Value-based decision making.
- When and how to analyze social settings and conditions.
- How to define key political issues and develop personal perspectives.
- Forms of civic participation.

Activities that enhance citizenship education include

- Going on field trips to government facilities and historical museums.
- Creating situations in which students can practice their citizenship skills.
- Developing scenarios for useful problem-solving practice.
- Discussing and debating current events.

# Geography

Geography is only one component of the subject of social studies, and it is as significant as the study of history. Students need a broad base of geographic knowledge as they grow and develop in an ever-changing global society. Just knowing where places are on Earth is not enough in our current world. The basic areas students need to know more about geography are as follows:

- Map skills and spatial organization of the world
- The places and regions of the world
- The physical and human systems
- The environment and society
- The uses of geography

Students need to

- Understand the relationships of places to one another and how people all over the world interact and affect each other's communities.
- Investigate the distribution of resources and products throughout the world.
- Comprehend how the use of these goods influences the people who consume them and the impact of these resources on the environment.
- Have a clearer understanding of how decisions that people make in their environments not only shape the present, but also the future.
- Know how places change over time and what their own role will be in the world.

The primary components of learning geography are patterns, regularities, and the reasons for spatial organization. Students must become adept at reading maps and demonstrate knowledge about the spatial relationships of people, places, and environments as well as the events that alter them.

## The World in Spatial Terms

According to the nationally recommended standards for geography, students must become "geographically informed" and learn how to organize information about the world in a spatial context. Becoming geographically aware and thinking in **spatial terms** means that students gain the ability to describe and analyze the presented spatial organization (the absolute or relative location of something) around the people and environments found on the Earth's surface. Students who acquire a strong foundation of geography vocabulary, map terms, and spatial organization phrases will be better equipped to learn the major concepts and apply their knowledge of this subject area.

Three standards from the National Education Goals of 2000 and the National Geography Standards of 1997 related to the **world in spatial terms** are summarized here:

1. Students should learn how to use maps and other geographic representations, tools, and technologies to acquire, process, and report information in a spatial context.
2. Students must know how to use mental maps to organize information about people, places, and environments in a more spatial context.
3. Students need to understand how to analyze the spatial organization of people, places, and environments on the Earth's surface.

Pertaining to the development of map skills and understanding spatial organization, examinees must be capable of aiding students in learning the following concepts of geography:

- The key concepts and legends that refer to pictorial or semipictorial symbols
- The relationships of geographical information and how places change over time
- The production of maps inclusive of geographical information
- The utilization of mental maps to connect people to places and make connections between objects and day-to-day life
- The spatial relationships among people, places, and the environment and how they influence each other
- The use of various types of reference works that are available

In order to instruct students regarding spatial organization, teachers must first analyze which students think in spatial terms. Not every individual has the ability to think using these terms and can learn to use visual representations or visual communications. Instruction should include hands-on map examples, models, and demonstrations. Identifying spatial organization terms will also aid students in being able to understand spatial organization. These terms may include *compass, directions, scale, location, latitude, longitude, prime meridian, equator, legend, symbol, time zones, hemispheres,* and *map projections*.

## Places, People, and Regions

The ability to function in the world is dependent upon the understanding and appreciation of similarities and differences of various places and regions in the world. Students must learn

- The physical and human characteristics of certain places and specific regions.
- The human relationships that exist and how these function in places and regions.
- The various regions and places to gain their ability to function in the world.
- To understand and appreciate the similarities and differences of the diverse places and regions across the continents.

In early 2000, the Joint Committee on Geographic Education of the National Council for Geographic Education, along with the American Association of Geographers, developed five specific themes in order to help focus student and teacher knowledge in geography. The themes are location, place, human-environment interaction, movement, and region. These specific themes help teachers concentrate on helping students to understand how the global community works.

Some ways to teach location include the following:

- Create a memory map of the world.
- Map favorite characters from literature (Harry Potter is from England, Madeline is from France, Dora the Explorer is from Latin America, and so on).
- Design a new country, include a map or the terrain, and describe the political and economic aspects.
- Make puzzle maps of specific regions for students to practice putting together.

Some ideas for teaching place include the following:

- Create postcards from areas and have students write as if they were vacationing there.
- Develop stamps for a specific place and have students include something that exemplifies that place.
- Construct weather reports on certain places from around the globe.
- Design ABC books describing a certain place (each letter of the alphabet represents a characteristic of the place).

Some ideas for teaching human-environment interaction include the following:

- Read literature that demonstrates the relationship between humans and the environment (for example, *The Lorax,* Dr. Seuss; *Just a Dream,* Chris Van Allsburg; *Uno's Garden and The Watering Hole,* Graeme Base; *Window,* Jeannie Baker; *The Great Kapok Tree,* Lynn Cherry; *Where Once There Was a Wood,* Denise Fleming; *Do Not Disturb,* Nancy Tafuri).
- Explore and research the history and growth of a local town to demonstrate how places change due to impacts.
- Examine the wants and needs of people and how those are met through goods and services as well as the use of resources.
- Discuss "what if" scenarios such as "what if this school was never built, how would the environment be different?" or "what if the town we live in was rural instead of urban?" or "what if you had to survive in the mountains all alone, how would you accomplish this with no electricity or technology?"

Ideas for teaching movement include the following:

- Research, graph, and explore where everyday products, goods, and services come from.
- Trace student families and find out how they came to America.
- Keep track of how many different license plates students see in a week or in a month and then place markers on a map to show the various license plate origins.
- Develop commuter maps to show how far people travel to school, work, the grocery store, the mall, and other places.

Ideas for teaching region include the following:

- Have students map their neighborhood and then the school and examine the differences in the regions. Utilize this technique for countries as well.
- Research stamps or currency from around the world and analyze the differences from region to region.
- Explore the various cultural regions of the United States and discuss how those developed (Northeast, Midwest, Southeast, Northwest, and Southwest).
- Study the various time zones around the country and the world and consider how this may affect travel and interaction from region to region.

# Physical and Human Systems

Since this area overlaps with science, it lends itself to instruction as a topic for integrated study. Students must learn how **physical systems** shape the Earth's surface and understand the concepts related to ecosystems and how they affect the world. They must gain knowledge about how to maintain and modify the Earth's environments, as these are critical to all human activity. By understanding how physical systems affect the Earth, students will begin to understand how the Earth serves as a home to plants and animals. Equally important is the history of **human systems,** which can be influenced and shaped by understanding geography. It is important for students to understand the historical and geographical values of human development. Viewing the past from both a historical and a geographical aspect aids in the understanding of physical and human events.

Students must learn

- How events (past and present) are formed by human perceptions of places and regions.
- To answer complex questions such as:

    What was the purpose of the Alaskan pipeline?

    Why was the Berlin Wall constructed?
- How the events of the past provide many insights into climate, resources, ecosystems, and migration of human ancestors.
- To explain why certain events happened in a certain way.

# Environment and Society

Humans are instrumental in the continuation of the environment, yet they can also be the destructors of certain environments, thus altering the world. Students must gain a sense of the interactions between humans and the environment in order to understand how the world changes and what their role will be.

Students need to understand

- That the consumption of resources and alterations of natural patterns both have consequences.
- How the building of structures that become part of the Earth's surface change the region.
- The variety of reasons why people compete for control of the Earth.
- How the modification of the natural environment causes changes in ecosystems.
- How relationships between nature and the people on Earth affect one another.
- How physical systems alter people's construction of their environment.
- The opportunities and constraints that the environment offers and how the costs of such properties/ characteristics are critical to the world.
- That the environment has a limited carrying capacity.
- How the intended and unintended repercussions of human interactions pertain to the Earth.
- The methods needed to synthesize and evaluate the ways that humans have used and adapted the environment to meet their needs.
- The development of skills necessary to interpret, evaluate, analyze, and synthesize the impact of humans on the environment and vice versa.

# Concepts and Skills

Students need to develop appropriate concepts and skills under the subject of social studies, which can include organizing data, problem solving, comparing and contrasting, model building, planning, forecasting, and decision making. Cause and effect is an extremely important component of social studies education. Learning the reasons why something occurs will help students begin to develop skills on how to prevent or plan for specific events. Students should be developing the following skills throughout the elementary years:

- **Geographic literacy**—Utilizing maps, cartographer tools, and interpreting various maps
- **Visual analysis**—Analyzing graphic data and images
- **Critical thinking and reading**—Identifying main ideas, sequencing, discerning cause and effect, making inferences, drawing conclusions, making valid generalizations, recognizing fact and opinion, analyzing source type (secondary or primary), identifying point of view and possible bias, problem solving, and comparing and contrasting
- **Communication**—Transferring from one medium to another, effectively stating a point, supporting a point or position, and unifying ideas

# Reference Works and Resources

Students need to know the various types of reference works that are available to them in order to find geographical information. Students will improve their ability to understand geographic information if they know where to find these tools, learn how to use them efficiently, and determine how to gauge the accuracy and reliability of the resources. Students also need to learn how to apply and interpret the information they seek, such as changing the information found on charts and graphs into a written form. These include such materials as encyclopedias, computer-based programs, almanacs, atlases, gazetteers, geographical dictionaries, statistical abstracts, and data compilations.

# Classroom Management

Overall classroom management in social studies—motivation, participation, inclusion, organization, fairness, and expectations—is much the same as for other subject areas. Strategies for establishing environments, developing and presenting lessons, managing behaviors, and accessing activities and materials all pertain to classroom management and essentially affect instruction. These are further reviewed in Chapter 1.

Social studies teachers can weave lessons into classroom management and structure that cover topics such as laws and regulations, citizenship and individual rights, government, and control. Teachers should incorporate classroom systems where students

- Work together to problem solve.
- Develop rules and guidelines.
- Make democratic decisions.

# Content Pedagogy

This section relates to map and globe skills, inquiry-based instruction, decision making, and models. Additional information regarding pedagogy may be found in Chapter 1.

## Map Knowledge and Map-Reading Skills

Maps are an essential component of learning the subject of geography. Maps require the use of different types of skills, both in language and reading. Map-reading skills can be developed through **direct instruction** and **repeated practice.** Often students have trouble making connections and drawing relationships between map symbols and information presented on the map. Helping students to move from concrete to abstract concepts and promoting practice from the simple to more complex tasks will be valuable for successful student achievement.

According to Piaget, the three stages of map-reading skill development are:

1. **Topographical stage**—The ability to understand different areas, but no specific place
2. **Projective stage**—The ability to locate an object or place in relation to self
3. **Euclidian stage**—The ability to use strong spatial relationship skills

Bruner's cognitive theory complements Piaget's findings by stating that students must go through a concrete interaction with space, an active process where learners base their ideas and concepts on current or past knowledge. Then learners begin to transform information and make decisions that are not just based on the given information by using icons or images from past experiences, thus moving into the iconic state. After this, the learner moves into the symbolic stage in which the child can categorize, think logically, and solve problems. The use of maps allows students to discover, interpret, and connect information and concepts on their own (or with minimal guidance), thus making the information more likely to be remembered and internalized.

Students need to acquire skills on how to read and understand the **symbols** and **key concepts** of maps. They need to learn how to view certain maps and to determine which maps to use when searching for specific information. They must be able to create a representation of information on a map, know if the properties depicted are correct, and understand which properties are misshaped. Critical to map reading is the ability to read the legends, understand the symbols, use the scales, determine directions, and comprehend the details.

Reading maps requires specific skills; for example, students must be able to understand the scale or units of measurement being used (inches, meters, and so on). The following strategies may assist students in acquiring these important lifelong competencies:

- Create simple maps to begin instruction (map of class, student's house, school, community, 50 states).
- Instruct on the simple symbols used (direction, landmark, grids).
- Require students to construct a map or three-dimensional model.
- Create maps of the classroom or school and have the students use the maps and map legends to give directions to one another.
- Use the animated maps on the Web to help assist in visual comprehension, motivation, and hands-on instruction.
- Teach orienteering to bridge the abstract with the concrete and physical interpretations of map reading.

# Geographic Representations

Knowledge about geographic representations helps students make sense of the world. They learn to store and recall information about the shapes and patterns of physical and human features of the Earth. Students may internalize one or more aspects of the Earth's surface based on previous knowledge and new concepts.

When students learn how to produce maps with geographical information, they are better able to understand the spatial organization of the world. In order to become proficient at map usage, they must feel comfortable with the four aspects of maps: symbols, scale, directions, and grid.

Map studies are often focused in the third grade, but can begin earlier with learning to use simple maps. The study of maps should continue with reading and creating more complex maps as students move past the third grade.

Geographic representations may be constructed of maps, globes, graphs, tables, diagrams, aerial photos, and satellite images. These tools provide valuable information on spatial terms and relationships, and can be used as supplements to the existing classroom materials. However, there are limitations in using geographic representations; some may not be understood by students, certain lessons on the content and use may need to be developed on these specialized mapping tools, and some may be difficult to access depending on the location.

# Uses of Geography

Geography is the study of the Earth that includes people and how they live, work, and play. It is the study of the environment as well as the cultures and how people adapt to certain areas. When students delve into the topic of geography they learn how to locate people and places, map resources, exploit resources, identify a location in relation to self, map landmarks, map barriers or dangers, and identify specific geographic formations.

Students learn to use geographic knowledge to understand what has happened to the world, its people, and its resources in the past; how those functions have affected the present; and how they can plan for the future. They can learn to use information about historical events and processes, apply knowledge to current events and issues, and develop ways to conduct urban planning, resolve social and community issues, and develop goals regarding future challenges such as pollution, resource consumption, and populations.

The Joint Committee on Geographic Education proposes that students learn the following specific set of geographic skills:

- Ask geographic questions.
- Acquire geographic information.
- Organize geographic information.
- Analyze geographic information.
- Answer geographic questions.

| Applications of Geography | Concepts and Skills Mastered |
|---|---|
| Spatial organization | * Patterns and reasons<br>* Movement between places and regions<br>* Local, national, and global interactions<br>* Diversity of areas and people<br>* Systems in locations |
| Ecological focus | * Patterns and processes<br>* Ecosystems and biomes<br>* Physical connections—local and global environments<br>* Human impact and relationship to environment |
| Geographical understanding | * Analyze and make informed decisions<br>* Gain knowledge about destinations<br>* Learn ability to function at home and abroad<br>* Predict consequences of interactions |

# Instructional Strategies for Social Studies

Instructional strategies used at the elementary level may vary according to teacher, but in general the strategies may be used across the curriculum. One key method for social studies instruction is to embed the content in other subject areas in an integrated curriculum style. For example, when reading short stories in the language arts program, the teacher should provide additional background content about the people, the lands, and the cultures in the stories.

The following three lists provide the examinee with information about recommended lesson types strategies and techniques, as well as activities that may be used. These lists are not totally inclusive of all possibilities.

Three types of essential lessons for social studies instruction:

1. **Utilize primary sources**—Include actual items from the period or place studied, such as original documents, artifacts, maps, newspaper articles, photos, clothing, music, and tools.
2. **Incorporate fiction**—Include the use of books, stories, and integrated readings, such as in the study of oral traditions or for storytelling and the outlining of events.
3. **Use timelines**—Depict the dates and sequential order of events, such as those specific to an area, certain historical events, or a people.

Strategies and techniques for use in social studies education:

- Deliver instruction using multiple-lesson formats.
- Utilize cooperative learning sessions, such as group projects, interview projects, and think-pair-share activities.
- Include inquiry learning periods to aid students in developing problem-solving skills, using reflective thinking skills, and learning through discovery. Inquiry is particularly useful in social studies, as it supports students in learning to use resource materials. In order to pursue inquiry learning, students may need access to resources such as atlases, encyclopedias, almanacs, magazines, newspapers, and electronic media.
- Impose a group investigation strategy, which is the use of both cooperative learning and inquiry learning.
- Provide scaffolding instruction and small or large group work.

Suggested activities to enhance social studies education:

- Consider historical investigation.
- Use diagrams, charts, maps, graphs, dioramas, and tables.
- Debate team topics.
- Utilize critical thinking activities.
- Require group models, presentations, and reports.
- Develop partner or team activities.
- Provide current event topics and study.
- Access information from newspaper and other media sources.
- Establish career days or job-shadowing opportunities.
- Identify types of work and monetary use around the world.

# Social Studies Assessment

There are many different types of assessments used in elementary education, and the purpose of assessment is the same in all subjects. The details regarding the topic of assessment are further explained in Chapter 1.

Conducting assessments helps teachers to determine the performance levels of their students and aids in developing the social studies curriculum in order to provide more appropriate activities to the students. When assessing for social studies understanding, a teacher should seek to collect data about students from a variety of sources (quizzes, homework, presentations) in different formats (group projects, individual research) and collect the data on a regular and ongoing basis.

Authentic assessments are popularly used in social studies and may include the following:

- Complete a project (use a criteria form).
- Make a presentation or give an oral report (use a rating scale).
- Submit a research paper (use in portfolio collection).
- Develop a mass-media presentation (use a rubric to evaluate).
- Maintain a journal (use a rubric to evaluate).
- Develop a portfolio (use a consistent format).
- Evaluate homework or an essay (use a set criteria).
- Use a nonwritten project such as developing a chart or maps (use observation or a rubric to evaluate).

Other more standardized assessments may be used, such as chapter quizzes, unit tests, and semester exams.

# Chapter 5
# Science Curriculum, Instruction, and Assessment (0011/5011)

Science is everywhere in the world, so students are exposed to it on a daily basis. Science concepts reach far beyond the academic subject, though the attitudes people gain about science are based on the knowledge and experiences they have. To help children develop strong, positive attitudes about science concepts and applications, educators must provide them with successful experiences and exciting opportunities to study, research, investigate, think about, ask questions, and draw conclusions.

What students learn about science in school is influenced by how it is taught. Students generally move from the concrete level of science knowledge to the abstract level as they mature and their understanding is actively constructed through individual and social processes. The key to acquiring scientific knowledge is for students to participate in science activities; by doing so, they will learn concepts, principles, and laws. Furthermore, multidisciplinary and integrated approaches need to be utilized to further increase science comprehension (the study of the history of science, reading about science in language arts, and so on).

The standards set forth for science instruction according to national science organizations are based on five primary principles:

1. The vision of science education described by the standards requires changes throughout the entire system.
2. What students learn is greatly influenced by how they are taught.
3. The actions of teachers are deeply influenced by their perceptions of science as an enterprise and as a subject to be taught and learned.
4. Student understanding is actively constructed through individual and social processes.
5. Actions of teachers are deeply influenced by their understanding of and relationships with students.

Furthermore, the instructional standards encompass the following:

- Teachers of science plan an inquiry-based science program for their students.
- Teachers of science guide and facilitate learning.
- Teachers of science engage in ongoing assessment of their teaching and of student learning.
- Teachers of science design and manage learning environments that provide students with the time, space, and resources needed for learning science.
- Teachers of science develop communities of science learners that reflect the intellectual rigor of scientific inquiry and the attitudes and social values conducive to learning science.
- Teachers of science actively participate in the ongoing planning and development of the school science program.

The eight broad categories for student educational standards recommended by the National Science Teachers Association (NSTA) and identified in Chapter 12 are available for further detailed review and provide educators with an overall view of the needs of students in this academic subject area. Each standard assumes the knowledge and skills of the other standards. The NSTA is involved with science education transformation in this country and has two primary goals:

1. Master scientific literacy for all.
2. Strengthen the supply of scientists, engineers, and science teachers.

Other organizations related to science education expound upon the beliefs that children should be provided with less scientific content and more opportunities for discovery. Children should be allowed to investigate, study, gain access through interdisciplinary topics, be offered inquiry, and be stimulated not only by the topics of science, but through the methods of science instruction.

The American Association for the Advancement of Science (www.aaas.org/) promotes the improvement of science and human progress. This organization has many resources that are utilized by schools in science education programs as an aid to teachers in the development of science curriculum, as it outlines what students should know in the areas of science, mathematics, and technology in the various grade level groupings: K–2, 3–5, 6–8, and 9–12.

The NSTA (www.nsta.org/) created the National Science Education Standards and Assessment, a document that outlines the standards and describes the expectations for student knowledge and achievement. Additionally, the National Association for the Education of Young Children provides guidelines for developmentally appropriate practices for children ages 3–8 years and is a resource to consider when developing a science program at the early childhood level.

Other organizations helpful in securing information about science education are as follows:

- The National Institute for Science Education (NISE) http://archive.wceruw.org/nise/
- The Council for Elementary Science International (CESI) www.cesiscience.org
- National Institutes of Health—Office of Science Education (NIHOSE) science-education.nih.gov
- The National Center for Science Education (NCSE) http://ncse.com
- The National Science Foundation (NSF) http://nsf.gov

The science portion of the Praxis II elementary education exam (0011/5011) assesses an examinee's overall knowledge and application of information regarding curriculum, instruction, and assessment, specifically focused on the unifying concepts and processes, inquiry, technology, health principles, and pedagogy. In this section of the study guide, examinees will find content specific to these science topics; the more general elementary practices are found in Chapter 1. Use both of these sections to study for this exam as well as a review of Science Content Knowledge 0014/5014, Chapter 12.

The 0011/5011 exam measures the extent to which an examinee knows how to develop and deliver instruction based on science content knowledge. This exam employs examples of elementary situations through multiple-choice questions. This section of the study guide includes the information necessary for the examinee to clearly utilize the content of 0014/5014 in the implementation of curriculum and instruction and the use of assessments in science education.

# Curriculum Components and Instruction

The more basic elements of instruction and curriculum design are found in Chapter 1 of this book. That section includes curriculum components such as scope and sequence, appropriate materials, technology, and learner objectives. This information is used in all elementary subject areas and can be adapted and modified for science. The content in this portion of the study guide is related to more specific science education topics.

Curriculum must be carefully addressed at each specific grade level and aligned with state and national standards. The content of any science curriculum should be integrated with other academic subjects as well as the areas of fine arts and physical education. The scope of the curriculum should establish parameters for the topics covered and the material should be sequenced logically to promote concept and skill acquisition. Inquiry-based learning and authentic assessments are critical to science education at the elementary level.

The disciplines of science are vast and comprehensive. Each discipline depends on another discipline. For this reason, many science educators and researchers believe that the sciences should be taught using the science-technology-society (STS) perspective, which is the integration of all areas of science. Science-technology research endorses the study of social, political, and cultural values and their impact on scientific research and technological innovation as well as society, politics, and culture as a whole.

| Curriculum Content | |
|---|---|
| **Approach** | **Description** |
| Historical | Studies the history of science at a human level |
| Philosophical | Studies the nature of science and the different viewpoints |
| Issues-based | Studies the factors of science that affect the environment and society |

Most educators who teach science believe that it is better to teach the processes than just the products of science. The laws, facts, and content of science are best discovered through learning the processes. It can be said that science *is* process rather than just part of it. The products of science should be derived from the process. Many educators believe that science instruction must be integrated with not only the other areas of science, but also with other academic areas. Incorporating language arts, mathematics, social studies, and fine arts into science education provides a richer curriculum and more experiential education opportunities for elementary children. This method provides a more realistic view of the world and the situations they will face in the future.

# Content-Specific Pedagogy

Research demonstrates the effectiveness of promoting the concept of scientific products first before teaching the scientific processes at the elementary level. Selecting those products of most interest to elementary students is the recommended method for then teaching the processes. When children are active participants in scientific exploration they arrive at their own conclusions, which become more meaningful to them.

Two of the most recognized theories useful to the instruction of science are:

1. Constructivism
2. Inquiry-based learning

Based on the work of Jean Piaget, **constructivism** is where the student constructs his or her own learning by using existing knowledge in order to create new knowledge. This theory is closely related to inquiry-based learning. Science is the process of construction and reconstruction, so students study existing knowledge and reconstruct their idea base when new information is discovered. A basic premise of science education is that children learn science best when they construct meaning by merging prior information with new information, as they must observe, think, infer, and process the information.

**Inquiry-based learning** is at the forefront of contemporary science education programs. Research demonstrates that when students are involved in hands-on tasks, are active in discovery, and participate in their own learning, they will retain knowledge for longer periods of time. If learning makes more sense to the student, it drives the learner toward higher levels of participation and achievement.

The three methods of imparting scientific knowledge to young children are:

1. Expository method
2. Free-discovery method
3. Guided-inquiry method

The **expository method** is a completely teacher-dominated and directed way to instruct children. Usually a summary of the information and an evaluation are included in the expository method. The teacher may manage the science classroom by providing lectures, delivering demonstrations, or imparting explanations of science topics. Some topics in science may require the expository method as the information and presentation may be standardized for all children. Delivering concepts, explaining procedures, demonstrating experiments, describing safety procedures, and distributing content information are all examples of topics that may require the use of the expository method.

The following challenges may be encountered while using the expository method:

- Motivation and attention of students may wane.
- Opportunities for differentiated instruction are limited.
- Pacing of instruction and that of student learning appears stilted.
- Some topic discussions may not be relevant to all students.
- Application of knowledge may not be available.

The **free-discovery method** is based on child-directed instruction. This method promotes the implementation and the direction of the inquiry as well as the knowledge acquisition where students may be involved and motivated in the learning process and in using the materials. Children create the situation of learning that is meaningful to them and where they may better apply the knowledge they have absorbed.

There are advantages and disadvantages of the free-discovery method. The advantages include the use of the constructivist model and how the children may be actively engaged in the learning. The disadvantages include the appearance of a lack of structure or organization; the need for additional time, materials, equipment, and resources; and the need for the implementation of strong classroom management principles.

**Guided inquiry** is a method on the continuum between the expository and free-discovery methods. In guided inquiry, the teacher may choose the topic of study and identify the process, by delineating questions and activities, while allowing students to construct their own investigations, determine their needed resources, find the answers to their questions, and organize the information. The teacher facilitates the instruction by leading the students in experimentation, investigation, and exploration of teacher-selected topics, and by encouraging students through use of inquiry and open-ended questions based on the specific activity. The teacher may guide the students in the direction of their findings but permits them to be the "doers" of science.

Other methods pertinent to the instruction of science at the elementary level are universal design, blending integrated subjects and interdisciplinary studies, incorporating the multiple intelligences, and including literature studies.

Universal design should be utilized in addition to inquiry or constructivism as it provides accommodations for diverse learners, necessary to meet each student's needs as related to science concepts, processes, and activities.

Integrated subjects and interdisciplinary studies focus on including other academic areas and disciplines into the study of science. Because the world is not fragmented into separate subjects, it is recommended that science education be delivered in elementary classrooms as a broad approach to learning. For example, when studying the water cycle (science), students may construct a poster to advertise a movie about the cycle (art and language arts).

The multiple intelligences theory was first identified by Howard Gardner, who believed that humans have at least nine intelligences (see definitions in Chapter 1) and these intelligences are revealed differently in each individual. Therefore, teachers should create a variety of activities and utilize different instructional methods to address every student in the classroom, which focuses on each student's areas of strength. Students may use a combination of the intelligence strands to become more successful in school and teachers should challenge students to utilize the less-used intelligence areas by combining them randomly in their lessons.

Instructional styles to recognize in the area of science include the following:

- **Inductive** (from specific to general)—Instruction begins with a study of the more finite information on which to base general conclusions or make broad generalizations about the subject or item.
- **Deductive** (from general to specific)—Instruction begins with the study of the broad topic of information and then focuses down to the more detailed information on the subject.

Additional pedagogy is outlined in Chapter 1 for elementary education.

# Strategies and Activities

The majority of elementary science teachers use a combination of methods, strategies, and activities for science instruction. It is valuable for educators to vary the presentation of science as it helps them cover all of the content and maintain motivation of the students. A highly recommended format, inquiry-based learning, utilized across the country, leads students toward mastering higher-level analysis skills and using logical thinking skills. Many publishers of science materials are incorporating this type of format in their printed materials.

Science educators refer to an instructional cycle and a series of steps that may be followed with students as active learners. This series of steps aligns with the EEI model of instruction defined in Chapter 1.

Following is the outline of the **instructional cycle** for science instruction:

- **Discrepant event**—An unusual phenomenon is demonstrated or described to students. This aids students in developing the hypothesis and experimental design.
- **Question**—A question that integrates the variable for the selected investigation is posed. Example of question format: When does (independent variable) impact (dependent variable)?
- **Inquiry**—Experiments may be constructed by the students based on the investigated variable. The format may be through question/answer, the collection of more data, or by inferences/comparisons. The experiments should follow an outline:
  - State the question that will be investigated.
  - Formulate a hypothesis.
  - Describe the independent (condition to be changed) and dependent (what is being measured, with suggested tools) variables.
  - Indicate the controls; identify the constant variables.
  - Collect data; organize and carefully gather data to ensure accuracy of results through use of tables, charts, and graphs.
  - Organize and correlate the data to determine how to present the gathered information. The use of line or bar graphs and solid communication helps students learn presentation skills regarding experimentation results.
  - Use mathematical applications; science and math terminology may be used, as well as math equations and tools.
  - Provide a conclusion; present a summary of the experiment, the process, and the results.
  - Include enrichment activities. For some learners an extension of the basic experiment may be quite beneficial. It may include readings, additional research, further experiments, or a project to enrich student knowledge base.

Several methods of instructional delivery are available to teachers, depending on the specific science topic and the types of students. Some of the more common methods of instructional delivery include the following:

- **Demonstration**—This provides students with models or visual examples of the information. It may precede an experiment or inquiry-based activity or it may be incorporated into a lecture or group presentation.
- **Lecture**—The teacher imparts the information to the students and may use multimedia to deliver the content. It is a structured format generally not recommended for elementary students, as inquiry-based learning is not represented through lecture.
- **Inquiry-based or inquiry-guided learning**—Evidence of high retention rates, this format is often facilitated or guided by the teacher. The process of learning is managed by the students. Often used for small group projects, this method may also be useful for experimental investigations and gathering data regarding a hypothesis.

- **Cooperative learning activity**—A group activity using homogeneous or heterogeneous combinations of students, selected by the teacher, it aids students in gaining problem-solving, communication, and critical thinking skills.

- **Small group instruction and presentations**—Students work in small groups of two, three, or four individuals to gather information and develop a presentation that is then delivered to the whole group. Students take on roles in the small group, such as being the presenter, recorder, defender, organizer, or researcher.

- **Whole group discussion**—Similar to the lecture format, the teacher often facilitates and manages the discussion while the students communicate with one another. Students are responsible for regurgitation of the information learned, while also analyzing the content, thereby presenting opinions or asking questions of others.

- **Laboratory experimentation**—This is generally a large group activity as all students participate in the same experiment, and therefore, inquiry is not a part of the learning process. Sometimes the activity follows a textbook or experiment manual or the ideas collected from teacher experiences.

- **Research projects**—These activities can be part of the overall assignments for the entire class or used as enrichment for students who need additional and extended content information.

- **Literature review**—Either used as a whole class project or for individual assignments, students use additional resources besides the textbook, by selecting books and materials via the library, the Internet, or the classroom.

# Unifying Concepts and Processes

Unifying concepts and processes provide students with the knowledge, procedures, and ideas of how the natural world works. These concepts and processes are described as a primary science standard and are carried out and repeated throughout all the science standards.

Unifying concepts and processes include the following:

- Systems, order, organization
- Evolution, equilibrium, cycles
- Evidence, models, explanation
- Form, function, structure
- Change, constancy, measurement

NSTA states:

> *"In early grades, instruction should establish the meaning and use of unifying concepts and processes—for example, what it means to measure and how to use measurement tools. At the upper grades, the standard should facilitate and enhance the learning of scientific concepts and principles by providing students with a big picture of scientific ideas—for example, how measurement is important in all scientific endeavors."*

# Science as Inquiry

Inquiry takes the student a step beyond science as a process and introduces skills such as conducting observations, making inferences, and performing experiments. Students should be engaged in these activities that promote and help formulate scientific reasoning and critical thinking during this period. Inquiry activity involves the student in the task and teaches the student to

- Ask questions.
- Plan and conduct investigations.
- Use tools and techniques to gather data.
- Draw conclusions between evidence and explanation.

- Construct and evaluate alternate explanations.
- Form and communicate scientific arguments.

**Science inquiry** should promote the following:

- Comprehension of scientific concepts
- Appreciation of history of scientific knowledge
- Understanding the nature of science
- Acquisition of the skills needed to become independent thinkers of the natural world
- Increasing the tendency to use the skills, abilities, and attitudes associated with science

# Physical Science

This is the first domain of science, in which the tangible, material world is studied. Instruction should focus on facts, concepts, principles, theories, and models of science. Physical science includes:

- Properties of objects, materials, matter
- Motion and force
- Light, heat, electricity, magnetism
- Energy (transfer, consumption, production)

# Life Science

The second domain of science examines the existence of organisms. Instruction should focus on facts, concepts, principles, theories, and models of science. Life science includes:

- Characteristics of organisms, behavior and regulation, diversity and adaptation
- Life cycles, reproduction, heredity
- Structure and function in living systems
- Organisms and environments, populations, ecosystems

# Earth and Space Science

This is the third domain of science, in which properties and the structure of the Earth are studied as well as the universal structures. Instruction should focus on facts, concepts, principles, theories, and models of science. Earth and space science includes:

- Properties and structure of Earth systems
- Earth's history
- Earth within the solar system
- Objects in space
- Changes in Earth and space

# Health Science

The fourth domain of science encompasses the vast topic of health education. Not only will the student benefit from the instruction, but families, communities, and environments will also improve. The primary goal is for students to attain and maintain a healthy lifestyle, and while in school, good health impacts student learning and achievement.

School health education should utilize community resources to promote educational opportunities, establish an environment conducive to appropriate health practices, empower students to demonstrate effective healthy routines, work with families to encourage change for health benefits, and maintain health messages that ultimately motivate students to adopt healthy habits.

When educators develop the health education program, it is essential to focus the curriculum on the following:

- Promoting behaviors and conditions that ensure proper health as well as reducing at-risk behaviors (communicable diseases, substance abuse, and personal safety and well-being)
- Instilling skills to use the behaviors or establish the conditions in personal lives
- Teaching attitudes, values, and knowledge of healthy behaviors and conditions
- Providing opportunities to practice and acquire the skills

The health education curriculum is sometimes taught separately, but often it is integrated into subjects or classes like science, physical education, consumer education, or social studies. Instruction should focus on facts, concepts, principles, theories, and models of science. Integrating the health content is particularly beneficial at the elementary level. It offers a more meaningful and detailed study of the concepts, and students are more apt to retain the critical information and make changes to their habits.

## Science in Personal and Social Perspectives

This area of science curriculum helps students obtain the tools and understanding to act on personal and social issues. These perspectives promote, encourage, teach, and allow students to develop decision-making skills. The perspectives also incorporate the technology of science, in which students will learn the process of design in science and how science is intertwined with technology. Students will gain strong foundations on which to base decisions they will encounter as citizens. Science in personal and social perspectives includes:

- Personal health
- Populations, resources, environments
- Natural hazards, local challenges, risks, benefits
- Science and technology, technological design, artificial versus natural designs

## History and Nature of Science

In this area of science curriculum, students must recognize and understand the symbiotic web of science and history. Science reflects history and is a continual and ever-changing enterprise. This standard examines the role science has played in the development of various cultures and the human aspects of science. History and nature of science includes:

- Science as a human endeavor
- History of science
- Nature of science

## Use of Materials and Technology

Science materials are instrumental to science instruction, particularly with the use of inquiry-based strategies. The use of science materials in elementary classrooms is an area educators should carefully evaluate. Storage is a critical need. The materials vary for the topics covered; some items are large with multiple parts. Using inexpensive, safe, and easily obtainable materials for experiments will enhance science instruction. Equally important is to obtain science tools that will withstand multiple uses even though they may be more expensive, such as microscopes, thermometers, or telescopes.

Technology is a strong component of a science education program. It is considered one of the disciplines of science and can be utilized to enhance student achievement. Students must be proficient in their use of technology tools and methods in order to sufficiently use them to benefit from instruction. Technology encompasses the media (films, videos, audio recordings), three-dimensional tools (charts, displays, models, manipulatives), electronic tools (calculators, lab equipment), and computers (databases, distance learning opportunities, software).

Six reasons for the use of computers and technology in an elementary science education program are:

1. Computers are available and used throughout the world.
2. Students are comfortable with electronic equipment and media.
3. Information is readily available and new information is constantly obtainable.
4. Electronic equipment provides opportunities for investigation and research not possible before.
5. Students' learning needs may be addressed by the use of technology.
6. Technology is a vehicle of science that scientists use.

# Model Building and Forecasting

**Models** in science provide concrete, visual representations of something that cannot otherwise be seen, such as the solar system or the human body. Students can investigate scientific phenomena to create or build a model that represents the object or process based on their research. They learn observation, measurement, comparison, and investigative skills by building and using models.

Building models helps students comprehend the size and use of an object or understand a process in the field of science. Spatial relationships are the most difficult aspect of building models, because most models are based on science objects or processes that are either incomprehensibly large or so minute (nano-scale) that they cannot be seen without powerful microscopes. It becomes a mathematical challenge to replicate some models with accuracy, and with some models reconstruction is not even possible.

**Forecasting** consists of discovering, simplifying, and applying patterns in scientific discovery. Students need to learn how to proceed with finding, collecting, and using data about the patterns they find, specifically in the natural and manufactured worlds. Forecasting is a method of making statements about events whose actual outcomes have not yet been determined or discovered. The act of forecasting is a process of prediction, and students may use graphs, charts, or equations to communicate their findings. Forecasting skills are used in weather reporting, the aviation field, and in studying the Earth.

# Analysis of Work Assessment

The National Science Education Standards (NSES) establishes assessment standards that include the evaluation of process skills, the assessment of inquiry, the evaluation of attitude, and the evaluation of content.

For most educators, the evaluation of content is primary to instruction. Teachers probably agree that in order to proceed with next-stage concepts in any subject, students must demonstrate that they comprehend and can utilize the recently presented information. It is essential in science that students are able to show their knowledge base of one concept before moving on to the next concept, as many of the concepts are interrelated and dependent upon the prior information. Teachers should be able to assess a classroom of students quickly each day to ensure that students grasp critical concepts.

Naturally, quizzes and tests are used in all subjects and provide benefit in science education. These evaluation tools may even be required by the state, district, or school as a measure of accountability regarding the curriculum process or plan and the standardization of the materials and instruction. However, there are other assessments (alternative and authentic) that are useful for science education. These may include the following:

- Presentations
- Games
- Research papers
- Journals
- Literature reviews
- Interviews
- Laboratory techniques
- Small group discussions
- Discussion formats
- Checklists
- Science projects
- Portfolios
- Homework

More on the topic of assessments used for all subject areas is explained in Chapter 1.

In addition to the content knowledge of science, an evaluation of the process skills is ultimately important to students' overall abilities to master science topics. When children perform these skills, teachers may observe the indicators to evaluate their mastery. Helpful to teachers in identifying indicators is the use of a checklist, observation, or interview, as not all indicators are required at every grade level. Identifying the expectations for the age group and the grade are necessary in determining student proficiency.

**Process indicators** at the elementary level may include the following:

- Observing
- Classifying
- Communicating
- Measuring
- Predicting
- Inferring
- Identifying content
- Controlling variables
- Formulating a hypothesis
- Interpreting data
- Researching information
- Experimenting
- Constructing models
- Using math operations
- Presenting findings

Another area of assessment critical to science education is the student's proficiency of the inquiry method. When a teacher provides an open-ended task, students must use their skills in investigation, communication, and processing data to complete the activity. Teachers generally develop a list of the inquiry indicators that suit the class, the age, and the content. Some specific skills to evaluate include the following:

| | | |
|---|---|---|
| Initiates investigation | Presents ideas and findings | Exhibits self-evaluation |
| Investigates questions | Challenges ideas | Uses prediction |
| Discusses processes | Uses a variety of resources | Applies learning to life |

Since one of the primary goals of elementary science education is for students to become more interested in the subject and perhaps select a science-related career for this fast-paced world, an assessment of the student's attitude about science will relay critical information to the teacher about how well the student is performing or will perform. The indicators to assess in the area of attitude are based on the student's characteristics, the program available, the community resources, and the existing attitudes. Some indicators include the following:

| | |
|---|---|
| Enjoys science and the investigation process | Acts curious about the topic or activity |
| Participates in additional science activities | Displays verbal skills |
| Inquires about science-related topics | Wants more time to participate |

# Chapter 6

# Arts and Physical Education Curriculum, Instruction, and Assessment (0011/5011)

## Physical Education

The National Association for Sport and Physical Education (NASPE) recognizes the importance of physical fitness at the elementary level. It has developed national standards focused on the learning of skills, knowledge, and behaviors that will enable children to be physically active throughout their lives.

These skills emphasize learning so students will

- Enjoy physical activity.
- Become positive participants in both organized and informal physical activities.
- Become aware of fitness concepts and exercise goals.
- Develop skills and knowledge regarding meaningful physical activity.

The Council on Physical Education for Children (COPEC) has written guidelines suggesting that elementary-aged children

- Should participate in 30–60 minutes of developmentally appropriate physical activities on all or most of the days of the week.
- Are encouraged to have an additional 60 minutes or more of free play per day.
- Should participate in daily activities that include 10–15 minutes of moderate to vigorous action with brief periods of rest and recovery.

A key concept at the elementary level regarding physical education and activities is to integrate motor activities throughout the day. In some elementary schools, the classroom teacher may be responsible for promoting these activities and may do so by integrating movement into core subject areas, assisting students during unstructured recess times, and developing after-school programs that include physical activity. These opportunities help students improve memory and attention, promote decision-making and problem-solving skills, and develop social learning and creativity. Physical education contributes significantly to students' education.

## Developmentally Appropriate

As with any subject, children must utilize and practice skills to become more proficient and to develop finely tuned abilities. Developmentally appropriate physical education acknowledges that children progress at various rates and possess a multitude of abilities. The environment, when focused on being developmentally appropriate, is a crucial component in motor skill development.

There are four levels at the elementary level for developmentally appropriate activities.

| Level | Activity |
|-------|----------|
| 1 | * Involves large muscle skill development and movement<br>* Has little formal organization<br>* Includes lifestyle activities |
| 2 | * Is aerobic (for example, biking or swimming) and includes basic skills (for example, pedaling or swimming strokes)<br>* Includes recreational activities and formal sports<br>* Considered cardiovascular activities |

| Level | Activity |
|---|---|
| 3 | * Reinforces fitness concepts of muscular strength and flexibility<br>* Improves development of specific skill exercises |
| 4 | * Considered "quiet" time<br>* Includes rest and inactivity |

In the **K–5** grades, the focus should be placed on spatial awareness, effort, and peer relationships. It is during this period of development that a strong foundation for physical activity should be established through movement concepts and skill themes.

In the **6–8** grades, the focus relies heavily on the foundation that was set in the early years. During this later period, the emphasis shifts to the use of skills and concepts in a multitude of movement techniques. Exploring the many possibilities of movement and activity is primary in stimulating a lifetime interest in fitness.

## Basic Concepts

The purpose of physical education is to steer youngsters into the practice of becoming physically active throughout their lifetimes. Studies demonstrate that when additional physical activity is included in school curricula, students improve their academic achievement and their ability to gain knowledge.

Physical education and sports are essential for elementary students because both help to build confidence and self-respect, increase social interactions and abilities, and prepare youngsters to cooperate and function together. Schools are the primary place where students acquire basic concepts about healthy habits and nutrition, and where students gain the fundamental skills necessary for competing and participating in physical activities.

The basic concepts in physical education include motor development, body awareness, and social adjustments and interactions. Students gain fitness skills, knowledge about sports and games, and learn to work with others through physical education activities and programs.

Physical education terms include the following:

- **Body composition:** The number of fat cells in comparison to the number of lean cells within a person's body mass. It can be measured by skin-fold thickness. Body fat percentage is determined by heredity, nutrition, and activity level.
- **Cardiovascular efficiency:** The body's capacity to maintain vigorous physical activity for a period of time, which is developed through activities that increase the heart rate for extended lengths of time.
- **Flexibility:** The ability of a joint to move through its range of motion, which can be increased through stretching of muscles, ligaments, and tendons. Flexibility is specific to each joint and will differ from person to person.
- **Muscular endurance:** The length of time or duration that a muscle can produce force.
- **Muscular strength:** The amount of force that a muscle can produce.
- **Physical fitness:** The body's ability to function efficiently and effectively during both work and leisure. It includes the function of a healthy body that resists disease and can handle emergency situations. Health-related fitness encompasses muscular strength, muscular endurance, flexibility, cardiovascular efficiency, and body composition.

Increased physical activity has been proven to aid in academic achievement, such as higher mathematics scores, increased concentration, enhanced memory, reduction of inappropriate behaviors, and improved reading and writing scores. Other specific areas that aid children during their daily lives and are a focus for physical education courses include locomotor skills, body management, social discipline, game/sport skills, and learning about healthy lifestyles.

# Locomotor Skills

Locomotor skills aid the student in traveling or moving some distance. Locomotion is the foundation for participation in games or sports as well as a fundamental skill for accessing home, school, and community. Locomotion follows chronological stepping stones of development and progresses from beginner to mastery level. Elementary students must obtain these basic skills in order to progress to higher levels.

In progression from low to high, locomotor skills at the elementary level include the following:

- Walking
- Running
- Hopping
- Leaping
- Sliding
- Galloping
- Skipping
- Jumping

Assessment of locomotor skills can include the following:

- Informal observation
- Authentic assessment
- Formal observation
- Standardized testing

# Body Management

**Body management** is the ability of an individual to control his or her physical self, handle personal movements, recognize spatial conditions, and develop body-space relationships. Body management includes the following:

- Spatial awareness
- Concept of direction
- Concepts of levels
- Pathways
- Extensions in space
- Body parts

# Social Discipline

This topic centers on improving social skills through the use of appropriate behaviors. It entails having the entire class on the same task or activity while productively engaged and actively focused on the task being taught. There are two branches essential to managing social discipline.

**Proactive**—Intended to be used prior to the occurrence of the inappropriate behavior:

- Positive interaction—The teacher communicates with the students using praise or compliments acceptable behaviors. (For example, the teacher states "I really like the way Haley is walking to line up at the door.")
- Eliminate differential treatment—The teacher does not single out students for either positive or negative reinforcement. (For example, instead of stating "Andrea, please be quiet," the teacher states "I will wait for the class to listen.")
- Prompting—Reminding students of expectations and behaviors in a positive manner. (For example, "Remember to place your equipment in the bin.")

**Reactive**—Intended to be used after the inappropriate behavior occurs:

- Ignore the behavior—The teacher does not engage in the student's inappropriate actions. (For example, Eric calls out an answer without raising his hand; his answer is ignored, and another child whose hand is raised is called upon.)
- Nonverbal interactions—The teacher uses techniques such as proximity, specific signals, or redirection. (For example, Justin veers from the task at hand so the teacher walks over and stands near him for the rest of the instructional period.)
- Person-to-person dialogue—The teacher sets up a time outside of class to discuss behavior. (For example, the teacher asks a student to attend a lunch or after-school meeting.)

# Game and Sports Skills

Children must understand specific concepts in order to participate in games or sports. These skills can be taught by using four levels of assessment:

1. **Precontrol** (beginner)—The movement or equipment moves the child instead of the child being in control. (For example, in trying to catch a ball, a child misses the ball and must chase it.)
2. **Control** (advanced beginner)—The movement seems to be more controlled, and the skill seems to be repeated in a similar manner each time it is demonstrated. This level involves strong concentration on the part of the child. (For example, when shooting a basketball, the ball goes in the general direction of the hoop.)
3. **Utilization** (intermediate)—The movements or skills are carried out with intensified instinctive actions. (For example, a child learns to dribble a basketball against an opponent.)
4. **Proficiency** (advanced)—The movements or skills become natural and are completed without thought. (For example, when a football is overthrown, a student can quickly change directions, track the football path, and make a successful catch.)

# Healthy Lifestyles

Incorporating physical activity at an early age increases the likelihood that the child will become a lifelong lover of movement. Early physical activity also helps to decrease or eliminate the ill effects of a sedentary lifestyle. Positive nutrition and activity levels also assist children in leading healthy lifestyles.

The 1996 Surgeon General's report concluded that "people of all ages, both male and female, who are physically active derive many benefits; reduction in the risk of premature mortality, in general, and of coronary heart disease, hypertension, colon cancer, and diabetes mellitus, in particular. Consistent influences on physical activity patterns among adults and young people include confidence in one's ability to engage in regular physical activity, enjoyment of physical activity, and support from others, positive beliefs concerning the benefits of physical activity, and lack of perceived barriers to physical activity. Physical activity also appears to improve health-related quality of life by enhancing psychological well-being and by improving physical functioning in persons compromised by poor health."

# Curriculum

Physical education contributes to students' overall health and well-being in addition to supporting academic achievement. Standards-based physical education programs support students in gaining positive social skills, developing a strong self-concept, instilling cooperation, building a fitness skill base, and accepting responsibility. Including physical education and activities in the school curriculum allows students the opportunities to gain knowledge, develop skills, and enhance self-confidence to lead an active lifestyle.

When designing curriculum in physical education, these three concepts must be considered:

1. Children develop motor skills at different rates; do not expect all children to be able to perform the same tasks with the same accuracy.
2. A child's age does not predict motor ability. Although some children may seem to be naturally skilled in athletics, motor skill is obtained not through heredity but through use and practice.
3. Children develop motor skills naturally through play; informal play helps motor skills develop as well as involvement in structured physical education programs or sports.

The curriculum used for physical education should have a set scope and sequence with goals that are appropriate for all children. Activities should result from this plan that are both meaningful and age-appropriate, and that include some relation to previous experiences. The program should reflect cognitive development and support the diversity of individuals.

The **multi-activity curriculum approach** is most suitable for the elementary grades as it includes a variety of content and activities for students. Educators can develop team sports, small group functions, and individual activities. Teachers can also create adventure activities, fitness activities, and those activities that require specific skills (such as dance).

Many other types of curricula are possible in physical education, although some have a stronger focus for older students. Types of physical education curricula include the following:

- **Movement education**—Students gain knowledge about human movement, such as dance, gymnastics, and games.
- **Fitness approach**—Students learn more about the physiological aspects of the body and focus activities on endurance, flexibility, strength, and so on.
- **Academic-discipline approach**—Students learn by this problem-solving approach about healthy lifestyles and how to maintain recreational activities in their lifetimes.
- **Social-developmental model**—Students focus on personal growth and social skills as individuals.
- **Sports-education model**—Students build knowledge about sports (both as participants and officials) and seasons, so working as a team and increasing specific skill areas are important, as well as learning that competition can be fun.
- **Adventure-education approach**—Students learn about outdoor recreation and safety, and develop lifelong interests.
- **Eclectic approach**—Students gain from the combination of the many types of curricula available depending on the school, the students, the location, and the physical education teacher.

## Assessment of Physical Education

In order for physical education to be meaningful, it is important to be able to identify at what skill level the students are working. Physical education is different than most other subject areas because physical education touches on all three domains: the psychomotor domain, the cognitive domain, and the affective domain. It is important to be able to address and assess all three domains in each lesson to have a clearer understanding of where each student falls in each area of the curriculum and to be able to address the individual needs of all students.

Following are examples of assessments:

- Teacher observation
- Exit/entrance slips
- Homework
- Peer observation

- Self-assessment
- Event task
- Videotaping
- Student illustrations
- Student displays
- Portfolios

## Website Resources for Physical Education

American Alliance for Health, Physical Education, Recreation and Dance (AAHPERD) www.aahperd.org

American Association for Health Education (AAHE) www.cnheo.org/aahe.htm

National Association for Health and Fitness (NAHF) www.physicalfitness.org

American Association for Physical Activity and Recreation (AAPAR) www.aahperd.org/aapar

National Association for Sport and Physical Education (NASPE) www.aahperd.org/naspe/

# Arts

There is a connection between the arts and academic achievement, particularly in mathematics, language arts, and science. The arts provide aspects critical to the development of the human mind and body. The vast array of disciplines in the arts nurtures human systems, which include the senses, cognition, emotions, social skills, and physical abilities.

Extensive research shows that using fine arts opportunities is the primary component in improving learning across all academic areas. Research in the cognitive sciences and brain studies confirms and recommends that the arts should be integrated across the curriculum, as it is essential for student success. Other studies have proven that offering the arts as part of the curriculum helps improve student attendance, behavior, motivation, interest, attitudes, and self-concept, which overall create individuals with a desire to learn. Studies focused on students currently involved in arts programs found that these individuals demonstrated superior skills in critical thinking, problem solving, creative thinking, self-expression, and cooperation when compared to peers who were not in arts-related programs.

However, even with the support of research and the organizations that declare their positive effects, the number of arts programs offered in schools diminishes every year. Experts highly recommend arts integration into the core school curriculum across all subjects each and every day. It is evident that the skills and abilities required for the arts (complex cognitive skills and foundational skills) are the same as those required for success in other subject areas. So, whether there is a program for the arts at a school or not, the elementary classroom teacher should be prepared to integrate core knowledge by using the arts throughout the curriculum.

Following is a list that demonstrates the overall importance of the arts. An arts program:

- Integrates other subjects and topics
- Develops independence, self-concept, and self-confidence
- Promotes symbol systems similar to science and mathematics
- Encourages the use of personal strengths and talents
- Motivates students and generates more ambition
- Improves language and literacy skills
- Enhances cultural awareness and engages diverse learners
- Uses higher-order thinking skills
- Promotes arts appreciation

- Helps students make connections
- Helps students achieve high standards across academic disciplines
- Allows creative self-expression and develops the imagination

## Standards

The arts are a common thread that connect other aspects of our society. The arts are based in the history of various cultures and should provide rich experiences for students that reflect the people and community of the greater society. Implementing activities that include the fine arts as an expansion of academic programs will substantially benefit students. The content should be based on academic standards and connect to the scope and sequence of each school's curricula.

Standards created by the Consortium of National Arts Education Associations with support from the National Association for Music Education (MENC) are divided into four categories by grade levels:

- Visual arts
- Music
- Theater
- Dance

The National Standards for Arts Education have outlined what is considered necessary for students upon completion of secondary school. They have identified two primary reasons for the standards of arts education: 1) to help define what arts education should provide, and 2) to ensure that schools support the arts.

The standards promote that students should be able to do the following:

- Communicate at a basic level in the four arts disciplines (dance, music, theater, and visual arts).
- Communicate proficiently in at least one art form.
- Develop and present basic analysis of works of art.
- Have an informed acquaintance with exemplary works of art from a variety of cultural and historical periods.
- Relate various types of arts knowledge and skills within and across the arts disciplines.

## Arts Integration

Research studies support the idea that integration of the arts promotes academic achievement and gains on standardized tests. These studies reveal that students learn better and improve when the arts are integrated into the core curriculum, connecting it with other subjects (literature, science, social studies, and math). Some believe that the inclusion of fine arts stimulates brain development and that similar cognitive skills are as necessary for art education as for academic subject content. Further studies focus on the positive gains made by lower socioeconomic groups and those at risk for school failure.

Standards that reflect the integrated arts are divided into three main categories with one primary goal for each of the categories. The various grade levels include a series of goals and objectives that pertain to that age group and to the content for that age level:

- **Creating arts**—Students know and apply the arts disciplines, techniques, and processes in original or interpretive work.
- **Arts as inquiry**—Students reflect upon concepts and themes, and assess the merits of their own work and the work of others.
- **Art in context**—Students analyze works of art from their own and other cultures and demonstrate how interrelated conditions (social, economic, political, historical) influence the development and reception of thoughts, ideas, and concepts in the arts.

A **parallel process** is one that blends an arts-related activity with an academic subject activity. Examples of parallel processes for integration of the arts with academic areas include the following:

- Use journal writing, adding drawn pictures for the content.
- Read literature and observe the famous paintings mentioned.
- Learn fractions by using drama to act out the number of parts.
- Study and learn the dances of historical periods for social studies.
- Play simple keyboard passages on the recorder for poetry accompaniment.
- Incorporate the use of clay to create science structures (volcanoes, cells, and so on).

# Curriculum

The curriculum used for the arts should be aligned with the scope, sequence, and academic goals appropriate for all children. Multiple art forms may be integrated throughout the curriculum to cultivate the special talents and interests demonstrated by all students. Using the added components of fine arts in a school curriculum complements the academic features of learning by adding an aesthetic focus. It is possible that additional materials, equipment, and possibly staff would be needed to integrate the visual and performing arts, but even at the elementary level, these will provide enrichment in all areas of the curriculum.

Adding an emphasis on the arts (drama, music, dance, visual arts) provides students with opportunities for personal and academic expression. This focus on fine arts education may be achieved through the integration of academic subject areas and by creating opportunities after school. The addition of arts in a school classroom also addresses the issue of providing differentiated instruction and should include field trips that deliver opportunities some children may not have otherwise.

**Fine arts** is the general subject area that encompasses art (drawing and other mediums), music and movement, singing, creative dance, and drama. Including these forms of art at the elementary level will allow children a distinctive method to process information, to express themselves, and to gain academic success. The arts can help students develop skills, gain foundational skills, become innovative thinkers, and develop attitudes about the world that they may not acquire in other ways. They can actively participate in learning experiences, using visual, auditory, and kinesthetic processes, when integrating arts into the curriculum.

# Basic Concepts

The study of the arts is an indispensable topic for elementary students because this content acquisition aids in their development and academic achievement. Students learn the basic concepts and skills related to the fine arts in school programs, and therefore may be more motivated to learn when art is integrated with other content areas. The fine arts need to be integrated with other subjects so they are more fully appreciated.

Schools should focus on the fundamental value of fine art experiences. The arts are useful in the study of literature, writing, learning mathematic concepts, understanding science, and learning about historical events. Educators must implement arts education into classroom practice to promote appreciation and to gain the multitude of skills that are related to the arts, yet applied to other subject areas. The purpose of arts education is to encourage students to become participants and observers, and to appreciate the arts throughout their lifetimes.

## Visual Arts

Arts education, which is recommended as part of the general education program, is based on visual or tangible arts such as painting, using clay or pottery, designing sculptures, drawing, or using fabrics. Students may be involved in activities or select opportunities based on the standards that are related to or integrated into the core curriculum. These experiences should allow students to express themselves while showing appreciation of the art form.

Classroom activities must allow students to explore the visual arts and the varieties of materials. Students should be encouraged to share their ideas through this form of expression, knowing that what they create is acceptable.

Students will gain a sense of accomplishment as they control this form of creative expression, instilling stronger self-confidence. Students' products should be on display often to build upon their self-concept.

The environment is crucial for implementing the visual arts. There needs to be ample physical space, a variety of accessible materials, and support from the adults who refrain from correcting a child or changing the work. There are developmental stages related to the arts, and not all children will move through those stages at the same time.

## Music

Music fills children's lives outside of school, but they may learn to appreciate it from the educational opportunities and experiences they receive in school. Music offers repetitive, sequential patterns and an emotional connection to information. Music should be present in elementary classrooms not only for pleasure, but for learning about the rhyme, rhythm, and patterns it may contain. Students should learn to sing, dance, and play instruments for variety. The use of music will help children grow in all five developmental domains: cognitive, language/literacy, social-emotional, self-help/adaptive, and physical. According to research, music has a particularly special connection to learning mathematics and developing literacy skills.

Music can provide students with integrated activities that promote the development of motor skills, physical health, coordination, social interactions, communication, and creativity. A classroom teacher might utilize learning centers for individual and small group instruction, incorporating music to enhance the study of math, language/literacy, science, and history. Even using background music in the classroom during a variety of learning periods has a profound effect on individual learners.

## Drama and Dance

Drama and dance engage children in movement activities, which help develop coordination and other physical skills. Students can use dance and drama to communicate their emotions, interpret a poem, share a historic moment, or tell a story. They may create a set routine to share or use interpretive and impromptu improvisational movements. Teachers may have music, costumes, props, and a small staging area available in the classroom. Students should learn to describe, compare, interpret, and evaluate performances in order to learn how to appreciate these art forms.

## Instruction

Implementation of the arts requires a variety of approaches and a host of strategies. Students gain competencies differently, since they enter programs with different skills, talents, and desires. In order for students to adequately learn the vocabulary, the concepts, and the perspectives and use the tools and techniques that are related to the various art forms, they must progress and build upon their abilities each year. The arts need to be included in successive years of schooling, from preschool to grade 12, in order for students to gain the most from those opportunities.

Instruction should acknowledge the varying abilities of individuals and be delivered using the developmentally appropriate practices (DAP) approach. This method acknowledges that children develop at a variety of rates, possess an array of abilities, and confirms that the environment and materials are critical components to learning. DAP allows students to learn and perform at their own rate in their own style.

Academic achievement is broadly improved when arts instruction is included. There is evidence of improved

- Higher-order thinking skills.
- Concentration and memory.
- Verbal expression.
- Attention spans and retention rates.
- Interpersonal and intrapersonal skills.
- Self-discipline.
- Teamwork and cooperation.

- Intuition and reasoning.
- Manual dexterity and physical health.
- Motivation and social behaviors.

## Strategies

There are endless opportunities for delivering instruction in the area of fine arts and for combining this instruction into the existing curriculum across all subject areas. Educators need to be aware of students' skills and abilities, as well as their interests, as they incorporate the arts into classrooms. The materials needed and the training necessary to use various mediums of the arts are essential for student success. Permitting students to participate in designing the assignments, allowing individual freedom of expression, and creating authentic learning situations will help make learning memorable and enjoyable.

Examples of utilizing the arts in an integrated approach include the following:

- Reenact historical events, math story problems, or literary works.
- Learn about the music and dance that reflect various cultures in history.
- Invite community artists to share their work.
- Participate in community events that feature the arts.
- Utilize visual arts to convey scientific processes.
- Use drama to communicate mathematics principles and concepts.

## Pedagogy

The No Child Left Behind (NCLB) legislation describes the necessity of arts education and has included it as one of the core subject areas in school. The majority of states have produced a set of standards for the fine arts. However, NCLB also requires accountability—which is being met in states by use of standardized testing in subject areas—but there is no standardized assessment for the arts. The omission of the arts in the accountability system has become a current educational issue.

Several theories support arts in education:

- **Discipline-based art education**—Allows students to study western art and construct their own artwork based on themes and movements of art history.
- **Visual culture art education**—Delivers attention to the visual record of human experience within the art curriculum.
- **Progressive education theory**—Promotes the arts as aesthetic. John Dewey believed that art objects and experiences of the local community culture should be studied.
- **Multiple intelligences model**—Addresses the various types of intelligences, specifically the musical intelligence, the visual intelligence, and the kinesthetic intelligence, and has supported the rationale for the integrated arts models in teaching and learning.
- **Metacognitive approach**—Encourages the transfer of knowledge and skills across disciplines by controlling a student's own learning.
- **Kodaly approach**—Encourages physical instruction with music instruction and endeavors to instill a lifelong interest in music.

Two names worth mentioning in regard to arts education are Harry Broudy and Elliot Eisner. Broudy was an advocate for the arts, which he felt improved and developed the imagination, an essential component of learning. He promoted the integration of arts education into all subjects. Eisner believed that the arts were critical to cognition and that they helped students understand the world on a broader and deeper level.

# Assessment

Arts education should include ongoing evaluations, both formative and summative, incorporated within the core curriculum. Often, teachers use authentic or performance-based assessments to evaluate students on dance, music, drama, or visual arts work.

Students should have the opportunity for feedback on their performances and their work, even though these are personal forms of expression. Teachers may use oral feedback, written comments, and portfolios to indicate progress on specific work.

For other forms of art, teachers may select various assessment tools and methods. Students should know ahead of time what type of assessment their work will be based upon. They need to know the components of a rubric, a rating scale, or a checklist before they delve into composing their artwork. Observations may be conducted periodically during the class and for the length of a project, but it is best to organize an observation with a previously developed checklist or rating scale as a guide. Students will then know what behaviors are appropriate for their performances and works and seek to achieve those as goals.

| Performance Assessments | Forced Answer Tests |
|---|---|
| Checklists | Vocabulary |
| Essays | Completion |
| Rubric scales | True-false |
| Observations | Multiple-choice |
| Portfolios | Matching |
| Rating scales | |

# Website Resources for the Fine Arts

American Alliance for Health, Physical Education, Recreation and Dance (AAHPERD) www.aahperd.org

National Art Education Association (NAEA) www.arteducators.org/

National Association for Music Education (NAfME) www.nafme.org/

National Dance Education Organization (NDEO) www.ndeo.org/

Dance Educators of America (DEA) www.deadance.com/

**PART II**

# CONTENT AREA EXERCISES (0012)

# Chapter 7

# Overview Content Area Exercises (0012)

The Praxis II exam for Content Area Exercises (0012) is comprised of essay questions that cover the topics of curriculum, instruction, and assessment at the elementary school level. The responses to these essays are written by the examinee based on personal knowledge and experience in the content areas of reading/language arts, mathematics, science, social studies, and the arts and physical education (although these subjects play a vital role in elementary education, physical education and fine arts are not included on this exam as separate subject areas).

This exam was designed to evaluate and measure how well an examinee can respond to specific situations in a thoughtful, well-written response. The essays encompass all four subject areas as well as interdisciplinary instruction. The scenarios are meant to be viewed as an event or situation that may occur in an elementary classroom setting. An examinee may be asked to discuss instructional approaches, develop instructional goals, solve instructional problems, or outline procedures necessary to achieve a desired academic outcome.

Many different situations arise within an elementary classroom, and the examinee must be prepared to handle each situation in a competent and thorough manner. Part of the fun of teaching is being consistently challenged and having new experiences surface each day. Some possible scenarios and situations are included in the individual sections of this study guide. Examinees should become familiar with these and practice writing lengthy and complete exercises to prepare for this examination.

## Examination Information

**Time restriction:** 2 hours

**Format:** 4 essay questions

**Scoring:** Since this exam is in an essay format, a rubric has been created as a standard scoring guide used by examination readers to determine the competence of the examinee's knowledge as evidenced in the answers. A sample has been included here.

**Rubric:** This scoring format is used consistently across the states and based on levels from 0 to 6, with 6 being the highest, or representative of a well-constructed narrative answer.

The expectations at each level in the scoring rubric are summarized here.

| Score | Level of knowledge and understanding demonstrated | Description |
|-------|---------------------------------------------------|-------------|
| 6 | Superior | Essay is answered clearly and concisely, with all portions of the questions addressed; answer includes well-organized key ideas and supportive details. |
| 5 | Strong | Essay answer is well organized, and key ideas are explained clearly with examples to support the ideas. |
| 4 | Adequate | Essay is answered accurately, with clear description of the main ideas and relevant supportive materials, although the answer is limited in content and in illustrating key points. |
| 3 | Some | Essay answer includes basic explanations of the key ideas, but lacks clarity and only a few relevant details support the answers. |
| 2 | Limited | Essay answer gives unclear or underdeveloped explanations that include inaccuracies, deficiencies, and lack of details or supporting examples. |
| 1 | Serious lack of | Essay answer is inadequately addressed and poorly written, provides no appropriate examples or details, and is incoherent and unorganized. |
| 0 | Poor | Essay answer is unwritten, illegible, or completely inappropriate to the topic given. |

It is recommended that examinees carefully study the examples of situations provided in the individual content sections included in this chapter and practice writing answers to them. These questions may be answered in many different ways, but the primary factor to being successful on this exam is to write answers that are clear and concise, while demonstrating a **superior** or **strong** knowledge base. As a study tool, examinees are encouraged to ask an experienced teacher or mentor to review their written answers using this scoring rubric and share feedback prior to taking the actual examination.

# Content Area Exercises (0012)

The Praxis II exam (0012) assesses an examinee's ability to apply the knowledge gained in the content knowledge section (0014/5014) as well as that found in the curriculum, instruction, and assessment information (0011/5011). Examinees will have two hours to answer four essay questions. One question will be focused on each of the subject areas: reading/language arts, mathematics, social studies, and science. Review the information from the chapters about the Praxis II 0014/5014 and 0011/5011 for each subject area in this study guide.

There are endless possibilities of questions that may be presented on this Praxis II exam, so examinees should prepare for this exam by considering how to use the individual subject area content information they already know. Examinees should read through the following list of questions that relate to each of the four subject area topics at the elementary level and try to answer these questions using a separate sheet of paper. Examinees will notice that answers are not provided, as there are many different ways to answer these open-ended questions.

The exercises posed on the actual exam will assess the examinee's ability to prepare an extended, in-depth written response to one question in each content area. When preparing to answer questions on the exam, examinees should remember that some of the questions presented may have multiple components and therefore require multidimensional answers. Concentrating on the content of each answer and addressing all components requested will aid in attaining success on the exam. A rubric is used in the scoring of the actual exam and is explained earlier in this chapter.

## Reading/Language Arts Content Area Exercises (0012)

Samples of possible reading/language arts essay questions for the Praxis II exam (0012):

1. Discuss how to integrate language arts into a unit of study on scientists at the fourth grade level. List the learner objectives for language arts, describe three activities, explain how to assess students on those activities, and outline how parents might be involved in this unit specifically related to language arts.

2. Identify the five stages of the writing process, and with a third grade class in mind, write a developmentally appropriate activity to implement those skills that will reinforce the students' knowledge of each stage and their ability to make generalizations and apply the skills.

3. Compare and contrast the following terms: read-alouds, shared reading, sustained reading, guided reading, choral reading, and reader's theater. Identify how these different methods would be used in a fifth grade elementary classroom, and state the benefits of each.

4. This question requires knowledge of Bloom's Taxonomy and its application to writing and implementing lesson plans. Use the Bloom's Taxonomy structure to design a lesson plan for a fourth grade class that is studying the various types of figurative language (select one type, such as alliteration, expressions, simile, metaphor, hyperbole, slang, or idioms).

5. Explain what role the home environment plays in a child's literacy development. Cite specific examples of those components that play a vital factor in literacy development (for example, adult attitude toward literacy).

6. Informal assessments can provide invaluable information to teachers about students and their individual needs. Read the list of three informal assessments for reading, describe how each type of assessment is used, what type of information it will provide, and how this information may be used to help structure instruction. Informal assessments: 1) running record; 2) miscue analysis; 3) informal reading inventory.

7. Invented spelling has its place in the stages of spelling development. Define invented spelling, and identify its importance in the overall process of learning to spell. Then explain four ways that teachers may nurture spelling in the classroom for elementary students.

8. Children enter classrooms with diverse skills in reading, and this range requires teachers to utilize differentiated instruction to meet each learner's needs. Given that some children will be below grade level and some will be above grade level in reading, create two activities to address the various needs of these groups at the second grade level related to vocabulary development: one focused on remediation and one that emphasizes enrichment.

9. The use of journals is an effective strategy in the area of language arts at all elementary grade levels. For grades K–6, describe how journals could be implemented, identify the differences for use as well as the possible objectives at each grade level.

10. Graphic awareness plays a key role in establishing early literacy. Define graphic awareness and explain how it is an important prerequisite to invented spelling, decoding, and independent reading.

## Mathematics Content Area Exercises (0012)

Samples of possible mathematics essay questions for the Praxis II exam (0012):

1. Design an instructional activity using either of these mathematics tools, Cuisenaire rods or tens frames, to teach elementary students how to extend numbers.

2. A group of parents from your first grade class are concerned about your instructional choice of topics in mathematics. They want you to be teaching operations and fractions to their children, as they believe their children are gifted in math. You have discussed this issue with your principal, who wants you to compose a letter that explains the state standards, the district's curriculum, developmentally appropriate practices, and how you might address advanced learners. Draft the letter that you will use to help parents understand the goals you have for your students and how you think you will accommodate them.

3. Discuss how to integrate mathematics at the fourth grade level into a thematic unit about the ocean. Include two curriculum goals, three objectives related to math instruction, and list four activities that may be used in an effort to integrate math with other subjects in this unit, such as science, social studies, or language arts. Then explain how to best assess students using both formative and summative formats.

4. Create a lesson plan that integrates the fine arts into teaching equivalent fractions at the third to fourth grade level, using the format of the Hunter model.

5. The fifth grade class you are teaching is studying decimals. Identify and explain three different authentic assessments that could be used to evaluate and measure a student's performance on this mathematical concept.

6. The Constructivist Theory is widely recommended in education and it especially applies to elementary mathematics education. Describe how this theory enhances the study of math and describe two learning activities that may be implemented at two different grade levels based on the application of this theory.

7. The topics of measurement, percentages, and estimation are critical topics for students to learn at the elementary level as these are foundational lifelong math skills. Using the method of instruction called *task analysis* describes how to proceed with the instruction of these math concepts.

8. Three students in your third grade class have begun to demonstrate acting-out behaviors specifically during math lessons. Your class is currently studying multiplication and division. You believe the antecedents for the undesired behaviors are directly related to the students' lack of acquisition of the foundational math skills of addition and subtraction in the third grade. Identify what assessment process you could use to verify their lack of skills and knowledge of these math operations. Then describe how you will address their behaviors and skills, and improve their attitude toward mathematics. (One of the students is also linguistically diverse.)

9. An outstanding and recommended approach for teaching geometry at the elementary level is the van Hiele Model. It is a five-level hierarchy (visualization, analysis, informal deduction, deduction, and rigor) to advance sequentially the thoughts and ideas of students regarding geometry. Identify the concept of focus on the level of visualization and construct a learning activity to promote this idea.

10. Bloom's Taxonomy relates to all subject areas. Use this process to outline a lesson for a second grade class on telling time by using a standard clock.

# Social Studies Content Area Exercises (0012)

Samples of possible social studies essay questions for the Praxis II (0012) exam:

1. As an elementary teacher, you have just completed a unit of study on exploration and the explorers of North America. Explain three informal assessment techniques and three authentic assessment techniques that you would use during this unit to evaluate student comprehension and retention. Explain why these types of assessments help evaluate student understanding better than giving a multiple-choice, 100-question test.

2. While studying Native American tribes and cultures, your fourth grade class asks whether they can design a school-wide Native American festival to show everything they have learned. Explain the student objectives/ goals for a project of this magnitude and write an outline of five activities, two of which are integrated subject areas, that could be included in the festival.

3. Explain how an elementary teacher should integrate poetry into the study of U.S. history in a fifth grade classroom.

4. Describe how an elementary teacher would integrate math and science into a unit of study on the classical civilizations during the study of world history.

5. It is a presidential election year and, as an elementary teacher, you are teaching topics in political science to your class. Write a lesson plan on the electoral process. Include learner outcomes, materials, and assessment techniques.

6. Economics can be a difficult topic to cover for elementary students. Identify at least five activities that will help promote an interest in this topic and explain why these would be motivational to students.

7. Incorporating children's literature to support social studies instruction is an effective method. If you, the elementary teacher, were to develop a unit on transportation for a second grade class, how would you utilize children's literature? Provide examples of literature and activities and indicate how you would address diversity throughout this study.

8. A primary goal of social studies is to teach students positive citizenship and community participation. Create a community service project that your third grade class may use to improve their knowledge about the community and work toward gaining skills that support good citizenship.

9. Howard Gardner recommends that educators utilize the nine intelligences when creating lessons for students. Identify four of the nine intelligences and explain how you would include them in a lesson on map-reading skills for third-graders.

10. An elementary class has just completed the study of famous inventors from the mid 1800s to the mid 1990s. Using a cooperative learning approach, what are some of the project possibilities for students to complete as a form of authentic assessment? Describe two different assignments and identify the objectives, the process, and the materials needed.

# Science Content Area Exercises (0012)

Samples of possible science essay questions for the Praxis II (0012) exam:

1. As the elementary teacher of a first grade class, you are planning instruction about plant growth and want to include experiments in your unit. Write a learner goal for the class on this topic. Outline and explain an experiment you would conduct with your students to help them achieve the learner goal about plant growth.

2. Explain when and how to use manipulatives in science at the elementary level. Provide specific examples for two different science topics.

3. The second grade class you are teaching is studying biomes. Explain five specific authentic assessments that could be used to evaluate and measure the students' comprehension and retention of the subject information.

4. Using Bloom's Taxonomy, design a lesson for a sixth grade class that is learning about the complexities of human anatomy.

5. Discuss how you would integrate technology into a unit of study about the food chain. Outline learner objectives and explain how you would assess student comprehension.

6. Explain how you would integrate math, language arts, fine arts, and social studies in the unit study on the solar system. In addition to this explanation, provide an example of one activity for each subject area mentioned.

7. The Constructivist Theory of education, formed by Piaget, enhances the study of science. Describe how this theory relates to the subject of science and explain the various activities that could be utilized in an elementary classroom based on the application of this theory.

8. A fourth grade class is studying the Earth's four principle components: atmosphere (air), lithosphere (land), hydrosphere (water), and biosphere (life). Create and outline a cooperative learning activity that includes a list of materials and how the activity will be assessed. Then identify how the teacher should address differentiated instruction in implementing this cooperative learning activity.

9. Healthy living is a concept related to health education that may have a lifelong impact on students. Identify five activities that an elementary teacher might use to engage and motivate students at the fifth grade level to begin making healthy personal choices.

10. A student enrolls in your elementary classroom four months after the beginning of school. This student demonstrates both cultural and linguistic diversity. Outline and describe four instructional methods that should be utilized to help this student learn the science concepts that have already been covered and address how to continue to engage this student.

# PART III

# ELEMENTARY EDUCATION: CONTENT KNOWLEDGE (0014/5014)

# Chapter 8
# Overview Elementary Education: Content Knowledge (0014/5014)

The Praxis II Content Knowledge examination for elementary education (0014/5014) is a comprehensive and detailed investigation of the core information that an examinee possesses pertaining to the following topics: language arts, mathematics, social studies, and science. This multiple-choice exam was constructed to assess the base knowledge across these subject areas of individuals who plan to teach at the elementary level.

Examinees should plan on a 2-hour exam of the content categories that comprise the four main subjects in an elementary classroom. The information in this exam is based on the content that is included in curricula at all elementary grade levels. Whether an individual plans to teach second grade or fifth grade, all elementary subject matter must be clearly understood.

This guide provides in-depth content for the Praxis II exam (0014/5014) divided by the four main subject areas, but it is not inclusive of the entire breadth of the content available at all grade levels. After reviewing and studying the content in this guide, if an examinee feels that further study is necessary, reference to subject areas through the Internet, utilization of library information, or examination of college texts should be considered.

Examinees should review the description of the content in the following list, along with the percentages and number of questions, to determine the areas that may need the most concentrated study. When taking the actual exam, the questions are situated in the test booklet and on the computer according to each subject area. A scientific or four-function calculator is permitted for use on this exam.

The Praxis II Elementary Education: Content Knowledge 0014/5014 is divided as follows:

| Language Arts | 30 questions | 25% of the test |
|---|---|---|
| | Understanding Literature | 30% |
| | Text Structures and Organization for Reading and Writing | 5% |
| | Literacy Acquisition and Reading Instruction | 30% |
| | Language in Writing | 25% |
| | Communication Skills | 10% |
| Mathematics | 30 questions | 25% of the test |
| | Critical Thinking | none given |
| | Number Sense and Numeration | 31% |
| | Algebraic Concepts | 23% |
| | Informal Geometry and Measurement | 23% |
| | Data Organization and Interpretation | 23% |
| Social Studies | 30 questions | 25% of the test |
| | Geography | 15% |
| | World History | 10% |
| | United States History | 25% |
| | Political Science | 20% |
| | Anthropology, Sociology, Psychology | 15% |
| | Economics | 15% |

| Science | 30 questions | 25% of the test |
|---|---|---|
| | Earth Science | 25% |
| | Life Science | 25% |
| | Physical Science | 25% |
| | Science in Personal and Social Perspectives | 10% |
| | History and the Nature of Science | 5–10% |
| | Unifying Processes | 5–10% |

It should be noticeable that this exam covers a vast array of information on these four topics. It may seem difficult to know what to study, although the outline given of the percentages will provide a good start in preparing for the number of test questions that will be included on the exam in the four topic areas. On the actual exam, there may be diagrams, charts, equations, story problems, definitions, readings, poetry, or examples of materials or lessons used in a classroom. Examinees will want to make sure they study the broad content of these subject areas and concentrate on the specific areas where they feel they may lack knowledge.

A practice test for 0014/5014 is found at the end of this guide and should help with further study. An additional 0014/5014 practice test is located on the CD-ROM. Not only are the answers provided, but a general explanation as well. It is helpful to use the practice tests to decide which areas to study and the depth of those studies.

No matter what is studied for this exam, the amount of information retained will be invaluable in the examinee's career as a teacher. Innumerable times, students ask for information about the subjects or topics being studied, and it is a wise teacher who is able to provide the details and facts to answer student questions.

Reading and language arts are essential to the success of all learners. Students must be familiar with the English language, its uses, and its functions in order to succeed in school and participate in a meaningful life. Understanding the structures and functions of the language allows learners to comprehend text, read and write coherently, and improve critical thinking skills.

## Understanding Literature

Literature is generally based on the ideologies and the values of a certain era, often deeply linked to the time period in which the piece was written. Literature is unique as a form of writing as it often does not provide a direct message for the reader, but embeds its message in a rather discreet and often concealing manner. Throughout time authors have asserted their own beliefs and values through their work, and the work may be influenced by these biases. It is up to the reader to uncover, analyze, and interpret the meaning.

There are four processes/stages essential to readers in the interpretation of literature:

1. **Initial** (construction stage): The reader has initial contact with content, structure, genre, and language of the text. The reader uses prior knowledge to begin to build an understanding of the literature.
2. **Developing** (extending stage): The reader dives into the text world and uses text and background knowledge to build understanding of the literature. New information is taken in and immediately used to ask questions about the literature.
3. **Reflection/Response** (extension of reading stage): The reader uses text knowledge to reflect on personal knowledge. What is read impacts as well as is reflected in the reader's own life, the lives of others, and the human condition.
4. **Critical Analysis** (examining stage): The reader reflects on and reacts to the content of the literature. The reader judges, evaluates, and relates to the literature.

## Types of Literature

There are many types of literature, each possessing unique characteristics. Knowing the type of literature one is reading can help the reader better understand the text as well as better extract meaning from what is being read. Following is a brief list of the most common forms of literature:

**Allegory**—A narrative in which the characters and events represent an idea or truth about life in general.

**Autobiography**—A narrative in which the author writes about his or her own life.

**Biography**—A narrative in which an author writes about another person's life.

**Comedy**—A genre of literature in which life is dealt with in a humorous manner, often poking fun at people's mistakes.

**Drama** (play)—A genre of literature that uses dialogue to present its message to the audience and is meant to be performed.

**Essay**—A nonfiction piece that is often short and used to express the writer's opinion about a topic or to share information on a subject.

**Fable**—A short story, often with animals as the main characters, that teaches a moral or lesson to the reader.

**Fantasy**—A genre of literature in which the story is set in an imaginary world, involving magic or adventure, in which the characters often have supernatural powers.

**Folktale**—A story that has been passed down orally from one generation to another; the characters usually follow the extreme (all good or all bad) and in the end are rewarded or punished as they deserve.

**Myth**—A story that was created to explain some natural force of nature, religious belief, or social phenomenon. The gods and goddesses have supernatural powers but the human characters often do not.

**Novel**—A fictional narrative of book length in which characters and plot are developed in a somewhat realistic manner.

**Parable**—A simple, short story that is used to explain a belief, moral, or spiritual lesson.

**Poetry**—A literary work that uses colorful, concise, rhythmic language and focuses on the expression of ideas or emotions.

**Prose**—A literary work that is in ordinary form, without metrical structure, and uses the familiar structure of spoken language, sentence after sentence.

**Realism**—A type of writing in which the reality of life is shown.

**Science fiction**—A genre of literature, often set in the future, in which real or imaginary scientific developments and concepts are prevalent.

**Short story**—A narrative that can be read in one sitting. It has few characters, often with one conflict or problem, but the characters usually go through some sort of change by the end of the story.

**Tall tale**—A humorous and exaggerated story often based on the life of a real person. The exaggerations increase and build until the character can achieve impossible tasks.

**Tragedy**—A genre of literature in which there is a downfall of the hero due to a tragic flaw or personal characteristic and that results in an unhappy, melancholy, or tragic ending.

# Narratives

A narrative is a story that has a beginning, middle, and end. The sequence of events or time is found within a narrative along with descriptions of setting or characters. Characters are an important ingredient within the sequence of events, which helps to propel the narrative forward.

Certain components must be present in order to make a piece of writing a story. These essential components are the elements of a narrative:

- **Pace**—How the details are placed and how transitions are made within the story. Pacing of a narrative consists of episodes or scenes that function to "move" the story along.
- **Tone**—The attitude or feeling that a piece of literature conveys through its characters, word choice, and writing style; for example, humorous, sad, serious, or satiric.
- **Point of view (POV)**—Who is telling the story or what angle the story is being told from. The POV impacts reader response to the story and the characters. There are five basic POVs:
  - **Objective**—The story is told through actions and dialogue; the reader must infer what the characters think and feel; the narrator is a detached observer.
  - **Third person**—The story is told through an outside voice (the narrator is not one of the characters) but informs the reader about how the characters feel.
  - **First person**—The story is told through an inside voice (the narrator is participating in the story as a character). The reader receives information from a narrator who is directly involved in the action, and the narrator may or may not be reliable or trustworthy; the narrator is biased.
  - **Omniscient**—The story is told by an all-knowing narrator who knows everything about all characters (inner thoughts included).
  - **Limited omniscient**—The story is told by a narrator whose knowledge is limited to knowing the inner thoughts and feelings of one character (major or minor).

- **Characters**—People, animals, or objects that participate in the sequence of events within a story. Characters are presented in myriad ways to the reader. They can be major or minor and either static (unchanging) or dynamic (changing). Readers learn about characters through physical traits, dialogue, actions, response to situations, opinions, beliefs, and POV. There are two divisions that pertain to the most important characters in a story:
  - **Antagonist**—The person or force that works against the hero (protagonist) in the story.
  - **Protagonist**—The main character in the story who is often good or possesses heroic qualities.
- **Setting**—The location of the events and the time in which the narrative takes place. The setting is created through vivid and descriptive language, which details the sights, sounds, colors, and moods of the environment.
- **Theme**—A view on life and of how people conduct themselves. In a narrative, the theme is not always directly presented but rather left up to the reader to extract from the characters, events, and setting.
- **Plot**—The plot is the sequence of events and the reason that the events occur within the story. A plot pulls the reader into the lives of the characters and allows the reader to understand the decisions and choices made by the characters. Eight elements make up the plot:
  1. **Exposition**—The introduction, in which the reader is introduced to the setting, tone, characters, and initial understanding of the story.
  2. **Inciting force**—The character or event that triggers or incites the central conflict.
  3. **Conflict**—The event(s) from which the plot is derived. There are seven types of narrative conflicts:
     - **Character versus Self**—Conflict in which the main character faces an internal struggle or problem.
     - **Character versus Character**—Conflict in which two characters face each other in an external problem (protagonist and antagonist).
     - **Character versus Society**—Conflict in which the main character or a group of main characters face a conflict with social traditions or concepts.
     - **Character versus Nature**—Conflict in which the main character faces the forces of nature (mainly survival themes).
     - **Character versus Supernatural**—Conflict in which the main character faces ghosts, spirits, or other supernatural forces (mainly horror stories).
     - **Character versus Technology**—Conflict in which the main character faces man-made entities that may possess artificial intelligence.
     - **Character versus Fate (Destiny)**—Conflict in which the main character faces the challenge of breaking free of a predetermined path that has been chosen for the character by another entity, force, icon, God, or unknown being.
  4. **Rising action**—The series of events that build up from the conflict ending with the climax.
  5. **Crisis**—The turning point of the conflict that is most intense between the two opposing forces in the story, either right before or at the same time as the climax.
  6. **Climax**—The point at which the outcome of the conflict can be predicted. It is the highest point of the story and often the one with the greatest emotion.
  7. **Falling action**—The series of events after the climax, that wrap up the story.
  8. **Resolution**—The conclusion of the story and the rounding out of the action.

# Nonfiction

Nonfiction is writing in which the information is presented as fact or truth. This does not necessarily mean that the information is accurate or valid. Some examples of nonfiction writing include, but are not limited to, the following:

Almanacs

Biographies

Book reports

Dictionaries

Encyclopedias

Essays

Historic papers

Journals

Letters

Literary critiques

Memoirs

Menus

Scientific papers

Textbooks

User manuals

# Poetry

Poetry is a creative form of writing that employs many literary techniques. Poems are meant to be read aloud, and therefore, must utilize many devices to ensure aesthetically pleasing reads. Poetry is written in groups of lines called stanzas. Following are the techniques or devices used in poetry.

| Technique | Definition | Examples |
|---|---|---|
| Rhyme | A scheme of how words are organized into patterns | aa bb cc |
|  | Internal rhyme—The rhyming of words within the line | ab ab ab |
|  | (Example: Peter, Peter, pumpkin-eater). | aaba bbcb ccdc |
|  | End rhyme—The rhyming of words at the end of a line |  |
|  | (Example: How now / Brown cow) |  |
| Meter | The rhythm of the poem; the pattern of accented and unaccented syllables | I love my little hat / My little hat loves me / and when I wear my hat / I'm as happy as can be |
| Alliteration | A repetition of the beginning consonant sound | The green grass grows slowly |
| Assonance | A repetition of vowel sounds | What's the story morning glory |
| Consonance | A repetition of consonant sounds anywhere within words | Bobo boxed Baby's blue baboon |
| Onomatopoeia | When a word sound relates to its meaning | buzz, hiss, woof, zip, swish |
| Repetition | The stating of a word or phrase more than once, which adds rhythm or focus | "I do not like them in a house. I do not like them with a mouse. I do not like them here or there. I do not like them anywhere. I do not like green eggs and ham." |

Poems are written in a unique structure that can enhance the tone and flow of the poem as well as the overall aesthetic effect. There can be formal poems and informal poems, as well as free-formed or formed poetry. The following is a list of poetic structures.

| Structure | Definition | Example |
|---|---|---|
| Foot | One unit of meter. There are five basic feet in poetry: | |
| | **Iambic**—An unaccented syllable followed by an accented syllable (da-dum, da-dum) | Whose woods / these are / I think / I know |
| | **Trochaic**—An accented syllable followed by an unaccented syllable (dum-da, dum-da) | Peter, Peter, pumpkin-eater |
| | **Spondaic**—Two accented syllables (dum-dum, dum-dum) | Well-loved of me / discerning to fulfill |
| | **Anapestic**—Two unaccented syllables followed by an accented syllable (da-da-dum, da-da-dum) | 'Twas the night before Christmas and all through the house |
| | **Dactylic**—An accented syllable followed by two unaccented syllables (dum-da-da, dum-da-da) | Woman much missed / how you call to me |
| Verse | A line of poetry written in meter and named for the number of feet per line. There are eight common types of verse: | **Monometer**—One foot<br>**Dimeter**—Two feet<br>**Trimeter**—Three feet<br>**Tetrameter**—Four feet<br>**Pentameter**—Five feet<br>**Hexameter**—Six feet<br>**Heptameter**—Seven feet<br>**Octameter**—Eight feet |
| Stanza | The sections or lines of a poem.<br>There are six common stanzas: | **Couplet**—Two lines<br>**Triplet**—Three lines<br>**Quatrain**—Four lines<br>**Sestet**—Six lines<br>**Septet**—Seven lines<br>**Octave**—Eight lines |

There are many forms in which a poem may be written. The form of a poem aids in the overall effect that the poem creates: It can set the tone, alter the flow and meter, and impact the way the poem is read. Following is a list of some common poetic forms.

| Forms of Poetry | |
|---|---|
| **Form** | **Description** |
| Acrostic | The letters of a word are used to begin each line in the poem; it can be comprised of adjectives or phrases. |
| Ballad | A poem usually written in quatrains that tells a story. Lines 1 and 3 are four accented syllables and lines 2 and 4 are three accented syllables. |
| Blank verse | A poem that is unrhymed but has a regular meter. Each line is usually 10 syllables and is in iambic pentameter. |
| Cinquain | A poem that is five lines in length. There can be both syllable and word cinquains. |

(continued)

| Form | Description |
|------|-------------|
| Couplet | Two lines of verse that often rhyme and convey one complete idea. |
| Elegy | A poem about death or the sadness related to the death of an important person (important to the author). |
| Epic | A poem of lengthy proportions that is a story or tells the adventures of a hero; it must have both a hero and a villain. |
| Free verse | A poem without regular meter or a rhyme scheme. |
| Haiku | A form of Japanese poetry, often about nature. It contains stanzas of three lines with 5, 7, 5 syllables. |
| Limerick | A humorous poem of five lines. Lines 1, 2, and 5 rhyme and lines 3 and 4 rhyme. The syllables are 9, 9, 5, 5, 9. |
| Lyric | A short poem with personal feelings; most often put to music. |
| Ode | A long lyric with much imagery and many poetic devices. |
| Sonnet | A 14-line poem that states the poet's personal feelings. There are different types of sonnets:<br>• **Shakespearean (English)**—Has three quatrains (four lines), a rhymed couplet with a rhyme scheme of abab cdcd efef gg<br>• **Petrarchan (Italian)**—Has an octave (eight lines) and a sestet (six lines) with a rhyme scheme of abbaabba and cdecde, cdccdc, or cdedce |

# Resource and Research Materials

The type of research being done leads to the type of resources needed. Many resources are available in today's world and a myriad of avenues exist to pursue information. When evaluating literature from a research perspective, the reader must keep in mind the validity and reliability of the source. There are two general categories for source information: primary and secondary.

**Primary sources** are original sources that give the reader firsthand knowledge (knowledge that was experienced by observing or participating in the activity). Primary sources offer firsthand ideas and details and will often allow the reader to get closer to the truth about a subject. A primary source can be traced back no further than its author.

There are five major types of primary sources:

1. **Interviews**—An activity that allows one to talk directly with a person who has expert knowledge about a subject or topic.
2. **Presentations**—Lectures, displays, and exhibits provide firsthand information.
3. **Surveys**—Questionnaires help gather opinions and preferences directly.
4. **Diaries, journals, and letters**—Personal writings supply an excellent way to gather information firsthand.
5. **Observation and participation**—Watching an event, people, or activity in person furnishes the observer with a firsthand account. Actively taking part in an event or activity yields the participant with firsthand experience and information.

A **secondary source** shares information from a primary source. Facts and data can be collected and gathered from a variety of primary sources and then organized, summarized, and presented in a new format. A secondary source can be traced back beyond its author to at least one other person and often more than one person. Some examples of secondary sources are magazines, books, newspapers, news programs, encyclopedias, online sources, and business presentations.

Readers are responsible for making an informed assessment about the resources they use to gain facts, opinions, and ideas. Information is everywhere in today's society: television, Internet, newspapers, magazines, libraries, schools, neighbors, coworkers, friends, and so on. It is up to the reader to judge whether or not the information provided is reliable and trustworthy. The reader must look at the source that provides the information and ask key questions to analyze the reliability of the source. The following questions are recommended when assessing sources:

*What type of source is this?* Whether the source is primary or secondary can play a large role in determining the validity and reliability of the information. Did the source actually witness or experience the information or did it simply relate it to the reader secondhand?

*Who is the source?* Anyone can write literature or an essay and post it on the Internet, claiming the information is valid. Check to see if the source is an expert or authority on the subject or topic before judging the validity. Explore the background of the individual providing the information.

*Is the information accurate?* The information provided needs to be clear, concise, and of high quality. Check to see if there are other sources that express similar information.

*Is the information up-to-date?* Make sure that the information given is the most current. Check for recent additions to the content as well.

*Is the source biased?* Check to see whether the source is an objective observer/participant or if the source has something to gain by using the facts and providing the information (for example, politicians, TV infomercials, drug company findings).

# Text Structure and Organization for Reading and Writing

**Structure** is the way authors organize written work. Authors must construct what they have to say in a pattern or form in order to convey their messages to the reader clearly and concisely. Understanding the organization of a piece of writing helps the reader comprehend the text and glean the information being presented.

Specific patterns can be found within fiction, poetry, and nonfiction. The structure often can be used as a type of formula when reading various forms of literature. If the reader understands the organization of the literature, the message that is being portrayed by the author will be more easily extracted and understood.

Following is a list of the patterns of organization found within each type of literature.

| Fiction | Poetry | Nonfiction |
| --- | --- | --- |
| Story and plot | Poetic devices | Description and details |
| Theme and meaning | Rhythm | Main idea and supporting details (introduction of the subject and the support to prove it) |
| Conflict and climax | Verses | Compare and contrast |
| Resolution and epiphany | Stanzas | Chronological order (time pattern) |
| | Diction | Cause and effect (situations/events and the reasons they occur) |
| | | Process (describes how an event happens) |

# Literacy Acquisition and Reading Instruction

Literacy acquisition is obtained through a variety of practices such as letter knowledge, familiar word reading, and symbol or picture reading. Literacy acquisition is essential for readers as it leads the reader into procedural knowledge (knowing how) and conceptual knowledge (knowing why). When children are able to assess themselves as readers as well as assess the text, their literacy and comprehension will flourish.

There are three components of the acquisition of language:

- **Letter knowledge**—Giving sounds for an individual letter and writing letters in response to their individual sounds
- **Logographic foundation**—Reading and recognizing familiar and common words (sight words)
- **Alphabetic foundation**—Reading aloud and having the student write the letter spoken based on the sound spoken or the letter name uttered

Reading is the foundation upon which all formal education is constructed. Reading skills and proficiency pervade all aspects of life and are specific to elementary education. Academic success, employment, and personal autonomy are dependent on reading and writing proficiencies.

# Foundations of Literacy and Reading Instruction

Development of literacy skills is dependent on language and listening skills. There are many ways to practice literacy and encourage the construction of literacy foundations:

- **Learn to listen**—Make eye contact and attend to the speaker; distinguish background noise from foreground sounds; develop attention span, social listening skills, mental imaging, and auditory memory.

- **Time to speak**—Practice social speaking skills; be aware of audience; take turns; develop vocabulary, sentence structure, and descriptive language; use predicting, planning, recalling, and analyzing.

- **Memory and music**—Develop rhythm, voice control, articulation, turn-taking, sense of time and beat, cooperation with others, auditory memory, language patterns, and prediction skills.

- **Learning about print**—Understand the function of print, recognizing the alphabet and letters, reading and writing concepts, and using sight words and high-frequency words.

- **Harmony with sound**—Use listening skills, learning the awareness of language, the recognition of rhyme and rhythm, the use and impact of poetic devices within language, and the influences of basic skills such as phonemic awareness, blending and segmenting, and phonics.

- **Development of writing**—Develop and hone in on motor skills, hand-eye coordination, letter shapes and formations; develop hand and finger muscles and control of pencil or pen.

## Foundations

Reading encompasses the acquisition of a wide array of skills. If students gain these skills early and have basic foundations set at an early age, they will continue to be successful in school and experience greater overall achievement in work and in life. The process of reading is complicated and detailed, but instruction in this area should be focused on the general principles.

The core of reading instruction should include the following four areas:

1. Understanding of psychology and development
2. Understanding of language structure
3. Application of best practices in all aspects of instruction
4. Using reliable, efficient, and validated assessments

Good readers process the letters of each word in detail unconsciously and very quickly, which can appear as skimming text. Because word recognition is accurate and fast, the reader's mind is able to expend energy mulling over the meaning of the text rather than focusing energy on decoding words. Sound symbol mapping allows the reader to develop word recognition, which leads to comprehension. Good readers are familiar with and possess linguistic structure, recognize patterns, and connect letter patterns with sounds, syllables, and meaningful word parts.

The detailed foundations are included here.

| Foundation | Definition | How to Obtain the Foundation |
|---|---|---|
| Print concepts | Letters have sounds, and letters form words. | Structure of a book<br>Learning through repeated reading and exposure to text/print |
| Phonemic awareness | Speech is broken into individual sounds; in the English language, there 44 sounds using the 26 letters of the alphabet. | Exposure to nursery rhymes or common jingles<br>Use of oral language and sound patterns |

| Foundation | Definition | How to Obtain the Foundation |
|---|---|---|
| Alphabetic principle | Letters represent sounds and speech. | Exposure to text and print |
| Word identification | Various strategies are used to recognize vocabulary. | Decoding by sound<br>Decoding by comparison to known words<br>Using sight words |
| Fluency | Reading is done with expression and is automatic and flowing (does not require comprehension). | Practice reading |
| Comprehension | Critical thinking and processing of the content read. | Practice reading and writing qualities.<br>*Reading qualities* may include the use of background knowledge, summarizing, visualizing, forming inference, making connections, asking questions, synthesizing, and determinging the main idea.<br>*Writing qualities* refer to ideas, organization, voice, word choice, sentence fluency, and mechanics. |

# Children's Literature

A literary genre designed especially for young children, **children's literature** is defined as literature that is read and selected by children. Early literature exposure provides an appreciation for reading and the different varieties of literary work, such as poems, limericks, and short stories. Children's literature is also used in schools to fulfill a number of niches that traditional curriculum materials cannot: as a language development resource, a medium for metacomprehension assessment, an instrument for discussing equity issues, an alternative text, an extension tool for gifted students, and an instrument for children with disabilities.

There are six basic categories of children's literature:

1. **Early childhood**—Picture books, concept books (counting and alphabet), pattern books, and nonprint books
2. **Traditional**—Myths, fables, folk songs, legends, tales (fairy and folk), rhymes
3. **Fiction**—Fantasy, historical, science, contemporary materials
4. **Biography and autobiography**—Stories about the lives of various people
5. **Nonfiction and reference**—Encyclopedia, dictionary, almanac, historical, scientific resources
6. **Poetry and verse**—Collections or anthologies

Children's literature gives children a chance to take ownership in their language acquisition by providing narratives and stories that are directly related to the interests, ideas, and concerns of children. Exposure to children-specific literature fosters comprehension, discussion, writing skills, and an emotional connection to text. It also allows children the chance to learn how to read for personal reasons, become actively involved in literature, and to reach a level of gaining deeper meaning from what is read.

# Strategies for Word Recognition

Readers use certain techniques to identify printed text and words. These techniques are crucial to text comprehension and reading foundations.

**Instant recognition**—Readers are able to easily identify words leads to text comprehension. There are 100 words that make up 50 percent of the words read by adults and children. These high-frequency words should be learned so they may be instantly recognized to assist students in reading fluency and comprehension.

Examples: the, to, from, in, said, he, it, she, read, you, me, and, by, or, as

**Context clues**—Readers are able to use words, meanings, and context to extract the meanings of unknown words leads to understanding. Context clues alone are not enough to predict word meaning, and therefore must be accompanied by other clues such as phonics, comparisons, or word structure.

There are three types of context clues that readers may use:

- **Semantic clues** (meaning)—Based on the subject read, the reader can determine what type of language will be used. Example: When reading a story about dogs, the reader will expect to see words such as *teeth, woof, bark, tail, ball, play, ears*. Within sentences (*My dog likes to _____.*) the reader can use context to determine reasonable vocabulary: *run, bark, play, jump*.

- **Syntactic clues** (word order)—Based on the order and structure of words, the reader can determine meaning based on the part of speech. (Example: *My dog likes to _____.*) Since the missing word is at the end of the sentence, the reader can reason that the word needed is a verb to make a complete sentence.

- **Symbolic clues** (pictures)—Illustrations and graphics can provide assistance with the identification of words. (Example: If a dog is chasing a ball in the picture, the word *play* seems a reasonable choice for the sentence *My dog likes to _____.*)

**Word structure clues**—Readers are able to recognize frequent letter groups; included in this category are prefixes, suffixes, and inflectional endings. These clues help readers become more rapid and efficient word identifiers.

**Analogy clues**—Readers are able to draw connections between patterns, simple words, and syllables. Being able to compare known words to unknown words helps readers determine sounds and the make-up of new words.

## Strategies for Comprehension

Reading comprehension is the level of understanding of a specific passage of text. Many reading strategies are available for students to use:

- **Think and read**—Before reading, the reader asks him- or herself what is already known about the subject, skims the text, pauses throughout the text to take notes or write questions, and reads difficult parts aloud; after reading, the reader writes or tells what was learned and summarizes the reading.

- **Inferential reading**—Utilizing prior knowledge, the reader draws conclusions and makes inferences, and the reader recognizes the effects that personal experiences, biases, and points of view may have on analyzing text. Examples include context clues, pronoun recognition, POV, details of setting, evaluation of author's message, making connections between text and life, and drawing conclusions from information.

- **Annotating text**—The reader develops questions in response to text, analyzes and interprets elements of poetry, draws conclusions based on literal and figurative meaning, labels and interprets literacy devices, determines and labels main ideas and supportive details.

- **KWL**—K represents "what do I *know*," W represents "what do I *want* to know," and L represents "what I *learned* or want to *learn*."

- **Metacognition**—During reading, an individual mentally includes these processes: thinking about thinking, monitoring understanding, clarifying purpose, identifying difficulty and planning to solve, looking through text to review key concepts, and adjusting reading speed depending on the difficulty of text.

- **Graphic organizer**—Organizers help readers focus on text structure, show relationships within a text, organize ideas for better summarizing, and illustrate concepts. Some examples include Venn diagrams, storyboards, chain of events, story maps, story webs, graphs, charts, and cause-and-effect tasks.

- **QAR (question-answer relationship)**—Readers learn how to answer questions, delineate between explicit and implicit information, and draw on background knowledge. There are four types of questions:

- ■ "Right there" questions within the text that ask the reader to find the answer that is located in one place as a word or simple phrase.

- ■ "Think and search" questions that force the reader to recall information directly from the text. The answer is found in more than one place, requiring the reader to search the text.

- ■ "Author and you" questions that require the reader to use what he or she already knows coupled with what he or she has just learned from the text.

- ■ "On your own" questions based on the reader's prior knowledge and background knowledge that the text may not be helpful in answering.

- ■ **Summarizing**—Identifies and/or generates main ideas, connects main ideas, eliminates unneeded information, and recalls what was read.

- ■ **Story structure recognition**—Recognizes patterns within literature, which aids in developing comprehension; identifies categories of content; recognizes the type of literature based on elements; and understands the organization of text.

# Language in Writing

Language is the foundation upon which writing is based, so having a firm grasp of language allows the writer to express meaning in a clear and concise manner. There are many facets to writing, which must be studied and understood in order to develop the ability to communicate effectively.

# Grammar and Usage

Grammar can be defined as the rules and guidelines that are followed in order to write and speak in an acceptable manner. In the English language, parts of speech assist an individual in the understanding of words and how to use words.

## Parts of Speech

There are eight parts of speech in the English language: noun, verb, adjective, pronoun, adverb, preposition, conjunction, and interjection. Every word in our language can be labeled as a part of speech.

## Noun

A **noun** is a word that names a person, place, thing, concept, idea, act, or characteristic. Nouns give names to everything that exists, has existed, or will exist in the world. There are eight ways of classifying types of nouns.

**Common nouns** refer to *general* ideas, objects, places, and concepts and are NOT capitalized. Examples: girl, man, house, bridge, class.

**Proper nouns** refer to *specific* ideas, people, concepts, places, and objects and ARE always capitalized. Examples: Haley, Chip, White House, Golden Gate Bridge, English.

**Concrete nouns** name things that are physical and able to be touched. Examples: desk, bottle, phone, space shuttle.

**Abstract nouns** name something that cannot be seen or touched but can be thought or felt. Examples: love, hate, Buddhism, happiness, sickness.

**Collective nouns** name a group or collection of people, things, places, concepts, or characteristics. Examples: tribe, family, team, flock, gaggle, litter, bunch, dozen.

**Compound nouns** are made up of two or more words. Examples: basketball, middle school, mother-in-law.

**Singular nouns** refer to only one thing, person, place, idea/concept, or characteristic. Examples: dog, teacher, dress, test, giraffe.

**Plural nouns** refer to more than one thing, person, place, idea/concept, or characteristic. The following rules apply when making nouns plural:

- For most words, simply add *s*. Examples: teachers, stethoscopes, drinks.
- If a word ends in *ch, s, ss, x,* or *z*, add *es*. Examples: boxes, witches, dresses.
- If a word ends in a *y* preceded by a consonant, change the *y* to *i* and add *es*. Example: butterflies, stories, flurries.
- If a word ends in *o* with a vowel right before the *o*, add *s*. Example: radios, igloos, radicchios.
- If a word ends in *o* with a consonant right before the *o*, add *es*. Example: echoes, buffaloes, tornadoes.
- If a word ends in *f* or *fe* in which the final sound is a *v* sound, change the *f* or *fe* to *ve* and add *s*. Examples: lives, loaves, knives.
- If a word ends in *f* and the final sound remains the *f* sound, add *s*. Examples: roofs, cutoffs, bluffs.

Nouns can be used in a variety of ways within a sentence. The chart delineates the specific usage for nouns and provides examples for clarity.

| Noun Type | Definition | Example |
|---|---|---|
| Subject noun | The noun does something or is being talked about within a sentence | The **dog** ran quickly around the fence to catch the red ball. |
| Predicate noun | The noun repeats or renames the subject | A classroom is a great **place** to learn new things. |
| Possessive noun | The noun shows ownership | My **mother's** face beamed with pride at **my** book's success. |
| Object noun | When the noun is used as the direct object, the indirect object, or the object of the preposition | You will love the **sandwich** on wheat **bread**. |

## Verb

A **verb** is a word that shows **action**(s) or a state of being. Some action verbs are *jump, hop, skip, scream, throw, call,* and *divide*. Verbs can also be **linking verbs,** which link the subject to the words that describe it, such as *is, has been,* and *was*. Samples of both action and linking verbs are identified in the chart.

| Action Verbs | Linking Verbs |
|---|---|
| Mabel **chases** squirrels. | Mabel **is** happy. |
| Mabel **barked** in the yard. | Mabel's face **was** dirty. |
| The squirrel **shrieks** at Mabel. | The dog treats **were** on sale. |
| The squirrel **fell**. | The sun **has been** bright today. |

**Helping verbs** are words that aid in the formation of a verb tense. Helping verbs may include *shall, will, should, would, could, must, can, may, have, had, has, do, did, is, are, was, were, am, being,* and *been*.

**Verb tenses** help clarify the period of time in a sentence. Verbs have three principle tenses: past, present, and future. Verbs must be conjugated into these different tenses depending on the time that the action takes place.

- **Present tense**—Shows the action is happening now
- **Past tense**—Shows the action happened in the past; generally the verb uses the ending *ed*
- **Future tense**—Shows the action will happen; generally words such as *will* or *shall* are added to the verb.

| Present | Past | Future |
|---|---|---|
| Chip **enjoys** his vacation. | Chip **enjoyed** his vacation. | Chip **will enjoy** his vacation. |
| I **jump** over the rock. | I **jumped** over the rock. | I **will jump** over the rock. |

Verbs in a sentence should agree with one another by coinciding or matching time sequences. If an action happened at the same time as another action, the verbs must have the same tense. This holds true within sentences, paragraphs, and narratives. Examples:

Justin *sleeps* while his dog *runs* up and down the stairs. (both present) CORRECT

Justin *slept* while his dog *runs* up and down the stairs. (past and present) INCORRECT

Justin *slept* while his dog *ran* up and down the stairs. (both past) CORRECT

**Present perfect tense** is used when the action begins in the past but concludes in the present. (Add *has* or *have* to the past participle.) Example: It *has taken* a very long time to write this book.

**Past perfect tense** is used when the action begins in the past and is completed in the past. (Add "had" to the past participle.) Example: I *had hoped* to be finished by November.

**Future perfect tense** is used when the action will begin in the future and will be completed by a specific time in the future. (Add *will have* to the past participle.) Example: By the end of the year, we *will have completed* the manuscript.

Verbs can also be **regular** and **irregular**. Regular verbs follow a distinct pattern and are predictable (past = *ed*, future = *will*). Irregular verbs have their own individual form for each tense that does not follow a pattern.

The chart identifies some common irregular verbs in the various tenses.

| Irregular Verbs to Know | | |
|---|---|---|
| **Present (Base form)** | **Past Simple** | **Past Participle** |
| be | was, were | been |
| begin | began | begun |
| break | broke | broken |
| bring | brought | brought |
| catch | caught | caught |
| choose | chose | chosen |
| do | did | done |
| eat | ate | eaten |
| give | gave | given |
| go | went | gone, been |
| grow | grew | grown |
| know | knew | known |
| lay | laid | laid |
| lie | lay | lain |
| ride | rode | ridden |
| ring | rang | rung |
| see | saw | seen |

*continued*

| Present (Base form) | Past Simple | Past Participle |
|---|---|---|
| sleep | slept | slept |
| speak | spoke | spoken |
| take | took | taken |
| tear | tore | torn |
| wake | woke | woken |
| write | wrote | written |

The **voice** of a verb explains whether the subject is *doing the action* or *receiving the action*. There are two separate types of verb voice.

- **Active voice**—The subject is doing the action in the sentence. Example: I found the treasure chest in the sand.
- **Passive voice**—The subject is receiving the action in the sentence. Example: The treasure was found in the sand.

Verbs can be used in many ways. The verb type allows the reader to better comprehend the meaning of what is being read. If the reader recognizes the use of the verb it may help in the understanding of the sentence content.

| Verb Uses | | |
|---|---|---|
| **Verb Type** | **Definition** | **Example** |
| **Transitive verb** | When the verb transfers its action to an object; the noun must receive the action of the verb for the verb meaning to be complete | The girl **threw** the ball. (*Threw* transfers its action to the ball. Without the ball, the meaning of the verb *threw* is incomplete.) |
| **Intransitive verb** | When the verb completes its action without an object | His shoulder **felt** sore. (*Sore* is a predicate adjective, not a direct object.) |
| **Transitive and intransitive verbs** | When the verb can be either transitive or intransitive, depending on the sentence | He **read** the paper. (transitive)<br>He **read** aloud. (intransitive) |

**Verbals** are words that are made from verbs, have the power of a verb, but act like another part of speech.

- **Participle—(present or past)** A verb that ends in *ing* or *ed*, and is used like an adjective. Example:
  The *shaking* windows broke in the aftermath of the tornado. (*Shaking* modifies *windows*.)
- **Infinite**—A verb preceded by *to* used as an adjective, noun, or adverb. Example:
  *To climb* Mount Everest is one of my goals. (*To climb* is used as a noun and is the subject of the sentence.)
- **Gerund**—A verb that ends in *ing* and is used as a noun. Example:
  *Screaming* is pointless. (The noun *screaming* is the subject.)

## Adjective

An **adjective** is a word used to describe a noun or pronoun, such as *purple, loud, minuscule, gigantic, colorful,* and *sweet.*

> The *purple* shirt is *pretty.*
> The child was *loud.*
> A *minuscule* fish rides on the back of a *gigantic* whale in the *tumultuous* ocean.

A **proper adjective** is formed by a proper noun and is always capitalized. Example: The *San Francisco* bridge stretches a long way.

A **common adjective** is any adjective that is not proper and is not capitalized. Example: The *long, elegant* bridge stretches for miles across the *angry* sea.

| Types of Adjectives | | |
|---|---|---|
| **Type** | **Description** | **Example** |
| **Demonstrative adjective** | An adjective that singles out a specific noun: this, that, these, those (a noun must immediately follow) | **This** lake is huge, but **that** ocean is larger. |
| **Compound adjective** | An adjective that is made up of two or more words and is hyphenated | The **self-centered** boy refused to share his snack with the starving children. |
| **Indefinite adjective** | An adjective that gives the reader approximate information and does not tell exactly how much or how many | **Some** rivers flow quickly. |
| **Predicate adjective** | An adjective that follows a linking verb and describes the subject | The Colorado River was once **humongous,** but is now small. |

| Adjective Forms | | |
|---|---|---|
| **Form** | **Definition** | **Example** |
| **Positive** | When an adjective describes a noun or pronoun without comparing it to anyone or anything else. | Mountain biking is an **exciting** sport that requires skill and balance. |
| **Comparative** | When an adjective compares two people, places, things, ideas, concepts, or characteristics. The adjective usually ends in er. | Mountain biking is **better** than road biking. |
| **Superlative** | When an adjective compares three or more people, places, things, ideas, concepts, or characteristics. The adjective usually includes the word "most" or ends in est. | Mountain biking is the **most exciting** sport in the Olympics. or Mountain biking is the **hardest** type of biking. |
| | **Two-syllable Superlative/Comparative** | When the adjective shows comparison by the suffixes (er/est) or modifiers (more/most) spicy, spicier, spiciest or boring, more boring, most boring |
| | **Three- (or more) syllables Superlative/ Comparative** | When the adjective is three or more syllables long, it requires the words more/most or less/least to express comparison. more terrifying, most terrifying, less terrifying, least terrifying |
| | **Irregular** | When the adjective uses a completely different word to express the comparison good, better, best, bad, worse, worst |

## Article

An **article** is a word placed before a noun that introduces the noun as specific (*the*) or nonspecific (*a, an*). Using *the* delineates a specific person, place, thing, concept, idea, characteristic, or a plural noun. Example:

Please get *the* pencil from *the* desk.

Using *a* or *an* delineates a nonspecific person, place, thing, concept, idea, or characteristic. *An* is used for nouns that begin with a vowel. Example:

*A* car can travel faster than *an* elephant.

## Pronoun

A **pronoun** is a word used to replace a noun or is used in the place of a noun. Personal pronouns include the following:

> I, me, myself
>
> you, yours, yourself
>
> we, us, ours
>
> he, she, his, her, hers
>
> they, their, theirs
>
> it, its

Examples: As the ball sailed over the net, *it* spun to the left. (The word *it* replaces *ball.*) Poppy kicked *her* soccer ball after *it* was passed to *her*. (The word *her* refers to Poppy, and *it* refers to the soccer ball.)

The **antecedent** is the noun that the pronoun replaces or to which it is referring. Every pronoun has an antecedent. The antecedent can be used in the same sentence as the pronoun or in the previous sentences. All pronouns must coincide and agree with their antecedent in person, number, and gender. Example:

> The dog chased the squeaky ball in the park. When *she* brought *it* to *her* owner *she* was praised. (The word *dog* is the antecedent for *she* and *her,* while the word *ball* is the antecedent for *it.*)

**Personal pronouns** replace nouns in a sentence. There are three types of personal pronouns:

- **Simple**—I, you, we, it, he, she, they
- **Compound**—myself, herself, himself, itself, ourselves, themselves, yourself
- **Phrasal**—one another, each other

**Singular pronouns** express one person, place, thing, concept, idea, or characteristic. Examples: *I, you, he, she, it.*

**Plural pronouns** express more than one person, place, thing, concept, idea, or characteristic. Examples: *we, you, they, us, you all, them.*

The **person of the pronoun** tells the reader whether the pronoun is doing the action or speaking, experiencing the action or receiving the speaking, or is being spoken about:

- **First person** (I, me, we)—Used to show the pronoun is doing the action or is speaking; replaces the name of the noun. Example: *I* am writing.
- **Second person** (you, you all)—Used to show the pronoun is experiencing the action or is being spoken to. Example: Adrienne, will *you* please go kayaking?
- **Third person** (he, she, it, they)—Used to show the pronoun is being spoken about. Example: Basta needs to cook dinner if *she* wants to eat.

Pronouns can be used in many ways within a sentence. A pronoun can represent a subject, an object, or be used to show possession.

The pronoun can be used as the **subject** of the sentence (*I, you, he, she, it, we, they*). Example: *I* like to eat peanut butter and jelly sandwiches. (The word *I* is the subject.)

The pronoun can be used as the **object** of a verb or prepositional phrase (*me, you, him, her, it, us, them*). Example: "You hit *me*!" screamed Tony. (The word *me* is the object pronoun because it receives the action *hit.*)

The pronoun can show **ownership or possession** (*my, mine, our, ours, his, hers, their, theirs, its, your, yours*). Example: The red jacket was *hers*. (The word *hers* shows ownership of the *jacket.*)

| Pronoun Uses | | | |
|---|---|---|---|
| **Type** | **Definition** | **Example** | **Pronoun** |
| **Relative** | A pronoun that connects a subordinate clause to the main clause and is used as a connecting word | The girl **who** has curly hair is in fourth grade. (*Who* relates to *girl*.) | that<br>who |
| **Intensive** | A pronoun that emphasizes the noun it refers to; most sentences are complete without the intensive pronoun | The rattlesnake curls before it strikes and the snake **itself** can strike up to three times its body length. (*Itself* intensifies *snake*.) | itself<br>myself<br>himself<br>herself<br>yourself |
| **Demonstrative** | A pronoun that identifies the noun without naming it specifically | **This** was a fabulous party.<br>or<br>We bought **that** last week. | this<br>that<br>these<br>those<br>none<br>neither |
| **Interrogative** | A pronoun that asks a question | **Who** wants ice cream?<br>**Whom** would you take to dinner?<br>**Which** ice cream is your favorite?<br>**Whose** car will you take? | who<br>whom<br>which<br>whose |
| **Indefinite** | A pronoun that does not specifically name the antecedent | Will **somebody** make me dinner? | somebody<br>anybody<br>anyone<br>someone |
| **Reflexive** | A pronoun that places the action back upon the noun | A rattlesnake protects **itself** by rattling and then striking. | itself<br>herself<br>himself |

## Adverb

An **adverb** is a word that modifies a verb, an adjective, or another adverb. Adverbs tell how, when, where, why, how much, and how often. (Many adverbs, but not all, end in –*ly*.) Examples:

> The scorpion scurries *quickly* across the floor. (The adverb *quickly* modifies the verb *scurries*.)
>
> Bark scorpions are *very* venomous. (The adverb *very* modifies the adverb *venomous*.)
>
> Bark scorpions are *extremely* dangerous. (The adverb *extremely* modifies the adjective *dangerous*.)

There are three forms of adverbs.

**Positive adverbs** describe a verb, adjective, or adverb. Example: She performed *poorly* on her presentation.

**Comparative adverbs** compare two things. Example: He plays the drums *more loudly* than his brother.

**Superlative adverbs** compare three or more things. Example: Blue whales are the *largest* animals in the world.

| Adverb Uses | | |
|---|---|---|
| **Type** | **Definition** | **Examples** |
| **Time adverbs** | When the adverb describes how often, when, or how long | She will go kayaking **tomorrow**.<br>She **always** goes kayaking. |
| **Place adverbs** | When the adverb describes where, to where, or from where | The music blared **outside**.<br>The boy walked backward **out** the door. |

*(continued)*

| Type | Definition | Examples |
|------|-----------|----------|
| Manner adverbs | When the adverb describes how something is done (often ends in –ly) | The rock climber **meticulously** chose holds to use. The rock fell **slowly** down the mountain. |
| Degree adverbs | When the adverb describes how much or how little | I **rarely** eat sushi. |

## Preposition

A **preposition** is a word or group of words that explains position, direction, or how two ideas are related to one another. Examples:

> The phone slid *off* the wall.
>
> Chuck raised the fly rod *above* his head at a ninety-degree angle before casting his line.
>
> He walked *across* the grass.
>
> *During* the game, Andrea scored four goals.

A **prepositional phrase** contains the preposition, the object of the preposition, and the modifiers of the object. The phrase can function either as an adjective or adverb. Example:

Grayson snowboarded *down the long, perilous ridge*. (Within the prepositional phrase, *down* = the preposition; *long, perilous* = the modifiers; *ridge* = the object.)

The following chart provides a listing of the most common prepositions, but it is not a comprehensive listing.

| Common Prepositions | | | | |
|------|------|------|------|------|
| above | below | except | off | since |
| across | beneath | for | on | through |
| after | beside | from | on top of | to |
| against | between | in | onto | together with |
| along | beyond | inside | opposite | under/underneath |
| among | but | into | out | until |
| apart of | by | like | outside | up/upon |
| around | down | near | over | with/within |
| at | during | of | regarding | without |

## Conjunction

A **conjunction** is a word that joins together words or groups of words. Examples include *when, and, but, so, or,* and *because*.

There are three different types of conjunctions.

A **coordinating conjunction** joins a word to a word, a phrase to a phrase, or a clause to a clause. The words, phrases, or clauses joined must be equal or of the same type. These include *and, or, but, for, nor, yet,* and *so*. Example: If you want to hang out with me, we can go see a movie *or* get coffee.

A **correlative conjunction** is used in pairs. Example: *Either* you sit quietly *or* leave the room.

A **subordinating conjunction** connects two clauses that are not equal or the same type, connecting a dependent clause to an independent clause. They include *if, although, as, when, because, since, though, when, whenever, after, unless, while, whereas,* and *even though.* Example: Running a marathon is hard work *because* of the way it taxes your body.

## Interjection

An **interjection** is a word or phrase used to show strong emotion or surprise. Interjections are usually delineated by an exclamation point or commas. Examples:

> *Whoa!* Slow down.
>
> *Ah,* a shark!
>
> *Look,* a falling star!
>
> *Yippee!* I won a bike.
>
> *Look out,* there's a moose in the road!
>
> *Yea,* it's time for roller derby!

# Syntax and Sentence Types

**Syntax** is the manner in which words are organized and put together in a sentence. This arrangement shows the reader what type of sentence is being read and how to read the information presented.

A sentence must have a **subject** and a **predicate.** The **subject** is the part of the sentence that is doing the action or is being talked about.

There are three types of subjects:

- **Simple subject**—The subject without all the words that modify or describe it. Example: The team *sports* at school encourage cooperation and teamwork.
- **Complete subject**—The simple subject and all the words that modify or describe it. Example: *The team sports at school* encourage cooperation and teamwork.
- **Compound subject**—Two or more simple subjects joined by a conjunction. Example: *Basketball, volleyball, and football* are all team sports at school.

The **predicate** is the part of a sentence that discusses or adds information to the subject.

There are three types of predicates:

- **Simple predicate**—The predicate without all the words that modify or describe only the verb. Example: The snow *falls* heavily every night in the month of December.
- **Complete predicate**—The simple predicate with all the words that modify or describe it. Example: The snow *falls heavily every night in the month of December.*
- **Compound predicate**—The compound predicate has two or more simple predicates joined by a conjunction. Example: The snow *falls* and *sticks* to the ground.

**Direct objects** include nouns and pronouns that directly receive the action of the predicate and answer the question "what?" or "whom?". Example: Preschool *children* enjoy stories on a daily basis.

**Indirect objects** include nouns and pronouns that indirectly receive the action of the predicate and answer the question "to whom?" or "from whom?". If an indirect object follows a preposition, it is the object of the preposition, NOT an indirect object. Example: I read the *class* a book.

**Independent clauses** can stand alone as a sentence because they express a complete idea or thought. Example: *If the vegetables are picked, they could be used to make a delicious, organic salad.*

**Dependent clauses** cannot stand alone as a sentence because they do not express a complete idea or thought. Example: *If the vegetables are picked,* they could be used to make a delicious, organic salad.

**Phrases** are groups of words that are related but lack a subject, a predicate, or both, and are therefore not complete sentences. Example: *two girls* (lacks a predicate); *has dirt on it* (lacks a subject).

There are five types of phrases. Each type is named for the function it serves within a sentence:

1. Noun phrase
2. Verb phrase
3. Adverb phrase
4. Verbal phrase
5. Prepositional phrase

**Sentences** are made up of one or more words and express a complete thought. Sentences begin with a capital letter and end with a punctuation mark such as a period, a question mark, or an exclamation point.

There are four sentence forms that may be used.

| Form | Definition | Examples |
|------|-----------|----------|
| **Simple sentence** | A sentence with one complete thought or independent clause | My hand hurts. Her shoulders and arms are sore. |
| **Compound sentence** | A sentence with two or more simple sentences, which are joined by a conjunction and/or punctuation | I usually stretch my arms in the morning, but I forgot to this morning. |
| **Complex sentence** | A sentence with one independent clause and one or more dependent clauses | Since my arms are sore, I think I will not lift weights today. |
| **Compound-complex sentence** | A sentence with two or more independent clauses and one or more dependent clauses | My friend Haley wants to go running, but I want to go biking when we get together on Saturday. |

The type of sentence helps the reader recognize the voice and the mood of the text as well as determine meaning, which leads to the overall comprehension of text.

There are four major categories into which sentences can be divided:

**Declarative (.) sentence:** Makes a statement or tells something and ends with a period. Example: Charles Darwin wrote *The Origin of Species.*

**Interrogative (?) sentence:** Asks a question and ends with a question mark. Example: Who wrote the book, *The Origin of Species?*

**Imperative (.) sentence:** Gives a command, often with you as the understood subject and ends with a period. Example: Read this book.

**Exclamatory (!) sentence:** Expresses strong feeling or shows surprise and ends with an exclamation point. Example: I love this book!

# Orthography and Morphology

**Orthography** is the study of the spelling systems of language. It examines how letters are combined to represent sound and form words. In language, **morphology** is the study of the forms of words and examines how words develop.

# Semantics

**Semantics** is the study of word meaning within linguistics. It includes sense, reference, implication, logical form, word meaning, word relations, and the structure of meaning. Readers use semantics to help gain fluency, comprehension, and language acquisition.

An **affix** is an attachment to a base or root word. There are two types:

- **Prefix**—Word or letters placed at the beginning of a root or base word to create a new word or alter the meaning of the root. Examples: *un–, pre–, non–, a–, tri–, bi–, dis–.*
- **Suffix**—Morpheme added to the end of a root or base word to form a new word or to alter the meaning of the root. Examples: *–ing, –er, –tion, –fy, –ly, –it, –is.*

A **derivational affixation** occurs when affixes are added to root or base words, which modifies meaning and function. Examples: To the verb *sing* add *–er* to create the noun *singer.* To the adjective *slow* add *–ly* to create the adverb *slowly.*

A **digraph** is a combination of two letters possessing a single sound. Examples:

head = *ea*

chance = *ch*

swing = *ng*

graph = *ph*

A **diphthong** is two vowels in which the sound begins at the first vowel and moves toward the sound of the second vowel. Examples:

snout = *ou*

boy = *oy*

A **grapheme** is a letter or letters that represent one phoneme (includes every letter in the alphabet); the smallest meaningful unit within a writing system. Example: cat = c, a, t = three graphemes.

A **homonym** occurs when two words have the same pronunciation and spelling but hold different meanings. Examples:

| | | |
|---|---|---|
| left (direction, opposite of right) | left (past tense of *leave*) | |
| bear (animal) | bear (to carry) | |
| mouse (animal) | mouse (computer component) | |
| mean (rude) | mean (average) | mean (to define) |

A **homophone** is defined as two or more words that are spelled differently, pronounced identically, but have different meanings. Examples:

| | |
|---|---|
| two, to, too | hour, our |
| aero, arrow | air, heir, err |
| isle, aisle | ball, bawl |
| sweet, suite | holy, wholly |
| hear, here | pair, pear |
| pain, pane | rain, reign |
| rheum, room | sighs, size |

A **homograph** is defined as words that have the same spelling but different meanings and may or may not be pronounced differently. Examples:

| | |
|---|---|
| read (past tense) | read (present tense) |
| dove (bird) | dove (past tense of *dive*) |

close (shut)                    close (near)

wind (to turn)                  wind (blowing air)

tear (cry)                      tear (rip)

A **morpheme** is the smallest meaningful unit of speech that can no longer be divided. Examples: *in, come, on*.

A **phoneme** is a distinct unit of sound found within language that helps distinguish utterances from one another. Examples: bat: b = "buh" + at; pat: p = "puh" + at

# Vocabulary in Context

Context helps readers decode words, extract meaning, and comprehend text. There are five major clues readers can use to assist them while reading.

| Clue | Definition | Key Vocabulary | Example |
|------|-----------|----------------|---------|
| **Antonym clue** | Words or phrases that indicate the opposite of an unknown word or concept | but, however, unlike, yet, in contrast, instead of | Instead of singing in a mellifluous voice, she sang with a harsh and grating voice. |
| **Synonym clue** | Words or phrases that have a similar or the same meaning as the unknown word or concept | that is, in other words, sometimes called, or, known as | The ursine, commonly known as the bear, tore through the camp garbage. |
| **Definition clue** | Words or phrases that explain or define the unknown word or concept | means, the term, is defined as, can be delineated as a phrase by commas, italics or boldface | Raucous sounds, loud and harsh noises, can be heard in the jungle. |
| **General knowledge** | Meaning is acquired from background knowledge or prior experience of the reader | the information is either familiar or common | A plethora of balloons floated in the sky. There were a myriad of colors in the atmosphere. |
| **Word analysis** | Breaking down words into roots, the meanings of individual roots, prefixes, and suffixes to determine meaning | prefixes, suffixes (un- = not, -able = having a quality of) un– defeat – able —not having the quality of being beaten | The home team was undefeatable in their tournament play. |

# Figurative Language

Writing that compares one person, place, thing, idea, concept, or characteristic to another in order to improve, magnify, strengthen, refine, and clarify meaning. **Figurative language** is any language that goes beyond the literal meaning of the words used. It is usually a word or phrase that departs from the everyday life literal language for the sake of comparison, emphasis, clarity, or freshness.

**Alliteration** is the repetition of consonant sounds that occur at the beginning of words or within words; it creates mood and melody, brings attention to important words, and points out similarities and differences. Example: The coffee cup was carefully cradled in her convulsing arms.

**Hyperbole** is an exaggeration or overstatement that may or may not be realistic and is not meant to be taken literally. Examples:

It was such a cold winter that even the penguins were wearing jackets.

I was so tired I spoke in snores rather than words.

**Imagery** is language that appeals to the readers' senses; it describes people or objects by using the five senses. Example:

> I walked calmly to the dark side of the moon where the winds of time blew softly through my hair.

**Idiom** is when words are used in a special way that is different from their literal meaning. Examples:

> steal one's thunder (to take the credit away from someone else)
> cut corners (to rush through a project or job just to finish quickly)

A **metaphor** is a comparison of two unrelated objects, concepts, or ideas without using the words *like* or *as*. Examples:

> The cloud was a soft pillow of down.
> Bryce's words were bullets flying at my heart.

**Onomatopoeia** is the use of words that mimic sounds. Examples:

> buzz, hiss, crackle, achoo, boom, zoom, poof, swoosh, whiz

An **oxymoron** is the combination of two words with opposite meanings. Examples:

> jumbo shrimp
> act naturally
> small fortune
> minor crisis
> freezer burn

**Personification** is giving a nonhuman thing (object, idea, animal) human characteristics. Examples:

> The tree fell with a silent, crackling cry of relief.
> My last chance just walked out the door.
> The wind sang melodically as it danced across the tops of the sleeping meadow.

A **simile** is a comparison of two unrelated objects, concepts, or ideas using the words *like* or *as*. Examples:

> The dog ran like a pinwheel in the wind.
> Her glance was as cold as ice.

## Social, Cultural, and Historical Influences

Language, both written and spoken, plays a vital role in building societies, cultures, cities, and countries. Socially, humans gather together according to understandings and beliefs about the things and events around them. People have the capacity to respond to these situations and events and social bonding is generated through discussion and understanding. Communication is strong before, during, immediately after, and long after an event occurs. The ability to talk, discuss, and respond to such events develops social, cultural, and community cohesion.

# Communication Skills

Communication is the ability to impart and share knowledge, opinions, ideas, feelings, and beliefs. Communication can be spoken or written, explicit or implied, simple or complex, positive or negative, and passionate or reasonable.

## Means of Communication

| Means | Definition |
|---|---|
| Symbolic names | Names identify people and places with groups, differentiate communities, and declare known and recognizable groups. |
| Specific vocabulary Jargon Lingo | Cultures and communities develop a characteristic vocabulary. Being able to use this specific vocabulary demonstrates membership within the culture and society. |
| Heroes and villains | People in groups tend to single out certain people to talk about. Some are praised and their actions endorsed (heroes). Others are condemned and their actions reprimanded (villains). Both reflect a society's values and beliefs. |
| Proverbs | A set of values or sayings that impart wisdom within a culture and guide the society in their actions. ("A penny saved is a penny earned.") |
| Stories Myths Histories | Every culture, society, and community has symbolic narratives. Knowing the stories identifies a person as a member of the group. Most tell tales of success in crisis, the growth of a hero, or the defeat of a villain. |

## Types of Communication

Communication occurs in a variety of forms within a culture and society. There are written and spoken, direct and indirect, explicit and implied forms. There are four ways in which a society or culture communicates:

**Encounters**—Day-to-day communications occur as people interact within their environment. Encounters take place at school, home, work, grocery store, gas station, library, mall, TV, over the phone, and on the Internet.

**Rituals**—These can be meetings or other established times to gather as a group to hold discussions. They are used to demonstrate unity (holidays) and in response to situations (rally or protest). Rituals can be determined by the clock or the calendar (Martin Luther King, Jr. Day) or by the events of life (wedding).

**Crisis**—This is a time that demands communication and attention. Society is forced to deal with a pressing issue or situation. The society must cooperate and respond properly to ensure success and cohesion.

**Deviants**—Encountering misfits or people who deviate from the accepted societal norms also cause society and cultures to communicate. Communities must identify deviant behavior and delineate the norms of society (laws).

## Aspects of Speaking and Listening

**Listening** is an active process that requires the listener to hear, understand, and judge. **Speaking** requires the speaker to be knowledgeable, confident, clear, and concise. Being a good listener and a well-articulated speaker is dependent on an individual's grasp of language.

There are three components to listening, which are essential to comprehension:

- **Hearing**—Being able to repeat a fact or concept that was stated
- **Understanding**—Being able to process the information heard, ask pertinent questions, and form responses to the information presented
- **Judging**—Being able to form opinions and analyze the information stated

When presenting information the speaker must consider four points:

1. **Subject**—What information is being presented and how (direct or indirect)?
   a. Informative
   b. Persuasive
   c. Entertaining
2. **Audience**—What are the backgrounds, needs, and wants of the people in the crowd?
3. **Themselves as a speaker**—What preparations need to be made?
4. **Occasion**—Does the subject fit the occasion; the time and place of the speech or presentation?

# Stages of Writing Development

There are eight stages in the development of writing. Writers must progress through each stage in order to fully comprehend language and evolve in writing:

1. **Scribbling**—Appears as a random collection of marks on a paper. The marks may be large, circular, and resemble drawings. The marks do not resemble letters or print but are highly significant as the young writer uses the marks to express ideas.
2. **Letter-like symbols**—Letter forms begin to emerge at times although still randomly placed, and numbers may be strewn throughout. The writer is able to explain and tell about the "writing."
3. **String of letters**—Some letters are legible and are usually written as a capital letter. The writer is developing an awareness of sound-symbol relationships but does not necessarily match the letter to the sound.
4. **Beginning sound emergence**—The message within the writing begins to make sense and matches the picture drawn with it. The writer is beginning to see the differences between a letter and a word, although spacing may not be apparent.
5. **Consonants represent words**—Spaces are becoming more frequent between words and lowercase letters begin to appear with uppercase letters. The writer begins to write sentences that express ideas.
6. **Initial, middle, and final sounds**—Sight words, familiar names, and environmental print are spelled correctly and are frequently used. Most other words are spelled phonetically. The writer is writing legibly and the written work makes sense.
7. **Transitional phases**—The writing is readable and is beginning to advance toward conventional spelling. The writer begins to use standard form and standard letter patterns.
8. **Standard spelling**—Most words are spelled correctly in this stage. Understanding of root words, compound words, and contractions is developing. The writer is able to decode words and spell using analogies of known words.

The writing process helps students organize their thoughts in a reasonable manner so that they may write in an effective and efficient manner. There are generally 6 stages in the process, with variants arising at each stage. Below is a table outlining these stages.

| Stages of the Writing Process | | |
|---|---|---|
| **Stage** | **Description** | **Techniques Used** |
| Prewriting | Generate ideas for writing<br>Gather details | Brainstorm<br>Read literature<br>Create life maps<br>Webs<br>Story charts<br>Word banks<br>Determine form, audience, voice |
| Rough draft | Write ideas on paper<br>Ignore conventions | Notes<br>Outlines<br>Webs |
| Reread | Proof the work<br>Fit purpose<br>Order details | Read aloud to self<br>Peer edit |
| Revise | Improve how information is presented<br>Improve details | Remove unneeded words<br>Add details and adjectives<br>Accept peer suggestions<br>Add imagery |
| Edit | Review writing for mechanics and grammar usage | Spell check<br>Grammar check |
| Final draft | Prepare final copy | Review, rewrite, and type final copy |

## Spelling Development

Children navigate through various stages of spelling. Each stage is crucial to the development of language acquisition as well as to good spelling habits.

**Invented spelling** is the attempts of a young child to spell words using his or her best judgment. The child can identify letters and relate letter sounds to words.

| Stages of Spelling Development | | |
|---|---|---|
| **Stage** | **Description** | **Example** |
| Precommunicative | When symbols are used to represent the alphabet; letter-sound does not correspond, no deciphering of upper- and lowercase letters | scribbles<br>(elephant)<br><br>$eolsy$ |
| Semiphonic | When letter-sound correspondence begins to arise; single letters are used to represent words or sounds or syllables; initial sounds are used first to spell words, then final sounds, and lastly, medial sounds | single letters (U = you)<br>(elephant)<br><br>$INT$ |
| Phonetic | When every sound heard is represented by a letter or group of letters; vowels appear at this stage and can be interchanged | –ed endings are often written with a "t" or "d"<br>"dr" and "jr" sound the same<br>"ch" is written as "tr" and vice versa<br>LFENT (elephant) |

| Stage | Description | Example |
|---|---|---|
| Transitional | When the child stops relying on sounds and mapping alone to spell words; vowels appear in every syllable; all letters are present in a word but may not be in the correct order; conventions and rules of spelling are learned (long vowels, doubling of consonants, and social conventions) | gril = girl<br>elefent = elephant<br>Jhon = John |

Following are some basic spelling guidelines:

- *i* before *e* except after *c* or when the sound produced sounds like *a* (n*ei*ghbor); exceptions to this rule: counterfeit, either, financier, foreign, height, heir, leisure, neither, seize, sheik, species, their, weird.
- Silent *e* at the end of a word means to drop the *e* before adding the suffix that begins with a vowel (state = stating = statement; like = liking = likable; use = usable = useful).
- If *y* is the last letter in the word preceded by a consonant, change the *y* to *i* when adding a suffix (hurry = hurried; happy = happiness; beauty = beautiful).
- One-syllable words ending in a consonant preceded by one vowel, double the final consonant before adding a suffix that begins with a vowel (pat = patting; god = goddess; hum = humming).

Mathematics is the academic discipline centered around concepts such as quantity, structure, space, and change. Math draws systematic conclusions and explains relationships among numbers, patterns, solutions, and problems. It is used in many fields ranging from medical to educational to science to business to engineering to economics. Math is apparent in daily living situations such as balancing a checkbook, calculating sales percentages, determining food portions, following a recipe, grocery shopping, figuring mixtures, and paying bills.

## Critical Thinking

Critical thinking is the process of conceptualizing, applying, analyzing, synthesizing, and evaluating information. The information being processed is gained through observation, reflection, reasoning, experience, and communication. Critical thinking is not a general or universal skill found among humans. All individuals experience and observe in unique and personal manners. Critical thinking is an ability that must be continually practiced and encouraged throughout life. In mathematics there are three types of reasoning associated with critical thinking:

- Deductive
- Inductive
- Adaptive

### Deductive Reasoning

This is the process in which conclusions are made based on prior knowledge, facts, and truths. It is a step-by-step process of drawing conclusions. Deductive reasoning is only valid and reliable when all the premises are true and each step follows the previous step logically.

For example, imagine you have lived in California your whole life and experienced many earthquakes. One day you are at the store when the shelves begin to shake and the ground buckles. You reason that an earthquake is occurring.

### Inductive Reasoning

This process of reasoning is based not on proofs but on observation. Inductive reasoning is drawing conclusions based on a set of observations. It does not provide valid or reliable conclusions, but is used instead to develop hypotheses or ideas. After the ideas are formed, systematic methods are used to confirm or deny the ideas.

For example, you observe an ice cream shop one summer day. You notice that bubble gum–flavored ice cream is ordered by children. You reason that children exclusively order bubble gum ice cream.

### Adaptive Reasoning

This process is defined as the ability to justify strategies and to analyze the strengths and weaknesses of solutions proposed by others. It is the capacity to think logically about the relationships between situations and concepts. This reasoning is one of the key components of mathematical proficiency as it allows students to think logically, weigh alternatives, and justify what they are doing.

# Problem Analysis

Problem analysis is the ability to apply and adapt a variety of mathematical strategies to solve problems. It can include being able to recognize needed and unneeded information, determining the algorithms best suited for obtaining a solution, having a strong number sense foundation, understanding the meaning and use of the numbers involved, and recognizing the strategies needed to solve as well as the reasonableness of the answer.

# Number Sense and Numeration

Number sense is the ability to understand numbers and their relationships. This skill develops gradually through experiencing numbers in a variety of contexts, exploring numbers, and relating numbers. Number sense should encompass all kinds of numbers (whole, fraction, decimal, percent, integer, rational, and so on). It is also the capability to progress beyond basic numeration concepts and the reading and writing of numerals. Number sense should include the following:

- **Relative magnitude**—The size relationship between numbers; is the number smaller, larger, close, or the same?
- **Real-world connections**—How do numbers affect our lives; where do we use numbers; what do you do with numbers?
- **Approximations and rounding**—Estimation skills are important for mental computations and verification of solutions.

## Types of Numbers

In the subject of mathematics, numbers obviously play an important role. Numbers can be used in a variety of ways to construct mathematical problems and equations. There are several different types of numbers, which are categorized according to the following:

- **Natural numbers**—The counting numbers: 1, 2, 3, 4, 5, 6, 7, . . .
- **Whole numbers**—All the natural numbers and zero: 0, 1, 2, 3, 4, 5, 6, . . .
- **Integers**—The natural numbers, the negatives of the natural numbers, and zero: . . . –4, –3, –2, –1, 0, 1, 2, 3, 4, . . .
- **Rational numbers**—All integers are rational numbers. They are also fractional numbers or fractions, any quotient of an integer divided by a nonzero integer: $\frac{1}{2}, \frac{1}{4}, \frac{4}{1}, \frac{7}{8}, \ldots$
- **Prime numbers**—An integer, greater than one that has only two factors, itself and 1; a number that can be divisible only by itself: 3, 5, 7, 11, 13, 17 . . .
- **Even numbers**—An integer divisible by two: $2n$
- **Odd numbers**—An integer that is not divisible by two: $2n - 1$
- **Complex numbers**—The numbers with "$i$" in them: $6 - 2i$ where $i^2 = -1$

## Meaning and Use of Numbers

"Number" is a broad and expansive concept that requires continual study and practice. Students must develop a strong foundation of numbers in early grades in order to support the extension of operations, large numbers, facts, and computations. Key concepts in using numbers include the following:

- Counting tells how many items or objects are in a set or group.
- Numbers are related to one another through a multitude of number relationships.
- Number concepts are intertwined and essential to the world around us as they help us make sense of the world.

Number development in early grades relates to the following:

- Relationship of more, less, and the same
- Counting
- Number writing and recognition
- Counting forward and back

General number relationships important to elementary children include the following:

- **Spatial**—Learn to recognize sets of items in patterns and without counting to tell how many items are present.
- **More and less**—Begin with the one and two more or the one and two less.
- **Five and ten anchors**—Useful relationships to know as 10 plays a large role in the numeration system.
- **Part-part-whole (PPW)**—Learn to recognize that a number is made up of two or more parts, as this will help students construct, deconstruct, and process numbers.

# The Standard Algorithms for Four Basic Operations

An algorithm is a routine process used to obtain a result to a problem without using extreme concentration, thus freeing the mind to focus on more difficult and important tasks.

## Addition

Carrying (regrouping) is the basic algorithm used in addition. Count by ones in the right hand column, tens in the next column to the left, hundreds in the next column to the left, and so forth. Once the sum of two numbers in any column exceeds nine (reaches ten), the amount over ten is kept in that column and the rest carried into the next column on the left.

24 added to 67

Adding the first column 7 plus 4 yields 11 or one 10 and one 1. The 10 is carried to the left and the 1 remains in the column. Then add the tens column, 2 and 6 and 1, which yields the sum of 9 tens. Therefore, the sum of 24 and 67 is 91.

## Subtraction

Borrowing (regrouping) is the algorithm for subtraction. Subtract the ones column first and if the subtrahend (number subtracted from another) is larger that the minuend (number to be subtracted from), a unit (10, 100, 1,000, and so on) must be borrowed from the column to the left. Then subtract the tens column, then the hundreds, and so on, borrowing as needed.

42 subtract 17

First, subtract the units column 2 minus 7. The subtrahend is larger than the minuend, so we must borrow from the tens column. 40 now becomes 30 and the ten borrowed is moved to the 2 to make 12. Now the units column becomes 12 minus 7, which yields 5. Then move on to the tens column, 30 minus 10 equals 20, so the difference of 42 and 17 is 25.

## Multiplication

The algorithm for multiplication is labeled long multiplication or grade-school multiplication. When faced with a multiplication problem, multiply the multiplicand by each digit in the multiplier. Knowledge of place values and careful positioning will help keep numerals in the correct spot. Once this has occurred, add up the results. This algorithm is based on three concepts:

- Place value system
- Memorization of multiplication table
- Distributive property of multiplication over addition

27 multiplied by 5

27 is 2 tens and 7 units. 7 units taken five times is 35 and 2 tens taken five times is 10 tens (100); therefore, 100 and 35 added together gives the final product of 135.

## Division

The division algorithm involves the quotient, remainder, divisor, and dividend. The algorithm here is long division. The divisor (how many times to divide) is divided into the dividend (the number being divided) to yield a quotient (answer). When dividing, the operation is conducted from largest place value to the smallest place value (left to right). Division requires a firm grasp on basic multiplication facts, subtraction, and place value.

5412 divided by 4

The 4 can be put into 5 (in the thousands place) one time, leaving a remainder of 1. The 4 (in the hundreds place) is then dropped down to make 14. The 4 goes into 14 three times: since 4 times 3 is 12, there's a remainder of 2. The 1 (in the tens place) is dropped down to make 21. Then 4 can be put into 21 five times for a product of 20 and a remainder of 1. Finally the 2 (in the units place) is dropped down to yield 12. The 4 can be divided evenly into the 12 three times with no remainder. Therefore the quotient is 1353.

# Appropriate Computations, Strategies, and Reasonableness of Results

There is no one best strategy for every student and every problem. Computation strategies used are based on the numbers in a problem, the background knowledge of the individual person, and the number of the relationships known. Strategies assist students in being able to clearly and concisely write down work and solutions, keep track of steps, check work, and allow others to understand the process that was used.

Mental computation places emphasis on the mental processes used to reach an answer rather than on physically writing to solve a problem. Being able to explain how one arrived at an answer and then compare that strategy to others is essential to building mental computation acuteness.

As students build up their ability to do mental computations, they begin to understand the reasonableness of results. Checking solutions to see if they seem possible is a higher order process as students must analyze and evaluate their solutions. Encouraging students to walk through their computations enables them to self-check (analyze) and justify (evaluate) their answers. A keen grasp of number sense is essential to the ability to determine reasonableness of results.

27 + 69 =

When looking at this problem, students need to use their number sense and critical thinking skills to estimate or approximate a reasonable answer. Students should recognize that 27 is close to 30 and 69 is close to 70 and determine reasonability from that knowledge.

It is not reasonable for students to say 27 + 69 = 120.

It is reasonable for students to say 27 + 69 = 100 (estimated answer)

# Methods of Mathematical Investigation

Mathematical investigations allow students to examine math situations using various techniques. This process of discovery helps students develop skills that can be applied to other problems. When approaching a mathematical investigation, students must use mathematical processes to understand and comprehend the problem.

Processes incorporated in mathematical investigations include the following:

| | | |
|---|---|---|
| abstracting | data collecting | hypothesizing |
| analyzing | evaluating | justifying |
| classifying | extending patterns | predicting |
| communicating | following patterns | proving |
| conjecturing | generalizing | symbolizing |

After students have developed the processes through mathematical investigations, they are better able to relay and apply the knowledge to new problems and situations.

# Number Patterns

A number pattern is a string of numbers that follow some logical rule or rules for the continuation of the string. Number patterns generally involve a progression of some form. The challenge of number patterns is not only to find and extend the pattern, but also to recognize a general rule that will produce the $n$th number in the pattern.

| Common Number Patterns | | |
|---|---|---|
| **Pattern** | **Name** | **Explanation** |
| 2, 4, 6, 8, 10, 12, . . . | Even numbers | $2n$ |
| 1, 3, 5, 7, 9, 11, . . . | Odd numbers | $2n - 1$ |
| 1, 4, 7, 10, 13, 16, 19, . . . | Arithmetic sequence | Add the same value each time; add 3 each time |
| 1, 4, 9, 16, 25, 36, . . . | Squares | Square each number in the pattern: $1^2, 2^2, 3^2$ |
| 2, 4, 8, 16, 32, 64, 128, . . . | Geometric sequence | Multiply by the same value each time; the previous number is multiplied by 2 |
| 1, 8, 27, 64, 125, 216, . . . | Cubes | Cube each number in the pattern: $1^3, 2^3, 3^3$ |
| 0, 1, 1, 2, 3, 5, 8, 13, 21, 34, . . . | Fibonacci numbers | The next number is found by adding the two numbers before it: $2 + 3 = 5$, $3 + 5 = 8$ |

# Place Value

Place value is a concept based on groupings of 10. It is an imperative concept for students to grasp, as it is the basic foundation for all mathematical operations.

| Whole Numbers | | | | | | |
|---|---|---|---|---|---|---|
| **Millions** | **Hundred thousands** | **Ten thousands** | **Thousands** | **Hundreds** | **Tens** | **Units** |
| 1,000,000 | 100,000 | 10,000 | 1,000 | 100 | 10 | 1 |
| 10 hundred thousands | 10 ten thousands | 10 thousands | 10 hundreds | 10 tens | 10 units | one |

Therefore, 78 is 7 tens and 8 units.

243 is 2 hundreds, 4 tens and 3 units.

**Place value** is also used for decimal concepts.

| Units | Decimal point | Tenths | Hundredths | Thousandths | Ten thousandths | Hundred thousandths | Millionths |
|-------|---------------|--------|------------|-------------|-----------------|---------------------|------------|
| 1 | . | .1 | .01 | .001 | .0001 | .00001 | .000001 |

# Equivalence

Equivalence is being equal in value or amount. Equivalences are used to demonstrate information in a variety of forms.

| Common Equivalences | | | |
|---------------------|---|---|---|
| **Simplified Fraction** | **Fraction** | **Decimal** | **Percentage** |
| $\frac{1}{5}$ | $\frac{2}{10}, \frac{3}{15}, \frac{4}{20}$ | 0.2 | 20% |
| $\frac{1}{4}$ | $\frac{2}{8}, \frac{3}{12}, \frac{4}{16}$ | 0.25 | 25% |
| $\frac{1}{3}$ | $\frac{2}{6}, \frac{3}{9}, \frac{4}{12}$ | $0.\overline{33}$ | $\approx 33\%$ |
| $\frac{1}{2}$ | $\frac{2}{4}, \frac{3}{6}, \frac{4}{8}$ | 0.5 | 50% |
| $\frac{2}{3}$ | $\frac{4}{6}, \frac{6}{9}, \frac{8}{12}$ | $0.\overline{66}$ | $\approx 67\%$ |
| $\frac{3}{4}$ | $\frac{6}{8}, \frac{9}{12}, \frac{12}{16}$ | 0.75 | 75% |

Note: The symbol $\approx$ means "approximately equal to."

# Factors and Multiples

Factors and multiples are used when comparing numbers and analyzing numerical value.

A **factor** is a prime or composite number that is multiplied to obtain a product. Factoring is the process of taking a number apart and expressing it as the product of its factors. A factor is a breakdown of a larger number.

Factors of 18 = 1, 2, 3, 6, 9, 18
Factors of 24 = 1, 2, 3, 4, 6, 8, 12, 24
Factors of 45 = 1, 3, 5, 9, 15, 45

## Factor Rules

1. 2 is a factor of ALL even numbers.
2. 10 is a factor of ALL numbers ending in 0.
3. 5 is a factor of ALL numbers ending in 0 or 5.
4. 3 is a factor of a number if it is also a factor of the sum of the individual digits found within the number.

$$65,331 \qquad 6+5+3+3+1=18$$
$$27 \qquad\qquad 2+7=9$$

5. 9 is a factor of a number if it is also a factor of the sum of the individual digits found within the number.

$$36 \qquad 3+6=9$$
$$89{,}172 \quad 8+9+1+7+2=27$$

6. 11 is a factor of a three-digit number if the middle digit is the sum of the two outside digits.

$$682 \quad 6+2=8$$
$$594 \quad 5+4=9$$

## Multiples

Multiples of a number are gathered by multiplying that number by a whole number.

Multiples of 3 are 3, 6, 9, 12, 15, 18, and so on.

Multiples of 25 are 25, 50, 75, 100, 125, 150, and so on.

## Least Common Multiples (LCM)

This is used when comparing two numbers. The LCM is a number that is a multiple of each of the two numbers being compared and is less than all other multiples.

6 and 4

The LCM is 12.

Multiples of 6 = 6, **12**, 18, 24, 30, 36, 42, 48, and so on.

Multiples of 4 = 4, 8, **12**, 16, 20, 24, 28, 32, 36, 40, 44, 48, and so on.

12 is the least common multiple because it is the least value multiple that both 6 and 4 have in common.

## Greatest Common Factor (GCF)

This is useful in solving math problems and also when comparing numbers. The GCF is the largest factor that divides two numbers.

24 and 32

The GCF is 8.

Factors of 24 = 1 and 24, 2 and 12, 3 and **8**, 4 and 6

Factors of 32 = 1 and 32, 2 and 16, 4 and **8**

8 is the greatest common factor because it is the largest factor that both 24 and 32 share.

# Ratio, Proportion, Percent

These three terms are imperative in not only mathematics, but in business and science as well. Each represents mathematical information in a similar manner yet each is distinct in its own way.

## Ratio

**A ratio** is a comparison between a pair of numbers. For example, if there are five dogs and three cats in a house, the ratio of dogs to cats is 5:3 or $\frac{5}{3}$ or 5 dogs to 3 cats.

## Proportion

A **proportion** is two ratios written with an equal sign between them; two ratios that are equal to one another (for example, $\frac{5}{3} = \frac{10}{6}$ or 5:3 = 10:6).

> The ratio of apples to oranges in a grocery store is 6:7, and there are 246 apples. How many oranges are there?

Set up a proportion.                                    $6 : 7 = 246 : x$

Write the proportion in fraction form.          $\frac{6}{7} = \frac{246}{x}$

Solve for $x$ using cross multiplication          $\left( \frac{a}{b} = \frac{c}{d} \rightarrow a \cdot d = b \cdot c \right)$

$6 \cdot x = 246 \cdot 7$

$6x = 1722$

Isolate the variable using division.          $x = 6\overline{)1722}$

$x = 287$

Therefore, there are 287 oranges in the store.

## Percent

Percent broken down means "per one hundred." A percent is represented by the % symbol. Percent can be written in three mathematical expressions; all are equivalent to one another:

$$\text{fifty percent} \quad = \quad 50\% \quad .50 \quad \frac{50}{100}$$

There are many ways to use percent in calculations.

> 1. What is 35% of 105?

35% of "something" requires a setup for multiplication. Simply stated, this means the percent multiplied by "the something." $(.35 \cdot 105 = 36.75)$

> 2. What percent of 105 is 36.75?

Set up the cross-multiplication fractions:

$\frac{x}{100} = \frac{36.75}{105}$  (cross multiply)

$105x = 3675$  (divide by 105 to isolate the variable)

$x = 35$

Therefore, $\frac{x}{100} = \frac{35}{100} = 35\%$

**3.** 18 is what percent of 20?

Divide the number you have by the number possible and multiply by 100% to obtain the percent:

$18 \div 20 = .9$

$.9 \cdot 100\% = 90\%$

**4.** A pair of shoes is on a 20% off sale rack. They have a sale price of $60. What is the original price?

The regular price is denoted by *x,* and the discount is 20% less than *x.* There is enough information to solve. The equation is written as follows:

$x - (0.20)x = 60$

$0.8x = 60$

$x = 60 \div 0.8$

$x = \$75$

Remember in the original equation, there is an invisible 1 in front of the first *x,* so it really states $1x - 0.2x = 0.8x$.

# Representations

There are many types of mathematical representations. A few types are mental representation, symbolic representation, models, physical representation, and numerical. Students should be able to do the following:

- Develop and utilize representations to organize, record, and communicate ideas.
- Choose, apply, and translate mathematical representations to solve a variety of problems.
- Use representations to model and interpret physical, social, and mathematical situations.

Mathematical representations help students do three things:

1. Identify the object.
2. Deduce some properties of the object.
3. Calculate something about the object mathematically.

# Calculator Strategies

The calculator allows students to solve problems that are both challenging and intriguing. The calculator is helpful in mathematics for all children as intellectual development is usually at a higher level than mathematical skill. Using calculators to support learning will help students develop a strong number sense.

Calculators provide the following educational supports:

- Support counting (skip counting—using the repeat function).
- Promote basic fact memorization (visual representation).
- Aid learning of place value (students can see the number on the screen in its column).
- Assist in computation (improves speed and accuracy and encourages self-reliance and autonomy).
- Show reasonableness of answers (allows students to validate their work).

# Number Lines

A number line is a one-dimensional illustration on which a list of integers is shown or placed at specifically indicated points, evenly spaced on the horizontal line. It is used as a tool for teaching addition, subtraction, and negative numbers. There are many variations on a number line, but normally each end has arrows depicting that the lines go on forever in either direction. "0" usually represents the origin and is placed in the middle of the line. Negative numbers are to the left of the 0 and positive numbers are to the right of the 0.

Number lines help students grasp the relationship between numbers and their relative magnitude.

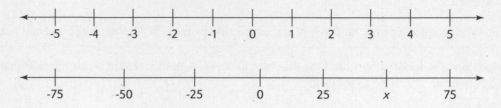

A child with number sense knows that $x$ is larger than 25 but smaller than 75.

# Algebraic Concepts

Algebraic concepts include expressions with numbers, variables, and arithmetic operations. It is a branch of math that studies structures, relationships, and quantities. Algebraic concepts at the elementary level introduce children to the fundamental ideas of adding/multiplying/subtracting/dividing numbers, variables, definitions of polynomials, factorization, and determining number roots.

## Algebraic Methods and Representations

Methods to solving algebraic equations and problems rely on the ability to represent unknown and missing quantities. Vocabulary is critical to understanding algebraic representations. Common phrases or key words alert students to the operations and skills needed to solve problems.

| Addition | Subtraction | Multiplication | Division | Equals |
|----------|-------------|----------------|----------|--------|
| more than | less than/fewer than | product | quotient | is |
| in addition to | decreased by | times | divided | are |
| exceeds | diminished | twice | separated | was |
| increased by | take away | of | distribute | were |
| altogether | difference | multiplied by | per | will be |
| sum | deduct | at this rate | out of | gives |
| and | Words that end with "-er" (heavier, faster, longer, shorter, father, and so on) | every | percent | yields |
| extra | | | ratio of | |
| combined | | | | |
| total of | | | | |

**Examples:**

| | | |
|---|---|---|
| 3 more than a number | = | $3 + x$ |
| 10 less than 5 times a number | = | $5x - 10$ |
| 2 times a number increased by 8 | = | $2x + 8$ |
| 4 less than a number divided by 3 | = | $\dfrac{(x-4)}{3}$ |

# Properties

There are four basic properties of number operation. Most mathematic systems/branches follow and obey these properties. Students must be familiar with these properties in order to solve algebraic problems.

## Associative Property

This property states that numbers can be grouped or regrouped in an operation in any manner without changing the answer; the order of the numbers or how the numbers are combined does not matter, the answer will always be the same. Both addition and multiplication are associative but subtraction and division are not.

### General addition property:

$$a + (b + c) = (a + b) + c$$

$$3+(4+6)=(3+4)+6 \qquad\qquad (-5+25)+10=-5+(25+10)$$
$$3+(10)=(7)+6 \qquad\qquad\quad (20)+10=-5+(35)$$
$$13=13 \qquad\qquad\qquad\qquad 30=30$$

### General multiplication property:

$$a \cdot (b \cdot c) = (a \cdot b) \cdot c$$
$$4\cdot(2\cdot6)=(4\cdot2)\cdot6 \qquad\qquad \left(\frac{1}{2}\cdot2\right)\cdot4=\frac{1}{2}\cdot(2\cdot4)$$

$$4\cdot(12)=(8)\cdot6 \qquad\qquad\qquad (1)\cdot4=\frac{1}{2}\cdot(8)$$

$$48=48 \qquad\qquad\qquad\qquad 4=4$$

## Commutative Property

This property states that numbers in an operation can change order without altering the end result; changing the order does not change the answer. Both addition and multiplication are commutative but subtraction and division are not.

### General addition formula:

$$a + b = b + a$$
$$60+15=15+60 \qquad\qquad (10+8)+(2+15)=(2+15)+(10+8)$$
$$75=75 \qquad\qquad\qquad\qquad 35=35$$

### General multiplication formula:

$$a \cdot b = b \cdot a$$
$$10\cdot5=5\cdot10 \qquad\qquad \frac{1}{2}\cdot\frac{1}{2}\cdot4=\frac{1}{2}\cdot4\cdot\frac{1}{2}$$

$$50=50 \qquad\qquad\qquad 4=4$$

## Distributive Property

To distribute means to share something or to deal out something (from the Latin *distribut*, meaning divided up). This property is used to multiply a single term and two or more terms inside a set of parenthesis. In math, this property is used to make equations simpler by distributing the value on the outside of the parenthesis to the terms inside the parenthesis. An easy way to remember this property is that it expands an expression into an equivalent expression.

## General formula:

$$a(b + c) = ab + ac$$

$$4(3+2) = 4(3)+4(2) \qquad 8(a+12) = 8(a)+8(12)$$
$$4(5) = 12+8 \qquad\qquad 8a+96 = 8a+96$$
$$20 = 20$$

# Transitive Property

This property states that when an operation is applicable between successive numbers in a sequence then it also applies to any two numbers taken in order; if $x$ is related to $y$ and $y$ is related to $z$ then $x$ is related to $z$.

## General formulas:

Whenever $a > b$ and $b > c$ then $a > c$.

Whenever $a < b$ and $b < c$ then $a < c$.

Whenever $a = b$ and $b = c$ then $a = c$.

For example:

If $5 > 4$ and $4 > 3$, then $5 > 3$.

If $3x + 2 = y$ and $y = 8$, then $3x + 2 = 8$.

# Additive and Multiplicative Inverses

The **additive inverse** of a number ($n$) is the opposite number or the number that when added to ($n$) results in a sum of zero. For example:

The additive inverse of $x$ is $-x$.

The additive inverse of 4 is $-4$ (because $4 + (-4) = 0$).

The additive inverse of 0.13 is $-0.13$ (because $0.13 + (-0.13) = 0$).

To calculate the additive inverse of a number, multiply the number by $-1$. $n \cdot -1 = -n$.

| Have Additive Inverses | Do Not Have Additive Inverses |
|---|---|
| integers | natural numbers |
| rational numbers | cardinal numbers |
| real numbers | ordinal numbers |
| complex numbers | nonzero whole numbers |

The **multiplicative inverse** for any number ($n$), except zero, is the reciprocal or a number that when multiplied by $n$ results in the product of 1. For example:

The multiplicative inverse of $x$ is $\frac{1}{x}$ or $x^{-1}$.

The multiplicative inverse of 6 is $\frac{1}{6}$ or $6^{-1}$ $\left(\text{because } 6 \cdot \frac{1}{6} = 1\right)$.

The multiplicative inverse of 0.25 is 4 (because $.25 \cdot 4 = 1$).

The multiplicative inverse of $-3$ is $\frac{1}{-3}$ $\left(\text{because } -3 \cdot \frac{-1}{3} = 1\right)$.

# Function Machines

Functions are expressed using words, graphs, equations, and tables. They describe relationships between sets of numbers and are often thought of in terms of input and output (algorithms). When a number is plugged in (input) to a function, and steps are followed, then a solution (output) is obtained. A function has two requirements:

**Consistency**—Every time the same input is plugged in, the same output is received.

**One output**—Each input will produce only one possible output.

Function machines allow students to picture algorithms/functions as little machines.

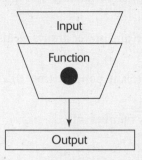

If you place a x = 4 into your machine along with the function of y = 6 + x, what is the outcome?

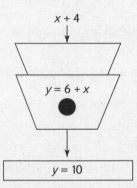

Not only can you work from input to obtain output, but you can also work inversely from the output to gain the input.

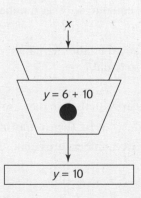

$x = 4$ because $10 - 6 = 4$.

# Properties of Zero and One

Zero and one are unique numerals. They possess special properties that no other numbers have. Here is a list of their important properties ($x$ = any number):

- **Addition property of zero**—Adding a 0 to a number does not change its value.

  $x + 0 = x$ or $0 + x = x$

- **Multiplication property of zero**—Multiplying a number by 0 always results in the product of 0.

  $x \cdot 0 = 0$ or $0 \cdot x = 0$

- **Multiplication property of one**—Multiplying a number by 1 does not change its value.

  $x \cdot 1 = x$ or $1 \cdot x = x$

- **Powers of one**—The number 1 raised to any power always yields the value of 1.

  $1^x = 1$ ($1^5 = 1 \times 1 \times 1 \times 1 \times 1 = 1$)

- **Powers of zero**—The number 0 raised to any power (except 0) always yields the value of 0.

  $0^x = 0$

- **Zero as a numerator**—0 divided by any number is 0.

  $\dfrac{0}{x} = 0$

- **Division by zero**—Any division problem with 0 as the denominator or divisor is undefined.

- **Quotient of one**—Any number other than 0 divided by itself equals 1.

  $x \div x = 1$

- **Additive inverse yields zero**—Any number added to its opposite equals 0.

  $x + (-x) = 0$

- **Multiplicative inverse yields one**—Any nonzero number multiplied by its reciprocal yields a product of 1.

  $x \cdot \dfrac{1}{x} = 1$

# Equalities and Inequalities

Equalities are relationships that indicate the expressions are the same on both sides of the equal sign without having to solve either side. There are six properties of equalities to remember ($x, y, z$ = any number):

- **Reflexive property**—Any number is equal to itself.

  $x = x$.

- **Symmetric property**—If one number is equal to another number, then vice versa.

  If $x = y$ then $y = x$.

- **Transitive property**—If one number is equal to another number and that number is equal to a third number, then the first and third numbers are also equal.

  If $x = y$ and $y = z$, then $x = z$.

- **Substitution property**—If two numbers are equal, then they are interchangeable in any situation.

  If $x = y$ then $x$ may be replaced by $y$; if $x = y + z$ then $x$ may be replaced by $y + z$.

- **Addition and subtraction property**—If two numbers are equal, then they will remain equal if the same value is added to or subtracted from them.

  If $x = y$, then $x + z = y + z$ or $x - z = y - z$.

- **Multiplication and division property**—If two numbers are equal, then they will remain equal if they are multiplied or divided by the same number (other than 0).

  If $x = y$, then $xz = yz$ or $x/z = y/z$.

Any mathematical problem containing <, ≤, >, or ≥ is called an inequality. Solutions to inequalities are any numbers that make the inequalities true. For example, 5 > 3 or 6 > 3 or 9 > 3.

**Addition principle for inequalities:** When the same quantity is added or subtracted to both sides of an inequality, the truth of the inequality does not change.

If $a > b$, then $a + c > b + c$.

**Multiplication principle for inequalities:**

If $a > b$ and $c$ is positive, then $ac > bc$.

If $a > b$ and $c$ is negative, then $ac < bc$. (Note the sign reversal.)

# Patterns and Algebraic Formulas

## Patterns

Patterns abound in the world. We use patterns to organize information that we see and hear, analyze data that we receive, and evaluate situations that we encounter. Recognizing patterns is an important problem-solving skill to help generalize specific concepts into broader solutions. Being able to find, describe, explain, and utilize patterns to make educated predictions is a vital skill in mathematics. Pattern recognition is dependent upon the individual perceptions of each person. Being able to communicate patterns effectively is an important concept to master. Algebra is a tool used to describe patterns in a universal manner.

Pattern recognition skills are as follows:

- **Finding**—Looking for repetition or regular features
- **Describing**—Communicating clearly and concisely
- **Explaining**—Determining why and how the pattern occurs
- **Predicting**—Foreseeing the next steps or future situation

For example, 15, 13, $x$, 9, 7, 5. . . .

1. **Find** the missing number—Look at the regular feature of odds.
2. **Describe** the pattern—The numbers are decreasing in a descending order by 2.
3. **Explain** the pattern—The difference between each number is 2, and every number is an odd number.
4. **Predict** the numbers—After recognizing a pattern, the missing numbers can be solved ($x = 11$).

## Algebraic Formulas

Algebraic formulas follow specific rules. Formulas are used in equation format, which helps state a fact or rule; formulas may use one or more variables. A formula can be solved for any of its variables by using equation-solving rules. Here are a few of the fundamental formulas needed to be able to solve problems:

- **Absolute value**—The absolute value of a number is never negative. If $x$ is greater than or equal to 0, then the absolute value of $x$ will be the same as its usual value. If $x$ is less than 0, then its absolute value will be opposite $x$'s usual value. Absolute value is notated by $|x|$.

  The absolute value of 3 is 3 or $|3| = 3$.

  The absolute value of –6 is 6 or $|-6| = 6$

- **Difference of squares**—$a^2 - b^2 = (a - b)(a + b)$

- **Distance formula**—Given the coordinate points on a plane are $(x_1, y_1)$, $(x_2, y_2)$.

  $$d = \sqrt{(x_2 - x_1)^2 + (y_2 - y_1)^2}$$

- **Fundamental theorem of algebra**—Every polynomial equation that exists must have at least one solution.
- **Laws of exponents:**

  $(a^m)(a^n) = a^{m+n}$

  $(ab)^m = a^m \cdot b^m$

  $a^{-m} = \dfrac{1}{a^m}$

  $(a^m)^n = a^{mn}$

  $a^0 = 1$

  $\dfrac{a^m}{a^n} = a^{m-n}$

- **Midpoint formula**—Used to find the midpoint coordinates on a plane with two points.

  $((x_2 + x_1) \div 2, (y_2 + y_1) \div 2)$

- **Negative exponents**—Any nonzero number taken to a negative exponent is the same as one over that number with the corresponding positive exponent.

  $x^{-y} = \dfrac{1}{x^y}$     Example: $6^{-2} = \dfrac{1}{6^2}$

- **Parallel lines**—Nonvertical lines in a plane with the same slope. The symbol for parallel lines is //.
- **Perpendicular lines**—Two lines in a plane with the product of the slopes equaling –1. The symbol for perpendicular is ⊥.
- **Pythagorean Theorem**—Used to explain the relationship between the lengths of the sides of a right triangle. The sum of the squares of the lengths of two legs ($a$ and $b$) yield the square of the length of the hypotenuse ($c$); given any two values of the three, the third value can always be found.

  $a^2 + b^2 = c^2$

- **Quadratic formula**—The standard form of a quadratic equation is $ax^2 + bx + c = 0$. The quadratic formula is a tool used to solve the equation. The roots of the equation will yield where the graph intersects the $x$-axis (except when the discriminant, what is under the square root symbol, is negative).

  $x = \dfrac{-b \pm \sqrt{b^2 - 4ac}}{2a}$

- **Remainder theorem**—When a number is divided, the dividend = quotient · divisor + remainder. This is used to check division solutions.
- **Slope**—Given two points, $(x_1, y_1)$, $(x_2, y_2)$, to find the slope ($m$) of the line through the points, use $\dfrac{y_2 - y_1}{x_2 - x_1}$.
- **Slope intercept formula**—$y = mx + b$ ($m$ = slope, $b$ = $y$-intercept, and $x$ = $x$ value, $y$ = $y$ value). The graph of this formula is a straight line.
- **Standard form of an equation**—$A$, $B$, and $C$ are variables, and $x$ and $y$ are unknowns.

  $Ax + By = C$

# Informal Geometry and Measurement

Geometry and measurement pervade the world around us. These math topics help students develop critical thinking skills, basic reasoning abilities, and knowledge of spatial relationship concepts.

## Real-World Properties and Relationships in Figures and Shapes in Dimensions

The field of geometry encompasses a wide array of topics. It is the study of properties and the relationships of points, lines, angles, surfaces, and solids.

# Figures and Shapes in Two Dimensions

A two-dimensional figure is also called a plane figure. It is defined as a set of lined segments (sides) and/or curved segments (arcs) lying within a single plane.

| Parts of a Two-Dimensional Figure | | |
|---|---|---|
| **Part** | **Description** | **Illustration** |
| Edges | The sides or arcs of the figure that are one-dimensional | |
| Vertices | The endpoints or corners of the figure that are zero-dimensional | |
| Angles | Formed when two sides meet usually at a vertex measured in degrees | |

Two-dimensional figures include the following:

| | | |
|---|---|---|
| chevron | kite | scalene triangle |
| circle | parallelogram | square |
| ellipse | rectangle | trapezoid |
| equilateral triangle | rhombus | |
| isosceles triangle | right triangle | |

**Polygons** are two-dimensional figures in which

- All edges are segments.
- Every vertex is the endpoint of two edges.
- No two sides cross each other.

Polygons are named and classified according to the number of sides they possess (which also equals the number of vertices). Polygons can be both regular (all sides and angles are equal) or scalene (sides and angles are unequal).

| Common Polygons | |
|---|---|
| **Number of Sides** | **Name** |
| 3 | triangle |
| 4 | quadrilateral |
| 5 | pentagon |
| 6 | hexagon |
| 7 | heptagon |
| 8 | octagon |
| 9 | nonagon |
| 10 | decagon |
| 11 | undecagon |
| 12 | dodecagon |
| $n$ | $n$-gon |

## Figures and Shapes of Three Dimensions

A three-dimensional figure is also called a **solid figure.** It is defined as a set of surface regions (faces that are two-dimensional) and a set of plane regions all lying within a three-dimensional space.

| Parts of a Three-Dimensional Figure | |
|---|---|
| **Part** | **Description** |
| Edges | The arcs or sides of the faces |
| Face | The surface region that is two-dimensional |
| Vertices | The endpoints of the edges that are zero-dimensional |

Three-dimensional figures include the following:

| | | | |
|---|---|---|---|
| cone | ellipsoid | prism | sphere |
| cylinder | ovoid | pyramid | |

**Polyhedrons** are three-dimensional figures or shapes in which

- All faces are plane regions.
- Every edge is a straight edge and the intersection of two faces.
- Every vertex is the vertex of three or more faces.
- No two faces cross each other.

Polyhedrons are classified and named by the number of faces they possess.

| Common Polyhedrons | |
|---|---|
| **Number of Faces** | **Name** |
| 4 | tetrahedron |
| 6 | cube |
| 8 | octahedron |
| 12 | dodecahedron |
| 20 | icosahedron |

# Pythagorean Theorem

The **Pythagorean Theorem**, also called the Pythagorean Formula, was discovered by the Greek mathematician, Pythagoras. This equation presents a simple relationship among three sides of a right triangle so that if the lengths of any of the two sides are known, the length of the third side can be found.

**The square of the hypotenuse of a right triangle is equal to the sum of the squares of the other two sides:**

$a^2 + b^2 = c^2$

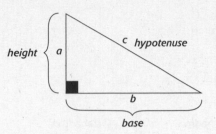

# Transformations

A **transformation** (transform equals "to change") is the general term for the ways to manipulate a shape or line or point. It changes the position of a shape upon a coordinate plane, places it in a different position but the shape keeps the same angles, size, area, and line lengths. The shape moves from one place (coordinate) to another.

There are three basic transformations:

| Name | Description | Illustration |
|---|---|---|
| Rotation (turn) | The shape is turned on a 360-degree axis from a center of rotation. | |
| Reflection (flip) | The shape is a mirror image. | |
| Translation (slide) | The shape moves by sliding to another area in the plane. | |

# Geometric Models

Geometric models are used to define and illustrate the shape and properties of an object in geometrical terms and concepts. Geometric models can be built for any object, any dimension, and any space.

# Nets

A geometrical net is when a three-dimensional shape is broken down into a two-dimensional or plane diagram. The edges of the net should never intercept. There are five regular solid shapes that can be broken into a net. They are known as the cosmic figures or Platonic figures.

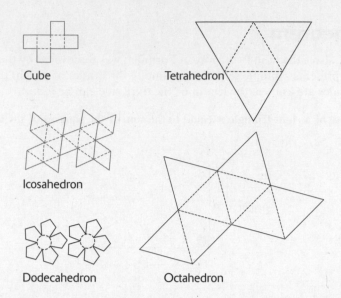

## Standard Units of Measurement

Students at the elementary level first learn measurement by using informal units of measure, but they soon advance to learning about the standard units of measurement. These involve using specific types of measuring tools, devices, containers, and units. They are used for measuring the length, area, volume, capacity, and weight of objects. The key for students is to understand what is being measured and what is needed to complete the task. Both customary U.S. and metric systems include various units that can be used in standard measurement.

### Metric Units and Conversions

The most common prefixes you will see within the Praxis II Elementary Exam and within schools are kilo-, hecto-, deka-, (unit), deci-, centi-, and milli-. It is easy to remember the order by using a simple sentence such as the following:

**K**ing **H**enry **D**oesn't **U**sually **D**rink **C**hocolate **M**ilk

The unit refers to the measurement you are using: grams (mass), meters (length), or liters (volume/capacity). Metric measurement is usually written using decimals and whole numbers. When converting between the various sized units you simply move the decimal point as you travel along the chart.

| kilo- | hecto- | deka- | unit | deci- | centi- | milli- |
|-------|--------|-------|------|-------|--------|--------|
| 0.001 | 0.01 | 0.1 | 1 | 10 | 100 | 1000 |

For example, convert 1000 mL to L.

Look at your chart and count the number of moves you need to make. You need to move three spaces to the left:

1.000 L or 1 L = 1000 mL

Convert 68.94 cm to kilometers.

Look at your chart and count the number of moves you need to make. You need to make five moves, which means moving the decimal point five spaces to the left and then adding three zeros for your space holders:

0.0006894 km = 68.94 cm

# Customary Units and Conversions

Customary measurement is what we use in the United States. Customary measurements are usually written in fractions and whole numbers. There are four categories for customary measurement: length, weight, volume, and time.

## Units of Length

Inches      Feet      Yards      Miles

1 foot (ft. or ') = 12 inches (in. or ")

1 yard (yd.) = 36 inches (in.)

1 yard (yd.) = 3 feet (ft.)

1 mile (mi.) = 5,280 feet (ft.)

1 mile (mi.) = 1,760 yards (yd.)

## Units of Weight

Ounces      Pounds      Ton

1 pound (lb.) = 16 ounces (oz.)

1 ton (T.) = 2,000 pounds (lbs.)

## Units of Volume/Capacity

Fluid Ounces      Cups      Pints      Quarts      Gallons

1 cup (c.) = 8 fluid ounces (fl. oz.)

1 pint (pt.) = 2 cups (c.)

1 quart (qt.) = 4 cups (c.)

1 quart (qt.) = 2 pints (pt.)

1 gallon (gal.) = 4 quarts (qt.)

## Units of Time

Seconds      Minutes      Hours      Days      Weeks      Months      Years

1 minute (min.) = 60 second (sec.)

1 hour (hr.) = 60 minutes (min.)

1 day = 24 hours (hr.)

1 week (wk.) = 7 days

1 year (yr.) = 52 weeks (wk.)

1 year (yr.) = 12 months (mo.)

1 year (yr.) = 365 days

## Coordinate Graphing

Coordinate graphing is a visual method for demonstrating relationships between numbers. Coordinate graphing uses a coordinate grid, which has two axes (perpendicular lines). The horizontal axis is called the $x$-axis and the vertical axis is called the $y$-axis. The origin is where the $x$- and $y$- axes intersect. A coordinate grid uses numbers to locate points. Each point is identified by an ordered pair of numbers: an $x$ coordinate and a $y$ coordinate. When writing ordered pairs, the $x$ coordinate always comes first and the $y$ coordinate is second. The pair is written in parentheses with a comma between the two coordinates: $(x, y)$.

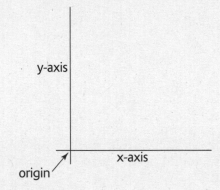

## Perimeter, Areas, Volume

| Rectangle | Perimeter | $P_{rect} = 2l + 2w$ |
| | Area | $A_{rect} = lw$ |
| | | $l = \text{length}$ <br> $w = \text{width}$ |
| Triangle | Perimeter | $P_{tri} = s_1 + s_2 + s_3 \text{ or } a + b + c$ <br> $s = sides$ |
| | Area | $A_{tri} = \frac{1}{2}bh$ <br><br> $b = base$ <br> $h = height$ |
| | Pythagorean Theorem (right triangle) | $a^2 + b^2 = c^2$ |
| | Angles | $\angle_1 + \angle_2 + \angle_3 = 180°$ |
| Square | Perimeter | $P_{sqr} = 4s$ |
| | Area | $A_{sqr} = s^2$ <br> $s = side$ |
| Circle | Perimeter (Circumference) | $C_{cir} = 2(\pi)r \text{ or } \pi d$ |
| | Area | $A_{cir} = (\pi)r^2$ <br><br> $r = radius$ <br> $d = diameter$ |

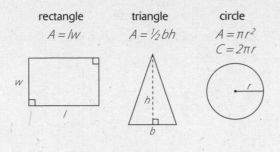

$(\pi$, or pi, is the number approximated by 3.14159 or $\frac{22}{7}$.)

## Volume

The volume of an object is measured in cubes and is the number of cubes that is required to fill the object completely.

| Common Volume Formulas | |
|---|---|
| **Shape** | **Formula** |
| Cube | $a^3$<br>$a = side$ |
| Rectangular prism | $l \cdot w \cdot h$<br>$l = \text{length}$<br>$w = \text{width}$ |
| Prism | $B \cdot h$<br>$B = \text{base area}$<br>$h = \text{height}$ |
| Pyramid | $\frac{1}{3}B \cdot h$<br>$B = \text{base area}$<br>$h = \text{height}$ |
| Cylinder | $\pi r^2 h$<br>$r = \text{radius}$<br>$h = \text{height}$<br>$\pi = 3.14$ or $\frac{22}{7}$ |
| Cone | $\frac{1}{3}\pi r^2 h$<br>$r = \text{radius}$<br>$h = \text{height}$<br>$\pi = 3.14$ or $\frac{22}{7}$ |
| Sphere | $\frac{4}{3}\pi r^3$<br>$r = \text{radius}$<br>$\pi = 3.14$ or $\frac{22}{7}$ |

**Volume**

rectangular solid         right circular cylinder

$V = lwh$             $V = \pi r^2 h$

# Rates

The **rate** explains a relationship between a pair of numbers. It is the amount of one thing needed to find the amount of another. To find the rate of speed, divide distance by time.

$$\text{rate} = \frac{\text{distance}}{\text{time}}$$

Rate is written as a fraction with the distance units as the numerator and the time units as the denominator.

To find **time,** use $\text{time} = \frac{\text{distance}}{\text{rate}}$.

To find **distance,** use distance = rate · time.

Be sure to keep the units organized and consistent. Sometimes, time will need to be converted in order to make the units match.

For example:

If a heart beats 152 beats a second for 4 minutes, what is the rate per minute? $d = 152$ and $t = 4$, so $r = \frac{152}{4}$ or 38 beats per minute.

If a car travels 65 mph for 7 hours, what is the distance it travels? $r = 65$ mph and $t = 7$ hours, so $d = 65 \cdot 7$ or 455 miles.

If a train travels 5400 miles at 90 mph, how many hours is it traveling? $r = 90$ mph and $d = 5400$ miles, so $t = 5400 \div 90$ mph, or 60 hours.

# Angles

An angle consists of two rays that share the same endpoint (vertex). The two rays are the sides of the angle. Angles are usually measured in degrees.

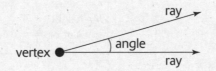

There are many types of angles:

**Acute angle**—Any angle that is less than 90 degrees but greater than 0 degrees.

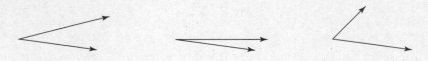

**Obtuse angle**—Any angle that is greater than 90 degrees but less than 180 degrees.

**Right angle**—Any angle measuring exactly 90 degrees. Two lines that meet at a right angle are said to be perpendicular.

**Complementary angle**—When two angles are measured, the sum of their degrees is equal to 90 degrees.

30 degrees + 60 degrees = 90 degrees

**Supplementary angles**—When two angles are measured, the sum of their degrees is equal to 180 degrees (straight line).

90 degrees + 90 degrees = 180 degrees

# Data Organization and Interpretation

Organizing data into a usable form and interpreting the meaning are critical skills to possess. There are many ways to record, organize, and communicate data. Students must learn how to use charts, tables, and graphs in order to better organize and interpret collected data.

## Visual Displays of Quantitative Information

Visual displays of quantitative information simply refer to different types of informational graphics that display measured quantities. These include but are not limited to the following:

| | | |
|---|---|---|
| illustrations | maps | 3-D computer graphics |
| diagrams | photographs | interactive models |
| tables | pictograms | charts |

Graphics (visual displays) are used to reveal data, often in a more precise and direct manner than conventional computations. The most common visual representation used in math is the graph.

| Types of Graphs | Description | Illustration |
|---|---|---|
| Line graph | Uses either vertical or horizontal lines to connect plotted data points. This graph shows change or information over a period of time. | 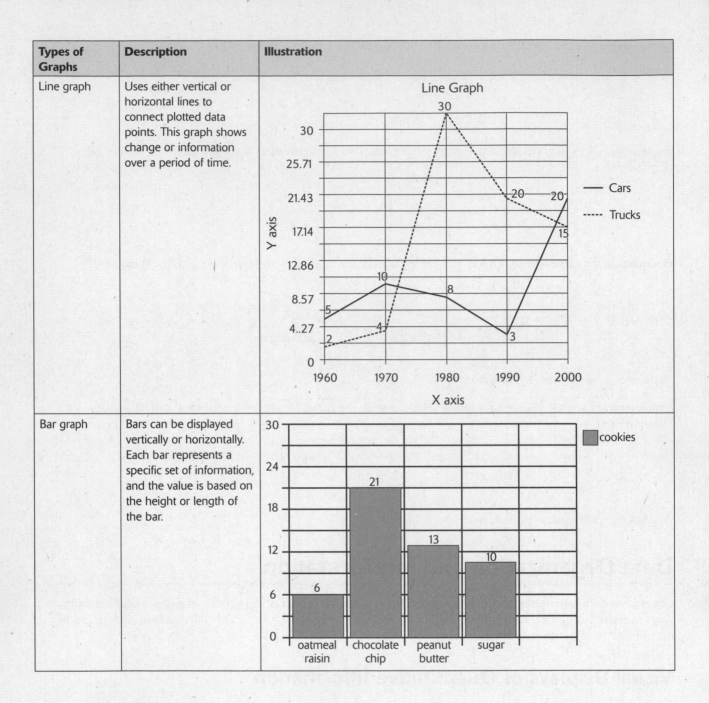 |
| Bar graph | Bars can be displayed vertically or horizontally. Each bar represents a specific set of information, and the value is based on the height or length of the bar. | |

| Types of Graphs | Description | Illustration |
|---|---|---|
| Pie chart | Has the shape of a circle and displays the information in relation to a whole. Data is usually shown in percentages. | 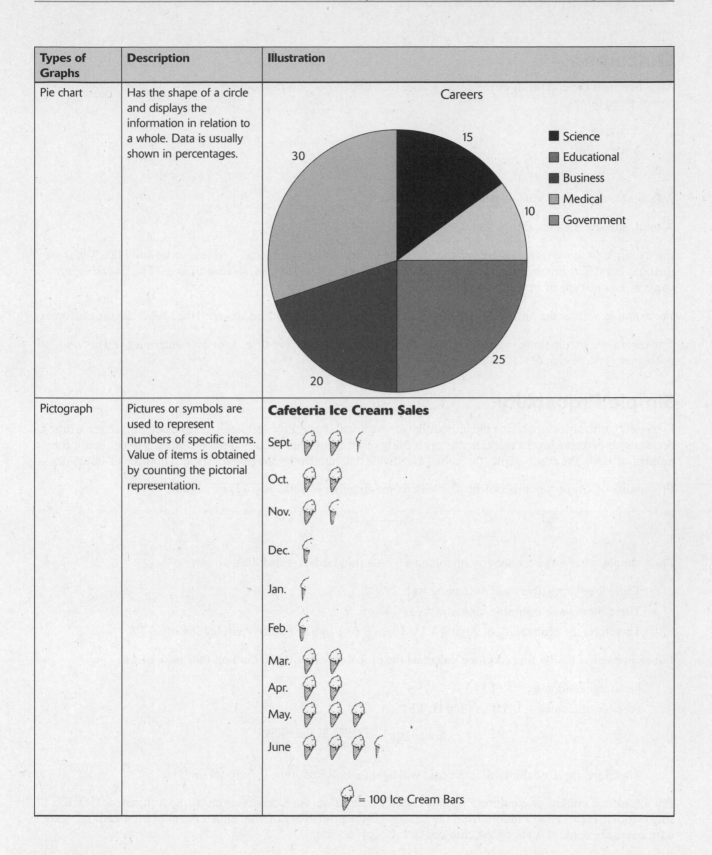 |
| Pictograph | Pictures or symbols are used to represent numbers of specific items. Value of items is obtained by counting the pictorial representation. | |

# Outcomes

An outcome is the end result or the consequence of a single trial of a random experiment. A possible outcome is one of three things:

1. A choice
2. A possibility
3. A result

A **favorable outcome** is what someone wants to happen.

A **total outcome** is all the things that could happen.

For example, at a restaurant, there are the following choices of drinks: coffee, iced tea, soda, and juice. What are the outcomes? The outcomes are the four choices of drinks: coffee, iced tea, soda, and juice. The favorable outcome is the one type of beverage chosen or desired.

For example, what is the probability of rolling an even number on a standard six-sided die? What are the outcomes?

The favorable outcomes are even numbers {2, 4, 6}. Therefore, there are three *favorable* outcomes and six *total* outcomes {1, 2, 3, 4, 5, 6}.

# Simple Probability

Probability is the measure of the likelihood that an event will occur. Probabilities are expressed as fractions, ratios, decimals, or percentages. To calculate the probability of an event when all outcomes are equally likely, count the number of times the event is true (favorable) and divide that number by the possible (total) number of outcomes.

Probability of Event = number of favorable outcomes/number of total possible outcomes

$$\text{Formula: } P_{\text{event}} = \frac{O_f}{O_p}$$

For example, what is the probability of rolling a 3 on a standard six-sided die?

There are six possible total outcomes = {1, 2, 3, 4, 5, 6}

There is only one favorable outcome = {3}

Therefore, the probability of rolling a 3 is 1:6 or $\frac{1}{6}$ or 1 to 6 or approximately .1666 or 16.7%.

For example, if a coin is flipped twice, calculate the probability that it will land on tails both times.

Favorable outcomes = 1 {TT}

Possible outcomes = 4 {HH, HT, TH, TT}

$$\text{Solve: } P_{\text{tails}} = \frac{\text{favorable outcome}}{\text{possible outcome}}$$

Therefore, the probability that the coin will land on tails each time is $\frac{1}{4}$ or 1:4 or 25%.

For example, a cookie jar contains 5 peanut butter, 3 oatmeal raisin, 8 chocolate chip, and 4 sugar cookies. If a single cookie is chosen at random from the jar, what is the probability of choosing a peanut butter cookie? An oatmeal raisin cookie? A chocolate chip cookie? A sugar cookie?

What do you know?

Outcomes = peanut butter (5), oatmeal raisin (3), chocolate chip (8), sugar (4)

Total number of cookies = 20

Probabilities: $P_{pb}$ = # of peanut butter cookies to choose from/total # of cookies = $\frac{5}{20} = \frac{1}{4}$

Probabilities: $P_{or}$ = # of oatmeal raisin cookies to choose from/total # of cookies = $\frac{3}{20}$

Probabilities: $P_{cc}$ = # of chocolate chip cookies to choose from/total # of cookies = $\frac{8}{20} = \frac{4}{10} = \frac{2}{5}$

Probabilities: $P_{s}$ = # of sugar cookies to choose from/total # of cookies = $\frac{4}{20} = \frac{1}{5}$

The outcomes in this example are not equally likely to occur due to the different values. The most likely outcome is chocolate chip and the least likely outcome is oatmeal raisin.

## Events

An event is the set of outcomes found within a probability; it is the occurrence (one or more outcomes) of a probability.

The probability of an event is written $P_{event} = \dfrac{\text{\# of ways an event can occur}}{\text{total \# of possible outcomes}}$.

For example, Megan grabs a sock from her drawer at random. The drawer has 6 white, 5 black, 4 blue, and 2 red socks. What is the probability she will grab a black sock?

One event of this probability is grabbing a black sock.

Another event of this probability is grabbing a white sock.

Another event of this probability is grabbing a blue sock.

Another event of this probability is grabbing a red sock.

Another event is grabbing a primary colored sock (red or blue).

To find the probability that Megan will grab a black sock, plug the information into the formula:

$P_{event} = \dfrac{\text{\# of ways an event can occur}}{\text{total \# of possible outcomes}}$.

5 is the number of ways the black sock can occur and 17 is the total number of socks (possible socks).

The probability that a black sock will be chosen is $\frac{5}{17}$ or approximately 29%.

## Sample Spaces

Sample space refers to the set of all possible outcomes of an event. The number of different ways something is chosen from the sample space is the total number of possible outcomes.

Since probabilities are fractions (decimals and percentages) of a sample space, the sum of the probabilities of all the possible outcomes is equal to 1. Therefore, the probability of the occurrence of a specific event is always 1 minus the probability that it does not occur. Within the sample space, the probability of any outcome is equal to the product of all possibilities along the path, which indicates the outcome on the tree diagram. Tree diagrams are discussed in the section below.

For example, a moose has 3 moose calves. How many outcomes in the sample space indicate the combinations of the gender of the moose calves? (Assume that the probability of male (M) and female (F) is each $\frac{1}{2}$.)

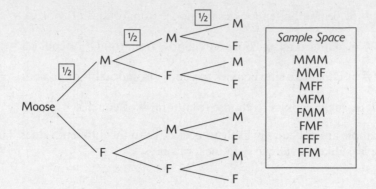

The probability of each outcome is $\frac{1}{2} \cdot \frac{1}{2} \cdot \frac{1}{2} = \frac{1}{8}$. (There are 8 outcomes in the sample space.)

## Counting Techniques

The fundamental counting principle, also called the multiplication principle, states that the total possible number of ways, in a sequence of events, for all events to occur is the product of the possible number of ways that each individual event can occur.

## Tree Diagrams

A tree diagram is used in math to decipher the probability of obtaining specific results. Tree diagrams are graphical representations that list all possible outcomes of an event. It helps organize the possible outcomes in an orderly manner beginning with event 1 and branching off into sequential events thereafter. Final outcomes are determined by tracing each branch to its end.

For example, a tree diagram shows the following possible outcomes when flipping two coins:

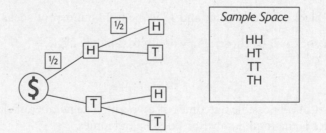

## Combinations

A **combination** is a selection of numbers or objects from a given set in which order is not important and there is no repetition.

$$C_{(n,r)} = \frac{n!}{[(n-r)!r!]}$$

$n$ = total number of objects     $r$ = size of selection     $C$ = combination

The ! symbol means a factorial; the number counted down multiplied.

For example, $5! = (5 \cdot 4 \cdot 3 \cdot 2 \cdot 1)$

1. How many different groups of 4 dogs can be chosen from a group of 15?

$n = 15$ $\qquad\qquad$ $r = 4$

$$_nC_r = \frac{15!}{[(15-4)!4!]}$$

$_nC_r = 15 \cdot 14 \cdot 13 \cdot 12 \cdot 11 \cdot 10 \cdot 9 \cdot 8 \cdot 7 \cdot 6 \cdot 5 \cdot 4 \cdot 3 \cdot 2 \cdot 1 \div (11)!4 \cdot 3 \cdot 2 \cdot 1$

$_nC_r = \dfrac{1307674368000}{(39916800)24}$

$_nC_r = \dfrac{1307674368000}{958003200}$

$_nC_r = 1{,}365$

In order to simplify the equation, reduce the fraction. You know that 11! is found in both the numerator and denominator so that can be eliminated from each:

$$\frac{15!}{11!4!} = \frac{15 \cdot 14 \cdot 13 \cdot 12 \cdot 11!}{11!4!}$$

$$= \frac{15 \cdot 14 \cdot 13 \cdot 12 \cdot \cancel{11!}}{\cancel{11!}4!}$$

$$= \frac{15 \cdot 14 \cdot 13 \cdot 12}{4 \cdot 3 \cdot 2 \cdot 1} = 1365 \qquad \text{There are 1,365 different groups.}$$

---

**2.** There are 7 colors of cars. How many different combinations of 3 cars can be chosen?

---

$n = 7$ $\qquad$ $r = 3$

$_nC_r = \dfrac{7!}{(7-3)!3!}$

$_nC_r = \dfrac{5040}{(4)!6}$

$_nC_r = \dfrac{5040}{144}$

$_nC_r = 35$

There are 35 different combinations.

# Permutations

A permutation is an arrangement of numbers (objects) in which order is important and there is no repetition. A factorial is a number that is successively multiplied down to the number 1, denoted by !.

For example, 5! is $5 \cdot 4 \cdot 3 \cdot 2 \cdot 1$.

The **Formula of Permutation** is

$$_nP_r = \frac{n!}{(n-r)!}$$

$n$ = total number of objects $\qquad$ $r$ = size of selection $\qquad$ $P$ = permutation

---

**1.** How many ways can 5 students from a class of 10 be lined up for a photograph?

---

$n = 10 \qquad\qquad r = 5$

$${}_nP_r = \frac{10!}{(10-5)!}$$

$${}_nP_r = \frac{3628800}{120}$$

$${}_nP_r = 30{,}240$$

The students can be arranged in 30,240 ways.

Reducing could also be used in the above problem by eliminating 5! from both the numerator and denominator and leaving only $10 \cdot 9 \cdot 8 \cdot 7 \cdot 6$.

---

**2.** How many three-letter permutations can you make from the word BEND?

$n = 4 \qquad\qquad r = 3$

$${}_nP_r = \frac{4!}{(4-3)!}$$

$${}_nP_r = \frac{24}{1}$$

$${}_nP_r = 24$$

There are 24 three-letter permutations for the word BEND.

# Mean, Median, Mode

Mean, median, and mode are used in math to determine three kinds of averages.

To determine the **mean,** add up all the numbers in the set and divide the sum by the number of numbers. For example, the mean of 3, 6, 9, 12, 15 is found as follows:

> $3 + 6 + 9 + 12 + 15 = 45$
>
> Divide 45 by 5 (there are 5 numbers in the set).
>
> The mean is 9.

To determine the **median,** which is the middle value in an ordered set of numbers, list the numbers in numerical order from highest to lowest or from lowest to highest. For example, the median of 5, 8, 3, 16, 12 is found as follows:

> Place in numerical order: 3, 5, 8, 12, 16.
>
> The median is 8.

If the set has an even number of numbers {3, 5, 8, 12, 16, 20}, add the two middle values together and divide by 2 to obtain the median $\left( 8 + 12 = 20,\ \frac{20}{2} = 10 \right)$.

The **mode** is the number that occurs most often. If there is no number that is repeated, then there is no mode. For example, in 1, 1, 2, 3, 5, 6, 10, the mode is 1.

The **range** is the difference between the greatest and least values. For example, the range of 13, 24, 7, 32, 29 is determined as follows:

> $32 - 7 = 25$

---

**1.** Find the mean, median, mode, and range of the following list of values.

21, 16, 13, 7, 5, 11, 2

---

Mean = (21 + 16 + 13 + 7 + 5 + 11 + 2) ÷ 7

75 ÷ 7 = 10.7 (rounded)

Mean = 10.7 (rounded)

Median = 2, 5, 7, 11, 13, 16, 21

Median is 11

Mode = There is no mode.

Range = 21 – 2 = 19

Range = 19

---

**2.** Chip is a racer in slalom snowboarding. He needs to maintain an average race time of 56 seconds to qualify for an event. In his last five races, his times have been 55, 58, 56, 54, and 59 seconds. What time does he need to get on his last race to maintain his qualifying average of 56 seconds?

Let $x$ represent the unknown value that is needed.

Set up the formula.

$$\frac{(x+55+58+56+54+59)}{6} = 56$$

Multiply each side by 6.

$$\frac{(x+282)}{6} \cdot 6 = 56 \cdot 6$$

Solve for $x$ by subtracting 282 from each side.

$x + 282 - 282 = 336 - 282$

$x = 54$

Chip needs to get a race time of 54 seconds to qualify.

# Chapter 11
# Social Studies Content Knowledge (0014/5014)

The National Council for Social Studies (NCSS) defines social studies as "the integrated study of the social sciences and humanities to promote civic competence." These social sciences may include anthropology, archeology, economics, geography, history, political science, religion, and sociology.

The NCSS believes that teachers need to provide students with the content knowledge, intellectual skills, and civic understanding to better prepare individuals to participate as informed citizens in an active democracy. The NCSS has provided the following statement regarding the study of social studies in the educational system: "The primary purpose of social studies is to help young people develop the ability to make informed and reasoned decisions for the public good as citizens of a culturally diverse, democratic society in an interdependent world."

The NCSS created 10 standards for social studies education that are used to clarify the concepts and core knowledge of this subject area.

These 10 standards are organized into themes related to social studies disciplines, and those themes include the following:

1. Culture
2. Time, Continuity, and Change
3. People, Places, and Environments
4. Individual Development and Identity
5. Individuals, Groups, and Institutions
6. Power, Authority, and Governance
7. Production, Distribution, and Consumption
8. Science, Technology, and Society
9. Global Connections
10. Civic Ideals and Practices

## Geography

The national standard that is reflected in this section focuses on the theme of People, Places, and Environments, which helps students understand the importance of location and aids them in developing a geographic perspective so they may decipher current social situations and conditions.

Geography is the study of places and encompasses four main components:

- Physical characteristics (for example, lands and vegetation)
- Geopolitical information (such as boundaries and capital cities)
- Demographics (for example, size, density, and population)
- Economic information (that is, agricultural and manufacturing)

Approximately 15 percent of the Praxis II elementary exam (0014/5014) assesses specific geography content knowledge that includes the following:

- Map skills and spatial organization of the world
- Places and regions of the world
- Physical and human systems

- Environment and society
- Uses of geography

There are five themes of geography pertinent to its study. These themes were developed in the early 1980s by the National Council for Geographic Education and the Association of American Geographers to aid in the organization and implementation of geographic study in schools. From this listing, the eighteen National Geographic Standards were designed in the mid 1990s. [See Chapter 4, "Social Studies Curriculum, Instruction, and Assessment (0011/5011)."]

| Five Themes of Geography Study | | |
|---|---|---|
| **Theme** | **Definition** | **Example** |
| Location | Where something happened; relative location (compared to another place) or absolute location (latitude, longitude). | The Rocky Mountain region of the NW; latitude 55° to 70° north. |
| Place | Physical and human characteristics of a location. | An arid climate in the Southwest provided few possibilities for growing crops. Therefore, early Native Americans developed irrigation devices to grow corn, using the resources of the desert (constructed adobe homes and used plants for food and medicine) to survive. |
| Interaction of people and environment | People adapt, modify, and depend on the environment, which can cause changes in the environment. | People in the Northwest created dams to maintain a water source to survive, redirecting the natural flow of the rivers. |
| Movement | How people, goods, cultures, and ideas move around the globe. | Tribes dependent on water sources may seek relocation. |
| Region | An area with similar characteristics, that include folklore, foods, and language. | Appalachia is considered a region since the people have preserved traditions and culture. |

# The World in Spatial Terms

This topic covers one of the national geography standards and suggests that students should learn how to use maps and other representations to acquire and use information about the world, as well as learn how to analyze the organization of people, places, and environments in the world. Geographers suggest that the combination of the aspects of the Earth's surface and the activities that occur on Earth are considered **phenomena.** These phenomena may be physical or human related or they may occur together. Understanding and using the proper geographic terminology becomes essential for students.

# Map Knowledge and Skills

A **map** is a visual representation of a particular area. A map can depict visible surface features such as rivers, coasts, roads, and towns, or underground features such as tunnels, subways, and geographical formations. Maps also show how information about physical and human features are located, arranged, and distributed in relation to one another. Maps are designed by topographers who use points, lines, symbols, and colors to define and describe areas.

Maps can be a mixture of objective knowledge and subjective perceptions. They can portray such abstract features as population density, lines of longitude and latitude, political boundaries, and agricultural products. Maps may be used to analyze the spatial organization of people, places, and the environment on the Earth's surface.

However, there are limitations to using maps. They cannot accurately represent a sphere on a flat surface without distortion of the distance, direction, size, and shape of water and landforms. Globes are one way to meet this problem, as they can illustrate the most precise representation of the Earth in size, shape, distance, area, and directions.

Examples of map types include:

- **Climate map**—Displays weather and typical climatic conditions of a region
- **Conformal map**—Presents land masses and the retention of proper shapes, but these maps are often distorted
- **Equal-area map**—Shows land areas with relatively proper sizes; however, distortion can occur
- **Fact-book maps**—Examines the actual facts of events or activities in certain regions or specific places such as life expectancy rates and energy consumption
- **Historical map**—Illustrates the people of an area and the population such as trade routes and religions
- **Mental map or sketch map**—Conjures a sketch in a person's mind and is constructed mentally without any particular references; demonstrates what a person knows about locations and characteristics of places
- **Outline map**—Shows some geographic features but does not include others
- **Physical map**—Reveals the features of actual geographical surfaces, such as mountains or rivers, and the underlying geological structures, such as rocks or fault lines
- **Political map**—Demonstrates government boundaries and territorial borders for major countries, states, territories, and provinces
- **Relief map or topographical map**—Exhibits a three-dimensional variation in the topography of land and water areas
- **Thematic map**—Demonstrates the location of specific ideas or distributions such as populations of children, languages of the world, and time zones

Following are some terms related to maps important at the elementary level:

- **Compass**—A tool used for determining specific directions on the Earth's surface
- **Compass rose**—The precise directions on a map or globe (north, south, east, west, northeast, northwest, southeast, southwest)
- **Coordinates**—Numbers or letters used on a map as a system to focus on finding specific locations
- **Direction**—A concept of space and location (right-left, up-down, north-south) to aid in reading map information
- **Grid**—A system on a more detailed map that shows the exact locations of places or landforms
- **Latitude**—The horizontal lines that run parallel to the equator and measure the distance in degrees north and south from the equator; based on 90° in each direction
- **Legend**—A listing of icons that explain what the symbols mean on each map
- **Longitude**—The vertical lines that run parallel to the prime meridian and measure the distance in degrees east and west from the meridian; based on a 360° system, but written as 180° in each direction
- **Scale**—The measurement used to describe the size of real objects represented on a map (miles, structures, and land masses)
- **Symbols**—The pictures or icons representing some item on a map (land masses, population), but the same icons and pictures are not consistently used the same on all maps

## Spatial Organization

Another component of geography is the ability to understand spatial relationships and the organization of people, places, and environments that exist in the world. In particular this knowledge includes knowing major areas and locations of the world and the specific terms that define examples of spatial organization.

The world is divided into sections and areas according to commonalities. These include continents, oceans, and regional areas. Examples include the following:

- **Seven major continents**—About 30 percent of the world is comprised of land mass, which is divided into separate continents, each unique to its area and its people. These continents are large and continuous plots of land usually separated by water. In order of size from largest to smallest, they are Asia, Africa, North America, South America, Antarctica, Europe, and Australia.

- **Five major oceans**—Oceans cover 70 percent of the Earth's surface and provide 97 percent of the world's water supply. In order of size from largest to smallest, they are the Pacific, Atlantic, Arctic, Indian, and Southern oceans.

- **Three major seas**—Seas are defined as large areas of water that are partly enclosed by land. The three major seas include the South China Sea, the Caribbean Sea, and the Mediterranean Sea.

- **Major deserts**—Deserts are land areas that are very dry and barren, mostly covered with sand and having specific plants and animals known only to that area. Some provide little possibility for human living conditions. The main deserts known in the world include Arabian, Atacama, Australian, Iranian, Kalahari, Namib, North American, Patagonian, Saharan, Sonoran, Takla Makan-Gobi, Thar, and Turkestand.

## Other Major Geographical Places

| Bays | Capes | Canals | Canyons |
|---|---|---|---|
| San Francisco Bay (U.S.) Bay of Pigs (Cuba) Hudson Bay (Canada) Bay of Banderas (Mexico) Chesapeake Bay (U.S.) Bay of Bengal (India) | Cape of Good Hope (Africa) Cape Horn (S. America) Cape Cod (U.S.) Cape Morris-Jesup (Greenland) | Panama Canal (Central America) Grand Canal of China Suez Canal (Egypt) | Bryce Canyon (Utah) Grand Canyon (Arizona) Waimea Canyon (Kauai) Chaco Canyon (New Mexico) Zion Canyon (Utah) Copper Canyon (Mexico) Hell's Canyon (Idaho) Canyon de Chelley (Arizona) Yarlung Tsangpo (China) Cotahuasi (Africa) Black Canyon (Colorado) Cheddar Gorge (England) |

| Gulfs | Islands | Lakes | Mountain Ranges |
|---|---|---|---|
| Persian Gulf or Arabian Gulf (Saudi Arabia and Iran) Gulf of California (U.S.) Gulf of Mexico (U.S.-Mexico) Gulf of Aden (between Red Sea and Arabian Sea) | Greenland Great Britain New Zealand Aleutian Islands, Alaska Hawaiian Islands Philippine Islands (7,100 islands) Venice, Italy (built on 118 islands) Caribbean Islands Galapagos Islands Falkland Islands British Isles Japan Azores | Great Salt Lake (Utah) The Great Lakes (U.S.) Caspian Sea (Iran) Tangan Yika (Africa) Victoria Lake (Africa) | Kangchenjunga (India-Nepal) Rockies (U.S.) Alps (Europe) Mount Everest (Nepal-China [Tibet]) Sierra Nevada (U.S.) Appalachian (U.S.) K–2 (Pakistan-China) Mount McKinley/Denali (U.S.) Matterhorn (Switzerland-Italy) Mount Cook (New Zealand) Kilimanjaro (Tanzania) Cascades-Mount Rainier (U.S.) |

| Peninsulas | Seas | Waterfalls | |
|---|---|---|---|
| Florida Italy Panama Baja (U.S.-Mexico) | Arabian Sea Black Sea Coral Sea Greenland Sea Red Sea Sea of Japan Tasman Sea | Niagara Falls (U.S.-Canada) Angel Falls (Venezuela) Barron Falls (Australia) Victoria Falls (Africa) Yosemite Falls (U.S.) | |

- **People**—The people of the world are diverse and offer a rich contribution to global unity. They live throughout the regions of the Earth's surface and sometimes are the primary means to defining an area. People are categorized in many ways in order to better describe them as related to their specific characteristics. Knowing information about the people of certain regions will help in understanding their relationships to the spaces of the world:

  Tribes (Navajo, Inuit, Aborigines, and so on)

  Cultures of people (Appalachians, Hispanics, and so on)

  Regions of people (Texas ranchers, Florida citrus farmers, and so on)

  Defined countries or states of people (French, Hawaiians, Filipinos, and so on)

Following is a list of individuals who study geography:

- **Anthropologist**—Studies the history of people such as their culture and language
- **Cartographer**—Studies the science or practice of map drawing
- **Geographer**—Studies land formations and the Earth's composition
- **Meteorologist**—Studies climates and the affects upon the Earth
- **Sociologists**—Studies the behaviors of people and how they impact the world
- **Topographer**—Designs, describes, and develops maps

# Places and Regions

Places and regions help humans understand and function in a global community. Land masses may be separated into enormous areas (places and regions), which espouse specifically defined characteristics. These two important features of geography help students learn about the world one area at a time as the concepts help delineate the various areas of the world according to sets of traits or qualities. Understanding the differences that set regions and places apart can also lead to understanding of interactions at the global level.

A **region** is a geographical unit of measure and is defined as a specific area consisting of unifying characteristics. Each region exudes unique and distinct attributes related to both the human and physical characteristics of the area. Boundaries between regions can often be vague, ambiguous, and generalized. Regions can also vary greatly in size; they can be as large as a continent or as small as a neighborhood or classroom. Regions may be described according to three types:

- **Formal**—Defined in two ways through either common human features such as language, religion, nationality, or culture (for example, the cattle ranches of Texas and the Four Corners region) or common physical features such as climate, landform, or vegetation (for example, the Mediterranean climate and the wine country of California).
- **Functional**—Organized around a central hub with the surrounding areas connected to the center by transportation systems, communication systems, manufacturing, or trading. The most common functional region is a metropolitan area. For example, Sydney, Australia, is linked by an established harbor area with commuting patterns, trade flows, TV and radio broadcasting, newspapers, travel, and goods commencing in this one region.
- **Perceptual**—Constructed around human feelings and attitudes of the area, these regions are defined by peoples' subjective images of an area and can be based on biases and stereotypes that may be incorrect or inappropriate. For example, the Appalachian region of the United States is perceived as an isolated, rural area, where the people are modest, appear undereducated, exhibit chronic poverty, promote oral traditions, and entertain strong religious beliefs.

Regions are cultural groupings not dependent on government or political rule. They are formed by a common history and geography as well as shaped by economics, literature, and folklore. Within each region, there are unique demographics, dialects, languages, and attitudes based on heritage and geography.

According to the United States Embassy, there are six regions of the United States. Several states comprise each region with special landforms, people, climates, and resources:

- **New England**—Connecticut (CT), Maine (ME), Massachusetts (MA), New Hampshire (NH), Rhode Island (RI), Vermont (VT)
- **Mid-Atlantic**—Delaware (DE), Maryland (MD), New Jersey (NJ), New York (NY), Pennsylvania (PA)
- **The South**—Alabama (AL), Arkansas (AR), Florida (FL), Georgia (GA), Kentucky (KY), Louisiana (LA), Mississippi (MS), North Carolina (NC), South Carolina (SC), Tennessee (TN), Virginia (VA), West Virginia (WV)
- **The Midwest**—Illinois (IL), Indiana (IN), Iowa (IA), Kansas (KS), Michigan (MI), Minnesota (MN), Missouri (MO), Nebraska (NE), North Dakota (ND), Ohio (OH), South Dakota (SD), Wisconsin (WI)
- **The Southwest**—Arizona (AZ), New Mexico (NM), Oklahoma (OK), Texas (TX)
- **The West**—Alaska (AK), Colorado (CO), California (CA), Hawaii (HI), Idaho (ID), Montana (MT), Nevada (NV), Oregon (OR), Utah (UT), Washington (WA), Wyoming (WY)

**Place** is defined as the physical and human characteristics of a location. Places are generally large sections created by humans on the surface of the Earth. Each place possesses a certain bordered area, whether specific or imaginary, in which meaning has been allocated by the humans who reside there. Some examples of place include continents, islands, countries, states, territories, cities, neighborhoods, and villages. Because each place has a name, boundary, and a specific set of characteristics, it is set apart from others and seen as an individual entity. Places can change due to evolving human characteristics as well as the restructuring of the physical characteristics in an area. Since places are defined and generated by humans, people gain a sense of self based on where they reside.

Two categories are used to define a place or region: physical characteristics and human characteristics. **Physical characteristics** can include water systems, animal life, plant life, landforms, and climate. **Human characteristics** can consist of values, religious beliefs, language systems, political structures, economic methods, and socioeconomic status.

## Physical Characteristics

The Earth's surface is riddled with unique features that set it apart from other planets. Physical features are visible characteristics or attributes. Basic categories of physical features are landforms, bodies of water, vegetation, soil, and climate. Physical characteristics studied in geography are the natural features of the Earth. These may include elements found on the Earth in a natural state such as animals, plants, and landforms (mountains, rivers, and so on). Following is a list of terms students need to know to study landforms:

- **Archipelago:** A chain or group of islands in a sea or ocean
- **Atoll:** A ring or partial ring of coral that forms an island in a sea or ocean
- **Bluff:** A cliff with a broad face
- **Butte:** A high, isolated flattop rock or hill with steep sides formed by the impact of tectonic plates
- **Canyon:** A deep valley carved by a river with very steep sides; includes a deep gorge with a running stream or river
- **Cape:** A narrow pointed piece of land that juts out from a coastline into a body of water
- **Cave:** A large hole or hollow in the ground or side of a mountain
- **Cavern:** A cave that is especially large, dark, and deep
- **Cliff:** A high, steep face of rock and soil
- **Col:** A mountain pass; a depression in the summit line of a chain of mountains
- **Continent:** A large mass of land, of which there are seven on Earth, that covers a specific area of the Earth's surface
- **Delta:** A flat silt, sand, and rock area that is formed at the mouth of a river and often shaped like a triangle; often produces fertile soil
- **Desert:** A very dry barren area with little to no rainfall; mostly sand covered

- **Dunes:** A hill or ridge made of sand and shaped by wind
- **Equator:** An imaginary circle around the Earth halfway between the poles that divides the Northern and Southern hemispheres; 0° latitude
- **Hill:** A raised area or mound of land smaller than a mountain
- **Island:** A small area of land surrounded by water on all sides
- **Isle:** A small island or peninsula
- **Islet:** A small island, usually isolated
- **Isthmus:** A narrow strip of land connecting two larger pieces of land with water on two sides
- **Mesa:** An isolated land or hill usually in a dry area with a flat top and steeply sloping sides
- **Mountain:** A very tall natural place on Earth that rises above the surrounding levels of land
- **Peninsula:** A body of land surrounded by water on three sides
- **Pinnacle:** The highest point of rock, ice, or land
- **Plains:** A flat land area with very small changes in elevation, most often a level track of treeless country
- **Plateau:** A flat area of land higher than the surrounding area
- **Prairie:** A wide, flat area of land with grasses and a few trees
- **Summit:** The highest point of a mountain
- **Tundra:** A cold, treeless area, considered the coldest biome
- **Valley:** A low place between mountains
- **Volcano:** A mountainous vent of the Earth's crust where lava, steam, or gases may erupt in intervals
- **Wetland:** A damp area of land often with wet soil that is low in oxygen (swamp, riparian, bog, moor, peatland, mire, fen, marsh, slough)

Following is a list of terms important to the study of water:

- **Bay:** An area of water smaller than a gulf that is partly enclosed by land
- **Canal:** An artificial waterway constructed for irrigation, drainage, river overflows, water supplies, communication, or navigation
- **Channel:** A body of water that connects two larger bodies of water
- **Cove:** A horseshoe-shaped body of water along the coast surrounded by land formed of soft rock
- **Estuary:** The location where a river meets the sea or ocean
- **Fjord:** A long narrow sea inlet bordered by steep cliffs
- **Geyser:** A natural hot spring in which water boils intermittently and shoots streams of water and steam into the air
- **Glacier:** A slow-moving river of ice
- **Gulf:** A part of an ocean or sea larger than a bay that is partly surrounded by land
- **Lagoon:** A shallow body of water located alongside a coast
- **Marsh:** A freshwater, brackish water, or saltwater wetland with plants growing out of the water found along rivers, ponds, lakes, and coasts
- **Ocean:** A large body of salt water that surrounds a continent
- **Pond:** A body of water smaller than a lake that is surrounded by land on all sides
- **River:** A large flowing body of water that empties into a sea or ocean
- **Sea:** A large body of salt water connected to an ocean, partly or completely surrounded by land
- **Sound:** A wide inlet of sea or ocean that is parallel to the coastline; it separates coastlines from nearby islands
- **Strait:** A narrow body of water that connects two larger bodies of water
- **Swamp:** A type of freshwater wetland that consists of spongy, muddy land full of water

- **Tributary:** A stream or river that flows into a larger waterway
- **Waterfall:** A waterway created when a river falls steeply off a cliff

**Climate** is the long-term pattern of weather in a specific area on Earth. Climate determines what plants and animals will survive in a region. There are five primary climates:

1. **Tropical**—High temperatures year-round with large amounts of rain
2. **Dry**—Limited rain with wide daily temperature ranges (semiarid and arid)
3. **Temperate**—Warm and dry summers with cool and wet winters
4. **Cold (continental)**—Seasonal temperatures that vary widely with low overall precipitation; found on the interior of large land masses
5. **Polar**—Extremely cold with permanent ice and tundra present

A **biome** is a large geographical area of distinctive plant life and animal life groups that have adapted to that particular environment. A region's biome is determined by climate and geography. There are nine major biomes:

| Name | Climate | Description |
| --- | --- | --- |
| Alpine | Snow, high winds, ice, and cold | Mountain regions around the world with an altitude of 10,000 feet or above and lies below the snow line of a mountain. |
| Chaparral (deserts) | Hot and dry (fire and droughts are common) | Located on most continents (west coast of U.S., west coast of South America, Cape Town region of South Africa, western tip of Australia, and the coastal area of the Mediterranean) with flat plains, rocky hills, and mountain slopes. |
| Deciduous forest | Four separate seasons: spring summer, fall, and winter | Generally located near an ocean, which aids in the wind and precipitation. Found throughout the world (eastern half of North America, Central Europe, Southeast Asia, southern part of South America, southeast coast of Australia, all of New Zealand). |
| Desert | Two types: a) hot and dry with little rainfall b) extreme cold and snow, mostly barren | a) Located in the Tropic of Cancer and the Tropic of Capricorn, b) Found near the Arctic. |
| Grassland | Two types: a) tall grass, humid, and very wet b) short grass, dry and hot summers, with cold winters | With large rolling terrains of grasses, flowers and herbs, also known as prairies; located in the interior of continents and in the middle latitudes. |
| Rain forest (Rain forests produce 40 percent of the Earth's oxygen.) | Year-round warmth and high rainfall levels | Almost all lie near the equator, located in northern South America, central Africa, and southern Asia. |
| Savanna (near the equator and around the edges of tropical rainforests) | Warm temperatures year-round with two seasons a) winter (long and dry) b) summer (short and wet) | With rolling grasslands and scattered shrubs and isolated trees found in Africa (Serengeti Plains-Tanzania), South America, northern Australia, and India. |
| Taiga (boreal forest) (the largest biome in the world) | Winters are cold with much snow and summers are warm, humid, and rainy | With a needle-leaf forest that is cold and barren; stretches across northern Europe to northern Asia and northern North America (Alaska and Canada) located at the top of the planet just below the tundra biome. |
| Tundra (world's coldest and driest biome) | Cold, dark winters with soggy, warm summers in which the sun shines 24 hours each day | A vast and treeless area covering the northern part of the world from latitude 55° to 70° north; located in the Northern Hemisphere; the ground is permanently frozen and trees cannot grow. |

# Human Characteristics

**Human characteristics** support the study of physical characteristics in geography as they comprise all that is people-centered. It can consist of man-made structures (such as buildings), values, religious beliefs, language systems, political structures, economic methods, and socioeconomic status. Human characteristics may be especially impacted in a particular area or specific region. In these places this may include the clothing, diet, shelter, transportation, monetary use, social organization, and employment of the people.

As an example, students can study a certain tribe in a particular region of the world. The Inuit people of the Arctic region in North America (Canada, Greenland, and Alaska) traditionally are of short stature and wear heavy clothing made of thick animal skins and furs. They live in homes made of ice blocks or stones covered with moss. They must hunt for food and may eat fish, seal, and walrus. They travel by kayak, dog sled, and by foot. The monetary system consists of the trading of furs, ivory, and arts. They have a social organization that is comprised of a strong family structure of multiple generations in the same homes. Employment for the Inuit is quite limited.

# Physical and Human Systems

A **system** is a set of connected parts functioning together. There are two primary systems critical to the ongoing changes on the Earth: physical systems and human systems.

## Physical Systems

Physical systems, which are comprised of processes, shape the Earth's surface and interact with plant and animal life to create, maintain, and change the ecosystems. For example, changes in the Earth's surface may occur due to the following physical systems conditions: tsunami, earthquake, volcano, typhoon, hurricane, water or wind erosion, and weathering.

There are five concepts that explain the interaction and impact of physical processes on the Earth:

1. System
2. Boundary
3. Force
4. State of equilibrium
5. Threshold (point of change)

For example, the Water Cycle (system) occurs between the hydrosphere and atmosphere (boundaries). Gravity (force) pulls the water down to the Earth's surface. Friction (force) erodes the Earth's surface, causing new landforms. After the water evaporates, it condensates in the atmosphere and is released back to the Earth (equilibrium). When the condensation that saturates the atmosphere is too much, the atmosphere releases the water (threshold is reached). After the rain, the cycle begins again (equilibrium).

An ecosystem is a key element in the viability of Earth as a home. Populations of different plants and animals are called a **community.** When a community interacts with the three components of a physical environment it is called an **ecosystem,** which is an interwoven infrastructure that produces and consumes energy.

The physical, chemical, and biological cycles, functioning within an ecosystem, form the different environments on Earth. When changes occur to one ecosystem, other ecosystems may be drastically affected, positively or negatively. Ecosystems can maintain a natural stability and balance when left to function on their own. However, the balance of an ecosystem can be significantly changed by natural events, such as flooding or fire. When they are transformed, ecosystems can either recover and flourish or diminish and disappear.

The primary change an ecosystem experiences is through the impact of the human factor. For example, the Glen Canyon Dam reduced the amount of water flow and sediment that the Colorado River carries, thus destroying the ability to arrive at the delta in the Gulf of California. Before the dam, the water was warm and muddy with bottom-feeding fish. With the dam, the river is clear and cold with trout, which caused the migration pattern of the bald eagle to change. Non-native species of animals and plants have been established, which adversely affected native wildlife.

There are four physical processes that mold the shape of the Earth's surface. The Earth's landscape is constantly reshaped by this complex group of symbiotic physical processes:

- **Atmosphere** (air)—Climate and meteorology
- **Lithosphere** (ground and surface)—Rock formation, soil formation, plate tectonics, and erosion
- **Hydrosphere** (water)—Water Cycle, currents of rivers, and tides of oceans
- **Biosphere** (life)—Ecosystems, habitats, and plant and animal realm

## Human Systems

The interdependency of both the physical systems and human systems affect the Earth's environment. People affect the planet's topography, soils, vegetation, and ecosystems as well as the available natural resources. Humans rarely live isolated from other humans. It is the human condition to organize groups of others to live and function within settlements. These settlements focus on economic, communication, transportation, political, and cultural systems. Settlements are not the same around the world and represent cultural differences across the Earth's surface. Spatial organization is essential to these units, the most familiar being a city.

There are three primary ways that humans impact Earth:

1. By consuming natural resources and changing natural patterns
2. By building structures
3. By competing for control

This planet has a limited amount of resources, all of which are not all available on every continent. No one country is able to produce all of the resources necessary to survive. Due to this lack of natural resources, the people of continents, regions, and countries must communicate and trade with one another. This promotes the **consumption of natural resources** from one area to use in another, **changing the natural patterns** on the Earth. Meeting resource demands in the world causes a great toll on the Earth's physical systems.

In the early period of development across the Earth, humans began to establish places to live that affected both the physical and human systems of an area. Then as humans began to interact and live together, larger settlements sprouted, which led to the increased need for economic activity. These settlements were based on the specific region that was important to the natural resources, transportation, or the cultural systems. **Building structures** developed in order to produce and establish settlements that were conducive to meeting human needs. This created a change in the Earth's surface and impacted a variety of ecosystems. For example, the increase in construction caused deforestation, an overuse of a natural resource that destroyed a natural landform (a forest area) and an entire ecosystem (deciduous forest-animals-lands-weather).

The third way that humans have influence upon the Earth is through their participation in conflicts. As they **compete for control,** conflicts often revolve around the management of resources, the acquisition of land, the organization of transportation and migratory routes, and power over other people. These conflicts very often result in the division and the destruction of the Earth's surface.

The results of these three methods of human interactions result in

- Population growth.
- Urbanization increases.

- Consumption of natural resources (oil, gas, water, coal).
- Migration of humans (reshapes landscape and modifies cultures).

# Environment and Society

An environment impacts and affects human society. It also has influences upon itself. Natural disasters are not caused by humans but can have harmful consequences for humans and the environment. Volcanoes, earthquakes, floods, tsunamis, forest fires, tornadoes, insect plagues, and hurricanes are mostly unpreventable and unpredictable. The harmful impact that these natural disasters have upon humans can be lessened through improved construction design, public education, warning systems, and regulations of land usage.

Environments have a carrying capacity. Each environment or region differs in its capacity to withstand and sustain use. Environments, like ecosystems, must have equilibrium and balance between consumption and production.

Humans play an essential role in the structure and transformation of the environment in which they live. Human interactions have intended and unintended repercussions on Earth. Their influences may cause deforestation, loss of wildlife habitat, redirection of water to arid lands, transplantation of non-native vegetation, depletion of the ozone layer, and reduction of air pollution in some regions.

Human survival depends on the environment, but using and adapting the environment to meet human needs modifies nature's balance. The physical environments can bring prosperity to a region but also crises and environmental conflicts. Making decisions based on these relationships will be developed through geographical knowledge of the opportunities and limitations of the Earth's surface. For example, damming a river for settlement and agriculture can bring homes, livelihood, and mobilization of populations to an area, while at the same time alter the physical systems, wildlife, and vegetation. As the population increases, the physical systems must cope with accommodating and absorbing human by-products (trash, pollution, waste, and overuse).

In order for humans to live in a variety of environments, technologies and adaptations must be employed. This also encompasses spacial organization of an environment to utilize the resources provided by the Earth. For example, New Orleans was originally developed on the natural levies or high ground along the Mississippi as a port city and a hub for the slave trade industry. Its establishment on high ground and inland reduced its vulnerability to hurricanes and flooding. But in the early twentieth century, engineers developed a pump system that allowed the city to further expand into the low-lying areas, placing the city several feet below sea level.

Resources are *any* physical materials that make up part of the Earth that people need, value, or want. The three basic resources are land, water, and air. Consumption and value of resources (oil, coal, metals, and minerals) increase as humans seek them.

The results of how people and resources interact are as follows:

- Location of resources causes population movement and settlement.
- Location of resources causes activity (employment and technology).
- Demand of resources causes economic development.
- Consumption of resources are causes of wealth.
- Lack of resources causes conflict.

Following are three types of resources:

- **Renewable**—Resources that can replenish themselves after they are used (for example, animals and plants)
- **Nonrenewable**—Resources that can be cultivated and used only once (for example, minerals, oil, natural gas, coal)
- **Flow**—Resources that must be used when, where, and as they occur (for example, water, sunlight, wind)

**201**

# Uses of Geography

Knowledge of geography enables individuals to develop a better understanding of the relationships that exist among people, places, and environments. Students must be able to use geography to analyze the causes, meanings, and influences of the physical and human events that take place on the Earth's surface. They should learn to locate people and places, understand the locations and exploitation of resources, be able to map landmarks, and comprehend the barriers that exist around the world. The uses of geography imply that students have learned the content in such a way that they may apply their knowledge to the past, present, and future in relation to this subject.

Physical geography exists in order to explain the spatial characteristics of the diverse natural phenomena affiliated with the Earth's biosphere, hydrosphere, atmosphere, and lithosphere. Physical geography studies phenomena such as rocks and minerals, landforms, plants and animals, environment, water in all its forms/stages, climate and weather, atmospheric occurrences, and soil, as well as the correlation and relationship of these phenomena to human activity. Human geography is the study of how humans interact, use, and alter the world. It incorporates the organization of human activity as well as the relationship with the physical environment. Human geography focuses completely on the study of spatial patterns of human influences on the environment. Some topics studied in human geography include population, settlements, economic activities, transportation, recreation, religion, politics, social traditions, migration, agriculture, and urbanization.

Geography is also full of patterns, which can be recurring in random, chaotic, or predictable arrangements. The study of these patterns allows students to predict and infer future outcomes or situations. Once students learn the processes of geography they will be able to utilize this knowledge to describe the world around them.

# World History

The national standard that is reflected in this section focuses on the theme of Time, Continuity, and Change. This aids students in gaining knowledge about the significance of place and they may develop a geographic perspective about the social aspects of the world. In this section of the guide the content includes information about the history of the world such as:

- Early and classical civilizations
- European and non-European civilizations
- Twentieth-century developments and transformations
- European explorations

## Prehistory and Early Civilizations

The prehistory period was a time of unwritten records. Knowledge of the time and the gains made are only evident through the existence of continued achievements.

Early civilizations brought the following:

- Basic achievements included the invention of the wheel, alphabets, math, and time measurements.
- Art and architecture was influential.
- Alphabetic writing increased.
- Religions were defined and practiced.
- Commonality and diversity became known (separate geographically and culturally but all developed trade, writing, cities).

# Neolithic Revolution—c. 10,000 B.C.E.

- Began in the Middle East and spread into India, North Africa, and Europe
- Developed agricultural societies
- Improved economic, political, and social organizations
- Gave humans the ability to remain settled permanently
- Civilizations begin to form
- Developed alongside major rivers for agricultural production ("river valley")
- Created a basic set of tools
- Introduced writing, mathematics, and politics

# Tigris-Euphrates Civilization—c. 5,000 B.C.E.

- Originated in the valley of the Tigris and Euphrates rivers in Mesopotamia
- Started from scratch with no model or examples (Sumerian people)
- Created cuneiform (earliest form of writing)
- Developed astronomical sciences, religious beliefs
- Established political system with a king and organized city-states
- Improved agriculture through the use of fertilizer
- Used silver to conduct commercial trade
- Developed procedures for law courts and property rights
- Focused on a standard legal system

# Egyptian Civilization—c. 3,000 B.C.E.

- Emerged along the Nile River in northern Africa
- Modeled trade on Mesopotamia
- Built impressive architectural structures (Pyramid and Sphinx)
- Produced mathematical achievements
- Ruled by pharaohs
- Established effective government, defense, monetary, and transportation systems
- Centralized the community to meet the needs of citizens

# Indian and Chinese River Valley Civilization—c. 2,500 B.C.E.

- Developed along the Indus River
- Prospered in urban civilizations
- Traded with Mesopotamia
- Developed well-defined alphabet and artistic forms
- Maintained and regulated irrigation system
- Created advanced engineering and architectural technology

- Developed impressive intellectual establishments
- Constructed massive tombs and palaces
- Invaded and destroyed by Indo-Europeans

# Classical Civilizations

There were three recognized classical civilizations that contributed to the present day organization of civilization. Each of these major civilizations

- Expanded trade and provided other influences to areas outside their own borders.
- Reevaluated and restructured key institutions upon the decline and fall of empires or rules, policies, and values.
- Created new and varied religions.
- Increased agricultural options and opportunities.
- Extended the land territories and boundary areas.
- Integrated the people and societies (social cohesion).

## The Civilization of China (c. 1029 B.C.E.)

The China Civilization was the longest-lasting civilization in world history and one of the most influential. They had three dynastic cycles, Zhou, Qin, Han, all of which developed strong political institutions, created active economies, and promoted central tax systems. As one dynasty began to falter, the next rose and developed through a prominent general, peasant, or invader who took the lead role.

| China Civilization Accomplishments | |
|---|---|
| Political | Began bureaucracy training<br>Established a system of tax collection<br>Promoted mandatory labor services |
| Religion and Culture | Developed Confucianism and Daoism<br>Promoted personal ethics of acting with self-control, humility, and respect<br>Embraced harmony in nature<br>Stressed details in art and craftsmanship<br>Encouraged geometrical and decorative arts<br>Developed accurate calendars<br>Studied mathematics of music<br>Studied science for the practical uses |
| Economy and Society | Designated three main social groups: upper class, laboring peasants, unskilled laborers<br>Excelled in technologies<br>Established model for global trade and promoted trade as essential<br>Encouraged tight-knit family unit<br>Instilled patriarchal society (women subordinate to men) and demanded arranged marriages |

## The Civilization of Greece and Rome (c. 800 B.C.E.)

Both Greece and Rome were extremely powerful and influential throughout the world and they created a rise in the city-state. The Greeks set up large expanding colonial and trading systems or webs. Rome gained territory and power by acquiring lesser developed cultures, causing it to grow into an empire.

| Greece and Rome Civilization Accomplishments | |
|---|---|
| Political | Emphasized aristocratic rule, but democratic elements also present<br>Formed democracy in Greece<br>Promoted intense loyalty to state<br>Created uniform legal principles |
| Religion and Culture | Taught moderation and balance (Aristotle and Cicero)<br>Taught followers to have conventional wisdom using rational inquiry (Socrates)<br>Excelled in sculpture, architecture, and plays (Greeks)<br>Promoted geometry and anatomy (Greeks)<br>Made the greatest contribution to science—engineering (Romans) |
| Economy and Society | Developed systems for agriculture (farming)<br>Participated in extensive trade by using a structure of slavery<br>Promoted a unified family structure<br>Instilled a patriarchal community, although women could own property |

# The Civilization of India (c. 600 B.C.E.)

The development of India's Civilization was shaped by its topography since it is partially separated from Asia by its northern mountain range. Most agricultural regions were along the Ganges and the Indus rivers. Rule in India was sporadic and divided into widespread empires (invaders) and small kingdoms. During both types of rule, culture and economics advanced. The Mauryn and Gupta were the two most successful dynasties and were managed completely by Indians. India's culture spread widely due to its extensive trading practices, which allowed the open acceptance of outside influences. Buddhism crossed cultures and became a globally practiced religion.

| India Civilization Accomplishments | |
|---|---|
| Political | Practiced diversity and regionalism (still today)<br>Established a caste system (social classes)<br>Utilized a variety of languages |
| Religion and Culture | Promoted Hinduism and Buddhism<br>Taught religion, medicine, and architecture in universities<br>Excelled in science and mathematics<br>Developed concept of "zero," Arabic numerals, and the decimal system<br>Created lively and colorful art |
| Economy and Society | Established extensive internal and external successful trade practices<br>Promoted patriarchal society (dominance over women)<br>Emphasized family, group, or government, not individuals<br>Utilized a nonopposed social hierarchy (caste system) |

# The Rise of Non-European Civilizations

The advent of civilization furnished a framework for the majority of the developments in the world. Specifically, the rise of civilizations in Africa and the Middle East provided political structure and cultural systems. Numerous civilizations began during this period. Following is a list of some of the major civilizations and their contributions:

- **Mayans**—Astronomy and mathematics, elaborate written language system, architecture, and art
- **Mongolians**—Nomadic society with law code unification, strong military, but transmitted diseases across continents

- **Muslim/Islam**—Islamic religion, chemistry advances, high-quality maps, influential arts and sciences
- **Africa**—Stateless societies
- **Inca**—Artistic pottery and clothing, metallurgy, architecture, irrigation, road systems, supreme military organization, and agriculture
- **Sumerians**—Cuneiform writing, city-state government, adopted silver as a means of exchange, agricultural advances using fertilizer, and improvements on the potter's wheel
- **Kushites**—Skilled in iron use, metal technological advances in military and agricultural realms, extensive trade, strong economic systems, and establishment of cities
- **Phoenicians**—A merchant society, elaborate trading networks, early alphabet, manufacturing advances (dyes), and improved the Egyptian number system

# The Rise and Expansion of Europe

European Civilization began with the Greek and Roman empires. It is often said that these civilizations provided the foundation of Western culture and further civilization. The expansion from the coast inland occurred as the empires began extending their rule. As the various empires spread, so did religion, culture, language, politics, philosophies, educational systems, sciences, arts, and economic networks. The Venetians, Florentines, and Genoese all helped give rise to the great Atlantic economy. The Portuguese increased trade, which gave rise to northern European trade and commerce. The Dutch Empires were commercial and helped increase commercial trade with other countries as well as established colonies in Asia as business ventures. There were many internal conflicts that affected the rate of expansion of Europe within the continent. However, there were many circumstances that promoted and pushed European exploration and other foreign ventures. These included a population explosion, religious persecution, and financial and investment opportunities.

Movement in Europe is associated with a shift in life from the Mediterranean to the Atlantic Coast. Europeans crossed oceans in search of fertile lands to use for agriculture and international trade. This curbed the conquest of the new world and allowed the discovery of America to occur. The establishment and colonization of new areas overseas caused migration of populations. As expansion increased, people made improvements in communications and their means of transportation.

# United States History

The national standard that is reflected under the history of the United States focuses on the themes of Time, Continuity, and Change, which aids students in gaining knowledge about the significance of place so that they may develop a geographic perspective on the social aspects of the world. The breadth of this topic is vast and far-reaching, and deserving of further attention. This study guide will discuss many topics related to United States history as well as summarize these topics, but further study of specifics and details is highly recommended.

## European Exploration and Colonization

There were a variety of reasons that early settlers came to the United States looking for a new homeland: to escape religious persecution, to develop business ventures, to promote personal/economic gain, and for political reasons. Those people who made the pilgrimage from England to the new land brought with them certain animals (horses, cattle, hogs), trades, and diseases.

The Europeans established three types of colonies in the Americas. **Corporate** (charter) colonies were led by joint-stock companies. These were run as a business with the backing of wealthy investors. The more money the colony made, the wealthier the investors became. The investors voted on officials and elected the leaders in this type of colony. **Proprietary** colonies were owned by a single person or single family. These colonies were run more like a dictatorship, with the family appointing officials as they pleased. **Royal** colonies were under direct control of the king or queen. Royal governors were appointed to rule over these colonies and were under direct orders from the king or queen. English investors often financed the building of a colony for profit; therefore, when profits were slow to return or did not return at all, investors often pulled out of the venture. This resulted in the responsibility falling to the colonists to build their own lives, communities, and economies.

Most settlers and colonists did not rely on imports, but were self-sufficient. They were proficient in fur trading, trapping, fishing, and farming. By the eighteenth century, the colonists had created regional patterns in colonial development:

- **New England**—Relied on ship building, sailing, and fishing
- **Maryland, Virginia, South Carolina, and North Carolina**—Grew tobacco, rice, and indigo
- **New York, Pennsylvania, New Jersey, and Delaware**—Shipped crops and traded furs

The colonists set high standards of living for themselves, which surpassed the standards of living in England. Entrepreneurship was highly popular in this New World. By 1770, the colonies were economically and politically ready to become a self-sufficient entity. This caused disputes to arise with England over taxation and control. Mounting frustrations and quarrels grew and blossomed into turmoil. In 1775, the American Revolution began with the colonists rallying for "unalienable rights to life, liberty, and property" (John Locke's *2nd Treatise on Civil Government*).

The **13 Colonies** began with the founding of settlements called Jamestown (1607), Plymouth (1620), and Massachusetts Bay Colony (1629). In 1773, these were the established **13 Colonies:** New Hampshire, Massachusetts, Rhode Island, Connecticut, New York, New Jersey, Pennsylvania, Delaware, Maryland, Virginia, North Carolina, South Carolina, and Georgia.

Following is a list of famous explorers with which all students should be familiar:

- **1450–1499, John Cabot**—English explorer and navigator who explored the Canadian coastline looking for a northwest passage to Asia.
- **1451–1506, Christopher Columbus**—Italian explorer who took a voyage across the Atlantic Ocean in 1492 hoping to find a route to India. He sailed his three ships, the Niña, Pinta, and Santa Maria, and discovered North America.
- **1454–1512, Amerigo Vespucci**—Italian explorer who was the first person to realize that the Americas were separate from Asia, stating that the Americas were not the East Indies. In 1507, a mapmaker named the Americas after him.
- **1460–1521, Juan Ponce de León**—Spanish explorer and soldier who discovered the Gulf Stream and was the first European to set foot in Florida, while searching for the Fountain of Youth.
- **1485–1547, Hernán Cortez**—Spanish conquistador who wiped out the Aztec Empire and claimed Mexico for Spain.
- **1491–1557, Jacques Cartier**—French explorer who discovered Canada. He paved the way for the French exploration of North America.
- **c. 1496–1542, Hernando De Soto**—Spanish explorer who explored Florida and the southeastern United States. He is credited with the discovery of the Mississippi River.
- **1510–1554, Francisco Vásquez de Coronado**—Spanish conquistador who explored the American Southwest (AZ, NM, TX, OK, KS). He killed many Native Americans because they would not convert to Christianity.
- **1552–1618, Sir Walter Raleigh**—British explorer, poet, historian, and soldier who established English colonies in the Americas. He named the state of Virginia after Queen Elizabeth.
- **1565–1611, Henry Hudson**—English explorer who explored the Arctic Ocean and northeastern North America. The Hudson River, the Hudson Strait, and the Hudson Bay were named after him, and he is credited with founding New York.
- **1580–1631, John Smith**—Captain in the English military who founded Jamestown, Virginia. He explored Chesapeake Bay and the New England coast.
- **1681–1741, Vitus Bering**—A Dutchman who explored Alaska and Siberia. The Bering Strait bears his name.
- **1728–1779, Captain James Cook**—British explorer and astronomer who led expeditions to the Pacific Ocean, Antarctica, the Arctic, and around the world. He is credited with discovering Hawaii.
- **1734–1820, Daniel Boone**—An American pioneer, explorer, trapper, mountain man, and soldier who founded the first U.S. settlement west of the Appalachian Mountains. He also explored the Kentucky wilderness.

- **1755–1806, Robert Gray**—The first American-born explorer to circumnavigate the globe. He also explored the northwestern United States and helped obtain the Oregon territory.

- **1774–1809, Meriwether Lewis** and **1770–1838 William Clark**—They explored and mapped the American West and the Pacific Coast. They traveled through the Louisiana Territory (Missouri to Oregon Coast) and were led by Sacagawea.

- **1799–1831, Jedediah Smith**—An American mountain man, hunter, and fur trapper who was the first person to travel from New York to California through the Rocky Mountains and the Mohave Desert. He was also the first person to cross the Great Basin Desert via the Sierra Nevada Mountains and the Great Salt Lake.

- **1809–1868, Kit Carson**—An American explorer, guide, trapper, and soldier who explored the southwest and western United States with John Fremont. In 1863, Carson destroyed the Navajo settlement in Canyon De Chelley and forced Native Americans on the "long walk."

# The American Revolution and the Founding of the Nation

The founding of the nation took shape in the last half of the eighteenth century. Prior to that, settlers and colonists were under English rule (Great Britain) rather than being an autonomous society.

For the first part of the eighteenth century Britain was preoccupied with other European countries and paid little attention to the American colonies. During this time Britain left the colonies to run themselves with autonomy in both their economic and political systems. It wasn't until the end of the Seven Years' War in 1763 that Parliament turned its attention to the colonies. At this time Britain was experiencing heavy debts from the war and realized the colonies could be used for financial gain. Parliament launched new policies that exerted more control over the economic and political systems of the colonies.

In 1775, the 13 British colonies in North America rebelled against British rule because the people did not want continued taxation and government rule from England. Britain imposed a series of taxes upon the colonies and the colonists had no representation in the British parliament. The British colonists residing in the Americas did not believe that Great Britain represented their needs nor could govern them from across the ocean.

As frustration mounted and tensions grew, colonists began forming militia in preparation for the impending fight for freedom. The American Revolution (also known as the Revolutionary War or the American War of Independence) was triggered by an event that occurred in April 1775. The government of England sent soldiers to the colonies to maintain order and gain control. British soldiers collided with colonial militiamen in Concord, Massachusetts, during a raid on a colonial arms depot. When a shot was fired, the American Revolution began, which lasted from 1775–1783. It was a civil war between the kingdom of Great Britain and the 13 British colonies for their independence.

When foreign nations (France, Spain, and the Dutch Republic) became allies with the revolutionaries, the war became an international conflict. The writing of the Declaration of Independence in 1776 was a turning point in the formation of the nation. The Treaty of Paris, signed in 1783, ended the war and recognized the sovereignty and the independence of the United States of America. By 1787, the American government was formalized by the development of the U.S. Constitution.

## Major Battles of the American Revolution

- Battle of Lexington and Concord, April 19, 1775
- Battle of Bunker Hill, June 17, 1775
- Battle of Princeton, January 3, 1777
- Battle of Brandywine, September 11, 1777
- Battle of Yorktown, October 19, 1781

## Important Government Actions

- **1765, Stamp Act**—First direct tax placed on the colonies; required all printed media to have stamps
- **1767, Townshend Act**—Placed a tax on essential goods (paper, glass, tea)

- **1773, Tea Act**—Tax break to the British East India Company
- **1773, Boston Tea Party**—A protest of the Tea Act by American colonists
- **1774, Intolerable Acts**—Massachusetts Government Act; Administration of Justice Act, Boston Port Act; Quartering Act
- **1776, The Declaration of Independence**—Adopted by a vote of the 13 Colonies, which led to an alliance with France, followed by alliances with Spain and the Dutch province

## Important Documents in United States History

- **The Magna Carta (1215)**—The clauses of this document (63 total) explained and restricted the rights of the monarch.
- **The Mayflower Compact (1620)**—This compact, signed en route on the Mayflower, established a temporary majority-rule government for the Pilgrims.
- **The Declaration of Independence (1776)**—The principles set forth in this document justified the separation of the 13 American colonies from Great Britain and provided responsibilities to individuals, with a government ruled by the people.
- **Articles of Confederation (1781)**—The first constitution of the 13 American states was later replaced in 1789 with the ratification of the Constitution of the United States.
- **The Federalist Papers (1787–1788)**—This group of 85 articles was published in the New York newspapers to influence the decision to ratify the Constitution; even today it helps to explain the intent of the Constitution.
- **The U.S. Constitution (1789)**—The document that established the basic principles of the American government.
- **Emancipation Proclamation (1865)**—This announcement issued during the Civil War by President Lincoln confirmed the end of slavery in the Confederate states.

| United States Presidents | | | |
|---|---|---|---|
| 1789–1797 | George Washington | 1889–1893 | Benjamin Harrison |
| 1797–1801 | John Adams | 1893–1897 | Grover Cleveland |
| 1801–1809 | Thomas Jefferson | 1897–1901 | William McKinley |
| 1809–1817 | James Madison | 1901–1909 | Theodore Roosevelt |
| 1817–1825 | James Monroe | 1909–1913 | William Howard Taft |
| 1825–1829 | John Quincy Adams | 1913–1921 | Woodrow Wilson |
| 1829–1837 | Andrew Jackson | 1921–1923 | Warren Gamaliel Harding |
| 1837–1841 | Martin Van Buren | 1923–1929 | Calvin Coolidge |
| 1841 | William Henry Harrison | 1929–1933 | Herbert Clark Hoover |
| 1841–1845 | John Tyler | 1933–1945 | Franklin Delano Roosevelt |
| 1845–1849 | James Knox Polk | 1945–1953 | Harry S Truman |
| 1849–1850 | Zachary Taylor | 1953–1961 | Dwight David Eisenhower |
| 1850–1853 | Millard Fillmore | 1961–1963 | John Fitzgerald Kennedy |
| 1853–1857 | Franklin Pierce | 1963–1969 | Lyndon Baines Johnson |
| 1857–1861 | James Buchanan | 1969–1974 | Richard Milhous Nixon |
| 1861–1865 | Abraham Lincoln | 1974–1977 | Gerald Rudolph Ford |
| 1865–1869 | Andrew Johnson | 1977–1981 | James Earl Carter, Jr. |
| 1869–1877 | Ulysses Simpson Grant | 1981–1989 | Ronald Wilson Reagan |
| 1877–1881 | Rutherford Birchard Hayes | 1989–1993 | George Herbert Walker Bush |
| 1881 | James Abram Garfield | 1993–2001 | William Jefferson Clinton |
| 1881–1885 | Chester Alan Arthur | 2001–2009 | George Walker Bush |
| 1885–1889 | Grover Cleveland | 2009– | Barack Hussein Obama |

# Growth and Expansion of the Republic

The Proclamation of 1763 restricted American movement across the Appalachian Mountains into the frontier. Colonists ignored this and traveled westward, which led to the expansion of the United States and further migration across North America. The original territorial boundaries of the United States were set between Canada (north), Florida (south and controlled by Spain), Atlantic Ocean (east), and the Mississippi River (west). These boundaries were established with Great Britain and defined by the treaties of November 30, 1782, and September 3, 1783.

Difficulty arose when the colonists began claiming the unoccupied territory between the original 13 Colonies and the Mississippi River. Due to conflicting claims and the realization of impending difficulties, the Continental Congress passed a resolution in 1779 recommending the territories in dispute should be ceded to the government. This land included the total area that is now known as Ohio, Indiana, Illinois, Michigan, Wisconsin, Minnesota, Alabama, and Mississippi. When this was one large territory, the government held title to the lands and administered the laws upon them.

The original colonial territories began relinquishing boundary lines and control so new states could form. Once this occurred, the vast area west of the colonies to the border of the Mississippi River began forming as states. The majority of the remaining states had their boundaries defined under an act of Congress known as the Enabling Acts, which admitted them into the Union.

After exploration moved westward, the remaining land areas were divided into states, ratified, and admitted into the Union. Additions to the original territory brought forth the expansion of our country and helped form its present boundaries. These included the Louisiana Purchase (from France—1803), the Purchase of Florida (from Spain—1819), the Annexation of Texas (1845), the acquisition of the Oregon Territory (1846), the Mexican Cession (1848), the Gadsden Purchase (from Mexico—1853), the purchase of Alaska (from Russia—1867), and the Annexation of Hawaii (1898).

# Wars

- **American-Indian Wars (1587–1890)**—These struggles involved European settlers in the colonies who defeated Native Americans and tribes in order to expand ownership of land, resulting in the placement and confinement of Native Americans on reservations.
- **American Revolution (1775–1783)**—A struggle in which the United States won independence from Great Britain.
- **War of 1812 (1812–1814)**—Congress declared war on Britain, which resulted in increased national patriotism, united the states into one nation, and built confidence in U.S. military strength. The Star-Spangled Banner, the national anthem, was written.
- **Civil War (1861–1865)**—The two factions of the new nation, the North (Union) and the slave-owning states of the South (Confederacy), fought until the succession of the South was squelched, slavery was abolished, and the federal government increased its power by uniting the country.
- **World War I (1914–1918)**—Great Britain, France, Russia, Belgium, Italy, Japan, the United States, and other allies defeated Germany, Austria-Hungary, Turkey, and Bulgaria, overthrowing four empires (German, Hapsburg, Turkish, and Russian empires) that resulted in the birth of seven new nations.
- **World War II (1939–1945)**—The struggle in which the United States, Great Britain, France, the Soviet Union, China, and other allies defeated Germany, Italy, and Japan. Two atomic bombs were dropped on Hiroshima and Nagasaki, in Japan, to end the war. Of the many outcomes of the war there are a few to note: Germany was divided into four parts and controlled by the Allied powers; geopolitical power shifted away from western and central Europe; the United States and Russia became known internationally as superpowers; new technologies appeared (computer, jet engine, nuclear fission); and many global organizations sprouted (United Nations, World Bank, World Trade Organization, International Monetary Fund).
- **The Korean War (1950–1953)**—The struggle between communist North Korea (aided by China and USSR—former Russia), and noncommunist South Korea (aided by the United States, Britain, and the United Nations), resulted in the same boundaries between North and South Korea.

- **The Vietnam War (1945–1975)**—A long conflict in which communist North Vietnam (supported by China and the Soviet Union) tried to take over noncommunist South Vietnam (supported by the United States). It resulted in the defeat of South Vietnam, with North Vietnam imposing a socialist republic where the communist party now governs.
- **Persian Gulf War (1990–1991)**—The United States led a coalition of forces and destroyed much of Iraq's military forces, resulting in driving out the Iraqi army from Kuwait.
- **The Iraq War (2003–2011)**—The struggle in which the United States and Great Britain led a coalition of forces against Iraq to expel Saddam Hussein (dictator) and sought to establish a democratic society.

## Twentieth-Century Developments and Transformations

The twentieth century has provided humankind with many advancements and technologies. From radios to cellphones to artificial intelligence, the developments of the twentieth century have been overwhelming. These developments and technologies have both improved our lives and placed lives in peril.

| Developments of the Common Era: January 1, 1901 to December 31, 2000 | | | |
|---|---|---|---|
| Automobile | Radio | Missiles | Personal computer |
| Transistor | Laser | Electric refrigeration | Chemical weapons |
| Television | Wireless technology | Manned space flight | Quantum physics |
| Airplane | Radar | Magnetic tape | Theory of Relativity |
| Plastics | Air conditioning | Global networks | Xerography |
| Atomic bomb | Artificial intelligence | Fiber optics | Internet |

# Political Science

The primary goal of political science programs is to promote citizenship education, so students can learn to make informed decisions that improve and enhance society. As they mature, students will become involved, active citizens. These national standards focus on the themes of Power, Authority, and Governance and Civic Ideals and Practices, which provide students with knowledge about the forms of government and the importance of community participation in a society.

The National Standards for Civics and Government suggest five elements of citizen education, which form the basic content knowledge for political science that will be assessed:

- The nature and purpose of government
- The forms of government
- The United States Constitution
- The rights and responsibilities of citizens
- The state and local governments

## The Nature and Purpose of Government

Societies developed as people joined together to establish consistent ways to protect their rights as human beings. Formal governments have been around for more than 5,000 years, and the aspects of their function are about the same as those today. Governments were established to protect individual's liberties, properties, and lives from other people.

The most important function of a government is to provide laws or rules. These are essential to prevent conflicts between individuals and the groups who reside in the same country or land. Not only does the government make the laws, but it must enforce them as well. Governments also establish procedures to settle conflicts, and some create governmental bodies to manage the people. By using established laws the government can focus on order and provide security for its people, with the ultimate goal being peace between and among its constituents.

Depending on the size of a country or state, there may be several levels of government, which might include governments of local, county, district, state, regional, or national origin. Each provides services and order critical to its area and its people.

# The Forms of Government

The form of the United States government is a democracy. However, there are many other forms of government throughout the world. The main systems of government include the following:

| Systems | Description | Examples |
| --- | --- | --- |
| Anarchism | A lack of government based on the political philosophy by people who hold beliefs that the state is unnecessary, undesirable, and harmful and have attitudes that reject compulsory government. | Isocracy and Tribalism |
| Authoritarianism | A form of government that demonstrates strict control and may coerce and use oppressive measures to ensure obedience. | Autocracy, Communism, Oligarchy, Aristocracy, Dictatorship, Monarchy, Fascism, and Tyranny |
| Democracy | A form of government in which the people hold certain liberties and freedoms and retain the power and rule either directly or through representatives. | Republicism, Parliamentary system, and Democratic Socialism |

Within these main types of government are a variety of other more specific ruling entities. There is no inclusive list of the many forms of government, as there may be new types developing as countries change and borders are moved. A government may have one or more types of rule as its basis. For example, the United States is considered a democratic republic.

This list describes the basic guidelines of rule:

**Anarchy**   Rule by no one

**Autocracy**   Rule by one

**Oligarchy**   Rule by minority

**Republic**   Rule by law

**Democracy**   Rule by majority

**Socialism**   Rule by all

These are a few specific forms of government that are practiced around the world (this is not a comprehensive or complete list):

- **Communism**—A type of government in which the state designs and controls the economy under the power of an authoritarian party. It eliminates private ownership of property or individual capital in order to create a classless society where all goods are shared equally by all individuals.

- **Dictatorship**—A type of government in which a single ruler or small group has absolute power, not restricted by constitution or law, where citizens have no choice in the leadership.

- **Monarchy**—A type of government in which supreme and absolute power resides in the hands of a single monarch who rules over the lands for life through hereditary right.

- **Theocracy**—A type of government in which a deity is the ruler and the laws are interpreted by religious clergy.
- **Totalitarian**—A type of government that controls all political aspects, economic matters, attitudes, values, and beliefs of the population keeping the individuals subordinate to the state.

# The U.S. Constitution

The U.S. Constitution was written by the Founding Fathers in order to avoid the power of one single figure and to create a strong centralized government away from Great Britain. During the Constitutional Convention in 1787, delegates voted immediately to abandon the Articles of Confederation (the original doctrine of the United States) and draft a new constitution that would frame a new central government. Opponents of the new government feared that a centralized government would become too powerful. In order to prevent this, a system of divided power along with a system of checks and balances was designed. The delegates worked for four months to construct this new document. Melding ideas and concepts from the preestablished state constitutions, the Articles of Confederation, and the Northwest Ordinance, the U.S. Constitution was born. The new constitution, even though not entirely full of original ideas, was distinctive and unparalleled in that it integrated the idea of checks and balances, federalism, and separation of powers.

When the country broke away from the rule of England and established the first 13 Colonies, the people wanted order and freedom from strict monarch rule, so they created the Articles of Confederation. The Articles were in effect until 1789 when the U.S. Constitution was implemented as the law of the land. The Constitution outlined the three branches of government, their powers, and the rights of the citizens through seven Articles.

The seven Articles (principles) of the Constitution are as follows:

1. Legislative Power (Popular Sovereignty)
2. Executive Power (Republicanism)
3. Judicial Power (Federalism)
4. States' Powers and Limits (Separation of Powers)
5. The Process of Amendments (Checks and Balances)
6. Federal Powers (Limited Government)
7. Ratification (Individual Rights)

Ratification of the Constitution was achieved in June 1788, when New Hampshire became the ninth state to ratify. Virginia and New York soon followed. Most states agreed to ratify under the condition that a federal Bill of Rights be developed. In September 1789, the first U.S. Congress proposed 12 Amendments to the Constitution; these became the Bill of Rights after great debate in December 1791.

There are three branches of the United States government that were designed to work together, creating a system of checks and balances, ensuring that the rights of citizens and the management of the country are considered in decisions. The three branches of government are as follows:

- **Executive**—This branch of the government ensures that the laws of the United States are followed. The head of the Executive Branch is the President of the United States, who also commands the military. The President has assistance from the Vice President, Cabinet members, Department members, and federal agencies, all of whom help in carrying out policy and providing special services.
- **Legislative**—This branch of government is comprised of Congress and government agencies that provide support to the Executive Branch. Congress has the power to make laws for the United States and is divided into two parts: the House of Representatives and the Senate. The Senate allows for two representatives from each state and the House permits representatives from the states based on population, with a total of 435 seats.

- **Judicial**—This branch of government contains the court system. The highest court in the land is the Supreme Court and included in the system are the federal courts. The courts must ensure that the rules of the Constitution are upheld, so members of the courts interpret the meanings of laws and how they should be applied.

The components of the U.S. Constitution include a preamble, seven original Articles, twenty-seven Amendments, and certification of the enactment.

## The Preamble

The Preamble is the formal introduction to the Constitution. It summarizes the basic premises and explains the purpose of the Constitution. The preamble to the Constitution of the United States follows:

*We the People of the United States, in Order to form a more perfect Union, establish Justice, insure domestic Tranquility, provide for the common defence [sic], promote the general Welfare, and secure the Blessings of Liberty to ourselves and our Posterity, do ordain and establish this Constitution for the United States of America.*

## The Bill of Rights

The first 10 Amendments ratified in 1791 are considered the Bill of Rights. These amendments outline the rights of citizens and visitors, according to the law of the land, expressing the freedoms and culture of this country.

An **amendment** is a modification, addition, or deletion to a law or bill; amendments are incorporated into the meaning of the Constitution. The first 10 Amendments are listed here:

Amendment 1—Freedom of religion, press, assembly, expression

Amendment 2—Right to keep and bear arms

Amendment 3—Conditions for quarters of soldiers

Amendment 4—Right of search and seizure

Amendment 5—Provisions concerning prosecution

Amendment 6—Rights of accused in criminal prosecutions

Amendment 7—Rights in civil cases

Amendment 8—Bail, fines, and punishment

Amendment 9—Rights retained by the people

Amendment 10—States' rights

## The Rights and Responsibilities of Citizens

The first founding document of the United States of America that dissolved any connection of the 13 Colonies with Great Britain is the **Declaration of Independence,** adopted on July 4, 1776 (now called Independence Day). This declaration led to the development of the Articles of Confederation and later the U.S. Constitution, both of which served to outline the rights and responsibilities of U.S. citizens. The Constitutional Amendments further outline the various rights of citizens. In the Gettysburg Address of 1863, President Abraham Lincoln summarized the basic premise of the Declaration: "Four score and seven years ago our fathers brought forth on this continent, a new nation, conceived in liberty, and dedicated to the proposition that all men are created equal."

The United States federal system of government, a democratic republic, focuses on the right to life, liberty, and the pursuit of happiness; promoting equal opportunities; addressing the common good; and seeking truth and justice. In a democratic society the government has limited powers. It is the people who have the ultimate authority, which is exercised through elections and government representation, chosen by the people. Final decisions are based on majority rule.

**Citizenship** is defined as the way we act and live our lives. It includes how an individual makes decisions that may affect others and how individuals demonstrate their concern about the community and nation. The two social science disciplines included in citizenship education are civics and government. Civics portrays the rights and responsibilities of people and their relationship toward others and the government. Information about the political and legislative institutions of a certain place is included in instruction about government.

Three components are important to citizenship education:

- **Content**—Knowledge that helps promote good citizenship
- **Values**—Set standards of human behavior
- **Processes**—The practice of citizenship through activities and opportunities

# State and Local Governments

After the victory of independence resulting from the American Revolution, the 13 Colonies became 13 states and formed a league in which they could work together. This system of cooperation between states was outlined and established through the Articles of Confederation. In this type of government, the national body was very weak and retained little power, whereas the individual states held the majority of the power. However, this lack of unity in overall governing left the nation weak and noncohesive, so the Founding Fathers wrote the Constitution to replace the Articles of Confederation. The Constitution divided the power between the national government and the state governments, outlining the responsibilities of each and creating a federalist system.

**Federalism**—The sharing of power between the national government and the individual state governments. State governments have their own constitution, similar to the U.S. Constitution, but the laws of the individual states cannot conflict with the federal Constitution. Every state constitution reflects its individual history, needs, philosophy, and geography and is uniquely different from all other states.

When the United States first formed, it embraced a type of governing called **dual federalism.** Dual federalism is when the states govern the people directly and the national government governs foreign affairs. This type of governing eventually led to the Civil War because there was a disagreement among the states as to division of powers. As a direct result of the Civil War, a series of Amendments was passed that outlined the authority of the federal government over social and economic policy and the protection of citizen rights. These included the 13th, 14th, and 15th Amendments.

Dual federalism continued until the Great Depression of 1930. During this time, states were unable to deal with the economic troubles within the country. President Roosevelt's **New Deal** brought forth a system of cooperative federalism in which national, state, and local governments would work together on programs rather than assigning specific functions to each level.

The interaction between state, local, and national governments is complex, yet clearly and concisely outlined in the Constitution in order to maintain a productive and democratic country.

| Distribution of Power in the United States | | |
|---|---|---|
| **National Government** | **Both (State and National)** | **State Government** |
| Declares war | Create and enforce laws | Oversees export and import within its boundaries |
| Manages foreign relations | Set taxes | Manages public health and safety |
| Oversees international, foreign, and interstate trade | Borrow money | Ratifies amendments |
| Mints money in a treasury | | |

Students should be familiar with the following political science terms:

- **Alien:** Resident of another country who has not yet become a citizen of the country where the person currently lives
- **Amend:** To change the wording or meaning of a motion, bill, constitution, and so on by formal procedure
- **Census:** Periodic official count of the number of persons living in a country
- **Checks and balances:** Limits imposed on all branches of government by giving each the right to amend acts of the other branches
- **Citizen:** Member of a state or nation who owes allegiance to its government and is entitled to its protection
- **Civil:** Relating to citizens, occurring within the community
- **Congressional district:** Division or part of a state; each district elects one person to the House of Representatives
- **Constituent:** Person who is represented by an elected official
- **Delegate:** Person who acts for or represents another or others
- **Immigrant:** Person who moves from one country to another to live permanently
- **Indictment:** Formal accusation through a legal process
- **National:** Citizen of a nation who is entitled to its protection
- **Separation of powers:** System of dividing the powers and duties of a government into different branches
- **Veto:** Cancel or postpone a decision, bill, and so on

# Anthropology, Sociology, and Psychology

The Praxis II elementary exam (0014/5014) tests specific content knowledge of this subject area according to the following:

- Social institutions and cultural changes
- Socialization and acculturation
- Human growth and development

The national standards that are reflected in this section focus on the themes of Culture; Individual Development and Identity; Individuals, Groups, and Institutions; and Global Connections, which guide students in learning about the characteristics of cultures around the world, how cultures shape personal identity, what institutions influence lives, and how global connections affect societies.

The study of anthropology is divided into two major parts:

- **Physical anthropology**—The study of physical characteristics and differences between groups of people
- **Cultural anthropology**—The study and comparison of ancient and modern cultures and groups of people, which should include:
  - Food-getting structures
  - Economic systems
  - Social stratification
  - Patterns of residence
  - Political organizations
  - Religions
  - Arts

# Social Stratification and Cultural Changes

**Social stratification** is the distribution of rights and obligations, power and authority, and goods and services within a society. There are five main topics of social stratification:

1. **Family**—Families exist in every society in every part of the world in one form or another. Every human being is or was a member of a family. There are many different definitions of a family (biological, psychological, and social). Biologically, everyone has a mother and a father. Psychologically, people can identify with someone they define as a parent (grandparent, uncle, aunt, brother, or sister). Socially, people can identify with other individuals or other groups of people as a "family," such as a friend or workplace peer. There are a variety of family types, with the most common being the **nuclear family (elementary or traditional family),** which consists of two or more people who are united by ties of parenthood or partnership as well as their socially recognized children (biological or adopted) all of which reside in a single household and interact with one another in respective social positions. A nuclear family consists of a pair of adults who are usually, but not always, married. Anthropologists and sociologists depict families as structural institutions that exist to help the continuation of a society.

2. **Norms**—These include the general rules by which a society exists. Norms define the patterns and structures of family, kinship, and marriage within a society.

3. **Marriage**—All societies recognize and permit marriage in one form or another. The most predominant form of marriage in the world is monogamy (exclusive relationship between two people), and it is a universally recognized norm.

4. **Residence**—When people marry, they decide where to live, which is dependent on the societal norms and conforms to one of three patterns:
   - **Neo-local**—The couple chooses a place of residence separate from either set of parents (most common in the United States and Europe).
   - **Matrilocal (Uxorilocal)**—The couple lives with or near the family of the wife (for example, Hopi, Pueblo, Amazon, !Kung).
   - **Patrilocal (Virilocal)**—The couple lives with or near the family of the husband (for example, Turkey, Igbo).

5. **Authority**—Rules of power are often dependent on gender in most societies. The two different types of authority include:
   - **Patriarchal**—The male has the power and authority demonstrated in personal as well as governmental law (for example, Japan, Iran, and Thailand).
   - **Matriarchal**—The female has power and authority, often being the oldest maternal figure (for example, Mosuo of China, Nair of South India, and Wemale of Seram).

There are also three types of societies based on authority:

1. **Egalitarian**—No one social group has greater access to economic resources, power, or prominence than another. Economic differences hold no bearing upon prominence within the society. For example, a cook and a doctor have equal access to societal possessions.

2. **Rank**—Economic resources and power are equal to all social groups, but prominence is unequally distributed. Often a ruler or chief maintain the highest prominence and status.

3. **Class**—There is unequal distribution in economic resources, power, and prominence among social groups. It can be a closed system (no ability to move into a higher rank) or an open system (the ability to move into a higher rank).

# Socialization and Acculturation

Societies are often built upon certain beliefs. Members of a society must learn how to cooperate or tolerate one another as well as the various belief systems that make up a society. There can be hurdles to overcome when faced with a network of different beliefs. As more and more cultures interact, more and more information is shared and transferred. The following terms are often associated with the interaction of societies and people:

- **Socialization**—The acceptance and practice of the behavior patterns of a culture (following the norms).
- **Acculturation**—The modification and adaptation of an individual or group as a result of contact or interaction with another culture. It can also be the manner by which an individual learns a culture.
- **Stereotypes**—Unsophisticated and strongly held beliefs about the characteristics of a group of people.

# Human Development and Behavior

Human development can be viewed from the biological, anthropological, or psychological realm. As a society develops and progresses, so do the individual humans within that society.

The three main psychological models of development are as follows:

1. **Jean Piaget**—He believed there are structural schemas in which individuals fit personal experiences through assimilation:

   *sensori-motor* (birth–2 yrs.) Experience through action; grabbing, looking, touching.

   *pre-operational* (2–7 yrs.) Thinking is concrete, egocentrical, and language develops.

   *concrete operations* (7–11 yrs.) Thinking is logical, mathematics develops, classification of objects begins.

   *formal operational* (12 yrs. and above) Thinking can handle abstract concepts.

2. **Sigmund Freud**—His theory revolved around sexual development and reflects five stages:

   *oral* (infancy)

   *anal* (1–3 yrs.)

   *phallic* (3–5 yrs.)

   *latency* (6 yrs.–puberty)

   *genital* (after puberty)

3. **Erik Erikson**—He further developed Freud's theories into eight "either/or" stages:

   *Trust versus Mistrust* (birth–1.5 yrs.)

   *Autonomy versus Self-Doubt* (1.5–3 yrs.)

   *Initiative versus Guilt* (3–6 yrs.)

   *Competence versus Inferiority* (6 yrs.–puberty)

   *Identity versus Role Confusion* (adolescence)

   *Intimacy versus Isolation* (early adult)

   *Generativity versus Stagnation* (middle adult)

   *Ego-Integrity versus Despair* (later adult)

Anthropology has helped establish that gender or sexual inequality is not a biological fact but rather a cultural and societal one. Gender role is a task or activity that a culture or society assigns to the different sexes.

# Economics

Economics is one of the social sciences and is defined as a social science that examines, studies, and analyzes the production, distribution, and consumption of goods and services. The goal of economics is to explain how financial systems work and how the financial entities interact and function.

Together, three organizations promote economic education and have developed national content standards for economics: the National Council on Economic Education, the Foundation for Teaching Economics, and the National Association of Economic Educators.

An economic system is the organization in which a state or nation allocates resources or apportions goods and services to the community. The society must follow the set principles and abide by guidelines pertaining to economic resources.

The following basic economics content knowledge will be assessed on the Praxis II:

- Key terms and major concepts of the economic market
- Economic effects on population and resources
- Impact on individuals and the government
- Economic systems
- Economic influences on technological developments
- International economics

There are two main branches of economics: microeconomics and macroeconomics.

**Microeconomics** is the branch of economics that is concerned with single factors and the effects of individual decisions on the economy. It studies the effects of decisions and behaviors on supply and demand, processes, quantities, market failure, competition, equilibrium, and elasticity of products.

**Macroeconomics** is the branch of economics that studies the behavior of the economy as a whole community. It is focused on changes in unemployment, national income, inflation, price levels, gross domestic product (GDP), and the rate of growth. Macroeconomics is used to help create and evaluate economic policy and business strategy.

# Key Terms and Major Concepts

The National Content Standards in Economics recommends 20 standards with benchmarks for grades 4, 8, and 12. These are summarized here:

- Resources are limited, so individuals must make choices.
- Costs and benefits must be analyzed when making economic decisions.
- Economic systems are complex and involve several institutions.
- Economic systems have a specific nature.
- Supply and demand play a major role in the market.
- Profits, incentives, and prices support the market system.
- Private and public economic sectors are different.
- Employment opportunities are specialized.
- Exchange or money use has various forms.
- Income is determined by market conditions.
- Investment and entrepreneurship are complex topics.
- Government policy affects a market system.

**Economic theories** include the following:

- **Anarchist**—There is no established control or guidelines.
- **Capitalism**—Property is privately owned and goods are privately produced.
- **Communist**—Endorses the establishment of society based on common ownership of the means of production.
- **Industrialism**—Uses large industries rather than agriculture or craftsmanship to create a system.
- **Laissez-faire**—Promotes private production to maintain freedom, security, and property rights.

- **Mercantilism**—States that a nation must depend on its capital and that the world market is unchangeable.
- **Socialist**—System of social control regarding property and income rather than individual control.

Students should be familiar with the following economic terms:

- **Black economy:** An unreported sector of the primary economic system in which transactions are handled in cash only
- **Budget:** Management of current money that requires choices and an analysis of the situation
- **Consumption:** The use of resources
- **Depression:** A long period of financial and industrial decline
- **Fiscal policy:** A way to regulate economic activity
- **Inflation:** An increase in overall prices for products and services
- **Macroeconomics:** How the national economics function (income, consumption, and investment)
- **Microeconomics:** How specific markets function involving consumers and businesses
- **Monetary policy:** The way government controls the money supply, such as interest rates
- **Recession:** Period of slow economic growth plagued with high unemployment and minimal spending
- **Supply and demand:** The amount of goods and services, which is directly related to the request for them—when the request (demand) goes up, the amount (supply) must go up, and therefore, the price goes up
- **Value:** The basis for economics, used to describe and measure what is occurring in the market

# The Individual and the Market

The **basic law of economics** is that of supply and demand, and individuals must often make choices based on the availability of the resources and their ability to obtain them. Supply and demand is such a crucial component of market economy that it is often considered the backbone of economics.

**Demand** is how much (quantity) of a good or service is sought after by consumers. The quantity that is demanded is measured by the amount of product people are willing to buy at a certain price. *Demand relationship* is the correlation between price and quantity demanded. *The law of demand* asserts that if all other factors beside demand remain constant and equal, the higher priced a good or service is the less people will demand it. So the higher the price, the lower the demand, and thus the higher the opportunity cost of buying that good or service.

**Supply** is how much of a good or service the market can offer. The quantity supplied correlates to the amount producers are willing to supply when receiving a certain price. *Supply relationship* is the connection between the price of a good or service and how much of that good or service is supplied to the market. The *law of supply* states that the higher the price of a good or service, the higher the quantity supplied. Producers will supply more of a good or service when receiving a high price as it increases revenue. Supply is often time-based as suppliers must react to changes in demand or price in order to produce appropriate quantities of product.

Every individual is affected by economics on a daily basis. Learning economics helps an individual better understand his or her role in relation to local, state, national, and international policies. Citizens become better informed of issues, more involved in changes, and could be influenced to vote.

Although choices may be restricted or affected by laws and regulations, many economic decisions are made by individuals based on the costs and benefits to them personally. Individuals have a say in the amount of products produced and the costs, which is established by their rate of spending and desire for the items. This process creates competition and promotes the issue of supply and demand.

# Effect on Population and Resources

A free market economy, like that of the United States, is based on two premises, that of **competition** and **supply and demand.** This type of economy allows the businesses and consumers to decide what should be produced, what employees should be paid, how much a product or service should cost, and how much should be provided for the population.

According to the United Nations, over the next few decades the global population will be greatly reduced and the aged population will continue to increase. These two factors cause changes in the culture, health-care systems, and economic systems of this nation. It is estimated that the rising numbers of people, primarily in underdeveloped countries, will cause a drastic drain on resources. The acceleration of resource usage and the impact on the environment are primarily the result of the growing populations in China and India, and natural resources are diminishing. It is believed that food, shelter, water, and natural resources will be greatly affected and that the need for increased plans to address poverty, disease, and conflicts are necessary.

It is believed that to eliminate the economic burden, people will work longer and investigate other options of working situations, as well as impose the same plans worldwide to reduce population growth as was implemented for developing countries in previous years. Without careful planning and serious considerations, resources will be greatly diminished, migration will cause more concerns, and economies will be further strained.

## Government's Role

Most economic decisions in the country are based on consumers and producers of products. The government often refers to the "free enterprise system" as being the most positive for the state of the economy. Debates about government involvement in economic efforts abound. Yet, the government plays a role in the economic development and process in four areas: fiscal policy (taxes), regulation, spending, and monetary policy (credit).

Stabilization and growth are of primary concern, and therefore the government attempts to guide the economic activities in the country, which includes employment rates, prices, and overall growth. When the government adjusts the fiscal level, manages the supply of money, or controls the credit rates, the economy changes (up or down depending on the intervention).

Spending and taxes can be controlled by the President and Congress, which changes the status of the economy in the country and may influence economies abroad. The government's monetary policy is directed by the nation's central bank, the Federal Reserve Board, with involvement from the President and Congress.

Other types of economic government interventions are termed:

> **Anarchism:** Self-regulated market with voluntary trade
>
> **Capitalism:** Mostly private-owned for profit
>
> **Laissez-faire:** Strict free market with absence of government involvement
>
> **Socialism:** Cooperative- and labor-managed

## Economic Systems

An economic system pertains to a specific group of social institutions and people dealing with the production, distribution, and consumption of goods, services, and resources in the society.

The general economic systems are as follows:

- **Autarky economy (closed economy)**—Self-sufficient system that limits outside trade, relying on its own resources.
- **Dual economy**—Two systems (local needs and global needs) within one country, occurs mostly in underdeveloped countries.
- **Gift economy**—Believes that goods and services should be given without specific reason, such as for generosity.
- **Market economy**—Functions through the exchange in the "free market." It is not designed or managed by a central authority, but through privately owned production, in which the revenue is distributed through the operation of markets.
- **Mixed economy**—Considered a compromise system, as it allows publicly and privately owned companies or businesses to operate simultaneously.
- **Natural economy**—Operates on a bartering or trade system rather than a monetary foundation for the exchange of goods and services.

- **Open economy**—Allows export and import from the global market.
- **Participatory economy**—Guides the production, consumption, and allocation of resources through participatory decision-making of its society members.
- **Planned economy (directed economy)**—Is designed and managed through a primary authority.
- **Subsistence economy**—Is one in which the output of services and goods meets only the population consumption of the area and resources are renewed and reproduced.

## Impact of Technology

As technology increases changes are evident in the local as well as global economies. In the past, vast improvements were made in the transportation of goods (by automobiles, trains, boats, planes). Most recently, immense strides have been made in communications, enabling products and services to be more widely distributed. The use of computers and the World Wide Web has dramatically increased the abilities of economies to interact with one another. Customers around the world may shop and browse online, place orders, and pay from the comfort of their own homes. For example, a small T-shirt manufacturer can reach international customers more rapidly by creating a website and placing order forms online.

## International Economics

International economics is the interaction of economic practices and factors between countries. It includes the production of items, international trade (import-export), and investments. International economics influences labor standards, the monetary exchange rates, outsourcing of work, and resource policies (based on supply and demand). It may also affect wages and incomes for the people of the various countries. Globalization of the economy, in some areas of the world, causes conflicts and issues of safety for its people.

Another factor in the status of international economics is the establishment of the International Monetary Fund (IMF), which allocates short-term credit to countries that need to pay off a debt. They may do so by taking a loan, using reserves, or increasing exports. Countries generally need assistance from the IMF when their economy is out of balance.

# Chapter 12

# Science Content Knowledge (0014/5014)

The National Science Teachers Association (NSTA) formed the National Commission on Science Education Standards and Assessment (NCSESA) to develop national standards related to science education. Although available, these are not federally mandated nor are they part of any mandated national curriculum. This organization produced a document that outlines the recommended perimeters of science education to ensure that students receive the proper instruction and benefits from science programs. Their primary goal states:

> "All students regardless of age, sex, cultural or ethnic background, disabilities, aspirations, or interest and motivation in science should have the opportunity to obtain high levels of scientific literacy."

Several principles guide the science standards set forth by the NCSESA:

1. Science is for every student.
2. Learning science requires an active process.
3. Science education should emulate the intellectual and cultural traditions of contemporary science.
4. Education reform should include the improvement of science education.

The NCSESA, supported by NSTA, created eight categories of content standards for science at the elementary levels (K–4, 5–8) and the secondary level (9–12). The content standards include the following:

1. Unifying concepts and processes in science
2. Science as inquiry
3. Physical science
4. Life science
5. Earth and space science
6. Science and technology
7. Science in personal and social perspectives
8. History and the nature of science

Note: These are explained more fully in Chapter 5, "Science Curriculum, Instruction, and Assessment (0011/5011)."

# Prominent Scientific Laws

Many important laws and theories govern science. A scientific law is a statement of fact that is proven time and time again. A scientific theory is a statement, based on educated observations, tested, and then it may be proven. Educators should be knowledgeable about the laws and theories that support the processes and concepts of science.

Although these laws may not be formally taught in the early elementary grades, the general science concepts and instruction at that lower elementary level will lead to the understanding of these laws when they are more formally taught in upper elementary and secondary programs.

Prominent laws of science and explanations to support elementary science education include:

I.  Conservation Laws—Fundamental laws of all science.

> Conservation of Mass/Matter—Matter cannot be created or destroyed but can be rearranged.

> Conservation of Energy—Energy remains constant in a system and cannot be recreated, but can change forms.

> Conservation of Momentum—Total momentum remains the same unless acted upon by an outside force ($p = mv$).

> Charge Conservation—Electric charge can neither be created nor destroyed but is always conserved.

II. Gas Laws

Boyle's Law—For a specified amount of gas kept at a specified temperature, pressure and volume are inversely proportional (while one increases, the other decreases) ($PV = k$).

Ideal Gas Law—The state of an amount of gas is determined by its pressure, volume, and temperature ($PV = nRT$).

III. Einstein's Laws

Mass-Energy Equivalence—When a body has a mass it has a certain energy even if it is not moving ($E = mc^2$).

General Relativity—Gravitational attraction between masses is a result of the nearby masses. Gravity has waves.

IV. Newton's Laws

First Law: Law of Inertia—An object will remain at rest or in motion unless acted upon by an outside force.

Second Law: Law of Acceleration—An object will move in the direction of the force applied to it. The object's acceleration is proportional to the force applied to it and inversely proportional to the mass of the object.

Third Law: Law of Reciprocal Actions—For every action there is an opposite and equal reaction.

Law of Gravity—Any two objects in the universe exert gravitational attraction on each other. This force has a universal form and is directed along the line of centers for the two objects and is proportional to the product of their masses and inversely proportional to the square of the separation between the two objects. $F_g = G\,(m_1 \times m_2 \div r^2)$

V. Electromagnetic Laws

Ohm's Law—Measures voltage and current in electrical circuits. The current going through a conductor is equal to the voltage divided by the resistor. $\left(I = \dfrac{V}{R}\right)$

Faraday's Law of Induction—Explains the ways that voltage can be generated. Any change in the magnetic environment of a coil of wire will cause voltage to be produced. (EMF)

VI. Thermodynamics

Fourier's Law (Law of Heat Conduction)—The transfer of heat moves through matter from higher temperatures to lower temperatures in order to equalize differences.

Zeroth Law—If two systems are in thermal equilibrium with a third system then they are in thermal equilibrium with each other as well.

First Law—The change in a system's internal energy is equal to the difference between heat added to the system from its surroundings and work done by the system on its surroundings; all heat energy added to a system will either cause the system to do work or change the internal energy of the system. Basically, energy cannot be created or destroyed.

Second Law—It is impossible for a process to have as its sole result the transfer of heat from a cooler body to a hotter one; it puts constraints upon the direction of heat transfer and the efficiencies of heat engines. Basically, energy exhibits entropy and moves away from its source.

Third Law—All processes stop as you move closer to absolute zero; there is no energy.

VII. Darwin's Laws

Natural Selection—Individual organisms with favorable traits are more likely to survive and reproduce.

Evolution—The world is in a constant state of change.

Common Descent—Every group of living organisms on Earth descended from a common ancestor.

Multiplication of Species—Species split into or produce other species depending on geographical location.

Gradualism—Changes occur through the slow gradual change of population, not through fast sudden production of new beings.

VIII. Kepler's Laws (Planetary Motion)

Law of Ellipses—The path of the planets around the sun is an elliptical shape with the center of the sun being at the focus.

Law of Equal Areas—An imaginary line drawn from the center of the sun to the center of the planet will sweep out equal areas in equal intervals of time.

Law of Harmonies—Compares the orbital period and the radius of the orbit of a planet to the other planets, providing an accurate description of the time and the distance for the planets' orbit around the sun. The ratio of the squares of the periods of any two planets is equal to the ratio of the cubes of their average distances from the sun.

# Earth Science

This area of science examines the structure and function of the Earth. It also extends studies into space and the universe. Earth science is important to understand as it directly relates to human actions and behaviors. In this section are topics such as structures of the Earth, processes of the Earth, Earth history, the universe, and interactions of the Earth with the universe.

## Structure of the Earth System

The Earth is comprised of many complex systems. These systems make up the various components and layers of the Earth, both on the surface and above the Earth.

The following four principal components associated with the Earth work together in a constant complex system:

- Atmosphere (air)
- Lithosphere (land)
- Hydrosphere (water)
- Biosphere (life)

Five layers comprise the atmosphere, listed here from highest to lowest:

- Exosphere (outermost area composed of hydrogen and helium from 300–600 miles to 6,000 miles)—This layer is slender and interacts with solar winds. Solar winds can compress this layer or allow it to increase in depth. It ranges from 620 miles to 6,214 miles above the Earth's surface, where it then merges with interplanetary space.
- Ionosphere (265,000–285,000 feet to 400+ miles)—Energy particles (ions) from the sun and outer space create this electric layer. This layer extends approximately 430 miles above the Earth's surface.
- Mesosphere (160,000 feet to about 285,000 feet)—This layer usually burns up the meteors that fly toward Earth, keeping them from striking the surface. It extends about 52 miles above the Earth's surface and is extremely cold.
- Stratosphere (23,000–60,000 feet to about 160,000 feet)—Includes the ozone layer, which blocks the harmful ultraviolet rays of the sun, causing it to be warmer than the troposphere. It extends about 30 miles above the Earth's surface.
- Troposphere (23,000 to 60,000 feet)—Provides most of the Earth's weather and contains about four-fifths of the Earth's air. It extends about 11 miles from the Earth's surface at the equator but less at the poles. The Earth's structure is composed of four concentric spheres. These layers of the Earth include:
  - Crust—5–30 miles thick, not fixed, a mosaic of moving plates, outer shell
  - Mantle—1,800 miles thick, plasticity (ability of solid to flow), circulating currents, causing the plates to move (it is comprised of the asthenosphere and lithosphere)
  - Outer core—1,300 miles thick, viscous liquid, the Earth's magnetic field originates here
  - Inner core—800 miles to the center of the Earth, a solid

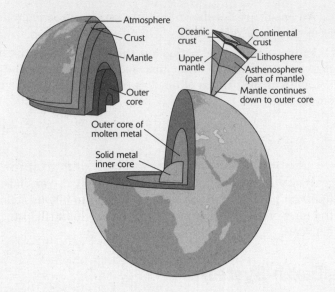

## Plate Tectonics

The Earth's crust is divided into about 20 plates, each varying in size and thickness. These plates continually drift and shift, changing the structure of the Earth's landforms. Plates are found under continents (continental plates) and beneath the ocean (oceanic plates).

## Plate Movement

There are three types of plate boundaries.

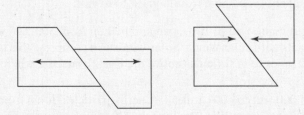

Divergent          Convergent

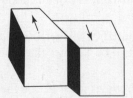

Transform

| Convergent (collision) | results in | mountains, volcanoes, ridges, recycling of crust |
|---|---|---|
| Transform (rubbing) | results in | earthquakes |
| Divergent (separating) | results in | new crust, rivers, oceans, lakes |

# Processes of the Earth System

The Earth functions as a result of various interrelated systems and is affected by their individual processes. Plants, humans, heat, weathering, erosion, the rock cycle, and the weather cycle each impact the Earth in different ways:

- **Plants** (biosphere) pull water (hydrosphere) and nutrients from the soil (lithosphere) and release oxygen and water vapor into the air (atmosphere).
- **Humans** (biosphere) build dams using rock materials (lithosphere) to control a lake (hydrosphere); as the water evaporates, it disperses into the air (atmosphere).
- **Heat** influences the Earth more than any other process in the universe. There are two sources of heat:
  1. Solar energy (the sun)—The Earth is on an axis, and the sun hits the surface at varying angles causing the major climates to occur on the planet. The sun affects and influences the type of life that exists in the various regions. It affects Earth's weather, which in turn affects the vegetation and erosion.
  2. Radioactivity (Earth's core)—Radioactivity is responsible for plate tectonics, most volcanoes, and earthquakes, which are located near plate boundaries. Radioactivity makes mountains, valleys, ocean basins, lake beds, islands, trenches, and most other landforms.
- **Weathering**—The process of changing structures through the effects of wind, water, ice, sun, and gravity.
- **Erosion**—The process of moving weathered materials by water or winds to another location.
- **Rock cycle**—All rocks come from the mantle except for limestone.

Following are three types of rocks:

- **Igneous**—Forms when magma cools (for example, granite and pumice)
- **Sedimentary**—Forms when layers of sediments are compressed (for example, sandstone, limestone, coal, and shale)
- **Metamorphic**—Forms through the transformation of igneous and sedimentary rocks through heat and pressure (for example, marble, slate, and quartzite)

The weather cycle occurs in the troposphere. There are three contributing factors to weather:

1. **Solar radiation:** Heat energy or infrared radiation from the sun hits the Earth's surface and changes into heat.
2. **Earth movement:** The seasons are caused by the orbit of the Earth around the sun and the rotation of the Earth upon its axis.

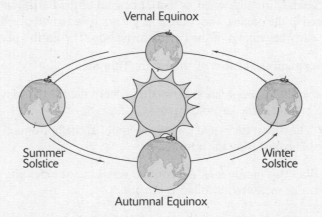

3. **Water Cycle:** A natural process in which water evaporates, condenses, and precipitates across the Earth's surface.

# Earth History

The Earth started as a giant, red-hot, roiling, magma ocean caused by the collision of space rocks. As the collisions slowed, the planet began to slowly cool, forming a thin crust on the surface. During this cooling, water vapor condensed in the air to form the Earth's atmosphere. Clouds formed and storms began to develop, bringing more and more water to the surface to cool it. The surface flooded with water, forming the oceans and seas.

Geological history, a type of science, investigates how the Earth and its life-forms have developed over time. The Earth is almost 5 billion years old. Currently, we know that 71 percent of the Earth's surface is ocean, with 97 percent of the Earth's water represented in the oceans. The continents known have moved over time and landforms known today have changed since the early beginnings of the Earth's formation. The Earth's plates move 2–5 cm per year.

There are two laws that help explain the history of the Earth. They are:

- *Principle of Uniformitarianism*—The scientific laws that govern the Earth today are the same since the beginning of time. The present is the key to the past.
- *Law of Superposition*—The oldest rocks and events are found at the bottom of formations, and the youngest are found at the top. The past is on the bottom.

The geologic time scale describes two major eons. An eon is a very long or indefinite period of time that explains the age of the universe and can be measured by billions of years:

- Precambian Eon—The period of time from the early formation of Earth (4.6 billion years ago) to the rise of life-forms, which are similar to present-day life-forms.
- Phanerozoic Eon—The period of time from the rise of life-forms to present day. Three eras are found within the Phanerozoic Eon:
  - Paleozoic: Early life, approximately 540 to 570 mya–245 mya—Trilobites, shells, mollusks, brachiopods, echinoderms, rise of first vertebrates, rise of land plants, rise of amphibians and large complex reptiles, and the beginnings of insects, seed plants, and trees.

- Mesozoic: Middle life, approximately 245 mya–65 mya—The rise of mammals and dinosaurs, the rise of birds, the extinction of dinosaurs, and the rise of flowering plants.
- Cenozoic: Late life, 65 mya–present day—The rise of primates, the rise of horses, the rise of hominids and modern man.

# Earth and Universe

The universe originated approximately 20 billion years ago from large amounts of matter that experienced a catastrophic explosion, which spread outward in all directions from the epicenter. The galaxies were formed into galactic clusters. The Milky Way galaxy is where the Earth is located. Everything that is seen in the sky with the naked eye belongs to this galaxy.

The sun and all bodies that revolve around it comprise our solar system. There are eight planets: Mercury, Venus, Earth, Mars, Jupiter, Saturn, Uranus, and Neptune. Pluto was once considered the ninth planet in our solar system but in 2006 there was a reclassification of space worlds. Since Pluto, Eris, and Ceres are more complex and developed than an asteroid but do not have the gravitational power to move and scatter objects near their orbits, they could not be classified as planets. These three worlds became the first dwarf planets identified in our solar system. Each planet revolves around the sun in an elliptical orbit at varying speeds. Each planet also has its own moon(s) that revolves around the planet and is caught in the planet's gravitational pull.

A meteoroid is a stony or metallic particle that revolves around the sun.

A meteor is created when meteorites burn through the Earth's atmosphere.

A comet revolves around the sun and possesses a tail and a nucleus. The tail always points away from the sun due to the solar winds.

Constellations are a type of boundary system astronomers use for organizing the night sky. There are 88 constellational regions and each region is named for the group of stars found within it.

## The Earth within the Universe

Earth has one moon, which takes one lunar month to revolve (28 days) around the Earth. The moon does not emit its own light but rather reflects the sun's light. The moon rotates upon an axis just like Earth, at exactly the same period and speed. Therefore, the same side of the moon is seen at all times. The moon phases are caused by the position of the moon relative to the sun.

## Moon Phases

The moon exhibits five different phases during its rotation around the Earth: new moon, crescent moon, quarter moon, gibbous moon, and full moon. During two of these phases the moon also exhibits waxing and waning. A waxing moon occurs when the sunlit portion of the moon is increasing and a waning moon occurs when the sunlit portion of the moon decreases. A waxing moon occurs twice in the 5 phases during both the crescent and the gibbous phases. A waning moon also occurs twice in the 5 phases during both the crescent and the gibbous phases.

New Moon  Waxing Crescent  First Quarter  Waxing Gibbous  Full Moon  Waning Gibbous  Last Quarter  Waning Crescent

An **eclipse** is the total or partial obscuring of a celestial body by another body, particularly involving the sun, the Earth, and the moon. An eclipse of the sun or moon occurs when the Earth, moon, and sun are aligned. There are three types of eclipses involving these celestial bodies.

During a **lunar eclipse,** all or part of the moon is blocked by the Earth's shadow and is no longer illuminated by the sun. A lunar eclipse only occurs during a full moon when the moon is directly opposite the sun.

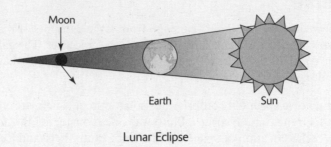

Lunar Eclipse

During a **solar eclipse,** the moon comes between the sun and the Earth, casting a shadow upon the Earth. During a total solar eclipse, the moon completely covers the vision of the sun and only the corona is visible.

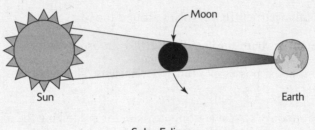

Solar Eclipse

An **annular eclipse** occurs when the moon is in the farthest orbit from the Earth and does not fully cover the sun, so part of the sun is visible as a ring around the moon.

# Life Science

This area of science involves the study of living things (biology) and their characteristics. It encompasses both plants and animals, the structure of a cell, reproduction and propagation of the species, physical structures, behaviors within environments, adaptations, and the interdependence of species. Millions of species exist and there are newly identified organisms discovered each year. These living things are categorized according to kingdoms.

There are five known kingdoms based in biology:

- Monera—Single-celled organism without nuclei (bacteria)
- Protista—Single-celled organism with nuclei (algae, protozoans)
- Fungi—Single-celled and multicelled organisms (mushrooms, molds, yeasts, lichens)
- Plantae—Multicellular plant organisms (mosses, ferns, conifers, dicots, monocots)
- Animalia—Multicellular animals (10–21 phyla)

The organization of living things is further studied according to a diagram that replicates a ladder or a pyramid. Within the traditional Linnean classification system, there are seven major levels or categories that are classified according to shared physical characteristics:

- Kingdom
- Phylum

- Class
- Order
- Family
- Genus
- Species

Each kingdom is broken down into smaller categories called phyla. A phylum contains organisms that are genetically related through common ancestry. Each phylum is then broken down into separate classes. A class is a more specific breakdown of organisms in which the group shares a common attribute, characteristic, or trait. Classes are further divided into orders, in which the class is specifically divided into smaller shared characteristics. Order then splits into smaller units called families, in which organisms possess multiple traits in common. Family is broken into genus, where the organisms share many common attributes. The last break is into species, in which organisms can interbreed and produce offspring that can propagate the species.

There are many mnemonic devices used to remember this breakdown of categories. Here are a few that may help you and your students:

**K**ing **P**hillip **C**ame **O**ver **F**or **G**ood **S**paghetti

**K**ids **P**laying **C**hicken **O**n **F**reeways **G**et **S**mashed

**K**ids **P**refer **C**heese **O**ver **F**ried **G**reen **S**pinach

**K**ings **P**lay **C**hess **O**n **F**ine **G**lass **S**urfaces

Carolus Linnaeus was an eighteenth-century Swedish botanist who developed the system of binomial nomenclature used for naming the various species. Each species is given a two-part Latin name, formed by affixing a specific label to the genus name. The genus name is capitalized, and then both the genus name and specific label are italicized (for example, common dog is *Canis familiaris*).

Following are examples of specific classifications:

| Human | Giant Panda |
|---|---|
| Kingdom: Animalia | Kingdom: Animalia |
| Phylum: Chordata (animals with backbones) | Phylum: Chordata |
| Class: Mammalia (with hair, female produces milk) | Class: Mammalia |
| Order: Primate (apes and monkeys) | Order: Carnivora |
| Family: Hominadae | Family: Ursidae |
| Genus: Homo | Genus: Ailuropoda |
| Species: Homo sapiens | Species: Ailuropoda melanoleuca |

# Structure and Function of Living Systems

According to the National Science Education Standards developed in 1996, "important **levels of organization** for structure and function include **cells, organs, tissues, organ systems, whole organisms,** and **ecosystems.** All organisms are composed of **cells—the basic unit of life.** Cells carry on the many functions needed to sustain life. Each type of cell, tissue, and organ has a distinct structure and set of functions. Human systems interact with one another. **Disease** is a breakdown in structures or functions of an organism."

The living systems include plants and animals that inhabit the Earth, and the characteristics of living things include:

- Made of protoplasm
- Reproduce, give rise to similar organisms
- Organized into cells

- Affected by the environment
- Use energy
- Adapt to the environment
- Capable of growth
- Respond to the environment
- Have definite life spans

# Cells

A cell is the fundamental unit that composes the structure and function of life. All living things are made up of cells. Following is the breakdown of a living body:

Tissue = a group of similar cells

Organs = a group of tissues working together

System = a group of organs working together

Organism = a group of systems

Functions of a cell:

- Manufacture proteins and other materials for building cells
- Manufacture energy
- Reproduce (mitosis and/or meiosis)

Plant cells manufacture their own food from water, minerals, and carbon dioxide.

| Parts of a Cell—Animal and Plant | |
|---|---|
| **Cell Part** | **Description** |
| Cell membrane | Made of lipids, permits inward passage of needed items/outward passage of waste |
| Nucleus | Control center of cell, "the brain" that contains DNA |
| Cytoplasm | Consists of all materials outside of the nucleus; supports and protects cell organelles |
| Endoplasmic reticulum (ER) | A system of transport canals that travel from the nucleus to cytoplasm |
| Ribosomes | Manufacture proteins |
| Mitochondria | Releases energy to cell through chemical reactions |
| Lysosomes | Hold enzymes to break down molecules |
| Golgi apparatus | Packages the proteins and transports them through the cell |
| Vacuoles | Store food, water, minerals, and wastes |
| Centrioles | Found only in animal cells; used during cellular division to organize the assembly of microtubles |
| **In addition to all those parts listed above, plants include the following:** | |
| Cell wall | Made of cellulose, provides rigid structure for plant, permits passage in and out of the cell |
| Chloroplasts | Consist of plastids that contain chlorophyll; function in photosynthesis; release oxygen |

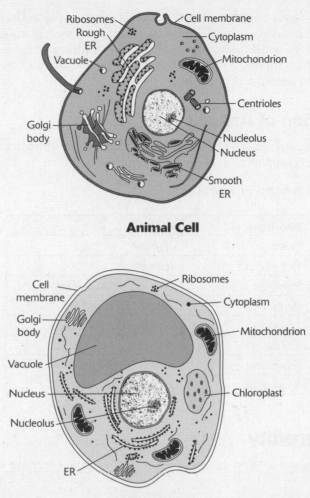

**Animal Cell**

**Plant Cell**

| Structure and Function of Plants ||
|---|---|
| **Part** | **Description/Purpose** |
| Roots | The anchor that absorbs water and minerals; functions in food storage |
| Stem | The transport that takes nutrients to the leaves; provides support to the leaves, flowers, and fruit |
| Leaves | The builder that manufactures food for the plant; main site of photosynthesis |
| Flower | The sex organ that is the site of reproduction of the plant |
| Fruit | The ripened ovaries of flowers; functions in the propagation of the plant through dispersal of the seeds |

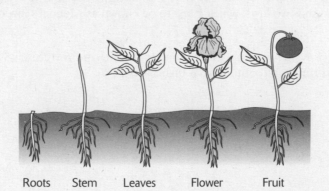

Roots        Stem        Leaves        Flower        Fruit

Flowers are the reproductive organs of plants. Insects and birds are attracted to the flower petals and help transport and disperse **pollen** for cross-fertilization. The **stamen,** which is the male reproductive organ, manufactures the pollen. The **pistil,** which is the female reproductive organ, has multiple parts: a **stigma,** which is the sticky top that captures pollen; **styles,** which transport the pollen to the ovary; and an **ovary,** which makes the ovules. When pollen joins the ovule, fertilized seeds are the outcome.

## Structure and Function of Animals

For animals to live and survive as a species, they must grow, reproduce, and interact with the environment. Animals must have systems that support each of their individual cells.

There are eight basic systems/functions of animals:

| Functions | System |
| --- | --- |
| Nutrition | Digestive |
| Respiration | Respiratory |
| Response | Brain and nervous system |
| Regulation | Glands and hormones |
| Excretion | Kidneys and other organs |
| Circulation | Circulatory |
| Movement | Nervous system and brain |
| Reproduction | Sexual and asexual |

# Reproduction/Heredity

Reproduction facilitates organisms to grow and to continue their species. There are two types of reproductive systems specific to organisms:

- Asexual—A cell that creates two identical pairs of chromosomes, splits, and forms nuclei around the chromosomes. The process of cell division is called **mitosis.** New cells are created using only one "parent" (for example, algae, bacteria, sponges, mold, fungi).

- Sexual—Requires the union of a male gamete and female gamete (a gamete is a reproductive cell). **Meiosis** is the process in which the gametes form. Each gamete has one-half of the chromosomes needed for reproduction. When the two gametes combine, they each donate one-half of the chromosomes to the new nucleus. When combined, the egg is fertilized with a full chromosome count.

DNA (deoxyribonucleic acid) carries the code of protein production, which is the code of life. Chromosomes are made of genes that are comprised of strands of DNA. Chromosomes come in pairs with a gene that contains a trait on each part of the pair. Traits can be dominant or recessive. The principles that govern heredity were discovered and outlined by a monk in the 1860s named Gregor Mendel. Mendel worked with pea plants and selected seven traits to study. He was able to manipulate certain traits and characteristics by cross-breeding and selective breeding. He discovered two laws, which came to be known as Mendel's law of segregation and law of independent assortment.

Mendel developed a reference system which used $D$ (dominant trait) and $R$ (recessive trait) as codes to demonstrate the possible traits offspring could obtain from their parents.

| DD | Dominant trait appears in organism. |
|----|--------------------------------------|
| DR | Dominant trait appears in organism, but organism carries recessive trait and can pass it on to its young. |
| RR | Recessive trait appears in organism. |

Examples of these traits follow:

- D traits—Brown eyes, curly hair, widow's peak, ability to curl tongue, freckles, unattached earlobes, dimples
- R traits—Blue or green eyes, straight hair, cannot curl tongue, no freckles, attached earlobes, no dimples

# Biological Evolution

Genetically, most offspring mirror their parents; however, abnormalities can sometimes occur. Abnormal or mutant genes occur by mistakes made during DNA duplication. This usually results in a nonfertilized egg that is discarded naturally. However, occasionally these mutations allow fertilization and in fact make the offspring more able to prosper or have a better chance of reproduction than offspring without the mutation. When this happens, most of the species will eventually possess the mutation.

**Biological evolution** is a scientific process in which inherited traits of organisms change from one generation to the next; it refers to the cumulative changes that occur in a population over time. There are two major beliefs regarding biological evolution:

- Natural selection—Producing and passing on traits that are helpful and necessary for the survival of the organism. Through natural selection, the most advantageous traits for a specific environment are kept or propagated forth while the traits that are disadvantageous are decreased.
- Adaptations—Large changes that occur after successive, small, and random changes or mutations in traits. This may cause permanent changes in the species or it may force the species to become extinct.

The basic principles of ecological evolution are as follows:

- **Survival of the fittest**—Organisms best adapted to an environment will generally produce the most offspring. Offspring that pose the more favorable traits will survive and reproduce, thus increasing the frequency of certain traits. For example:

  Polar bears are best suited to the cold regions of the world and continue to populate there.

  Mountain lions or cougars are adaptable to most regions of the world.

- **Natural selection**—This is the process in which individuals with favorable traits survive and reproduce. It shows how organisms become better adapted to survive environments while the organisms with less favorable adaptations or traits die out. For example:

  Camouflaged brown lizards living in the desert are more apt to survive than if they were black.

  An Arctic fox with white fur is more likely to survive the Arctic climate and its predators than a fox with black or brown fur.

# Interdependence of Organisms

Since there are numerous organisms that inhabit the Earth, they must learn to adapt and function in diverse environments located on the Earth's surface. Every species is linked either directly or indirectly within an ecosystem.

Plants often depend on animals for fertilizer, reproduction, or nutrients. Animals depend on plants for food, shelter, or nesting sites. Parasites can be both harmful and beneficial to their host. In general, on the Earth,

- Atoms and molecules cycle through the living and nonliving components of the biosphere.
- Energy travels through the ecosystem in a specific direction (the food chain cycle: photosynthetic organisms–herbivores–carnivores–decomposers).
- Organisms cooperate and compete within the ecosystem.
- Living organisms have the ability to produce populations of unlimited size; however, environments and resources are limited, and this interaction has significant effects on how the organisms react.
- Human beings live within the world's ecosystems and alter them by such things as population growth, technology, and consumption.

**Ecology** is the study of the interaction of organisms within their environment and with one another. This study helps foster an understanding of the interdependence of organisms. In order to understand the interaction of organisms, knowledge of the biosphere is essential. The *biosphere* is the larger environment in which living things exist (land, air, water). An *ecosystem* is the smaller community found within the biosphere of the living and non-living components. An ecosystem has energy flow and recycling of minerals. They can be large (desert or ocean) or small (pond or backyard).

There are three key characteristics of a balanced ecosystem:

1. Constant source of energy (sun—solar energy).
2. Energy is converted to glucose (needed by all living things).
3. Organic nutrients and matter are recycled successfully.

The Food Chain is the primary way ecosystems transmit and disperse energy.

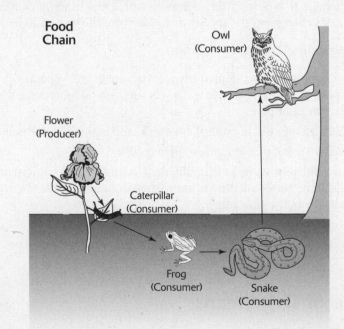

Ecosystem balance depends on the interactions between the species. The interdependence of organisms help to maintain a healthy world. Some conditions that change an ecosystem's balance include the following:

- Supply of energy changes
- Food cycle interrupted

- Organic matter and nutrients increase or decrease
- Natural disasters (floods, earthquakes, tornadoes, erosion)
- Natural phenomena (El Niño)
- Human contributions (air or water pollution, raw material usage, increased production of carbon dioxide, radiation, mining, deforestation)

## Life Cycle

Life cycles are a series of changes that an organism goes through during its growth and development as it progresses from birth to a mature state. Simple organisms (bacteria) start their life cycle when an organism is produced by fission and ends when the organism divides or splits. Organisms that reproduce sexually begin their life cycle with the fusion of reproductive cells forming a new organism. The cycle then ends when the new organism produces reproductive cells itself.

Every living organism moves through these life cycle stages:

1. Come into being, birth (sometimes a larvae state)
2. Growth
3. Metamorphosis
4. Maturation
5. Reproduction
6. Death

Some lower species exhibit additional juvenile and larvae stages, and these occur in order for the organism to develop into adults (for example, frog). In higher species, the fertilized egg develops directly into the adult (for example, dog, human).

# Physical Science

This is the first domain of science in which the tangible and material world is studied. This science focuses on analyzing the nature and properties of energy and nonliving matter. Instruction should focus on facts, concepts, principles, theories, and the models of science. Following are physical science components:

- Structures and properties of objects, materials, and matter
- Motion and force
- Light, heat, electricity, magnetism
- Energy (transfer, consumption, production)

## Structure and Properties of Matter

Materials found on Earth include elements, compounds, and mixtures.

- Atom— It is the basis of chemistry and so small it cannot be divided. Atoms make up all matter. An atom has a nucleus (protons and neutrons) and up to seven shells (orbiting electrons). An atom is comprised of neutrons (no charge), protons (positively charged), and electrons (negatively charged). The **atomic number** of an atom is the same as the number of protons found within the nucleus and also determines what element the atom is. The atomic number of a neutrally charged atom is also the same as the number of electrons. The **atomic mass** is figured based on the total number of protons and neutrons. Niels Böhr discovered the structure of the atom and developed the Böhr diagram, shown below.
- Nucleus—The center of the atom with a positive charge (+); it contains neutrons and protons.

- Proton—Located in the nucleus, it has a positive (+) charge and is symbolized by the letter "p."
- Electron—Located in the shells that orbit an atom's nucleus, it has a negative (−) charge and is symbolized by the letter "e."
- Neutron—Located in the nucleus, it has no charge and is symbolized by the letter "n."

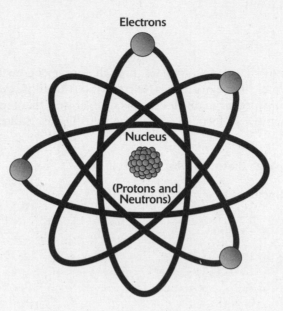

# Chemistry

Chemistry is the study of the science of matter, especially the properties, structures, composition, behavior reactions, and interactions of such components. Chemistry creates a connection between physics and other natural sciences.

Elements are the basic structures studied. An **element** is matter that cannot be separated into different kinds of matter. As of May 2011, there are 118 elements that have been discovered and identified on Earth. They are represented on the periodic table, developed by Dmitri Mendeleev in 1869. Elements are listed on the table according to similar properties (families) as well as by their atomic numbers (number of protons in the nucleus).

Common elements to know at the elementary level are listed below, in alphabetical order for convenience:

Aluminum = Al

Calcium = Ca

Carbon = C

Copper = Cu

Gold = Au

Helium = He

Hydrogen = H

Iodine = I

Iron = Fe

Lead = Pb

Magnesium = Mg

Nickel = Ni

Nitrogen = N

Oxygen = O

Potassium = K

Silver = Ag

Sodium = Na

Sulfur = S

Tin = Sn

A **compound** is formed by the chemical bonding of two or more elements.

Common compounds to know at the elementary level include:

Baking soda = $NaHCO_3$

Carbon dioxide = $CO_2$

Carbon monoxide = CO

Sand or glass = $SiO_2$

Table salt = NaCl

Water = $H_2O$

# Three Forms of Matter: Gas, Liquid, Solid

| State of Matter | Definition of Type of Matter | Shape | Example | Graphic Representation |
|---|---|---|---|---|
| Gas | Has weak molecular forces with no shape, color, or volume and can expand infinitely | Volume of container Shape of container | air | Gas |
| Liquid | Takes on the shape of the container that holds it and has definite volume with molecular forces weaker than a solid | Fixed volume Shape of container Free surface | milk | Liquid |
| Solid | Has defined shape and definite volume with strong molecular forces, and holds a shape | Fixed volume Holds shape | wood | Solid |

All matter can move from one of the three states of matter to another state, which is accomplished through temperature changes and/or pressure changes.

**Solid**    Decrease pressure → Increase energy → **Liquid**    Decrease pressure → Increase energy → **Gas**

States of matter include the following:

| Name of State | Starts from | Changes to |
|---|---|---|
| melting | solid | liquid |
| freezing | liquid | solid |
| boiling | liquid | gas |
| condensation | gas | liquid |
| sublimation | solid | gas (skips liquid stage) |
| deposition | gas | solid (skips liquid stage) |

# Energy

**Energy** is necessary to do work.

- **Work** (w)—When an object is moved through a distance in response to some force; energy is transferred from one object to another ($w = fd$ means work = force × distance).
- **Power**—The rate of doing work.

There are two types of energy:

- **Potential energy**—This is energy that could do work if released. For example, a ball resting at the top of a steep hill is in the potential energy position.
- **Kinetic energy**—This is energy that is doing work as it is occurring. For example, a ball rolling down a steep hill is displaying kinetic energy.

# Interactions of Energy and Matter

**The Law of Conservation of Matter** states that matter can neither be created nor destroyed. Einstein created the formula of $E = mc^2$ to show the relationship between energy and matter. $E$ is the amount of energy, $m$ is the given mass, and $c$ is the speed of light (300,000 km/s). It was discovered that the movement of the particles of matter could be accelerated enough to the point that they will gain in mass.

**The Law of Conservation of Matter and Energy** states that the sum of the matter and the energy in the universe remains the same.

- **Heat energy and states of matter**—The motion of particles within a substance causes heat.

  All objects are made up of atoms and/or molecules that are in a constant state of motion.

  The cooler an object is or becomes, the slower the motion of particles.

  The hotter an object is or becomes, the faster the motion of particles.
- **Melting**—When a solid reaches a point at which its particles move so rapidly that they escape their boundaries, they begin to move more freely and change to a liquid state.
- **Vaporization/evaporation**—When the particles in a liquid are heated to such a temperature as to make them uncontainable within liquid boundaries, they escape into a gas.
- **Diffusion**—The movement of particles from a high concentration to an area of low concentration. In a system, diffusion occurs until the concentrations in all areas are the same. This is called a state of equilibrium.

Most solids, liquids, and gases expand when heated due to the increase in the motion of particles. They contract when cooled due to the decreased motion of particles. For example, tire pressure increases when a person drives a vehicle on the road. Friction causes heat, but it decreases if the car is left in the shade (cooling off of air particles).

*Little known fact:* Ice is the exception to this rule, as it expands as it cools, due to the molecules of water arranging themselves into a crystalline matrix that occupies more volume as a solid than as a liquid.

## Force and Motion

Forces that cause changes in the motion of objects (Newton's First Law) are gravity, friction, air resistance, pushing, pulling, and throwing.

- **Gravity**—Acceleration of objects toward the center of the Earth.
- **Inertia**—The state of an object remaining at rest or in motion.
- **Friction**—The force between any two objects that come into contact with one another. Friction cannot be eliminated; for example, a parachute in the air, socks on a tile floor, and a bicycle wheel on a road.

## Energy and Matter

The universe is comprised of things made from energy and matter. **Energy** that cannot be created or destroyed can be defined by separating it into ten categories that relate to the forms of physical science: **kinetic, potential, heat, sound, light, magnetism, mechanical, electric, chemical,** and **nuclear.** All of these forms of energy can be changed into another form without the loss of any energy. **Matter** that cannot be created or destroyed can be converted into another form without losing its mass. Einstein created the **Law of Relativity,** which verified the laws of energy and matter, previously thought not to be possible.

**Kinetic** is a form of energy that is occurring because an object or substance or being is in motion or doing work.

**Potential** is a form of energy that has the ability or potential to occur. This energy usually occurs when an object, being, or substance is at rest and could display kinetic energy if prompted by an outside force.

**Heat** is a form of energy that can be produced in many ways, all of which cause an increase in the motion of particles of a substance.

Types of heat movement include:

- **Conduction**—Heat moves from warmer areas to cooler areas along materials that conduct heat (wire and rod).
- **Convection**—Heat is transferred through collisions of molecules and occurs only in liquids and gases as they circulate.
- **Radiation**—Heat is transmitted in the form of infrared radiation and occurs only in gases and empty space.

**Sound** is another form of energy controlled by vibrations. The speed of sound depends on the space between the molecules. It travels quickest through a solid and slowest through a gas.

**Rules of sound:**

- The more rapid the vibration, the higher the pitch.
- Sound travels through solids, liquids, and gases.
- Objects produce sound by causing a series of compressions and rare fractions or waves of molecules.

A **wave** is a longitudinal movement in which the compressions and rare fractions travel spherically outward from the source. A **wavelength** (the length of one complete wave) is the distance between two successive compressions (where the air particles are smashed together; high air pressure) or two successive rare fractions (where the air particles are spread apart; low air pressure).

The characteristics of sound are as follows:

| Characteristic | Definition | Cause |
| --- | --- | --- |
| Pitch | How high or low the sound | Rate of vibration |
| Amplitude | Loudness or volume of the sound | By force used to create the sound (the greater the force, the louder the sound) |
| Quality | A distinctive timbre | Source of the sound |

**Light,** another form of energy, travels through anything that is transparent or translucent. Following are the four rules of light:

- Travels in rays (straight lines).
- The more dense the object or medium, the slower light travels.
- Travels in transverse waves.
- Is an electromagnetic wave that is created by causing the electrons to move rapidly and emit energy.

A **transverse wave** has a series of crests and troughs; such as dropping a pebble into still water.

A **wavelength** is the distance between the crests or the distance between the troughs.

**Reflection** is caused by light rays bouncing off a surface.

**Refraction** is caused by the bending of light rays as they pass from one medium to another.

**Magnetism** is a form of energy that involves magnets. Magnets have two poles, a north (N) and a south (S). The rules of magnets are

- Similar poles repel (N-N, S-S).
- Opposite poles attract (N-S, S-N).

**Electric** energy can be found in different forms. Electricity is a kind of energy that can produce light, heat, motion, and/or a magnetic force. Electricity flows through a conductor as current.

Laws of electric energy include:

- Like charges repel one another (+ +, − −).
- Opposite charges attract one another (+ −, − +).

An **electric current** contains electrical energy and a conductor.

A **conductor** is the material that allows an electric current to flow, such materials include copper, gold, aluminum, or silver.

An **insulator** is a material that does not allow an electric current to flow through it, such examples include wood, rubber, or plastic.

**Voltage** (volt) is the amount of force of an electric current.

**Amperage** (amp) is the amount of electricity that flows through a conductor.

**Resistance** causes electron flow to do the work and decreases the flow of amperage in a circuit; the longer the conductor, the higher the resistance.

A **circuit** is the path that an electric current flows. Two types of circuits are:

- **Series**—The resistances are connected to one another, one following another. If one resistance is disconnected, the circuit fails to work.

- **Parallel**—Each resistance is connected to the main circuit with its own connection. If one is disconnected, the others still work.

**Static electricity** is a result of the accumulation of electric charges and the subsequent imbalance of positive and negative charges.

**Mechanical** energy relates to that action or power created by the use of machines.

A **simple machine** also utilizes energy. It is a tool with few or no moving parts that does work. **The Law of Simple Machines** states that the force put into the machine (effort force) times the distance the effort moves equals the output force from the machine (resistance) times the distance the resistance moves.

There are six types of simple machines.

| Machine | Purpose | Illustration |
|---------|---------|--------------|
| Lever | Magnifies force, increases speed, or changes directions and is used to lift things. Three types of levers follow:<br><br>• Class 1: Fulcrum is in the middle or between the effort and the load; for example, scissors and seesaw.<br><br>• Class 2: Fulcrum is at one end, so the load is between the fulcrum and the effort; for example, stapler, wheelbarrow.<br><br>• Class 3: Fulcrum is at the end, and the effort is between the fulcrum and the load; for example, tweezers, fishing rod. | 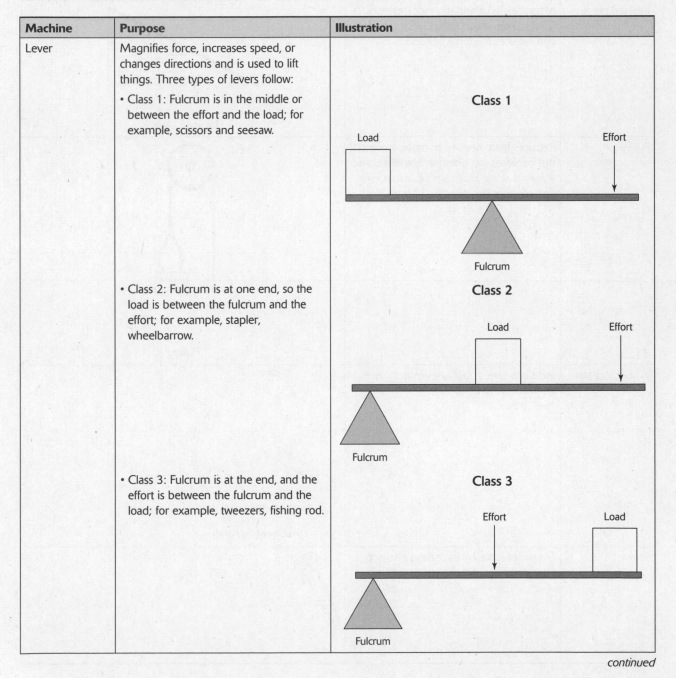 |

continued

| Machine | Purpose | Illustration |
|---------|---------|--------------|
| Wedge | Magnifies force, used to push things apart, or secure things together. | Wedge |
| Inclined plane | Magnifies force and distance increases. Is used to help move things up and down, and reduces the force needed. | Inclined plane |
| Pulley | Reduces force needed to move an object, but increases the distance. Is a wheel and a rope that moves things up and down, and changes the direction of force. | Pulley |
| Wheel and axle | Increases speed, facilitates motion, and the movement of objects. | Wheel & Axel |
| Screw | Magnifies force by increasing distance. | Screw |

**Chemical** energy is the result of a material found on Earth interacting with another material. Materials are either elements, compounds, or mixtures. A chemical element is a substance that is comprised of one type of atom. Everything within the universe is made of some type of element. There are 118 known elements; the first 94 are naturally found and the remaining 24 are man-made, all of which are radioactive. There are technically 30 elements that are artificially synthesized, but six of those are found in the natural world in trace quantities and are generally artificially synthesized.

A **compound** is the result of a chemical reaction of two or more elements. When two or more elements combine without a chemical reaction, it is known as a **mixture.**

In **nuclear** energy, the nucleus of the atom forms a different kind of element, producing increased energy. This change or disintegration of the nucleus represents the half-life of the substance. Radioactivity is a form of nuclear energy that can be used in the field of medicine, for creating electricity, or for powering generators.

Two kinds of nuclear reactions are known:

- **Fission**—When the nuclei of atoms are disintegrated, such as a nuclear reactor or an atomic bomb.
- **Fusion**—When two or more nuclei are combined together with increased force to form a different kind of nucleus, such as the sun or a hydrogen bomb.

# Science as Inquiry

**Science** is the process of obtaining and verifying knowledge. The subject of science permits educators to allow students to be curious, ask questions, discover information, and explore possibilities. When science is studied as inquiry, it supports skill development in critical thinking and learning scientific reasoning. When children are involved in seeking answers, as the Constructivist Theory emphasizes, the results have more meaning. It is recommended that science should be inquiry-based as this promotes the basic principles of organization and knowledge of science. Cognitive development and the acquisition of knowledge are enhanced through this process. The **scientific concept** includes the process of producing knowledge.

Features that exhibit valuable science inquiry:

- Identification and control of variables.
- Collection of data using various instruments.
- Interpretation of data through reliable and valid reasoning.
- Formulation and testing of hypotheses.
- Communication of procedures, methods, results, and interpretations.

# Twelve Processes of Science

Scientific theory includes the following processes, in order: observation, question, theory, experiment, data, results, and conclusion. Processes are a systematic chain of actions directed toward a conclusion, usually in the form of steps that clarify the concepts. These processes are the fundamental building blocks of science:

- **Observation**—Uses the five senses to watch the world and the movement within it
- **Classification**—Uses commonalities of objects to logically group items
- **Communication**—Utilizes the ability to share findings and results with others
- **Measurement**—Utilizes the ability to use appropriate tools
- **Prediction**—Uses prior knowledge and experiences to foresee what may occur
- **Inference**—Uses prior knowledge and experience to state why something may occur or why it is the way it is
- **Variable identification/control**—Determines the factors and stabilizes all the variables except one
- **Formulation of hypothesis**—Develops an assumption based on variables

- **Interpretation of data**—Uses gathered information and constructs it in charts, graphs, or narration to provide reasonable results
- **Define operations**—Applies mathematical equations and principles
- **Experimentation**—Uses prior knowledge and the hypothesis to try different solutions
- **Constructing models**—Identifies the need for a model and creates an accurate and appropriate model

## Science in Personal and Social Perspectives

This specific area of science helps students learn to connect with their world. They focus on the study of personal health, environmental issues, science/technology, and the greater society. This discipline allows students to develop decision-making skills by establishing a solid foundation on which to base judgments. Topics covered in this area include:

Personal health

Types of resources

Environmental changes

Natural hazards

Risks and benefits

Science and technology at the local level, including challenges faced

Changes and characteristics in populations

# History and Nature of Science

This is an area of science education that enhances the study of nature and includes history in science to promote an understanding of inquiry, science in society, and human relationships within science.

Science is the process used to produce knowledge. According to David Jerner Martin, there are six characteristics of science:

1. **Science rejects authority and authoritarianism.** Most science works to disprove hypotheses by not proving them correct. Elementary science should focus on trying to contradict theories, which in turn proves and affirms knowledge.

2. **Science is honest.** The scientific method and steps for experiments allow others to duplicate and disprove or prove theories. Flawed research will lead to failed theories.

3. **Science rejects supernatural explanations for observed phenomena.** Science looks for natural explanations of phenomena that can be tried and retried.

4. **Science is skeptical.** There is always some degree of uncertainty in the natural world as there is no "absolute truth."

5. **Science is parsimonious.** The simplest explanation of an observation is always chosen. Science should focus on the quality of understanding rather than the quantity of information presented.

6. **Science seeks consistency.** There are basic rules for the natural world and events will occur in consistent patterns.

Science gives us products such as jet engines, medical advances, cellphones, computers, drought-resistant crops, and ethanol. Technology and science go hand in hand. However, technology is defined as the means by which humans control or modify their environment. Technology has helped humans adapt to their world and environment, creating more sophisticated methods to meet their needs: metal tools instead of stone tools, cars for transportation rather than horses, e-mail for communication rather than telegraphs, and so on.

# Careers

Working with elementary students to excite them in the area of science, as well as technology, engineering, and mathematics (collectively known as STEM), should include the study of various careers in the field. Students should be provided with information about the many types of science careers in the many different categories of science: health sciences, space sciences, environmental sciences, science education, ocean sciences, and more. Acknowledging that not all science careers require a significant study of science and that there is a focus on gender equity in the field may help to entice diverse learners into the field. Providing school and community activities, descriptions of specific careers, and guest speakers will help establish the many possibilities of science as a career.

# Systems, Order, and Organization

Science is reflected in its systems and the order and organization of information. Establishing a method of arranging and categorizing data is a fundamental practice in science. There are universal methods to maintain the organization of science data collection and information. Some methods are listed in the following table.

| Systems | Examples | Purpose |
|---|---|---|
| Small units of the natural world used to investigate<br>Organized groups of related parts, objects, and components that form a larger whole<br>Have boundaries, input and output, parts and reactions<br>Two types:<br>  closed (not affected by external forces)<br>  open (able to be affected by external forces) | • machines<br>• education<br>• organisms<br>• transportation<br>• numbers<br>• galaxy | Keeps track of organisms, energy, mass, and events<br>Develops understanding of regularities, commonalities, reactions, and equilibrium<br>Extends knowledge of law, theories, and models |
| **Order** | **Examples** | **Purpose** |
| Statistically describes the behavior of matter, organisms, events, and objects | • probability | Develops knowledge of factors influencing matter, organisms, events, and objects<br>Promotes improved and increased observations<br>Creates advanced exploratory models |
| **Organization** | **Examples** | **Purpose** |
| Various types and levels<br>Gathering, grouping, and structuring of systems and information | • food pyramid<br>• periodic table of elements<br>• organism<br>• classification | Provides useful ways of thinking about the world<br>Shows interaction of systems<br>Demonstrates hierarchy |

**Measurement** is a process (method) in science that helps with certain types of order and organization. Measurement can describe length or distance, volume or capacity, mass, and temperature.

| Distance | Volume | Mass | Temperature |
|---|---|---|---|
| inches | ounces | pounds | Fahrenheit |
| feet | cup | grams (mg, cg, kg) | Celsius |
| yards | quart | | |
| miles | gallon | | |
| league | liter (ml, cl, kl) | | |
| meters (cm, mm, km) | | | |

## Tables of Measurement Conversions

**Length** is the distance between two points.

| Standard or Conventional Measure | Metric Measure |
| --- | --- |
| 12 inches (in) = 1 foot (ft) | 100 centimeters (cm) = 1 meter (m) |
| 3 ft = 1 yard (yd) | 1,000 millimeters (mm) = 1 meter (m) |
| 5,280 ft = 1 mile (mi) | 1,000 m = 1 kilometer (km) |
| 3 mi = 1 league (lea) | 2.54 cm = 1 in |

**Volume** is how much space something takes up.

| Standard or Conventional Measure | Metric Measure |
| --- | --- |
| 8 ounces (oz) = 1 cup (c) | 1 liter (l) = 1,000 milliliter (ml) |
| 4 c = 1 quart (qt) | 1 liter (l) = 100 (cl) |
| 4 qts = 1 gallon (gal) | 1 ml = 1 cubic centimeter (cc) |

## Mass versus Weight

**Mass** is the amount of material that comprises an object.

**Weight** is the pull of gravity on an object, and the amount depends on the strength of gravity.

| Metric Prefixes Chart | | | | | | |
| --- | --- | --- | --- | --- | --- | --- |
| **Milli-** | **Centi-** | **Deci-** | **Unit-** | **Deca-** | **Hecto-** | **Kilo-** |
| 1/1000 or .001 | 1/100 or .01 | 1/10 or .1 | 1 | 10 times | 100 times | 1000 times |

PART IV

# PRACTICE TESTS WITH
# ANSWER EXPLANATIONS

**Directions:** Read the following multiple-choice questions and select the most appropriate answer. Mark the answer sheet accordingly.

1. Read the following passage:

   The hikers prepared for a five-day trip into the canyon. They expected perfect weather with no hint of winds or rains. They were surprised when the storm came and flooded their camp the first night. *Nevertheless,* they continued on their morning journey and successfully made it to the planned destination.

   The word *nevertheless* in this passage is an example of

   A. a cohesive tie.
   B. expository text.
   C. figurative language.
   D. a comprehension link.

2. A third grade teacher selects a book about the oceans of the world for her students. Prior to reading, she asks the students what they know about the ocean and its creatures and then asks what else they want to know about sea life. When they are done reading, she asks what they learned about the ocean and the creatures. Following these procedures is a reading strategy used at the elementary level. What is this method called?

   A. metacognition
   B. K-W-L strategy
   C. reciprocal teaching
   D. literal comprehension

3. A first grade student can step with the opposite foot while throwing a ball. A classmate steps with the same foot as his throwing hand. This is an example of motor

   A. ability through heredity.
   B. ability delineated by age.
   C. skill development of variable rates.
   D. skill development through informal play.

4. The two main types of standardized tests can sometimes be interrelated. The primary difference between an aptitude test and an achievement test is

   A. The aptitude test is more reliable than an achievement test.
   B. The aptitude test has a scoring rubric; the achievement test uses stanine scores.
   C. The aptitude test predicts a student's ability; the achievement test measures mastery.
   D. The aptitude test shows outcomes through the validity of a score, and an achievement test uses the variability of a score.

5. Which answer BEST completes the following statement?

   Instructional activities utilized in each classroom should address federal, state, and district standards while also meeting the

   A. goals addressed in the textbook.
   B. outline of the yearly curriculum.
   C. individual needs of the students.
   D. specific policies of the district.

6. A component that is necessary for improving students' reading skills is the use of *imagery.* A recommended activity for teaching the use of imagery is

   A. the use of poetry and art.
   B. memorizing new vocabulary.
   C. reading and rereading passages.
   D. incorporating science and history.

7.  Look at the color wheel representing three categories of colors. The instructional concept about color relationships can be difficult for elementary children. Which of the following is the most appropriate method for teaching the concept of color and the vocabulary that includes hues, values, and intensity, as well as primary, secondary, and tertiary?

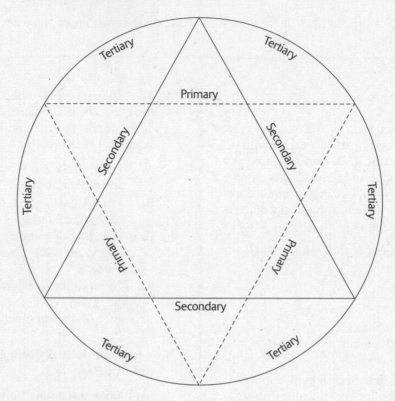

-   **A.**  science—mixing colored liquids
-   **B.**  social studies—designing a kaleidoscope
-   **C.**  math—teaching proper three-part vocabulary
-   **D.**  language arts—reading books about rainbows

8.  A kindergarten teacher uses nursery rhymes, songs, and fingerplays on a daily basis to instill reading ability and language development. What specific skill does this confirm for students?

-   **A.**  phonetics
-   **B.**  phoneme addition
-   **C.**  phonemic awareness
-   **D.**  phonetic demonstration

9.  One exemplar method used to instruct students in estimation is the use of

-   **A.**  a set of tens frames.
-   **B.**  simple graphs and tables.
-   **C.**  situations that resemble real life.
-   **D.**  specially designed manipulatives.

10. Educators believe that teaching the _____ of science should be completed along with teaching the processes.

-   **A.**  laws
-   **B.**  formats
-   **C.**  equations
-   **D.**  products

11. When a third grade teacher suggests that students should organize their seats, theater-style, for a brief lecture on plant and animal structures, she is using an instructional method best described as

-   **A.**  discovery.
-   **B.**  integration.
-   **C.**  expository.
-   **D.**  guided inquiry.

12. In order for a student to be able to use decoding skills, he must have adequate instruction in the areas of print concepts, letter knowledge, and

   A. reading fluency.
   B. classical literature.
   C. word comprehension.
   D. the alphabetic principle.

13. A theory exists that promotes that a child's very basic needs must be met before the child may partake in an educational experience that will be meaningful and permit learning to occur. These basic needs, at Level I on this hierarchy, include food, water, rest, and shelter. Who was the master behind this theory of human development?

   A. Freud
   B. Piaget
   C. Skinner
   D. Maslow

14. When teachers select children's literature and trade books in a leveled format to teach reading, they are implementing a reading approach called

   A. linguistics.
   B. basal reading.
   C. language experience.
   D. literature-based reading.

15. The most important reason for elementary students to obtain locomotor skills is to

   A. be able to compete in sports.
   B. increase cardiovascular efficiency.
   C. progress in development of physical fitness.
   D. build a strong foundation for the access of their environment.

16. A third grade teacher plans to assess the students on a social studies project involving the music and dance of other cultures. She wants to be sure students are prepared for the final exam, which is a forced-answer exam, on this unit of historical information. Which of the following might she do in preparation for their studies?

   A. Conduct a vocabulary test.
   B. Request the performance of a dance.
   C. Observe a cooperative learning activity.
   D. Use a checklist of the students' responses.

17. The transmission model in teaching citizenship is

   A. the acquisition of open-minded thoughts, values, and ideals.
   B. analyzing information, forming opinions, and acting upon these thoughts.
   C. learning government functions and following government rules.
   D. following laws, studying implications, and acknowledging rights.

18. A kindergarten teacher uses buttons to instill the concept of classification, a critical mathematical skill. This type of math manipulative may be identified as

   A. reflective.
   B. inflective.
   C. structured.
   D. unstructured.

19. A kindergarten teacher says /p/ /i/ /g/ to her students and asks them what she is saying. She suggests they do the same and sound out the hidden word. This is an example of

   A. phoneme identity.
   B. phoneme addition.
   C. phoneme blending.
   D. phoneme segmentation.

20. A third grade teacher notices that one of her students is playing with equipment when she is trying to provide instructions to the class. The best type of social discipline to use would be to

   A. move closer to the student in order to enable him to hear the lesson better.
   B. ask the student to remain after class so she may ask the student about the disruption.
   C. continue instruction, using the equipment the student has to demonstrate the next activity.
   D. stop the entire class to point out how the student is disrupting the class, causing other students to lose time for the activity.

21. A third grade teacher has determined that the new student just placed in her class is somewhat behind the others in the area of math, primarily because the student's previous learning experiences did not cover the same principles and standards. In order for this student to catch up with the other students, which of the following strategies would be most beneficial?

    A. retention
    B. prompting
    C. peer tutoring
    D. modifications

22. A fourth grade class is examining the family structure of the Maori tribe of New Zealand. This falls under which of the following social sciences?

    A. sociology
    B. economics
    C. psychology
    D. anthropology

23. Educators need to help students develop the reading and writing skills necessary to comprehend and use modern technology. The traditional reading and writing of texts exposes students to the linear format. New technology, however, requires that students also be exposed to _____ formats of materials

    A. advanced
    B. interactive
    C. culturally rich
    D. multidimensional

24. Music education at the elementary level is supported by extensive research about its benefits. Which of the following subject areas demonstrate substantial improvement when students have the opportunity to be exposed to music through school experiences and activities?

    A. mathematics and art
    B. mathematics and literacy
    C. science and social studies
    D. science and physical education

25. During a writing assignment, the teacher roams around the classroom observing the students' generalizations and use of skills. He makes notes about each of the students as they use grammar and spelling in their writing. The notes are used to make adjustments to the instruction for the next writing period or to address a specific skill with a particular student. This type of informal assessment is referred to as a(n)

    A. running record.
    B. notation record.
    C. anecdotal record.
    D. observational record.

26. Which of the following is the BEST example of an activity that promotes phonemic awareness?

    A. singing a song
    B. writing a story
    C. reading a note
    D. talking to someone

27. A fifth grade teacher has focused science study on the solar system. Students have learned the composition of the planets and compared them to the Earth. The teacher has divided the class into cooperative learning groups and assigned a project based on this topic. The project given to the students is to identify the planet they believe could sustain a life-form and describe how this creature would differ from humans in order to live on the planet. This is an example of which of the following stages of Bloom's Taxonomy?

    A. synthesis
    B. knowledge
    C. application
    D. comprehension

28. To help students learn _____, an elementary teacher created a set of cards that look like the following:

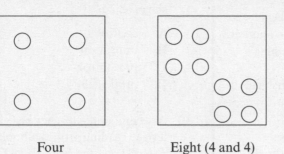

Four          Eight (4 and 4)          Five (4 and 1 more)

A. grouping sets
B. anchor numbers
C. counting objects
D. spatial relationships

29. A writing assignment has been given to a fifth-grade class of students. The students are to construct a written report on one of the inventions of the twentieth century that was studied during a unit on inventors. One of the students went to the library to gather some books on Thomas Edison. The student also began to list some words that seemed important to the report: light bulb, electricity, watts. Then the student designed a web of Edison's life. What stage of the writing process is this student in?

A. editing
B. revising
C. rough draft
D. prewriting

30. Which of the following is the most emphasized pedagogy in elementary science education and related to inquiry-based learning?

A. behavioral
B. sociological
C. constructivist
D. psychodynamic

31. Which of the following is a procedure often used to aid students in learning how to gain information from text?

A. presenting expository texts
B. utilizing content exercises
C. sharing literature readings
D. implementing reciprocal teaching

32. A key principle of No Child Left Behind (NCLB), the federal law mandated in 2002, is the

A. school accountability of adequate yearly progress.
B. inclusion of students with disabilities in classrooms.
C. provision for detailed scope and sequence in curricula.
D. involvement of parents in hiring highly qualified teachers.

33. The skills that a child acquires in language are based on his exposure to which of the following?

A. procedures and strategies
B. education and motivation
C. instruction and assessment
D. environment and experiences

34. A first grade teacher uses product containers, newspapers, and small signs to share new words with students. They have learned the words *exit, stop, florist, cereal, beans,* and *theater* in just one week. The use of these items to teach new words falls under the category of

A. instructional guides.
B. appositives sources.
C. environmental print.
D. classified groupings.

35. When students learn to measure the *weight* of an object, they are learning to

    A. determine when something may begin.
    B. compare the mass of one object to another.
    C. analyze the degree to which something changes.
    D. figure the quantity of three-dimensional objects and figures.

36. Which of the following learning theories supports the philosophy that students should build, design, and create their own artwork?

    A. ecological
    B. behavioral
    C. sociological
    D. constructivist

37. What is the highest level of Bloom's Taxonomy reached when a fifth grade student diagrams the consequences a new law will have on a local community?

    A. analysis
    B. synthesis
    C. knowledge
    D. understanding

38. An elementary teacher is reading *The Very Hungry Caterpillar* by Eric Carle. She is using dialogic reading to seek answers to questions such as:

    Who has seen a caterpillar before?

    Have you ever eaten an apple?

    What does a caterpillar change into?

    By conducting a reading session in this manner, what is the teacher trying to establish for the students?

    A. using prior knowledge to make connections to the text
    B. preparing for an assessment by learning the vocabulary
    C. providing a chance to use oral language with a large group
    D. allowing time for individuals to review the illustrations matching the text

39. If a student is able to dribble a basketball against an opponent, what sport skill level has she reached?

    A. control
    B. utilization
    C. precontrol
    D. proficiency

40. A second grade teacher has given one of her leveled reading groups a book titled *The Princess and the Horse Who Could Fly* and asked them to think about the name of the book. One of the students stated, "I think this book is about a young girl who lives in a kingdom with a very special horse. The girl loves her horse, and they have some fun adventures." What skill group is this student building upon?

    A. interpreting and predicting
    B. prereading and identifying
    C. imagery and understanding
    D. comprehending and translating

41. A sixth grade teacher uses peer assessment for her physical education class to identify the level of mastery of the volleyball skills each student possesses. Which answer is an example that best describes peer assessment?

    A. Two students take turns observing each other to determine their volleyball skill level.
    B. Students submit displays and essays on what they believe are their volleyball skill levels.
    C. The teacher walks around the class and observes students practicing their volleyball skills.
    D. The teacher videotapes the class to watch it later in order to determine the students' volleyball skill levels.

42. Read the following excerpt from a second grade writer.

> Won dey my mudr and my fadr tok me to the park. We saw sum duks. We fed thm bred. The duks wer green and blu. We had fun.

What does this child's writing reflect to the teacher?

A. The child should work on vowel sounds.
B. The child needs remedial spelling instruction.
C. The child uses invented spelling to deliver a message.
D. The child needs knowledge about grammar and sentence structure.

43. For students who are capable of participating in extended instruction or gaining additional information on a topic, the teacher might offer tiered lessons, or learning centers. These are examples of which of the following strategies?

A. motivation
B. assessment
C. enrichment
D. intervention

44. When a teacher observes a student who demonstrates difficulty remembering some of the letters in a word that is not only familiar, but easy to read, this may indicate that the student

A. does not apply context clues.
B. has not learned the correct spelling.
C. is not clear on the consonant-vowel rules.
D. lacks knowledge of letter-sound correspondence.

45. Models in science are useful to students as they can learn spatial relationships and meet mathematical challenges through these

A. inquiry assessments.
B. alternative activities.
C. simplified structures.
D. visual representations.

46. Which of the following is considered a parallel process related to arts education?

A. taking a test on music terms
B. reading about artists to improve literacy
C. constructing a model of a cell for science
D. visiting a museum and writing a story about it

47. As an elementary teacher, you are teaching a unit on map skills, and you want to address all learning intelligences. Which of the following would satisfy the needs of a kinesthetic learner?

A. singing a song about the different map components
B. reading a passage about the different map components
C. using manipulatives to learn the different map components
D. moving physically around the areas of the different map components

48. What is one of the best methods for teaching a student silent letters or letter patterns in words to help with memorization of more regular spelling?

A. Practice writing words multiple times until the student is able to write the word without a cue.
B. Compare different types of words and word endings to help the student choose the proper spelling.
C. Conduct regular assessments on students' abilities to spell the words in the weekly reading passages.
D. Point out words that have the same silent letters or patterns, especially in those words the student may already know.

49. An elementary teacher who is teaching the properties of geometric objects states, "If all four angles are right angles, the shape must be a rectangle. If it is a square, all angles are right angles. If it is a square, it must be a rectangle." This *if-then* reasoning reflects which of the following theories?

   A. van Hiele—informal deduction
   B. Gardner theory—logical intelligence
   C. Van de Walle approach—developmental teaching
   D. Piaget constructivist approach— "hands-on" learning

50. Piaget is responsible for describing and promoting which of the following theories of learning?

   A. cognitive
   B. ecological
   C. behavioral
   D. sociological

51. A fourth grade teacher prefers to divide his students into heterogeneous groups to conduct experiments. Which of the following is the name of this instructional format?

   A. control groups
   B. guided activities
   C. unifying presentations
   D. cooperative learning process

52. While studying the U.S. Constitution, as the elementary teacher, you take your class on a field trip to the National Archives to see the Constitution document. This is an example of which instructional strategy?

   A. scaffolding
   B. cooperative learning
   C. fiction incorporation
   D. primary source utilization

53. A fifth grade class is studying the cultures around the world. The teacher has incorporated the study of languages, foods, dances, dress, and customs by asking students to give various presentations during the unit. One particular student, who generally works well with others and participates in class, has demonstrated undesirable behaviors during these social studies lessons. Based on this information, what may be the cause (antecedent) of this student's inappropriate behaviors?

   A. afraid of other students
   B. not sure about the assignment
   C. unable to read the information
   D. embarrassed to perform in class

54. Multiplication can be a complex operation to learn. An elementary teacher places the following example on the board to teach a specific multiplication strategy related to another formal operation, addition. Which of the following specific strategies of multiplication is identified in this example?

   Example: $2 \cdot 4 = 8 \quad 4 + 4 = 8$

   A. fact families
   B. part-part-whole
   C. doubles equivalency
   D. whole number computation

55. A first grade teacher reads the story of *The Three Bears* to the class. When rereading the story, the teacher points out the initial consonants of the main vocabulary for words of the week and asks students to predict what the word is: *bears, porridge, house,* and *bed.* This is a strategy used to promote which type of knowledge?

   A. writing
   B. reading
   C. spelling
   D. phonics

56. Health education has become a component of science education at the elementary level. Its primary purpose is to

    A.    instill healthy lifestyles.

    B.    minimize at-risk behaviors.

    C.    motivate parents in proper nutrition.

    D.    demonstrate proper grooming routines.

57. One of the critical issues that teachers face related to high-stakes testing is the

    A.    scores only reflect last year's skills.

    B.    amount of time students need to study.

    C.    parents' outrage at the content in the exam.

    D.    "dumbing down" of curriculum and teaching to the test.

58. Under the theory of multiple intelligences, the one most closely tied to reading and language arts is

    A.    verbal.

    B.    logical.

    C.    existential.

    D.    kinesthetic.

59. Look at this computation:

$$\begin{array}{r} 19 \\ 4\overline{)436} \\ \underline{4}\phantom{00} \\ 036 \\ \underline{36} \\ 0 \end{array}$$

This error is an example of a student who has not adequately learned how to use

    A.    decimals.

    B.    place values.

    C.    division operations.

    D.    3-digit multiplication.

60. A third grade teacher instructs students on the five Great Lakes. To help the students remember the names of the lakes, the teacher uses the word "HOMES." Which of the following is the name of this instructional strategy?

    A.    chunking

    B.    prompting

    C.    mnemonics

    D.    task analysis

61. A critical design element of a curriculum is the _____, which includes decisions and planning about the information to be taught, as well as an outline of the grade levels at which the sequential skills and concepts are taught.

    A.    scope and sequence

    B.    pedagogical practices

    C.    instructional objectives

    D.    extension and remediation techniques

62. Students should learn how to record collected data using charts, tables, or graphs. A graph is a visual format of expressing and exploring numbers and information. Using a graph is most appropriately introduced at the

    A.    first grade.

    B.    second grade.

    C.    fourth grade.

    D.    fifth grade.

63. Which theory encompasses the following scenario? A child relates newly learned knowledge about the technology of the twentieth century to prior knowledge on developments of the classical civilization.

    A.    cognitive

    B.    sociological

    C.    developmental

    D.    psychodynamic

64. The domain of science that includes the properties of objects, materials, and matter is

    A.    earth science.

    B.    energy science.

    C.    natural science.

    D.    physical science.

65. A third grade teacher has assigned a cooperative learning activity for the study of haiku poetry. The teacher has based the student groupings on student performance throughout the poetry unit. Students are to work together in separate groups to develop a haiku, create an illustration, and present the haiku to the class using actions and props. This activity is an example of

    A.    integrating fine arts.

    B.    using written expression.

    C.    utilizing authentic assessment.

    D.    diagnosing post-learning goals.

66. When students are active in their education because they enjoy learning and they want to succeed and gain skills or knowledge in a particular subject, they are considered to have which of the following types of motivation?

   A. explicit
   B. implicit
   C. intrinsic
   D. extrinsic

67. Students have been asked to study four different plants that the teacher has brought into the classroom. They are to carefully examine the structure, identify the parts, and compare the properties. After they have gathered this specific information, they are to proceed with developing a generalization based on their knowledge of the plant kingdom to determine the habitat in which each plant must exist and how each plant may affect its environment. This is a form of which of the following teaching styles?

   A. inductive
   B. deductive
   C. reflective
   D. inflective

68. Using the trade book, *Silly Sally* by Audrey Wood, in a reading-aloud activity, a kindergarten teacher shares the pictures with the students as the story is read. The teacher asks students to predict what will happen next as they read the text on each page and look at the pictures. In reference to Bloom's Taxonomy, to which level does this refer?

   A. analysis
   B. synthesis
   C. application
   D. comprehension

69. A fifth grade teacher presents a lesson on the three branches of government. She asks her students to give five examples for each branch, paraphrases the information in the textbook, and expounds upon ideas the students have. What integration strategy is she utilizing?

   A. debriefing
   B. scaffolding
   C. whole class
   D. cooperative learning

70. A worksheet of fractions is given as homework with directions to chose the larger of the two and write the reason.

   #1. $\frac{3}{8}$ or $\frac{4}{10}$

   #2. $\frac{8}{9}$ or $\frac{7}{8}$

   #3. $\frac{7}{13}$ or $\frac{4}{13}$

   Which concept related to fractions is the teacher reinforcing?

   A. ordering
   B. reducing
   C. expanding
   D. comparing

71. A third grade teacher has just completed a thematic unit of study about the ocean. Which of the following types of assessments would be the most beneficial in planning instruction for the next unit?

   A. formative
   B. alternative
   C. summative
   D. observation

72. Scientific experiments follow certain steps in order to comply with scientific inquiry and discovery. Students are instructed on these steps prior to being permitted to conduct independent or small-group experiments. The primary steps include state the question, _____, describe the variables, and collect the data.

   A. gather the materials
   B. formulate a hypothesis
   C. organize the correlations
   D. establish the environment

73. A strategy that promotes listening and speaking skills in a classroom is

   A. mnemonics.
   B. phonics.
   C. guided practice.
   D. choral responding.

74. The anticipatory set that an elementary teacher could use to engage a second grade class while teaching citizenship would be to

A. give a short quiz on citizenship terms.
B. have the students create a diorama on citizenship.
C. deliver a speech or lecture about the basics of citizenship.
D. act out a scene from the playground that demonstrates citizenship.

75. As the anticipatory set, if a teacher writes these examples on the board for students to discuss, what math concept is the teacher planning to introduce?

It will be cloudy tomorrow.

A fish will die if it does not live in water.

Andrea and Justin will see a movie at 7:00 p.m.

A storm will begin on July 28.

Mabel will be about 6 years old next year.

A. number lines
B. algebraic equations
C. primes and composites
D. probability and estimation

76. One of the standards of assessment in science for elementary children, established by the NSES, is the evaluation of

A. attitude.
B. equipment.
C. experiments.
D. comprehension.

77. A fourth grade teacher has developed a consistent method of behavior management that includes modeling the desired behaviors and shaping the behaviors through a system of rewards and consequences. The teacher is using the model for behavior management developed by

A. Jones.
B. Canter.
C. Kounin.
D. Skinner.

78. A fifth grade teacher has created a unit on famous authors and, as an end-of-unit assessment, students are required to research the life of an author and write a report using the skills of writing acquired during the unit study. This demonstrates the use of which of the following types of assessment?

A. explicit
B. implicit
C. formative
D. summative

79. A third grade student whose parents are concerned about his abilities to keep up with the math content want regular contact with the teacher about the child's mathematics progress. The teacher would like to accommodate the parents and provide them with solid information. Which of the following assessment types would be best used to illustrate the student's progress over time?

A. an aptitude test
B. dynamic assessment
C. a portfolio assessment
D. a norm-referenced test

80. If a teacher asks his class "Why did the Revolutionary War occur?" and waits 1–3 minutes for a response, he is demonstrating

A. scaffolding.
B. processing time.
C. instructional pacing.
D. student response technique.

81. The instructional model created by Hunter that improves academic achievement by supporting diverse learners and structuring a sequence for learning is called

A. inquiry learning.
B. mastery learning.
C. direct instruction.
D. the traditional approach.

82. A fourth grade teacher is preparing to introduce the concept of decimals to the class, as they are learning about the U.S. monetary system, which is based on the decimal system. However, she is unsure whether all of the students are ready to learn this mathematics concept. In which area of math should the teacher assess students prior to teaching decimals?

   A. fractions
   B. operations
   C. percentages
   D. whole numbers

83. Which of the following formal measures should a teacher use to assess student progress on the terminology of the poetry unit?

   A. dynamic assessment
   B. criterion-referenced test
   C. ecological-based assessment
   D. performance-based assessment

84. An elementary student writes the following, making a consistent error.

   > This summer my family went to a palce in Canada. We went to a lake to go fishing. We stayed at a palce on the edge of the lake in a small cabin. Then we went to another palce in Oregon to go camping. We had lots of fun!

   Which of the following stages of spelling development does this passage demonstrate?

   A. phonetic
   B. transitional
   C. semiphonic
   D. precommunicative

85. One of the six principles established for school mathematics by the National Council for Teachers of Mathematics is

   A. equity.
   B. diversity.
   C. equivalency.
   D. objective thinking.

86. When evaluating a student's performance assessment, the best strategy is to use a prepared and predetermined _____ that establishes criteria and expectations on which performance will be judged.

   A. stanine index
   B. grading scale
   C. scoring rubric
   D. percentage chart

87. A fifth grade student has been demonstrating some behavior problems in class and could use a structured program of intervention. Of the following, which would offer the student the most involvement in learning to self-manage his off-task behaviors?

   A. modeling
   B. contingency contract
   C. implied consequences
   D. negative reinforcement

88. When a student writes the word "house" in the following manner, it is an example of which of these developmental stages of writing?

   ⊥O( )s4

   A. scribbling
   B. transitional letters
   C. letter-like symbols
   D. beginning sound emergence

89. A first grade teacher has asked her students to explain several of the basic math facts as a way of checking their skills. Which of the following levels of Bloom's Taxonomy is this activity an example of?

    A. synthesis
    B. knowledge
    C. application
    D. comprehension

90. When an assignment or skill is broken down into smaller sequential steps and each of those steps is taught one at a time, this strategy is known as

    A. chunking.
    B. task analysis.
    C. cloze procedure.
    D. scaffolded lessons.

91. In order to determine a student's reading strengths and needs, which of the following might the teacher conduct?

    A. reader profile
    B. parent interview
    C. curriculum survey
    D. teacher observation

92. A fourth grade teacher is designing the lessons for mathematics based on great diversity in his classroom. He has students with cultural and linguistic diversity, some who are also placed in special education, and some who receive services as gifted or talented students. What is the best way for him to accommodate all these learning needs?

    A. Request an assistant.
    B. Simplify the materials.
    C. Develop tiered lessons.
    D. Increase the assessments.

93. Students need to be assured that they are performing appropriately in math, and develop a strong self-concept and competence that inspires more positive attitudes for the future in math classes. Which of the following strategies will help students develop a positive attitude and a desire to learn math?

    A. skill drill
    B. time trials
    C. strategic instruction
    D. systematic feedback

94. An elementary teacher writes the following word parts on the board and assigns the students to blend the words and recite them to a partner. Then each student must write them as practice for both spelling and familiarity. What are these two collective forms called?

    | tr- | ack | bl- | ack |
    | tr- | ain | bl- | and |
    | tr- | am  | bl- | eak |
    | tr- | ash | bl- | end |

    A. onsets and rimes
    B. blends and rhymes
    C. segments and words
    D. prefixes and suffixes

95. The implementation of reading strategies has a different impact on the various abilities of student readers. Which of the following is the most comfortable for less proficient readers?

    A. choral reading
    B. guided reading
    C. reader's theater
    D. round-robin reading

96. Which of the following teaching styles offers the most autonomy to the learners?

    A. delegator
    B. facilitator
    C. demonstrator
    D. formal authority

97. A second grade teacher requires each student to complete a five-page research paper at the end of the second semester for the study of literature. Students have had difficulty achieving mastery of this assignment. The principal of the school has received numerous complaints from parents and peer educators about the complexity and use of this assignment. What did the principal determine was the reason the teacher should eliminate this requirement from this class?

    A. It was not developmentally appropriate.
    B. It did not adequately measure yearly progress.
    C. Not all of the students have access to resources.
    D. It was taking parents too much time out of their schedules to assist their children.

98. There are 10 general national academic standards for mathematics instruction. They are divided into two groups, with the first set of five standards relating to number and operations, algebra, geometry, measurement, and

    A. reasoning and proof.
    B. data analysis and probability.
    C. connections and representation.
    D. the processes of problem solving.

99. A fifth grade teacher works with a student to brainstorm some ideas for writing assignments and writes down some key words. The student orally states some of the sentences before writing them down. Then the student begins to write the sentences, and the teacher encourages rereading and revision. This is an example of instruction using the practice of

    A. drafting.
    B. dictation.
    C. guided writing.
    D. repeated writing.

100. To assess a reader's comprehension and use of reading skills and strategies, a teacher may present a passage using the following format. This is an example of _____.

    Rabbit and tortoise ran a _____. They each decided to _____ at their own speed. Rabbit could run very _____ and tortoise was very _____. But tortoise was wise. _____ was foolish and careless.

    A. context clues
    B. cloze procedure
    C. word recognition
    D. phonemic awareness

101. Which of the following equations is the BEST example of the basic facts of mathematics?

    A. $5 + 3 = 8$
    B. $24 \div 12 = 2$
    C. $44 - 11 = 33$
    D. $20 \cdot 11 = 220$

102. In a third grade classroom, during small group instruction, a student is having trouble reading the word "canyon" as the group reads about areas of the Southwest. Which of the following skills might show the area in which the student is having the most difficulty?

    A. content clues
    B. context clues
    C. phonetic clues
    D. phonemic clues

103. The primary reason that elementary teachers should use manipulatives to teach mathematics is because they enable students to

    A. visualize concepts.
    B. be more motivated.
    C. learn at their own rate.
    D. maintain concentration.

**104.** An elementary teacher is preparing to introduce geometry and shape relationships, which is a new concept for the class. The teacher should consider which of the following strategies to more appropriately help students in acquiring the proper skills related to this topic?

   **A.**   response cards
   **B.**   triad grouping
   **C.**   choral responding
   **D.**   scaffolded instruction

**105.** An elementary teacher receives the following paragraph from a student on an assignment about a favorite animal. This passage demonstrates that the student is having difficulty with which of the following?

> Katz kin be fun at hom. I lick to play iwth mi dog and berd too. Mi kat has a purple kolar. Mi dog kin run fast. Mi muder wil walk wit the dog but not the kat. Mi bab sistr wans a frog to play with. I lik to feed mi dog good food.

   **A.**   conventions
   **B.**   word choice
   **C.**   organization
   **D.**   sentence fluency

**106.** The following is an example of

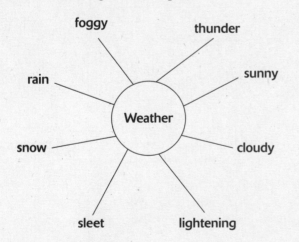

   **A.**   key scaling.
   **B.**   expository text.
   **C.**   semantic webbing.
   **D.**   background information.

**107.** A key component to effective classroom management when instructing in the subject of mathematics is to ensure that the lessons, activities, and assessments

   **A.**   offer self-paced instruction.
   **B.**   demonstrate ability groupings.
   **C.**   are developmentally appropriate.
   **D.**   are designed for independent learners.

**108.** Which of the following is the most preferred theory to implement in elementary mathematics education?

   **A.**   ecological
   **B.**   behavioral
   **C.**   constructivist
   **D.**   psychoanalytic

**109.** The recommended method of teaching grammar to elementary students is to use

   **A.**  an authentic and meaningful approach.

   **B.**  a system of direct instruction and practice.

   **C.**  familiar rules and guidelines.

   **D.**  periodic evaluations and altered instruction.

**110.** A third grade student, excited about learning new words, wanted to practice writing some words at home. Even though there was no homework assigned, he wanted to share his word list with the teacher. Based on this list that he created, what stage of spelling development is he in?

parkd     char (chair)
fishd     jragin (dragon)
changd   chrane (train)

   **A.**  phonetic

   **B.**  semiphonic

   **C.**  transitional

   **D.**  precommunicative

# Answer Key

| | | | |
|---|---|---|---|
| 1. A | 29. D | 57. D | 85. A |
| 2. B | 30. C | 58. A | 86. C |
| 3. C | 31. D | 59. B | 87. B |
| 4. C | 32. A | 60. C | 88. C |
| 5. C | 33. D | 61. A | 89. D |
| 6. A | 34. C | 62. B | 90. B |
| 7. A | 35. B | 63. A | 91. A |
| 8. C | 36. D | 64. D | 92. C |
| 9. C | 37. A | 65. A | 93. D |
| 10. D | 38. A | 66. C | 94. A |
| 11. C | 39. B | 67. A | 95. A |
| 12. D | 40. A | 68. D | 96. A |
| 13. D | 41. A | 69. B | 97. A |
| 14. D | 42. C | 70. D | 98. B |
| 15. D | 43. C | 71. C | 99. C |
| 16. A | 44. D | 72. B | 100. B |
| 17. C | 45. D | 73. D | 101. A |
| 18. D | 46. C | 74. D | 102. B |
| 19. C | 47. D | 75. D | 103. A |
| 20. C | 48. D | 76. A | 104. D |
| 21. C | 49. A | 77. D | 105. C |
| 22. A | 50. A | 78. D | 106. C |
| 23. D | 51. D | 79. C | 107. C |
| 24. B | 52. D | 80. B | 108. C |
| 25. C | 53. D | 81. C | 109. A |
| 26. A | 54. C | 82. A | 110. A |
| 27. A | 55. D | 83. B | |
| 28. D | 56. A | 84. B | |

# Answer Explanations

1. **A.** A word or phrase that creates a link between sentences or between a sentence and its content to make a connection for the reader is called a cohesive tie.

2. **B.** The K-W-L strategy is used to promote students' active thinking as they read passages. It stands for K, what do you *know;* W, *what* else do you want to learn; and L, what did you *learn* from the reading.

3. **C.** Even though both students are first graders, skill development will vary from individual to individual. Expecting children to develop the same skills at the same time is unrealistic. Age and heredity are not predictors of motor ability. Skill must be developed from use and practice.

4. **C.** An aptitude test is designed to predict how well a student will learn a skill or gain knowledge in a topic area, whereas an achievement test is used to measure what the student has already learned or to identify the skills the student has mastered.

5. **C.** It is critical to meet the needs of all students as lessons are presented and taught to ensure comprehension of the materials and competencies of the content. Some students will need accommodations and others may need enrichment. The other answers are areas a teacher should review, but none of these will separately guarantee that students will have what they need.

6. **A.** Teachers should read descriptive poetry lines to students and ask them to create a picture in their minds or ask students to write poetry that depicts a given scene. Teachers may also use art such as drawing pictures or making a collage to help teach imagery.

7. **A.** Having students mix colored liquids in science is the best selection, as the concept is visual and will be imprinted in their minds as they perform the activity. It is a positive method for integrating art into a subject area and using the vocabulary, as it is appropriate to the activity. The other options are related to color relationships, but would not offer the depth and concept development of the science lesson.

8. **C.** At a young age, students should be exposed to phonemic awareness, which is the ability to match the sounds of a word given orally to the knowledge that a word exists. This may be accomplished by using songs and rhymes to "play" with word and syllable sounds.

9. **C.** Estimation is an important lifelong skill that is used in figuring measurements and the quantities of objects. Teaching students by using typical daily situations will be more meaningful to understanding this concept.

10. **D.** Students are better able to learn the laws, facts, and content of science if they are first exposed to the inquiry of products. Understanding products and being active participants in the exploration aids students in being able to grasp the concepts of science processes.

11. **C.** The expository method of instruction is based on teacher-dominated activities, such as conducting a lecture, reading stories, showing videos, or demonstrating an activity.

12. **D.** The alphabetic principle is the concept that written language is comprised of letters that represent sounds in spoken words. This is essential to knowing how to decode.

13. **D.** Maslow's Theory of Hierarchy of Needs was created to show the various levels through which a person develops to become a self-actualized person who is capable of managing himself in society. The first level consists of basic needs, and Maslow believed that these must be met first for the person to continue up the hierarchy to more advanced stages and learn to be independent.

14. **D.** The literature-based reading approach supports children through various literature selections and a variety of trade books. These are chosen through the use of specific criteria that relates to grade levels. Research finds that this approach encourages children to read, as they are motivated and gain interest through the materials.

15. **D.** Children must obtain locomotor skills so that they may gain better access of their home, school, and community environments. While locomotor skills are required for participation in sports, aid in physical fitness, and improve the cardiovascular system, they are more importantly linked to a student's ability to navigate the world around them.

16. **A.** The teacher should conduct a vocabulary test to check student comprehension of the music terms, the dances taught, and the cultural aspects of the study. Although the other choices have potential for evaluating student progress, they are all performance-based assessments and not forced-answer assessments.

17. **C.** The two different models recommended in the teaching of citizenship are transmission and transformation. Transmission is the learning of government functions and following the rules. There are two perspectives in the transmission model: legalistic and assimilationist.

18. **D.** A mathematics manipulative that is considered unstructured is one that has various uses and may be applied to more than one concept in learning math. Buttons can be used to teach classification, ordered sets, math operations, and a variety of other concepts.

19. **C.** Phoneme blending is the strategy of providing a sequence of spoken phonemes and then using them to sound out and form a word. Examples include /t/ /a/ /p/ is *tap,* /m/ /o/ /m/ is *mom,* /d/ /e/ /n/ is *den*.

20. **C.** The best social discipline technique to use in this situation is one of a reactive nature since the distraction is already taking place. Nonverbal teacher instruction, in which the teacher uses the equipment the student is playing with to teach the next lesson, can be effective in reducing the inappropriate behavior without stopping the class.

21. **C.** For a new student who has yet to be introduced to the concepts and who needs to catch up to the other students in the class, the most beneficial strategy is peer tutoring. The use of this strategy allows the teacher time to observe the new student and allows the student to become comfortable in the class, while not feeling incompetent. Peer tutoring is conducted under the guidance of a teacher in which a student who needs assistance in an academic area works with a student who is more competent or knowledgeable in that particular area.

22. **A.** Sociology, a social science, is the study of human behavior and society specifically related to institutions, groups, social changes, communications, and relationships among people. Anthropology encompasses the study of the physical characteristics of people and cultural traits. Psychology is the study of human behavior and society but is also focused on perceptions and behaviors, individual differences, and emotions. Economics is considered a social structure of a society.

23. **D.** The new literacies of technology require complex skills that are different from those needed in the past. Students must be able to access information in multidimensional formats through a variety of technological tools, act on that information immediately, and deliver concise and clear information to others. Teachers must be trained to address these skills.

24. **B.** Research studies confirm that when students are exposed to music in structured standards-based educational opportunities and it is integrated into the curriculum, students reap the benefits in academic areas, particularly mathematics and literacy.

25. **C.** An anecdotal record kept during a writing assignment is helpful to a teacher in planning for future instruction in this area. It includes a description of meaningful information observed by the teacher and collected as notes so the teacher may interpret the information. The teacher may then modify and adjust instruction for individual students.

26. **A.** Phonemic awareness is the understanding that oral sounds in the language become words and that blending the sounds in a word make it possible to say the word.

27. **A.** Synthesis is the step in which students demonstrate the capability of creating something new from information they already know. Taking what they have learned in this example of the solar system, students can work together to identify a planet and create a life-form capable of inhabiting it.

28. **D.** Children understand how to recognize the amount in sets of objects when given patterned arrangements. Using cards such as those in the example help in teaching and grasping the concept of spatial relationships.

29. **D.** In the stage of prewriting, students generate ideas for their writing piece and gather details. They do so through reading literature, creating maps or webs of the information, developing word banks, or determining the audience for the piece.

30. **C.** The constructivist theory is based on Piaget's developmental stages and related to how children construct their own knowledge based on prior experience and investigation. The focus in elementary science education is inquiry-based learning, in which children utilize hands-on learning to discover the principles and concepts of science.

31. **D.** Students need practice in extracting information from texts in preparation for reading expository texts at the higher grade levels. The use of reciprocal teaching helps students learn how to read expository texts. A set process for implementing reciprocal teaching is important and includes predicting, reading, questioning, clarifying, summarizing, and predicting.

32. **A.** Under the NCLB law, states are required to create a system of accountability to ensure that all students are making adequate annual progress in prime subject areas. There is a measurement system in place that determines the school's adequate yearly progress, and each state establishes a system for remediation of schools.

33. **D.** A child's environment and experiences at an early age contribute to the development of the language domain and impacts future success specifically in reading and language arts.

34. **C.** Environmental print or text has been shown to be beneficial in literacy development. Sharing words from a child's daily world, such as those on product containers, in newspapers, ads, or small signs, contributes to rich vocabulary development.

35. **B.** The concept of weight measurement compares the mass of one object to another and is one of the first measurement concepts taught. Students may use informal units of measure such as their hands to determine mass when first learning this concept

36. **D.** The constructivist theory, regarded by the work of Jean Piaget, suggests that children learn best when they participate in hands-on learning, which is an appropriate selection for the area of arts education.

37. **A.** Analysis is the fourth level in Bloom's Taxonomy, in which students recognize patterns, organize parts, identify components, conclude, and clarify. Questions found at this level include "how" and "what."

38. **A.** The teacher is establishing the background for students by seeking answers to simple questions that relate to the book and to the students' lives and experiences. This aids the students in using their prior knowledge to make connections to the text.

39. **B.** At the utilization level, students are able to carry out movements and skills with more autonomy, and there is a purpose for each intentional movement or skill. Dribbling a basketball against an opponent is one example of the utilization level.

40. **A.** Interpreting and predicting are complex cognitive skills and important reading skills. Interpreting is the ability of a reader to use inference and apply literal information to his or her personal life. In this instance, the student must have some familiarity with horses. Predicting also involves the use of inference to make a deduction about what may happen next or what ideas are present. In this illustration, the student is imagining that there will be fun adventures, perhaps based on previous or desired experiences with horses.

41. **A.** Peer assessment is best described as two students who observe each other to determine whether they are each able to complete the predetermined skills on which they are being assessed. They must use a rubric for scoring created by the physical education teacher. Peer assessment is a positive assessment technique used to provide information to the teacher on individual student skill levels and supports the affective domain by having students work together to reach a goal.

42. **C.** The child is using invented spelling in this passage, which is an early spelling stage for young children. Children guess how a word might be spelled according to what they hear, using the spelling skills and knowledge they possess. Children should be allowed to use invented spelling. As they are exposed to more standard spelling instruction, they will improve their spelling skills.

43. **C.** Enrichment is an instructional method used for extending a lesson or unit for those students who are able to grasp more of the topic and who may need additional participation in the learning situation. Many of the students who require enrichment activities are found to be gifted or talented.

**44. D.** A student who shows problems with remembering some of the letters in a word that he can easily read may not have a complete understanding of letter-sound correspondences, so the word becomes difficult to remember.

**45. D.** Building models in science offers concrete, visual representations of structures and, frequently, things that cannot easily be seen due to the size of the actual object. Building models accurately requires skills in spatial relationships and mathematics.

**46. C.** Using art to create a model of something studied in science offers the best selection for a parallel process, which is the blending of an arts-related activity with an academic subject. This reflects a type of integrated activity.

**47. D.** A bodily kinesthetic learner acquires knowledge through body movements and physical activity; therefore, having the students physically move about an area to learn the map components would best meet the needs of these learners.

**48. D.** Showing the student some lists of other words with the same silent letters or letter patterns as words the student already knows aids in the memorization of these regular spellings. For example, *right, bright, tight, fight*.

**49. A.** Informal deduction is one of the sequential levels of the van Hiele theory of geometry. At this level the student can learn the properties of shapes and the relationships among the properties of geometric objects.

**50. A.** Piaget believed that individuals construct new knowledge based on prior knowledge, and there are distinct stages of learning. He promoted the cognitive theory, which encompasses the constructivist approach to learning, often used in science education.

**51. D.** Group activity using homogeneous or heterogeneous combinations of students, selected by the teacher, is considered cooperative learning as the students work collaboratively to derive outcomes. The cooperative learning process aids students in gaining problem-solving, communication, and critical thinking skills.

**52. D.** Primary source utilization is one of the three essential types of lessons used for social studies. It involves using the actual items from the period or going to a place that includes period items or relates to a period (for example, original documents, artifacts, maps, photos, clothing, music, tools, museums, libraries, and historical monuments).

**53. D.** Based on the information provided, this student may be embarrassed about performing a dance, using the languages, or dressing in costumes during the class. Teachers must take into account student abilities and interests when creating lessons and making expectations. This student may need an accommodation for this assignment. Asking the student about preferences and desires may help to promote trust and understanding, thus encouraging more participation.

**54. C.** This example is the multiplication strategy of doubles that are equivalent to doubles in addition problems.

**55. D.** When a teacher points out the initial consonants of vocabulary in a story to help students begin to predict a word, it encourages the use and development of phonics skills.

**56. A.** Health education has become a timely and important topic in the science curriculum. The primary goal is for students to attain and maintain a healthy lifestyle. While in school, good health impacts student learning and achievement.

**57. D.** Individuals believe that the high-stakes tests promote the "dumbing down" (a focus on lower-order skills) of the school curriculum by implementing rote memorization strategies in learning key concepts rather than emphasizing critical thinking skills and other more complex cognitive skills.

**58. A.** The verbal intelligence is most closely related to the subject area of reading and language arts, as it is the ability to express oneself orally or in writing.

**59. B.** This error shows a student who has forgotten to record the zeros (0), which then results in the misplacement of the digits of the quotient. Using column lines between numbers with place values in division will help students learn this concept.

60. **C.** Mnemonics is a strategy that enhances student memory by using key words, acronyms, or acrostics to highlight the information. "HOMES" stands for the following Great Lakes: Huron, Ontario, Michigan, Erie, and Superior.

61. **A.** Scope and sequence is an essential design component of a curriculum. It includes the plan for learning sequences and an outline of the sequential development of skills and concepts of the content.

62. **B.** Recording small amounts of data plotted on a simple graph is a skill that is reasonably introduced at the second-grade level.

63. **A.** Cognitive theorists believe that an individual constructs the acquisition of new information and skills based on prior knowledge. The internal mental processes included in this theory are problem solving, memory, and language.

64. **D.** The study of science is divided into specific domains, one of which is physical science. It includes the study of the tangible and material world, such as properties of objects, materials, and matter, motion and force, light, heat, electricity, magnetism, and energy.

65. **A.** This is an example of integrating fine arts into the reading and language arts content area. Having students compose an original piece (written expression) and then create an illustration (art) and perform before peers (drama) is one way to incorporate two or more subjects and meet additional goals and standards. Although written expression is one of the answers provided, it is not the BEST answer for this question as it represents only one of the components of the activity.

66. **C.** Students who participate in learning activities for the pleasure of doing so and complete assignments or participate in activities because they want to successfully master a subject or skill have intrinsic motivation, which comes from within the individual.

67. **A.** Inductive instruction is the process of moving from more specific to more generalized information. Students study detailed information on which to base a broad conclusion. In this example, students study specific plants and the details of each, which leads them to a generalized statement about where the plant must live and its purpose for being there.

68. **D.** This is an example of the comprehension level, as students are asked to predict, which demonstrates an understanding of the information and the ability to interpret the material.

69. **B.** Scaffolding provides a temporary support for a learner who is not ready to perform the task alone. The teacher is giving needed support at the beginning of her lesson by paraphrasing the textbook, asking questions, and exploring ideas. She will gradually decrease it as the students become more independent and gain higher-order thinking skills.

70. **D.** Through this activity, students are learning more about the top (numerator) and bottom (denominator) numbers and the relative sizes, which is the concept of comparing. Comparing requires that the student be able to understand the relationship between the numerals within the fraction rather than the arrangement of the fractions according to a specific sequence, pattern, or method (ordering).

71. **C.** A summative assessment is the best choice for an assessment utilized at the completion of a unit. It can be used to identify the future needs of learners and make decisions that support student achievement.

72. **B.** The second most important step in conducting an experiment is to formulate the hypothesis based on the first step of stating the question. The hypothesis is an educated guess as to the answer to the proposed question. The hypothesis is the basis for proceeding with the experiment and the concept to be proved or disproved.

73. **D.** Choral responding is an excellent strategy to use in the classroom to promote both listening and speaking skills. Choral responding is the oral response by a class of students to a question that is presented by the teacher. Students must listen to the question, interpret the meaning, form an answer, and respond orally.

74. **D.** The purpose of an anticipatory set, one of the essential skills, is to engage students and grab their attention, getting them motivated and interested in the subject matter. If a teacher were to act out a playground scene depicting citizenship, it would link the student's prior knowledge to current learning.

75. **D.** Using meaningful content in a discussion prior to introducing a new concept should be motivating to the students. If they discuss whether these sentences are true, impossible, or possible, it will support their understanding of the new concept to be introduced: probability and estimation.

76. **A.** It is important to establish the appropriate attitude about science at an early age so children will continue to pursue this subject area, regardless of their gender or culture. Elementary teachers should evaluate student attitudes and enhance the curriculum to address this area.

77. **D.** The Neo-Skinnerian Model, developed by Skinner, is described as the modeling and shaping of desired behaviors through the use of consistent rewards and consequences.

78. **D.** A summative assessment is the type of evaluation used at the end of a unit of study to check a particular skill or concept. The method of obtaining data may be left to the teacher, and in this instance the delivery of the report may be used as an authentic assessment and scored using a rubric.

79. **C.** A portfolio assessment is a collection of student work that may be selected by both the student and the teacher to demonstrate strengths, progress, skills, and completed assignments. It is a recommended method of assessment for use with parents, as it demonstrates ongoing progress, acquisition of skills, and actual performance on tasks.

80. **B.** Allowing learners the appropriate time between instruction/task presentation and responding to a question posed is called processing time, wait time, or think time. Time to pause and think should be based on the difficulty of the task and the age of the students.

81. **C.** Madeline Hunter is well known for her approach of direct instruction, which includes an instructional sequence for any subject and grade level, considering the diversity of learners. Students move along a sequence, supported by the educator, reviewing previous concepts and moving to the next step after mastery of the skills is complete.

82. **A.** The U.S. monetary system, as well as the system of scientific measures, is based on decimals. Students must have a solid grasp of fractions before beginning the study of decimals, as these are related and are not separate concepts. The teacher should assess the students' understanding of fractions prior to teaching decimals.

83. **B.** A criterion-referenced test is a formal measure that may be used to evaluate students on the specific information of the poetry unit by having students answer specific questions, such as those about terminology.

84. **B.** This passage is an example of the transitional stage of writing, in which all letters are present in the word, but the letters may not be in the correct order.

85. **A.** One of the six primary principles created by the NCTM for mathematics in the schools is *equity,* which focuses on the expectations and supports that should be available to students. The premise is that every student should have the same goals, supports, materials, and instruction in math in order for each student to reach the highest potential.

86. **C.** A scoring rubric is a predetermined outline of how the product will be scored. It offers several viable components in grading a performance assessment, including setting the criteria to be used to judge the performance, the range of quality that is acceptable, and the value of the score. Students know before completing the performance assessment the outline of the rubric criteria.

87. **B.** A contingency contract is a written agreement that is developed by the student and the teacher. It describes the expected performance and the kinds of reinforcers that should be used. The steps and procedures are discussed together, giving the student an active role in learning to self-manage off-task behaviors.

88. **C.** The word "house" in this example suggests the student is in the phase of letter-like symbols, which shows writing in which letters begin to emerge although still randomly placed with numbers mixed throughout.

89. **D.** Comprehension is the level that is best described as understanding the information, where students are able to explain, discuss, review, and summarize the information.

90. **B.** Task analysis involves creating a set of sequential steps to learn a specific skill, which helps students move to a preferred level of skills.

91. **A.** A reader profile may include a student interview of reading preferences, a miscue analysis, and a retelling and discussion of the materials. This is a beneficial tool in determining a student's reading strengths and needs.

92. **C.** Developing tiered lessons would be the best solution in this situation, as these provide accommodations for various learners, both at the lower end of the bell curve and at the higher end of the academic curve.

93. **D.** Systematic feedback provides regular positive reinforcement and confirms for the learner that his performance is adequate, which improves learning. In mathematics education, students need consistent and constant feedback so they know that they are performing the tasks appropriately, which helps them improve their skills.

94. **A.** Onsets and rimes are parts of words in the spoken language that are smaller than syllables. An *onset* is the initial consonant sound of a syllable, and a *rime* is the portion of the syllable with the vowel and is the remainder of the word.

95. **A.** Choral reading is used to involve several readers taking different parts as a specific selection is read aloud. These parts are rehearsed, and since more than one student reads the part at the same time, readers with less proficiency will feel more comfortable.

96. **A.** The delegator style of teaching is the choice that encourages greater autonomy in learners and makes the educator available as a consultative resource. It is useful with older age groups, who are more responsible.

97. **A.** When creating assignments for students in a class, teachers should refer to developmentally appropriate practices, which consider the level at which each student is presently functioning. The assignments selected should meet the expectations for the age group and the ability of the group.

98. **B.** Data analysis and probability are identified in the first five standards, and the other options given are all connected to the second set of five in the ten general standards.

99. **C.** Guided writing is the use of instruction that scaffolds the writing process for a student. As the teacher works with and models the steps in the writing process, the student will gain mastery and reach independence.

100. **B.** The cloze procedure omits about every fifth word in a passage and requires that the student supply the missing word to make sense of the passage.

101. **A.** Basic facts mean the addends and the factors in addition and multiplication problems that are less than 10. In subtraction and division, it means that the facts related to addition and multiplication and both parts equal less than 10.

102. **B.** The use of context clues should allow students to determine words that they have heard before, but may not know in print. If a student has trouble reading a word, he may lack the ability to use context clues.

103. **A.** Using manipulatives to teach mathematics provides practice in visualizing concepts, which helps students acquire math skills and retain the information.

104. **D.** Scaffolded instruction is a strategy that provides temporary support to the learner who is not yet ready to perform a task independently. The use of this strategy delivers support in the beginning, then gradually decreases the teacher participation as the student becomes more competent. It ends with independent practice as the student masters the skill. This is especially helpful when students are learning new concepts and must perform tasks related to those concepts.

105. **C.** Lack of organization is evident in this sample. This student needs additional training in how to organize ideas and compose a proper structure for a paragraph.

106. **C.** Graphic displays often aid students in learning new vocabulary words. Using semantic webbing can support a main concept and relate the new words to some words a student already knows. In this example, the main concept is weather and some of the eight vocabulary words may be known by the student. If a student knows the word rain, then new words such as sleet or snow will be easier to relate to.

107. **C.** Essential to the positive attitude students will gain regarding mathematics is that the lessons and activities, as well as the assessments, are developmentally appropriate for the students. If these are too difficult or too easy for the students, the interest and ability to achieve will decrease.

108. **C.** The constructivist theory, based on Piaget's work, relates to how children construct their own knowledge based on prior experiences and investigations. The emphasis for elementary mathematics education is based on hands-on learning so students may discover the principles and concepts of math and relate them to what they already know.

109. **A.** The recommended method of instruction for students to learn proper grammar and its use is to provide authentic and meaningful lessons to students. Demonstrating grammar through the design of poetry and other narratives will aid students in the use of correct grammar in the context of reading, writing, and speaking.

110. **A.** This student shows evidence of being in the phonetic stage of spelling development. He is attempting to write a letter for each sound that is heard. However, some of the endings, such as *–ed,* may become *d* or *t* in some words, and blends are substituted in some words.

## Introduction

> The content of this practice test is meant to aid the examinee in studying and preparing for the actual essay exam component of the Praxis II elementary exam (0012). The 0012 exam is unlike the other Praxis II exams described in this study guide. This exam requires that the examinee have extensive background knowledge about core subject areas, and the curriculum, instruction, and assessment used at the elementary school level, in order to apply this knowledge to various situations in written essay form.
>
> For each essay question presented, recommendations are provided in text boxes for examinees to consider in developing a written answer. These include key information and essential points that the examinee should include in the narrative. Since each examinee composes and answers essay questions in a different manner, based on prior knowledge and previous experiences, the answers for this practice test provide only an outline and some suggestions for potential answers on the actual exam. These answers should not be considered by the examinee to be complete or reflective of what is an acceptable answer on the actual exam.

Directions: Read each of the following essay questions and develop a complete, detailed, and supportive written answer. These answers will be scored according to a standard rubric.

## Essay 1

1. An elementary teacher is planning a unit for a fifth grade class about explorers. Write three learner goals that demonstrate the integration of the subjects of social studies, science, and mathematics for this unit. Then develop and compose an activity using the format of Bloom's Taxonomy that demonstrates the integration of two or more of these subjects with reading and language arts.

> *Note to Examinee:* Examinees should fully understand the meaning of **integration of subjects** prior to composing an answer to this question. For study purposes, the definition as well as the benefits of integration have been included here, although neither would be required as part of the written answer. This information should help an examinee study and prepare for the composition of a written answer to this question.

### Definition of Integration

**Integration** literally means "to combine into a whole," which helps to clarify the meaning when used in elementary education. When integrating subjects in the curricula, the focus is on comprehensive and whole understanding of concepts and topics rather than just individual topics. Integration means to help students gain comprehensive understanding across various disciplines. Furthermore, it is defined as the instruction of concepts that crosses disciplines and subjects, such as teaching mathematics through science activities, and literature through social studies activities.

### Benefits of Integration

- Helps supply students with an understanding of the relationships of all individual parts to the whole.
- Helps students to take ownership of their own learning and creates autonomy.
- Aids in social relationships and cooperation among students.

- Increases knowledge in all subject areas.
- Cultivates appreciation for all areas of study.

---

*Note to Examinee:* When writing the answer for this essay question, examinees should include information based on the definition, the benefits, and purpose of integration. Although the question only requires three learner goals, more are included for further consideration and study.

---

# Response 1

## Learner Goals

For social studies, the following should be considered appropriate learner goals:

- Compare and contrast the differences of ideas, values, behaviors, personalities, and institutions.
- Hypothesize about some of the greatest influences of the past (inventors, eras, civilizations, and so on).
- Explain the cause and effect of historical actions.
- Create timelines to show significant achievements in history, math, and science.
- Identify problems or dilemmas of the past.
- Propose alternative choices for addressing problems.
- Evaluate the consequences of decisions made by explorers that influence areas of science or math.

For math, the following should be considered appropriate learner goals:

- Measure using techniques of the past.
- Carry out conversions to standard measurements.
- Create and use representations to organize, record, and communicate mathematical ideas.
- Use statistical representations to model and interpret physical, social, and math phenomena.

For science, the following should be considered appropriate learner goals:

- Recognize the impact humans have on the environment (irrigation, roads, cities, and so on).
- Identify environmental changes caused by living things.
- Predict the effects of human actions and/or natural disasters during this period in history on the environment.
- Determine the importance of crops and farming over this period in history.
- Recognize the impact of society's use of nonrenewable resources over time.

---

*Note to Examinee:* As review, the examinee should be knowledgeable about Bloom's Taxonomy in order to clearly state activities that may reflect this philosophy. Benjamin Bloom was an educational psychologist who developed a classification of levels of intellectual behaviors important to learning. These levels should be incorporated into lessons, and the educator should strive to progress the students into the upper levels (analysis, synthesis, and evaluation).

---

## Bloom's Taxonomy

- Knowledge—Recall or recognize facts. (Use terms such as *arrange, define, label, list, name, order, repeat, relate, recall.*)
- Understanding (comprehension)—Grasp the meaning. (Use terms such as *classify, describe, discuss, explain, identify, indicate, locate, recognize, report, select, translate.*)
- Application—Use previously learned information in new situations to solve problems. (Use terms such as *apply, choose, demonstrate, employ, illustrate, operate, practice, sketch, solve, use, write.*)

- Analysis—Break down wholes into parts to identify causes, make inferences, or find evidence to support. (Use terms such as *analyze, calculate, compare, contrast, criticize, discriminate, distinguish, examine, question, test.*)

- Synthesis—Creatively apply prior knowledge and skills to produce a new whole. (Use terms such as *arrange, assemble, collect, compose, construct, create, design, develop, formulate, manage, organize, plan, report.*)

- Evaluation—Judge the value of material based on individual values and produce a final product. (Use terms such as *appraise, argue, assess, attach, compare, estimate, judge, predict, rate, select, support, value, evaluate.*)

## Activities

A multitude of activities could impart knowledge to students, but activities that encourage active learning should be promoted in order to reach Bloom's stages of application, analysis, and synthesis.

- Students study parts of a map and write a user's manual on map reading (social studies, language arts/reading) [*application & synthesis*].

- Students study the parts of a map: compass rose, legend, and so on, and create a map of the school using the parts studied (language arts/reading, math, social studies) [*understanding & application & synthesis*].

- Students map a specific explorer's course across his expedition using precise measurements, appropriate time frames, geographic entities, and major landforms, and then label each part of the map (social studies, math, and language) [*understanding & application & synthesis*].

- Students study travel media and then create a travel brochure to an explored region; this brochure should include climate, landforms, historical significance, and colorful, descriptive language to entice tourists (science, social studies, language arts/reading) [*understanding & application & synthesis*].

- Students study North American explorers and make a timeline of exploration, including illustrations (language arts, social studies, mathematics) [*knowledge & application & synthesis*].

- Students keep a journal as if they were explorers, complete with illustrations, dated entries, miles traveled, and comments on major discoveries (language arts/reading, social studies, mathematics) [*application & analysis & synthesis*].

- Students study explorer ships and design a ship of exploration; considerations include what size it must be, how to scale down the size into a model, the shape it must be, what supplies may be needed for a voyage, what tools and size of crew may be needed, and so on. Students will draw "blueprints" for the ship and then construct it on a small scale from a variety of materials (social studies, mathematics, language arts/reading, science) [*understanding & application & analysis & synthesis*].

- Students study an explorer, his contributions to society, and his negative effects on society, and write a report or give an oral presentation based on this information (language arts/reading, social studies, science) [*understanding & application & analysis & synthesis & evaluation*].

# Essay 2

2. The first grade team, of which you are a member, has designed a six-week social studies unit on community helpers. The principal has asked for a copy of the assessment plan for this unit. Outline a plan for assessment during this six-week unit that includes both summative and formative assessments. Describe five different types of student assessments that will be used and explain how each will specifically be used. Then describe what the teacher will be evaluating in this unit.

---

*Note to Examinee:* To aid in study for answering this question, the definition of assessment is presented along with information about the assessment selection process.

---

# Definition of Assessment

Many forms and types of assessments may determine student comprehension. **Summative assessments** are assessments given periodically to gauge students' comprehension of a particular skill at a particular point in time and includes standardized tests, end-of-chapter exams, and semester finals. **Formative assessments** are assessments that occur during the learning process so that the teacher may adjust and revamp teaching techniques and include portfolios, student record-keeping, observations, and student-led conferences.

Assessments allow learners to identify what they need to learn and what they want to learn. It also provides learners insight into their strengths and weaknesses. Assessments permit learners to see what they have learned, what they have retained, and how they have grown. An assessment gives students the chance to understand individual capabilities so that they may assess tasks and projects for themselves. This is an opportunity for students to gain a sense of what strategies work best for them personally and why those strategies are effective.

# Choosing Assessments

Assessments should not only be connected to learner backgrounds and interests but should be matched to the appropriate tasks and skills measured, linking the content to instruction. Teachers must consider these five points when selecting the proper assessments:

- A combination of assessments should be chosen to adequately evaluate each learner and the learning concepts presented.
- Some assessments focus on skills, some on strategies, and some on the acquisition of knowledge, so determining the purpose of the assessment aids in selection.
- It is important that authentic assessments concentrate on the application of skills as those pertain to learners' daily lives.
- Learners should participate in the decision of which tasks they need to work on and also in what kind of assessments they want to use to evaluate their skills (especially important in the higher grades).
- Self-assessment, conferencing, and reflections should be implemented at an early age in all subjects and disciplines to promote ownership of learning.

# Response 2

## Outline of Plan for Assessment

The teacher submits the following to the principal as an outline of the six-week plan for assessment:

1. Pretest on vocabulary and concepts related to community helpers one week prior to the beginning of the unit.
2. Collect artifacts from students such as reports, drawings, and journals for portfolios throughout six-week period and share with parents.
3. Conduct quizzes and trivia games to use each week as a culmination activity or review of the materials discussed and presented during the week for six weeks.
4. Present a mid-unit assessment at the beginning of the fourth week, using the pretest content as the basis for evaluation.
5. Evaluate the student work (classroom and homework) throughout the six-week period to include oral reports, class Q/A participation, and so on.
6. Present a final assessment at the end of the six weeks as a culmination of all concepts presented.

## Types of Assessments

The following five types of assessments may be used to evaluate first-graders during a community helpers unit of study.

**Memory matrix:** A formative assessment used to advance the organization of ideas and the illustration of relationships. Present a sheet of paper with rows and columns, with only the headings of each row filled in.

For the first-grader learning about community helpers, it may be as simple as placing the community helper in the appropriate row. (For example, the *helps people* column would include firefighter, police officer, and teacher; the *provides a service* column would include mail carrier, baker, and butcher.)

**Word journal:** A formative assessment used to examine the depth of comprehension and the ability to summarize information. Use a notebook of the learner's words, which are associated with the task at hand. The words are placed in alphabetical order (similar to a dictionary) and defined by the student.

For the first-grader learning about community helpers, the journal would be used to keep new or complex words associated with the unit. (For example, *hydrant, veterinarian, canine, feline, community, cooperation, language.*)

**Writing task:** A formative assessment used to analyze student understanding and the synthesis of the content learned. Present as an activity in which the student is asked to write something on a given topic to gauge comprehension.

For the first-grader learning about community helpers, it may be used as a functional writing assessment in which the student writes about a day in the life of a specific community helper, writes a job description of a community helper, or writes a song or poem about a community helper. To add to the written assignment, the student might illustrate the job of a community helper or paint a picture of the community helper.

**Test:** A summative assessment used at the conclusion of a unit or in a given time frame. Constructed in the format of a true/false, multiple-choice, essay, matching, or fill-in-the-blank test.

For the first-grader learning about community helpers, the test may include pictures or words related to community jobs and community helpers. The student must match the pictures or words to specific community helpers.

**Oral presentation:** A formative assessment used to evaluate student understanding, analysis, synthesis, and application of skills and content learned. Utilize a researched or planned presentation given on a specific topic related to community members.

For the first-grader learning about community helpers, the presentation may be a brief discussion about which community helper the student would most like to be when he or she grows up. This could be assessed through a simple one-on-one conversation with the teacher or through peer interviews. The teacher could use a simple rubric in assessing knowledge during this time.

# Essay 3

3. Measurement is a basic mathematics concept and necessary in daily life. Using Hunter's guide for the *essential elements of instruction,* write a lesson plan at the third-grade level for the instruction of standard customary liquid measures.

> *Note to Examinee:* Prior to developing the written portion for this question, consider the information needed. Study the components of a lesson plan and the Madeline Hunter format of essential elements of instruction.

# Introduction to Lesson Plan Development

Measurement knowledge is an essential skill, and the concept of measurement is complex. Students should be able to use the units, systems, and processes of measurement throughout their lifetimes. Using the proper tools, techniques, and formulas to determine measurement should be included in the instruction.

In third grade, students may learn about volume/capacity and the proper tools or containers used for measuring. Measuring volume and capacity relates to three-dimensional objects and figures. The standard units of measurement utilized for volume include ounces, cups, pints, quarts, and gallons. Students may also use containers to check the amount being measured, such as cups, boxes, and bowls.

# Response 3

*Note to Examinee:* The following is a summary of a lesson plan, but the examinee should include more details and explanations when writing the answer to this question. This is a sample of a simple lesson outline; all lessons written for this question will be clearly different.

## Lesson Plan Using Essential Elements of Instruction (Hunter)

| | |
|---|---|
| **Standards-expectations** | The students will be able to identify the various measurement tools used for measuring volume and capacity. |
| **Objectives** | The students will be able to compare the capacity of different containers used for measuring liquids. |
| **Anticipatory set** | Clear containers (cup, pint, quart) are set up on a center table as students gather for the lesson. The teacher has a pitcher of water and a set of food coloring drops. Water is poured into the cup and a few drops of coloring added. The water is poured into the pint container to compare the amount. More is added to the cup, which is then added to the pint. The same is done for the quart, so students may not only compare the amounts in each container, but see how the colors change by the amount added. |
| **Instruction** | The teacher delivers direct information:<br>• Provides names of containers and comparison of amounts.<br>• Demonstrates how various liquids and amounts can be measured.<br>• Uses a question and answer period to determine student understanding. |
| **Guided practice** | Cooperative groups are created to practice measuring amounts and charting what the different containers can hold. |
| **Closure** | The teacher plays a quick trivia game with students to check knowledge. |
| **Independent practice** | A learning center is created with measuring tools and various liquids. Students may practice measurements, comparisons, and conversions. |
| **Assessment** | The teacher will monitor student progress through observations during independent practice time. The teacher may engage students with questions regarding the tasks at hand to gauge individual comprehension and progress. |

# Essay 4

4. The National Reading Council and reading research suggest that five primary core skills are factors that contribute to the success of readers: phonemic awareness, phonics, fluency, vocabulary, and comprehension of text.

   Define each of these skills and describe how each skill relates to reading instruction. Write an activity for elementary students at grades pre-K to 2 that will promote each of these predictor skills in young children (a total of five activities).

# Response 4

*Note to Examinee:* These definitions should be written in more detail to answer this question appropriately. This information is offered as a guideline to show what to include as the main points.

## Definitions

- *Phonemic awareness:* The knowledge that speech sounds are found in the letters of the alphabet and that blending sounds can create words.
- *Phonics:* The relationship between the sounds in spoken language with the letters that represent the sounds when in a written format.
- *Fluency:* The ability to have flow when reading is done accurately and automatically with expression and a consistent rate.
- *Vocabulary:* The words that are either being learned or already known and used during reading.
- *Comprehension of text:* The specific strategies used in the processing of reading to understand the content, such as critical thinking.

*Note to Examinee:* The examinee should describe an activity for each of the five core skills listed in this question (phonemic awareness, phonics, fluency, vocabulary, and comprehension of text). The following are provided as suggestions on which to base an activity for students. These should not be considered as complete answers to this question.

## Activities

Activities for **phonemic awareness** could include the following:

- Use nursery rhymes.
- Include exposure to poetry, jingles, or rhyming phrases.
- Utilize songs with rhyme and rhythm.
- Play games with nonsense syllables.

Activities for **phonics** could include the following:

- Read new sight words.
- Compare new words to those with similar patterns.
- Practice blending words through onsets and rimes.
- Create word banks.
- Recite poetry and rhymes.

Activities for **fluency** could include the following:

- Practice oral reading periods.
- Use reader's theater opportunities.
- Provide a chance for choral readings.
- Use listening center, read-alouds, and models.
- Use sustained reading periods.

Activities for **vocabulary** could include the following:

- Use games and puzzles.
- Create word books.
- Instruct in the use of dictionary.
- Improve oral vocabulary usage.
- Compare types of words, such as homographs or homophones or homonyms.
- Instruct in the use of prefixes or suffixes and root words.
- Teach context clue strategies.
- Use descriptive words in speaking and writing.

Activities for **comprehension of text** could include the following:

- Practice using inferences.
- Use imagery.
- Learn to make connections.
- Understand question-answer relationships.
- Use K-W-L strategy.
- Practice summarizing what is read.

Note: On this practice test, examinees will experience a more intense assessment of basic knowledge as the subject matter has been mixed. In the actual examination the content is grouped together by each of the four subjects. The practice test on the CD (5014) follows the grouping together format.

**Directions:** Read the following multiple-choice questions and select the most appropriate answer. Mark the answer sheet accordingly.

---

1. What were the first civilizations called?

   A. Tigris
   B. valley
   C. river-valley
   D. Mesopotamia

2. What is the value of the $x$ on the following number line?

   A. 100
   B. 25
   C. 75
   D. 125

3. When a solid changes into a liquid, which of the following occurs?

   A. Pressure increases and energy increases.
   B. Pressure decreases and energy increases.
   C. Pressure increases and energy decreases.
   D. Pressure decreases and energy decreases.

4. A first grade student reads a story about a dog lost in the woods. When he is finished reading, he states, "I was lost in a store and couldn't find my mommy. It was scary. The puppy must have been scared, too. He missed his mommy." The first-grader is demonstrating which stage in the interpretation of literature?

   A. initial
   B. developing
   C. reflection-response
   D. critical analysis

5. The Earth's magnetic field originates in the thick, viscous part called the

   A. crust.
   B. mantle.
   C. inner core.
   D. outer core.

6. Which of the following was developed prior to the twentieth century?

   A. radio
   B. airplane
   C. firearms
   D. electronic refrigeration

7. The algorithms used in addition and subtraction both fall into which category?

   A. carrying
   B. borrowing
   C. regrouping
   D. consigning

8. The limited omniscient point of view is when the story is told by

   A. a narrator who is detached from the story and tells about the actions and dialogue.
   B. a narrator whose knowledge is restricted to knowing all inner thoughts and feelings of one character.
   C. a narrator who knows everything about every character, including all inner thoughts and feelings.
   D. a narrator who is directly involved in the story and action and may or may not be trusted.

9. The *exposition* of a narrative accomplishes which of the following tasks?

    A. tells the events of a story
    B. triggers the central conflict of a story
    C. concludes the events in a story
    D. introduces the characters, setting, and tone of a story

10. Which of the following did the classical civilizations contribute to present day?

    A. writing, trade, wheel
    B. time measurement, alphabet, art
    C. social cohesion, religions, agricultural options
    D. monotheistic belief, democratic rule, family structure

11. A third grade student demonstrates the use of which algorithm when he writes:

    $13 \times 7$ is one 10 and 3 ones taken 7 times, and the product is equal to 9 tens plus 1 unit.

    A. whole multiplication
    B. regrouping multiplication
    C. long multiplication
    D. distributive multiplication

12. A ball that is resting on the top of an inclined plane is said to have what type of energy?

    A. inertia
    B. kinetic energy
    C. potential energy
    D. conserved energy

13. Which of the following non-European civilizations brought forth the concept of present-day irrigation, road systems, and military organizations?

    A. Incas
    B. Islams
    C. Mayans
    D. Mongolians

14. The law that states *the effort force times the distance the effort moves is equal to the resistance times the distance the resistance moves* is the

    A. Law of Simple Machines.
    B. Law of Conservation of Matter.
    C. Law of Conservation of Energy.
    D. Law of Energy, Mass, and Substance.

15. User manuals are an example of what type of literature?

    A. poetry
    B. nonfiction
    C. fiction
    D. research

16. What is the missing number in the number pattern below?

    5, 15, 45, _____ , 405, 1,215

    A. 130
    B. 135
    C. 205
    D. 235

17. When using maps to teach distances between continents, one limitation to take into consideration is that they

    A. show landmasses without distortion.
    B. are used to analyze spatial organization.
    C. depict the most precise representation of the Earth.
    D. cannot accurately represent a sphere on a flat surface without distortion.

18. The illustration represents which number?

    A. 1,048
    B. 481
    C. 841
    D. 148

19. The following is an example of what poetic device?

    The rain falls mainly on the plains of Spain.

    A. alliteration
    B. assonance
    C. consonance
    D. repetition

20. When a student adds one drop of food coloring to a warm cup of water without stirring, but observes the food coloring changing the water into one solid well-mixed color, he is witnessing

    A. melting.
    B. diffusion.
    C. evaporation.
    D. vaporization.

21. Which type of map would be BEST used when teaching a sixth grade class about tectonic plates and fault lines?

    A. outline
    B. physical
    C. conformal
    D. topographical

22. The best characteristics to define sound are

    A. pitch, amplitude, and quality.
    B. wave, rare fraction, and amplitude.
    C. pitch, wave length, and compression.
    D. compression, wave length, and quality.

23. Which is a true statement of equivalence?

    A. One fourth equals six twenty-fourths.
    B. One fourth equals two sixths.
    C. One fourth equals twenty-six one-hundredths.
    D. One fourth equals twenty percent.

24. Geographically, the largest continent is

    A. Asia.
    B. Africa.
    C. Europe.
    D. North America.

25. Mutant genes can cause a disruption within the DNA of an organism that usually results in

    A. an aborted egg.
    B. unneeded eggs.
    C. a fertilized egg.
    D. unfertilized eggs.

Use the following poem to answer questions 26–28.

## JABBERWOCKY
### – Lewis Carroll

'Twas brillig, and the slithy toves
Did gyre and gimble in the wade;
All mimsy were the borogoves,
And the mome raths outgrabe.

"Beware the Jabberwock, my son!
The jaws that bite, the claws that catch!
Beware the Jubjub bird, and shun
The frumious Bandersnatch!"

He took his vorpal sword in hand:
Long time the manxome foe he sought—
So rested he by the Tumtum tree.
And stood awhile in thought.

And as in uffish thought he stood,
The Jabberwock, with eyes of flame,
Came wiffling through the tulgey wood,
And burbled as it came!

One, two! One, two! And through and through
The vorpal blade went snicker-snack!
He left it dead, and with its head
He went galumphing back.

"And hast thou slain the Jabberwock?
Come to my arms, my beamish boy!
O frabjous day! Callooh! Callay!"
He chortled in his joy.

'Twas brillig, and the slithy toves
Did gyre and gimble in the wabe;
All mimsy were the borogoves,
And the mome raths outgrabe.

26. This poem is an example of what common stanza?

    A. quatrain
    B. sestet
    C. octane
    D. triplet

27. The rhyme scheme of this poem is BEST represented by which of the following patterns?

    A.  aa bb cc dd ee ff gg hh
    B.  aaba bbcb ccdc dded
    C.  abab cdcd efef ghgh
    D.  aaaa bbbb cccc dddd

28. The figurative language device MOST employed in this poem is

    A.  onomatopoeia.
    B.  imagery.
    C.  metaphor.
    D.  personification.

29. Eleven is a factor of which one of the following three-digit numbers?

    A.  680
    B.  892
    C.  736
    D.  583

30. A cartographer is defined as which of the following?

    A.  a person who writes the history of the Earth
    B.  a person who studies the Earth's composition
    C.  a person who designs, describes, and develops maps
    D.  a person who studies the science or practice of map drawing

31. The ratio of girls to boys in sixth grade is 5:4, and there are 64 boys. How many girls are there?

    A.  69
    B.  75
    C.  80
    D.  16

32. Natural selection is BEST described as which of the following?

    A.  the basic principle of biological evolution
    B.  the survival of offspring with recessive traits
    C.  the dying out of mutant genes so the organism cannot reproduce
    D.  the process in which individuals with favorable traits survive and reproduce

33. If a basketball player shoots 77 percent from the free-throw line and during a game she is at the line 16 times, how many shots did she make? (Round to the nearest whole number.)

    A.  12
    B.  4
    C.  13
    D.  20

34. The following is an example of which type of sonnet?

    Weary with toil, I haste me to my bed,
    The dear repose for limbs with travel tired,
    But then begins a journey in my head
    To work my mind when body's work's expired;
    For then my thoughts, from far where I abide,
    Intend a zealous pilgrimage to thee,
    And keep my drooping eyelids open wide,
    Looking on darkness which the blind do see;
    Save that my soul's imaginary sight
    Presents thy shadow to my sightless view,
    Which, like a jewel hung in ghastly night,
    Makes black night beauteous and her old
        face new.
    Lo, thus, by day my limbs, by night my mind,
    For thee and for myself no quiet find.

    A.  German sonnet
    B.  Shakespearean sonnet
    C.  Petrarchan sonnet
    D.  Italian sonnet

35. When defining a region or place in the world, the two types of characteristics used are

    A.  physical and human.
    B.  human and regional.
    C.  physical and regional.
    D.  human and geological.

36. Within a garden ecosystem, if all the earthworms were to be removed, this changes the balance by

    A.  interrupting the food cycle within the ecosystem.
    B.  changing the supply of energy within the ecosystem.
    C.  producing a natural phenomenon within the ecosystem.
    D.  disrupting the organic matter and nutrients recycled within the ecosystem.

37. When tectonic plates collide, the result is the

    A.  formation of new crust.
    B.  formation of mountains.
    C.  occurrence of volcanoes.
    D.  occurrence of earthquakes.

38. A survey is an example of which kind of source?

    A.  written
    B.  secondary
    C.  observational
    D.  primary

39. Haley makes 6 peanut butter and jelly sandwiches more than Gill. Gill makes 2 sandwiches less than Tzvia. If Tzvia makes 15 peanut butter and jelly sandwiches, how many does Haley make?

    A.  13
    B.  19
    C.  21
    D.  23

40. Which of the following BEST defines a biome?

    A.  a large geographical area of distinctive plant life and animal life groups that have adapted to a specific environment
    B.  a large geographical area of nondistinct plant life and animal life groups that have adapted to a specific environment
    C.  a small geographical area of distinctive plant life and animal life groups that have adapted to a specific environment
    D.  a small geographical area of nondistinct plant life and animal life groups that have yet to adapt to a specific environment

41. A student brings in a rock with obvious layers and tells you it is a piece of marble. The type of rock he most likely has is

    A.  striated.
    B.  igneous.
    C.  sedimentary.
    D.  metamorphic.

42. A pattern of organization used in nonfiction is

    A.  story and plot.
    B.  metaphor and simile.
    C.  compare and contrast.
    D.  theme and meaning.

43. Which equation represents the statement, "2 times a number decreased by 6 and then distributed evenly 5 times"?

    A.  $(2A - 6)5$
    B.  $(2A + 6)5$
    C.  $(2A - 6) \div 5$
    D.  $(2A + 6) \div 5$

44. Which physical process includes rock formation, soil formation, plate tectonics, and erosion?

    A.  biosphere
    B.  lithosphere
    C.  atmosphere
    D.  hydrosphere

45. The consumption of natural resources from one area to be used in another area does what to the Earth?

    A.  depletes the ozone
    B.  changes natural patterns
    C.  increases resource demands
    D.  helps produce more resources

46. A kindergarten teacher reads a picture book aloud to her class every day. Before she begins the story each day, she discusses parts of the book (the front cover, the title, the author, the illustrator, and the back cover) with her students. The teacher is demonstrating which foundation of literacy?

    A.  print concepts
    B.  word identification
    C.  alphabetic principle
    D.  comprehension

47. The three most contributing factors of weather are

    A.  solar radiation, wind patterns, and the seasons.
    B.  the water cycle, wind patterns, and the seasons.
    C.  the Earth's movement, the water cycle, and wind patterns.
    D.  solar radiation, the Earth's movement, and the water cycle.

48. Which of the following is an example of the associative property?

   A. $(5 + 3) + 10 = 5 + (3 + 10)$
   B. $(5 - 3) - 10 = 5 - (3 - 10)$
   C. $(5 \cdot 3) + 10 = 5 + (3 \cdot 10)$
   D. $(5 \cdot 3) - 10 = 5 - (3 \cdot 10)$

49. The multiplicative inverse for 0.2 is

   A. $-0.2$
   B. 5
   C. $-5$
   D. $\frac{1}{2}$

50. Which of the following did *early* civilizations contribute?

   A. culture
   B. science
   C. petroglyphs
   D. alphabetic writing

51. The Law of Superposition is best defined as

   A. the scientific laws that govern the Earth today are the same scientific laws that have governed the Earth since the beginning of time.
   B. the law that proposes that the Earth and its life-forms developed slowly over a long period of time.
   C. the oldest rocks and events are found at the bottom of formations while the youngest are found at the top.
   D. the youngest rocks and events are found at the bottom of formations as they overtake any existing oldest rocks or events.

52. A third grade student is reading a story about a sloth. When he reaches an unknown word, *unobtrusive,* he sees that he recognizes the prefix (*un-*) and the root word (*obtrusive*) and is able to decipher the meaning. Which word recognition strategy is he displaying?

   A. context clues
   B. semantic clues
   C. analogy clues
   D. word structure clues

53. A fourth grade child is presented with the following number pattern. Using all previous knowledge and number sense, the student is able to figure out that the next value in the pattern is 13 and is able to write an equation to explain the pattern. What equation does he write?

   1, 3, 5, 7, 9, 11, ___ , 15, 17, 19

   A. $2n + 2$
   B. $2n$
   C. $2n - 1$
   D. $n - 1$

54. The three classical civilizations are

   A. India, Greece and Rome, Japan.
   B. China, Greece and Rome, India.
   C. China, Japan, Greece and Rome.
   D. Britain, Greece and Rome, Russia.

55. The BEST description of the solar system is

   A. the sun and the planets.
   B. the sun, the stars, and the planets.
   C. the sun, the comets, and the planets.
   D. the sun and all bodies that revolve around it.

56. While reading a story about a high school baseball player, a second grade student may use which of the following two context clues to determine the missing words of the following sentence?

   The young baseball player was good at _____ _____.

   A. semantic and symbolic clues
   B. symbolic and syntactic clues
   C. syntactic and semantic clues
   D. sequential and symbolic clues

57. When a fourth grader reads with expression while her reading flows automatically, she is demonstrating

   A. comprehension.
   B. fluency.
   C. word identification.
   D. phonemic awareness.

58. Solve: $(6^2)(6^4)$

    A. 7,776
    B. 46,656
    C. 1,296
    D. 279,936

59. Which of the following BEST describes the Townshend Act of 1767?

    A. the first land tax placed on the Colonies
    B. the tax placed on all media that required stamps
    C. the tax on essential goods like paper, glass, and tea
    D. the tax imposed by the East India Trading Company

60. When the sun lights the back of the moon, we are experiencing a

    A. full moon.
    B. new moon.
    C. solar eclipse.
    D. lunar eclipse.

61. Solve: 4,532 divided by 6

    A. 755
    B. 755.34
    C. $755\frac{1}{3}$
    D. 756

62. When a second grade student sees the word "giraffe" and states "that is the big yellow and black animal with a really long neck in Africa," she is demonstrating which foundation of literacy?

    A. word identification
    B. alphabetic principle
    C. print concept
    D. comprehension

63. The six basic processes of science are

    A. observation, classification, experimentation, prediction, hypothesis, methods.
    B. observation, communication, data, hypothesis, measurement, experimentation.
    C. observation, classification, communication, measurement, prediction, inference.
    D. observation, communication, inference, classification, experimentation, hypothesis.

64. Which of the following was a direct result of the War of 1812?

    A. Slavery was abolished.
    B. The national anthem was written.
    C. Four governments were overthrown.
    D. Boundaries were drawn between the North and South.

65. The Mayflower Compact was signed en route to the New World and established which of the following?

    A. rights of the monarch over the Pilgrims
    B. housing, communities, and schools for the Pilgrims
    C. the separation of the Thirteen Colonies from Great Britain
    D. temporary majority-rule government for the Pilgrims

66. Find the slope of the line segment joining the points (3,5) and (6,4).

    A. $\frac{1}{3}$
    B. $-1$
    C. $-\frac{1}{3}$
    D. 3

67. Words that are high frequency and should be learned to be recognized immediately are called

    A. sight words.
    B. instant words.
    C. dolch words.
    D. fluency words.

68. When a 10-year-old student watches a baby bird struggling to fly from a nest and states "the bird may fall but can begin to flap its wings before it hits the ground," she is using the scientific processes of observation and

    A. inference.
    B. prediction.
    C. measurement.
    D. communication.

69. The Earth and other planets revolve around the sun in a shape that most resembles a(n)

    A. circle.
    B. sphere.
    C. ovoid.
    D. ellipse.

70. The Proclamation of 1763 restricted American movement across the Appalachian Mountains but was ignored, which led to expansion

    A. eastward.
    B. westward.
    C. northward.
    D. southward.

71. A fifth grade student reads a text about Jamestown, Virginia. After reading about the settling of the colony, he remarks how difficult it must have been for the colonists to leave everything that was familiar to them in England and make a long journey to the New World. He concludes that the move must have been particularly difficult for children. He is demonstrating which comprehension strategy?

    A. think and read
    B. inferential reading
    C. metacognition
    D. summarizing

72. Which of the following is a plane figure?

    A. rhombus
    B. pyramid
    C. cylinder
    D. ovoid

73. The reasons that formal governments are established are to

    A. create laws, order, and security.
    B. establish rule, control, and protection.
    C. join together people, cultures, and rights.
    D. protect individual liberties, properties, and lives.

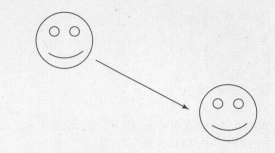

74. The preceding illustration represents what type of transformation?

    A. rotation
    B. translation
    C. reflection
    D. mutation

75. Concept books and pattern books are examples of which type of children's literature?

    A. traditional
    B. fiction
    C. nonfiction
    D. early childhood

76. The water cycle is a natural process in which water

    A. precipitates, dissipates, accumulates.
    B. evaporates, condensates, precipitates.
    C. accumulates, evaporates, precipitates.
    D. condensates, accumulates, dissipates.

77. The best explanation for the function of animals is that they are on the Earth to grow, reproduce, and

    A. die.
    B. adapt.
    C. interact with humans.
    D. interact with the environment.

78. A second grade student is struggling to read the word "complementary." She draws a connection between a word she already knows, "elementary," and is able to determine the pronunciation of the word. She has used which word recognition strategy?

    A. word structure clues
    B. context clues
    C. analogy clues
    D. phonemic clues

79. How many centimeters are in 47 kilometers?

    A.  470
    B.  4,700
    C.  4,700,000
    D.  470,000

80. An oligarchy is a form of government in which

    A.  no one rules.
    B.  a majority rules.
    C.  a minority rules.
    D.  a monarch rules.

Use the graph to answer questions 81 and 82.

### Use of Time on Saturday
Total time: 18 hours

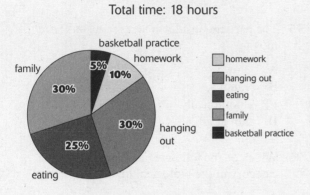

81. How much time was spent completing homework?

    A.  2 hrs
    B.  1.8 hrs
    C.  3 hrs
    D.  1.6 hrs

82. Which of the following is closest to the fraction of the total time spent with family and eating?

    A.  $\frac{2}{5}$
    B.  $\frac{3}{4}$
    C.  $\frac{1}{2}$
    D.  $\frac{1}{3}$

83. The Legislative Branch of the U.S. government is comprised of the

    A.  court systems.
    B.  president and his cabinet.
    C.  primary government contractors.
    D.  Senate and the House of Representatives.

84. The part of a plant that houses the reproductive organs is the

    A.  root.
    B.  fruit.
    C.  leaves.
    D.  flower.

85. Copper is a metal that allows electric current to flow through it, which is an example of a(n)

    A.  circuit.
    B.  conductor.
    C.  insulator.
    D.  accumulator.

86. Which of the following is the correct way to write "volcano" in the plural form?

    A.  volcanos
    B.  volcano's
    C.  volcanos'
    D.  volcanoes

87. What noun type is underlined in this sentence:

    The park is a great <u>place</u> to have a picnic.

    A.  predicate noun
    B.  subject noun
    C.  object noun
    D.  possessive noun

88. Which Amendment abolished slavery?

    A.  9th
    B.  10th
    C.  12th
    D.  13th

89. The Declaration of Independence led to the development of which two important documents?

   A. the Bill of Rights and the Gettysburg Address
   B. the Articles of Confederation and the Constitution
   C. the Constitutional Amendments and the Preamble
   D. the Magna Carta and the Articles of the Union

90. When you slide across a tile floor in your socks and come to a gradual stop, you are experiencing which force?

   A. inertia
   B. friction
   C. centrifugal
   D. momentum

91. The past tense of "lay" is

   A. lay.
   B. lain.
   C. lie.
   D. laid.

Question 92 refers to the following diagram.

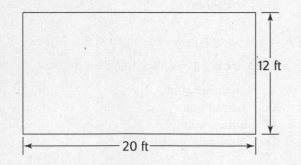

92. Mabel plans to install a wood floor in her living room. If each square foot of wood costs $12.25, how much will Mabel spend on her new wooden floor?

   A. $294
   B. $240
   C. $2,880
   D. $2,940

93. Which of the following figures is the greatest in value?

   A. 30% of 80
   B. 13% of 120
   C. 10% of 100
   D. 5% of 600

94. When comparing two tribes of Native Americans, if the class studies how food is obtained, they are using what type of anthropology?

   A. cultural
   B. physical
   C. economic
   D. behavioral

95. The particles inside an ice cream shake are moving

   A. slowly.
   B. rapidly.
   C. sporadically.
   D. not at all.

96. Which of the following is the most specific category in the biological taxonomy?

   A. class
   B. species
   C. kingdom
   D. phylum

97. What is the mean of 68, 45, 32, 90, 15?

   A. 40
   B. 45
   C. 50
   D. 55

98. Which of the following sentences is an example of a verbal gerund?

   A. She was hitting the boy.
   B. I am hitting the wall.
   C. Hitting is not an acceptable behavior.
   D. He was grounded because he was hitting others.

**99.** In the sentence, "That boy is smart when he wants to be," the word "that" is categorized as what type of adjective?

   **A.** demonstrative adjective
   **B.** compound adjective
   **C.** indefinite adjective
   **D.** predicate adjective

**100.** What is the volume of a square pyramid that has a base of 12.5 square inches and a height of 16 inches?

   **A.** $66\frac{2}{3}$ in$^3$
   **B.** $9\frac{1}{2}$ in$^3$
   **C.** 64 in$^3$
   **D.** 200 in$^3$

**101.** A society that has a strict free market with no government involvement can be said to have which economy?

   **A.** socialist
   **B.** anarchist
   **C.** capitalist
   **D.** laissez-faire

**102.** The three components of citizenship education are

   **A.** content, values, processes.
   **B.** rights, concern, community.
   **C.** democracy, equality, patriotism.
   **D.** responsibilities, relationships, justice.

**103.** Which of the diagrams best depicts the structure of a lunar eclipse?

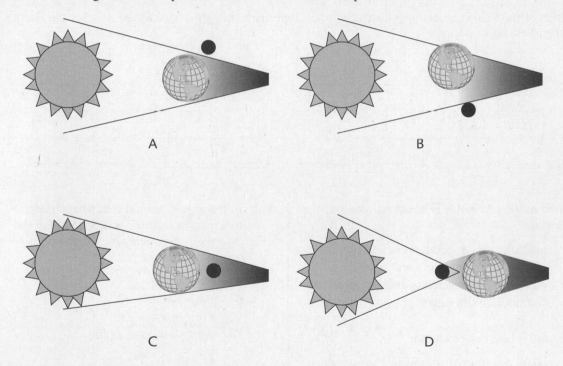

A     B

C     D

**104.** In the following sentence, what part of speech is the word "often?"

He often practices the electric guitar.

   **A.** noun
   **B.** adjective
   **C.** preposition
   **D.** adverb

105. Which of the following is a complementary angle for an angle measuring 40°?

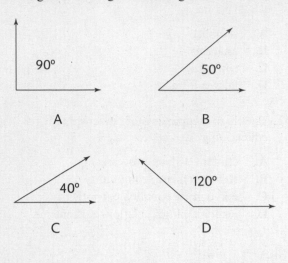

106. Justin puts his CDs on shuffle mode. The CD player holds 16 CDs at one time and shuffles the discs at random. He puts 4 country, 6 punk, 2 folk, and 4 rock CDs into the machine. What is the probability that a punk CD will play?

   A.  $\dfrac{3}{8}$

   B.  $\dfrac{5}{8}$

   C.  1 in 6

   D.  60%

107. Advances in technology have helped economies by

   A.  increasing the sales of computers.
   B.  bringing manufacturing costs down.
   C.  balancing social and economic gains.
   D.  creating a broader, more accessible market.

108. Which of the following tectonic illustrations best represents the formation of new rock for the Earth's surface?

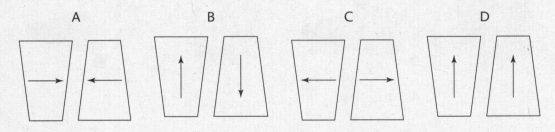

109. A free-market economy is based on which of the following?

   A.  identification of production and services
   B.  reference to population and resources
   C.  outline about businesses and development
   D.  competition through supply and demand

110. An atoll is best described as a

   A.  chain or group of islands in a sea or ocean.
   B.  body of land that is surrounded by water on three sides.
   C.  ring or partial ring of coral that forms an island in a sea or ocean.
   D.  narrow pointed piece of land that juts out from a coastline into a body of water.

111. In the typical animal cell, what structure functions as a canal or tube found in the cytoplasm, through which material is transported to the nucleus?

   A.  ribosomes
   B.  mitochondria
   C.  Golgi apparatus
   D.  endoplasmic reticulum

112. Which of the following is the world's coldest and driest biome?

   A.  taiga
   B.  alpine
   C.  tundra
   D.  chaparral

113. Which of the following structures are found in a typical plant cell, but not in a typical animal cell?

    A.  ribosomes, vacuoles
    B.  plastids, chloroplasts
    C.  mitochondria, nucleus
    D.  reticulum, Golgi apparatus

114. What is the complete predicate in the following sentence?

    The caged, restless, Siberian tiger roars loudly at the crowd of people.

    A.  Siberian tiger roars
    B.  roars loudly
    C.  roars loudly at the crowd of people
    D.  The caged, restless, Siberian tiger roars

115. Which of the following illustrations demonstrates a first-class lever?

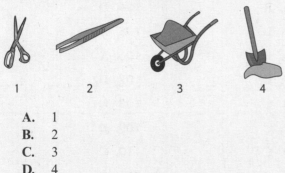

    1          2          3          4

    A.  1
    B.  2
    C.  3
    D.  4

116. Which of the following is the correct progression through the eight stages of writing?

    A.  pictures, letter-like symbols, string of letters, beginning sound emergence, initial-middle-final sounds, transitional phases, and standard spelling
    B.  beginning sound emergence, scribbling, letter-like symbols, string of letters, inventive spelling, initial-middle-final sounds, transitional phases, and standard spelling
    C.  scribbling, letter-like symbols, string of letters, beginning sound emergence, consonants represent words, initial-middle-final sounds, transitional phases, and standard spelling
    D.  letter-like symbols, scribbling, string of letters, beginning sound emergence, vowels represent words, initial-middle-final sounds, transitional phases, and standard spelling

117. Accurate listening comprehension is dependent upon which of the following three components?

    A.  hearing, understanding, and judging
    B.  visual contact, understanding, and a lack of distractions
    C.  hearing, speaker, and occasion
    D.  attention span, posture, and understanding

118. How many different groups of three t-shirts can be chosen from a selection of ten shirts?

    A.  3,600
    B.  120
    C.  1,200
    D.  30

119. Tony is a marathon runner. He wants to maintain an average time of 4 hrs. 20 min. In his last five marathons he has gotten times of 4 hrs. 45 min., 4 hrs. 55 min., 5 hrs. 5 min., 4 hrs., and 4 hrs. 15 min. What time does he need to get in his last race to finish with a 4 hrs. 20 min. average?

    A.  4 hrs. 20 min.
    B.  4 hrs.
    C.  3 hrs. 10 min.
    D.  3 hrs.

120. Transitional spelling is when

    A.  symbols are used to represent the alphabet, and letters and sounds do not correspond.
    B.  letters and sounds begin to correspond, and single letters are used to represent words, sounds, or syllables.
    C.  every sound heard is represented by a letter or group of letters.
    D.  conventions and rules of spelling are learned and all letters are present in a word, although the letters may not be in the correct order.

# Answer Key

| | | | |
|---|---|---|---|
| 1. C | 31. C | 61. C | 91. D |
| 2. A | 32. D | 62. D | 92. D |
| 3. B | 33. A | 63. C | 93. D |
| 4. C | 34. B | 64. B | 94. A |
| 5. D | 35. A | 65. D | 95. A |
| 6. C | 36. D | 66. C | 96. B |
| 7. C | 37. B | 67. A | 97. C |
| 8. B | 38. D | 68. B | 98. C |
| 9. D | 39. B | 69. D | 99. A |
| 10. C | 40. A | 70. B | 100. A |
| 11. C | 41. D | 71. B | 101. D |
| 12. C | 42. C | 72. A | 102. A |
| 13. A | 43. C | 73. D | 103. C |
| 14. A | 44. B | 74. B | 104. D |
| 15. B | 45. B | 75. D | 105. B |
| 16. B | 46. A | 76. B | 106. A |
| 17. D | 47. D | 77. D | 107. D |
| 18. D | 48. A | 78. C | 108. C |
| 19. B | 49. B | 79. C | 109. D |
| 20. B | 50. D | 80. C | 110. C |
| 21. B | 51. C | 81. B | 111. D |
| 22. A | 52. D | 82. C | 112. C |
| 23. A | 53. C | 83. D | 113. B |
| 24. A | 54. B | 84. D | 114. C |
| 25. D | 55. D | 85. B | 115. A |
| 26. A | 56. C | 86. D | 116. C |
| 27. C | 57. B | 87. A | 117. A |
| 28. B | 58. B | 88. D | 118. B |
| 29. D | 59. C | 89. B | 119. D |
| 30. D | 60. B | 90. B | 120. D |

# Answer Explanations

1. **C.** The first civilizations were developed alongside rivers for agricultural production and called river-valleys.

2. **A.** Based on number sense, the value of $x$ is 100 since the number line is divided into segments of 50.

3. **B.** For a solid to become a liquid it must incur a decrease in pressure to allow the molecules more free movement, along with an increase in energy as the molecules begin to move more quickly.

4. **C.** When a reader uses text knowledge to reflect on personal knowledge and then draw connections between text and personal experience, the reader is in the reflection-response stage. This first-grader is relating his personal experience and knowledge of his feelings when he was lost to those of the lost puppy in the story. In the initial stage, the reader has first contact with the tone, characters, and content. The developing stage is the extending stage in which the reader takes in the information and begins to ask questions about the text. During critical analysis, the reader reflects and reacts to the content by judging, evaluating, and examining the text.

5. **D.** The outer core is a thick viscous liquid that is rich in iron and produces the Earth's magnetic field.

6. **C.** Guns and the use of gunpowder began in the ninth century with Chinese alchemists who were searching for an elixir of immortality and happened upon the combination of the explosive mixture of sulfur, charcoal, and potassium nitrate. The radio, the airplane, and electric refrigeration were not developed until the twentieth century.

7. **C.** Regrouping is used in operations of both addition and subtraction.

8. **B.** When written from the limited omniscient point of view a narrator knows everything about only one character (major or minor). The reader must draw conclusions about other characters through this one point of view and setting and dialogue to get the complete picture and meaning of the story. With the objective point of view the narrator is a detached observer and tells only the dialogue and actions so that the reader must infer all inner thoughts and feelings. With the omniscient point of view the narrator knows all feelings and inner thoughts of all characters. With the first person point of view the narrator is directly involved in the story and may or may not be a reliable source for the reader.

9. **D.** The exposition occurs at the beginning of a story when the characters, setting, tone, and initial understanding of the story are presented to the reader. The plot explains the events of a story; the inciting force identifies the events that lead to the central conflict; and the conclusion ends the story by wrapping up all actions.

10. **C.** Classical civilizations developed many structures and institutions that are still present today. The three recognized classical civilizations contributed the following: expansion of trade, new and various religions, increased agricultural options, extended territories, and social cohesion (integrating people and societies).

11. **C.** Long multiplication, sometimes called elementary multiplication, is when the multiplication problem is broken down into its components (multiplicand and multiplier) and then added together to reach the product. Long multiplication is the algorithm used in multiplication.

12. **C.** The ball has potential energy because it possesses the ability to have energy even though it is at rest.

13. **A.** The Incas are considered a non-European civilization and are credited with contributing artistic pottery and clothing, metallurgy, architecture, irrigation, road systems, supreme military organization, and agriculture to present-day societies.

14. **A.** The Law of Simple Machines states that whatever force is exerted times the distance moved is equal to the output force of the machine times the distance the output force moves.

15. **B.** Nonfiction is writing in which information, factual or truthful, is presented as fact or truth. A user manual factually explains how to operate something. Poetry is a creative form of writing that is organized into stanzas and uses poetic devices. Fiction is an untrue story that contains certain elements. Research is not a type of literature but is a tool used to evaluate something.

16. **B.** This is a geometrical sequence in which the value is multiplied by three each time. $5 \times 3$, $15 \times 3$, $45 \times 3$, and so on. The missing value is the product of $45 \times 3$, which is 135.

17. **D.** Flat maps distort size, distance, direction, and the shape of the objects on the Earth.

18. **D.** Place value works on a base-10 system. Using manipulatives or diagrams to demonstrate this aids in student comprehension. The square is equal to 100, the bar is 10, and the single squares are equal to one. Therefore, the number represented is 148.

19. **B.** Because the vowel sound "ai" is repeated throughout the line, the correct answer is assonance. Assonance is the repetition of a vowel sound. Alliteration is the repetition of a beginning consonant sound. Consonance is the repetition of consonant sounds anywhere within the words. Repetition is the stating of a word or phrase more than once.

20. **B.** Diffusion is the movement of particles from a high concentration (the drop of food coloring) to an area of low concentration (plain water) until all areas are in a state of equilibrium (the same color).

21. **B.** Physical maps reveal the features of actual geographical surfaces, such as mountains or rivers, and the underlying geological structures, such as rocks or fault lines.

22. **A.** Pitch is how high or low a sound is made, amplitude is the volume of the sound, and quality shows the source of the sound.

23. **A.** The equivalence to $\frac{1}{4}$ is $\frac{2}{8}$, $\frac{3}{12}$, $\frac{4}{16}$, $\frac{5}{20}$, $\frac{6}{24}$, and so on. An equivalence is when numbers are equal in value. $\frac{6}{24}$ can be reduced to $\frac{1}{4}$ by dividing both the numerator and denominator by 6.

24. **A.** Asia is the largest continent in geographical terms. The following are the continents by size: Asia, Africa, North America, South America, Antarctica, Europe, and Australia.

25. **D.** Mutant genes most commonly result in unfertilized eggs because DNA strands cannot be fully developed.

26. **A.** Stanzas are the divisions of poems into lines and sections. A quatrain breaks lines into groups of four. This poem has seven quatrains. A sestet has six lines, an octave or octet has eight lines, and a triplet has three lines.

27. **C.** The poem has end rhyme, which follows the rhyme pattern of lines 1 and 3 (denoted by the letter "a"), 2 and 4 (denoted by the letter "b"), 5 and 7 (denoted by the letter "c"), 6 and 8 (denoted by the letter "d"), and so on. The rhyme scheme is therefore written abab cdcd and so on.

28. **B.** Imagery is language that appeals to the five senses and to the imagination of the reader. The most prolific types of imagery found in the poem "Jabberwocky" are visual and auditory. Even though most of the words are made up by Carroll, they provoke visual images in the reader's mind ("All mimsy were the borogoves" and "The Jabberwock, with eyes of flame"). Carroll also uses auditory imagery in the lines "Came wiffling through the tulgey wood/And burbled as it came!" as well as "The vorpal blade went snicker-snack!" Personification is attributing human qualities to objects, animals, or places; onomatopoeia is when a word sound relates to its meaning; metaphor is a comparison of two unrelated objects without using the words "like "or "as."

29. **D.** 11 is a factor of a three-digit number if the sum of the first and third digits is equal to the middle digit. In 583, $5 + 3 = 8$, so 11 is a factor.

30. **D.** A cartographer is someone who studies the science or practice of map drawing.

31. **C.** It is helpful to set up a proportion to solve this problem: $5:4 = x:64$ (let $x$ represent the unknown value of girls). Write the proportion in fraction form and solve using cross-multiplication.

$$\frac{5}{4} = \frac{x}{64}$$
$$320 = 4x$$
$$80 = x$$

**32. D.** Natural selection states that individuals become better adapted to survive environments through favorable adaptation and traits; those without such traits perish and do not reproduce.

**33. A.** Set up a proportion using percentages.

$$\frac{77}{100} = \frac{x}{16}$$
$$1232 = 100x$$
$$12.32 = x$$

Round your answer to 12; since 3 is not large enough to round up, you round the value down.

**34. B.** A sonnet is a 14-lined poem that states the poet's feelings. This sonnet is a Shakespearean sonnet (English), because it has three quatrains and ends in a rhymed couplet. It has a rhyme scheme of abab cdcd efef gg. A Petrarchan sonnet, also called an Italian sonnet, has an octave and a sestet with a rhyme scheme of abbaabba and cdecde, cdccdc, or cdedce.

**35. A.** Physical characteristics include water systems, plant/animal life, landforms, and climate. Human characteristics include values, religions, languages, and political and economic factors. Human and physical characteristics act together to define a region or place.

**36. D.** Earthworms, although part of the food chain, play a vital role in the breakdown of organic matter within an ecosystem. Removal of those creatures would cause nutrients to build up and disrupt the balance.

**37. B.** When plates collide, they force the crust upward, forming mountains.

**38. D.** A survey is a questionnaire used to help gather opinions and preferences based on firsthand knowledge. A primary source is when resources/research are gathered from an original source in order to give the reader direct, firsthand knowledge.

**39. B.** Using representational terms, you can organize your data to solve the problem. Let H = Haley, G = Gill, and T = Tzvia.

H = G + 6; G = T – 2; T = 15

Now substitute Tzvia into Gill's equation to solve for Gill: 15 – 2 = 13 (Gill makes 13 sandwiches). Lastly, substitute Gill into Haley's equation and solve for Haley: 13 + 6 = 19. Haley makes 19 sandwiches.

**40. A.** A biome is defined as a large geographical area of distinctive plant life and animal life groups that have adapted to a specific environment. A biome includes two entities (animal and plant) living together and modifying themselves to live in a certain environment. Biomes are determined by climate and geography.

**41. D.** Metamorphic rock forms through the heat and pressure of igneous and sedimentary rocks, resulting in layers. Marble is a type of metamorphic rock.

**42. C.** Literature is structured and organized in patterns so that authors can convey their message to the reader. Nonfiction is structured differently from poetry or fiction. Nonfiction follows a formula of description and details, main idea and supporting details (introduction of the subject and the support to prove it), compare and contrast, chronological order (time pattern), cause and effect (situations/events and the reasons they occur), and process (how an event happens).

**43. C.** The key terms to focus on are times (multiply), decreased by (subtract), and distributed evenly (divide). Therefore, (2A – 6) ÷ 5 is the correct answer.

**44. B.** The lithosphere is the ground and surface, atmosphere is air, hydrosphere is water, and biosphere is life. Therefore, rock formation, soil formation, plate tectonics, and erosion, which are part of the Earth's surface, are included in the lithosphere.

**45. B.** Natural physical patterns are changed when natural resources are consumed. Meeting resource demands across the world places great stress on the planet's physical systems, forcing changes in natural patterns.

46. **A.** When the teacher goes over the structure of a book and repeats the same vocabulary each time ("a book by," "illustrated by") she is demonstrating that letters have sounds and they form words, which is the foundation of print concepts. Word identification decodes words by sound; alphabetic principle shows letters represent speech; and comprehension is the processing of the content read.

47. **D.** Solar radiation causes heat, Earth movement causes seasons/wind, and the water cycle determines precipitation, thus resulting in weather conditions.

48. **A.** The associative property states that numbers can be grouped or regrouped without changing the outcome. "A" is the only equation that remains true as the numbers are regrouped:

$$8 + 10 = 5 + 13$$
$$18 = 18$$

49. **B.** The multiplicative inverse for a number is the reciprocal. When 0.2 is converted to a fraction, it is equivalent to $\frac{1}{5}$. In order to find the multiplicative inverse of a fraction, invert the fraction. In this case, this procedure would yield $5 \left( \frac{1}{5} = \frac{5}{1} \right)$. –0.2 is the additive inverse, –5 yields a –1, and $\frac{1}{2}$ produces a 0.1.

50. **D.** Early civilizations developed the following: basic achievements (wheel, math, time measurement), art and architecture, alphabetic writing, defined religion, commonality, and diversity.

51. **C.** The Law of Superposition is a geologic law that states the past will hold the position at the bottom, and the present will hold the position on the top.

52. **D.** When recognizing frequent letter groupings, prefixes, suffixes, and inflectional endings, a reader is using word structure clues to deconstruct the unknown word and construct a meaning from the parts known. The student has broken the word into parts he recognizes and knows and then reconstructed the unknown word to obtain its meaning. Context clues means to use words, meaning, and content to extract the meaning of the unknown; semantic clues are a type of context clue in which the reader uses the meaning of the text to decipher unknown meanings; and analogy clues are used to draw connections between known words and unknown words.

53. **C.** The student recognized the repeating pattern as an increasing odd repetition. The equation he wrote explains the pattern by taking any numeral and multiplying it by 2 and then subtracting 1 to obtain the odd number. For example: $(1 \cdot 2) - 1 = 1$, the first number in the sequence. To obtain the seventh number in the sequence: $(7 \cdot 2) - 1 = 13$.

54. **B.** The civilization of China (1029 B.C.E.), the civilization of Greece and Rome (800 B.C.E.), and the civilization of India (600 B.C.E.) are the three recognized classical civilizations.

55. **D.** The solar system encompasses all the bodies that revolve around the sun (planets, stars, comets, meteorites, and so on) and also the sun itself.

56. **C.** The reader uses the meaning of the text and the word order of the sentence to determine the appropriate words for the blank. Semantic clues are based on the content read and help the reader determine reasonable vocabulary associated with the content. Syntactic clues are based on the order and structure of the words in the sentence and help the reader determine meaning based on grammatical rules.

57. **B.** A reader is fluent when she reads with expression and automatically without unwarranted pauses or mistakes. Comprehension is the reader's use of critical thinking to process the information read. Word identification is a reader's use of word recognition strategies to pronounce or to determine word meaning. Phonemic awareness occurs when a reader is able to break words into individual sounds (phonemes).

58. **B.** The law of exponents (rule of exponents) explains that you need to combine the like terms and add their exponents by using this formula: $x^m x^n = x^{m+n}$:

$$6^{2+4}$$

$$6^6$$

$$6 \cdot 6 \cdot 6 \cdot 6 \cdot 6 \cdot 6, \text{which equals } 46,656.$$

59. **C.** The Townshend Act of 1767 was a tax on essential goods like paper, glass, and tea. These taxes were placed on the American colonies by the British in order to exercise control and authority over them.

60. **B.** A new moon is the phase of the moon that occurs as it passes between the Earth and the sun. It occurs when the sun is behind the moon, thus lighting the back of the moon. This causes the moon to appear to be invisible (as if there were no moon at all) or a thin, narrow sliver (crescent).

61. **C.** Using long division, the answer gained is 755.33 (with a repeating decimal) or 755 R2 (which is $755\frac{1}{3}$). The repeating decimal of 0.33 is equivalent to $\frac{1}{3}$. The problem does not ask you to round your answer.

$$
\begin{array}{r}
755.333 \\
6\overline{)4532.000} \\
\underline{42}\phantom{00.000} \\
33\phantom{0.000} \\
\underline{-30}\phantom{0.000} \\
32\phantom{.000} \\
\underline{-30}\phantom{.000} \\
20\phantom{000} \\
\underline{-18}\phantom{000} \\
20\phantom{00} \\
\underline{-18}\phantom{00}
\end{array}
$$

62. **D.** The student is processing the meaning of a word she has seen by using prior knowledge to describe the animal that the word refers to. Comprehension occurs when the readers use critical thinking and are able to process the information and words they have read. Print concept occurs when the reader understands that letters have sounds and they form words. Alphabetic principle shows letters that represent speech, and word identification is when a reader uses word recognition strategies to pronounce or to determine word meaning.

63. **C.** Observation uses the five senses to take in the surrounding world; classification uses commonalities of objects for grouping; communication allows someone to share findings and results; measurement promotes the ability to use appropriate tools; prediction taps into prior knowledge and experience to foresee what may occur; inference utilizes prior knowledge and experience to explain why something occurs.

64. **B.** The War of 1812 increased national patriotism, united the states into one nation, built confidence in the military strength, and brought forth "The Star-Spangled Banner," which later became the national anthem of the United States.

65. **D.** In 1620, the Mayflower Compact was signed to set up a temporary government for the Pilgrims, which operated on the majority-rule basis and was the beginning of our democratic republic.

66. **C.** Use the slope formula:

$$m = \frac{y_2 - y_1}{x_2 - x_1}$$

$$m = \frac{4 - 5}{6 - 3}$$

$$m = \frac{-1}{3}$$

67. **A.** Sight words are words that should be known to the reader as soon as they are seen. These words are seen so frequently that they make up 50 percent of what is read by both adults and children (for example, *said, the, read, these, what, when, she, have*).

68. **B.** The student is watching (observation) the bird and making an educated guess based on prior knowledge as to what may occur next (prediction).

69. **D.** The nine planets revolve around the sun in an elliptical pattern.

70. **B.** The proclamation of 1763 was ignored by colonists who then traveled westward across North America, leading to the expansion of the United States and further migration of the colonists across the West.

71. **B.** The student is drawing conclusions and making inferences based on his prior knowledge and the details of the story. In inferential reading, the reader makes conclusions based on the provided information and his prior knowledge. Think and read is done prior to reading, when the reader asks himself what he knows about the subject already. In metacognition, the reader thinks about thinking, monitors his own understanding, and identifies difficulties he is having. In summarizing, the reader identifies the main ideas and recalls the main points of what he has read.

72. **A.** A rhombus is a two-dimensional figure containing four edges, four vertices, and four angles. The pyramid, cylinder, and ovoid are all solid (three-dimensional) figures containing edges, faces, and vertices.

73. **D.** Formal governments have been around for more than 5,000 years and have maintained the same functions throughout time. Governments were established to protect individual liberties, properties, and lives. Governments do so by creating laws, establishing rule, maintaining control, and providing security for people of diverse cultures.

74. **B.** A translation is when the shape or object moves by sliding to another area in the plane. Reflection is a mirror image, and rotation is when the shape turns on a 360° axis.

75. **D.** The early childhood category encompasses picture books, concept books, pattern books, and wordless books. There are six basic categories in children's literature. The traditional category includes myths, fables, tales, folk songs, and legends. Fiction includes fantasy, historical, and contemporary. Nonfiction encompasses reference books, encyclopedias, almanacs, and historical books.

76. **B.** The water cycle involves the stages of evaporation (liquid turning into a gas), condensation (gas turning into a liquid), and precipitation (the falling of the liquid or solid) of water.

77. **D.** In order to survive as a species, animals must grow, reproduce, and interact with their environment. Maintaining survival is essential to Earth's biomes, ecosystems, and food chains.

78. **C.** The student is able to recognize patterns in the unknown word that she has seen before in other words. She compares the unknown word to the word she knows in order to determine sounds, which is the foundation of *analogy clues*.

79. **C.** There are 100 centimeters in a meter and 1,000 meters in a kilometer. To solve, multiply 100 times 1,000 times 47. This results in the correct answer of 4,700,000 centimeters.

80. **C.** An oligarchy is the type of rule in which the minority rules, such as in Sparta, Greece, and some African tribes.

81. **B.** Homework was done 10% of the time. The total time was 18 hours. Multiply 18 by 10% to obtain the answer. $18 \cdot 0.1 = 1.8$ hours.

82. **C.** The total time spent with family and eating is 55%. The closest fraction is $\frac{1}{2}$, which is equal to 50%. $\frac{2}{5}$ is equal to 40%; $\frac{3}{4}$ is equal to 75%; and $\frac{1}{3}$ is 33%—none of which come close to 55%.

83. **D.** The Legislative Branch contains Congress and other government support agencies. Congress incorporates both the Senate and the House of Representatives. Congress has the power to create laws (legislation), which is the main function of the Legislative Branch.

84. **D.** The flower is the sexual reproduction site of the plant, as it contains the stamen, the pistil, the stigma, and the ovaries.

85. **B.** Conductors are materials that permit electrical current to run through them. Gold, copper, aluminum, and silver are examples of conductors.

86. **D.** If a word ends in "o" with a consonant right before it, you must add "es" to make it plural. Apostrophe "s" ('s) is used to indicate singular possession, and the "s" apostrophe (s') is used to indicate plural possession.

87. **A.** A predicate noun repeats or renames the subject. Since the word "place" renames the word "park," it is classified as a predicate noun. A subject noun is defined as a noun that is being talked about within a sentence; a possessive noun shows ownership; and an object noun is a noun used as a direct object, indirect object, or object of the preposition.

88. **D.** The 13th Amendment to the U.S. Constitution was passed in 1865, under the presidency of Abraham Lincoln, and abolished slavery in this country.

89. **B.** After the Revolutionary War, the 13 Colonies wrote the Articles of Confederation to establish a federalist government. The Founding Fathers realized that the Articles gave all the power to the states and therefore created no cohesion or ability to control the nation as a whole, leaving it weak. The Constitution of the United States was written in order to create a stronger unified government.

90. **B.** Friction is the force between two objects that come into contact with one another. When someone slides on a tile floor wearing socks, the reason the person comes to a gradual stop is due to the interaction between the tile and the fabric of the socks and the opposing force.

91. **D.** "Lay" is an irregular verb, which does not follow a distinct pattern. "Laid" is both the past and future tense of "lay." "Lain" in the future tense of "lie," and "lay" is the past tense of "lie."

92. **D.** Use the area formula to determine how many square feet of wood Mabel will need to purchase.

$$A_{rect} = lw$$
$$A_{rect} = 20ft \cdot 12ft$$
$$A_{rect} = 240ft^2$$

After the total area is found, multiply the cost per square foot by the total area.

Total cost = $240 \cdot 12.25$

Total cost = $2,940

93. **D.** Divide each percent by 100 to obtain the decimal form and then multiply with the value "out of."

$$0.3 \cdot 80 = 24$$
$$0.13 \cdot 120 = 15.6$$
$$0.1 \cdot 100 = 10$$
$$0.05 \cdot 600 = 30$$

94. **A.** Cultural anthropology is the study and comparison of ancient and modern cultures. It includes the study of groups of people that includes food getting, economic systems, social stratification, patterns of residence, political organization, religion, and arts.

95. **A.** The cooler a substance, the slower the particles move. When a substance is warm or hot, the particles move more rapidly.

96. **B.** Species is the last biological classification and the most specific in the order. The following is the order of the system from general to specific: kingdom, phylum, class, order, family, genius, species.

97. **C.** The mean of a set of numbers is the average. To find the mean, add up all values and divide by the number of values in the set.

$$68 + 45 + 32 + 90 + 15 = 250$$
$$250 \div 5 = 50$$

98. **C.** A gerund is a verb that ends in "ing" and is used as the subject of a sentence. In the sentence *Hitting is not an acceptable behavior,* the word "hitting" is the noun and also the subject and not treated as a verb.

99. **A.** A demonstrative adjective singles out a specific noun ("that boy"). A compound adjective is made up of two or more words and is hyphenated; an indefinite adjective gives approximate information (some, few); and a predicate adjective follows a linking verb and describes the subject.

**100. A.** Use the pyramid volume formula, $\frac{1}{3} \cdot B \cdot h$, where $B$ = area of the base and $h$ = height.

$$V = \frac{1}{3} \cdot 12.5 \text{ in}^2 \cdot 16 \text{ in}$$

$$V = \frac{1}{3} \cdot 200 \text{ in}^3$$

$$V = 66\frac{2}{3} \text{ in}^3$$

**101. D.** Laissez-faire is an economy in which the government does not interfere or become involved, and it operates solely as a free-market system.

**102. A.** Citizenship is the way we act and live out our lives within society. Citizenship includes how individuals make decisions and demonstrate concern for the community and nation. Three components important to citizenship education are content (knowledge), values (standards of behavior), and processes (practicing).

**103. C.** A lunar eclipse is when the moon passes through the Earth's shadow (sun-Earth-moon).

**104. D.** Adverbs are used in a variety of ways: time adverbs, place adverbs, manner adverbs, and degree adverbs. In the sentence, the word "often" is used to tell how frequently something occurs, which makes it a time adverb.

**105. B.** The figure shows an angle measuring 50°. Complementary angles, when measured, have the sum of their degrees equal to 90°. 50° + 40° = 90°.

**106. A.** The favorable outcome is a punk CD, of which there are 6 and the total number of possibilities is 16 CDs. The probability formula is $P_{event} = \dfrac{number\ of\ favorable\ outcomes}{number\ of\ possible\ outcomes}$.

Therefore, $P_{punk} = \dfrac{6}{16}$ and when reduced, $\dfrac{3}{8}$ or 3 in 8 or 37.5%.

**107. D.** Technology such as the telephone and computers (Internet) has allowed markets to expand and reach a larger audience. This improvement in communication has enabled products and services to be more widely distributed.

**108. C.** This illustration shows the separation of the tectonic plates and the cooling of rising magma, which creates new rock or new crust.

**109. D.** A free-market economy, like that used in the United States, is based on the two premises of competition: supply and demand. This allows businesses and consumers to decide what should be produced, what employees should be paid, how much products or services should cost, and how much should be provided for the population.

**110. C.** An atoll is a ring of coral that forms an island. An archipelago is a chain of islands. A cape is a narrow piece of land jutting out from a coastline. A peninsula is a body of land surrounded by water on three sides.

**111. D.** The endoplasmic reticulum (ER) connects the cell membrane to the nucleus and is the transport tube for the materials to the nucleus.

**112. C.** The tundra has cold, dark winters with soggy, warm summers. It is a vast and treeless area covering the northern part of the world from latitude 55° to 70°. The ground is permanently frozen and trees cannot grow there. Precipitation in this biome is roughly 6–10 inches per year, which mainly falls as snow.

**113. B.** Only plants have plastids (tiny colored structures that give the plant color and are used for storage) and chloroplasts (plastids that contain chlorophyll).

**114. C.** A predicate is the part of the sentence that tells what the subject is doing or what the subject is. It adds the action to the sentence. The complete predicate includes the verb and all the modifiers. Therefore, the predicate is *roars loudly at the crowd of people*.

**115. A.** A first-class lever has the fulcrum (pivot) between the effort and the load, best illustrated by scissors.

116. **C.** Writers progress through specific phases. While children frequently draw pictures, this is not part of the writing process. The first stage is scribbling, in which the random marks placed throughout the page hold meaning for the child. Writers then progress to letter-like symbols. The next phase is strings of letters, then beginning sound emergence. The use of vowels to represent words is not a specific stage through which writers progress. Inventive spelling is a part of the initial, middle, and final sounds stages and not a stage itself. After beginning sound emergence, writers progress through the stage in which consonants represent words. The final three stages through which writers progress are initial-middle-final sounds, transitional phases, and standard spelling.

117. **A.** Because listening is a dynamic procedure, the most vital components are hearing so that the listener can retain what was heard, understanding so that the listener can ask significant questions and form suitable responses, and judging so that the listener can create opinions and scrutinize the information stated.

118. **B.** Use the formula for finding combinations since the problem does not require the objects be in a specific order.

$$_nC_r = \frac{n!}{(n-r)!\,r!}$$

Solve using $n = 10$ and $r = 3$.

$$_nC_r = \frac{10!}{(7)!\,3!}$$
$$_nC_r = \frac{3628800}{(5040)(6)}$$
$$_nC_r = \frac{3628800}{30240}$$
$$_nC_r = 120$$

119. **D.** Let $x$ represent the unknown value needed. It is easier to change the values into minutes in order to solve the problem. Set up an equation, using minutes:

$$\frac{x + 285 + 295 + 305 + 240 + 255}{6} = 260$$
$$\frac{x + 1380}{6} = 260$$
$$x + 1380 = 1560$$
$$x = 180 \ \text{min.}$$
$$x = 180 \ \text{min.} \div 60 \ \text{min.} = 3\,\text{hrs.}$$

120. **D.** Transitional spelling is the final stage of spelling before accurate spelling occurs. At this stage spellers begin to use rules of spelling to construct words. It is at this time that vowels appear in each syllable.

# Final Thoughts and Tips

Exam day approaches, so taking the preparatory steps regarding registration and completing quality study periods will ensure satisfactory success on these elementary education exams.

This section provides important information about preparing for these exams. All test-takers should review and address these issues prior to taking any of the Praxis II exams.

## Registration

Some examinees are required to complete more than one Praxis II exam for teaching elementary students. This obligation depends on the specific state's Department of Education requirements for teacher certification or licensure. Examinees should be sure to determine which exams are needed in the state where they plan to teach. If an exam regarding elementary education students is compulsory but not found in this study guide, check *CliffsTestPrep Praxis II Fundamental Subjects: Content Knowledge (0511),* also published by John Wiley & Sons, Inc., which has a series of other educational study guides for the Praxis II exams that might be helpful.

If more than one exam is a requisite, it is recommended that the examinee take only one exam per day to optimize specific study periods and to achieve success on each exam. The elementary exams can be complicated and fast-paced. Examinees should consider individual learning styles and study habits so goals set for adequate performance may be reached.

Review the following registration guidelines:

- Check exam dates and locations online at www.ets.org.
- Speak with a college or university financial aid officer to determine whether the fee(s) for the exam(s) may be waived.
- Check the online application process prior to completing registration if you think you might qualify for accommodations due to a disability.
- Register at least one month ahead of the exam date to secure a seat and location. (Many examinees find online registration to be the easiest, fastest, and cheapest.)
- Bring proof of registration to the testing center on the day of the exam.

## Study Tips

Because individuals learn in different ways, examinees will likely implement self-imposed personal methods for exam study. Studying early and preparing for each exam over the long term (1 to 3 months) is recommended, as there is a tremendous amount of information covered in the exams.

Practice tests are available in this guide to help examinees understand the types of questions and to learn how to pace themselves in developing answers in preparation for taking the actual exams.

Following are some recommended study tips:

- Review the Table of Contents to determine the topics that are covered on each of the exams.
- Assess individual strengths and needs regarding the exam content.
- Read the information about the exam format to become familiar with the multiple-choice questions, fill-in-the-blank questions, and the constructed response questions.

- Develop a personal plan for study based on your recognized individual strengths and needs. Use a calendar, a PDA, or a daily schedule to help stay on the planned course of study. Studying should be an enjoyable and motivational task, and the environment used should be comfortable, with study materials easily accessible (paper, pencils, study guide, computer, and so on). Some options that enhance studying include occasionally changing locations in which you study, taking a break, studying with a partner, utilizing background music, and enjoying a favorite beverage or snack.

- Study every day prior to the exam. Review the information studied the day before prior to studying any new material. Use an outline of information, flashcards, or vocabulary lists to support memorization of important facts and concepts. The outcome of this examination is very important for certification, so make studying a priority.

- Take the sample practice test(s) for the specific elementary topic either before or after using the study guide materials. Some examinees take the practice test first to assess their abilities and knowledge. Use the additional information provided in the answer explanations as a component of your study.

- Use the most effective individualized methods and strategies to study and prepare for the Praxis II exams.

# Exam WeekPrep

The day before the exam, do the following:

- Verify the location of the exam center on the ETS website.
- Access the directions for the location of the testing center and determine the amount of time necessary for travel.
- Check the specifics allowed at the testing location you will use, but remember that most testing centers do NOT allow cellphones, Blackberry devices, or other electronic equipment; personal items; backpacks; handbags; or student study materials.
- Print a copy of the admission ticket or authorization voucher.
- Participate in activities that do not distract from the materials studied for the Praxis II exam. The effects of partying and other strenuous activities the day before the exam may be felt on exam day, so avoiding these is recommended.
- Eat well and drink adequate water.
- Set out the items needed (proof of registration, identification, pencils, pens, comfortable clothing, and so on).
- Get a good evening of rest and sleep, and do not stay up late to cram for the exam.

The day of the exam, do the following:

- Awake early to get ready and avoid rushing around.
- Eat a healthy, well-balanced breakfast that includes protein, water, and/or juice.
- Remember to take the important items needed for the exam.
- Arrive 15 to 30 minutes early to the exam location.

# Notes

# Notes

# Notes

# Notes

# Notes

# Notes

# Notes

# Notes

# John Wiley & Sons, Inc.
# End-User License Agreement

**READ THIS.** You should carefully read these terms and conditions before opening the software packet(s) included with this book "Book". This is a license agreement "Agreement" between you and John Wiley & Sons, Inc. "Wiley". By opening the accompanying software packet(s), you acknowledge that you have read and accept the following terms and conditions. If you do not agree and do not want to be bound by such terms and conditions, promptly return the Book and the unopened software packet(s) to the place you obtained them for a full refund.

1. **License Grant.** Wiley grants to you (either an individual or entity) a nonexclusive license to use one copy of the enclosed software program(s) (collectively, the "Software") solely for your own personal or business purposes on a single computer (whether a standard computer or a workstation component of a multi-user network). The Software is in use on a computer when it is loaded into temporary memory (RAM) or installed into permanent memory (hard disk, CD-ROM, or other storage device). Wiley reserves all rights not expressly granted herein.

2. **Ownership.** Wiley is the owner of all right, title, and interest, including copyright, in and to the compilation of the Software recorded on the physical packet included with this Book "Software Media". Copyright to the individual programs recorded on the Software Media is owned by the author or other authorized copyright owner of each program. Ownership of the Software and all proprietary rights relating thereto remain with Wiley and its licensers.

3. **Restrictions on Use and Transfer.**

   (a) You may only (i) make one copy of the Software for backup or archival purposes, or (ii) transfer the Software to a single hard disk, provided that you keep the original for backup or archival purposes. You may not (i) rent or lease the Software, (ii) copy or reproduce the Software through a LAN or other network system or through any computer subscriber system or bulletin-board system, or (iii) modify, adapt, or create derivative works based on the Software.

   (b) You may not reverse engineer, decompile, or disassemble the Software. You may transfer the Software and user documentation on a permanent basis, provided that the transferee agrees to accept the terms and conditions of this Agreement and you retain no copies. If the Software is an update or has been updated, any transfer must include the most recent update and all prior versions.

4. **Restrictions on Use of Individual Programs.** You must follow the individual requirements and restrictions detailed for each individual program on the Software Media. These limitations are also contained in the individual license agreements recorded on the Software Media. These limitations may include a requirement that after using the program for a specified period of time, the user must pay a registration fee or discontinue use. By opening the Software packet(s), you agree to abide by the licenses and restrictions for these individual programs that are detailed on the Software Media. None of the material on this Software Media or listed in this Book may ever be redistributed, in original or modified form, for commercial purposes.

5. **Limited Warranty.**

   (a) Wiley warrants that the Software and Software Media are free from defects in materials and workmanship under normal use for a period of sixty (60) days from the date of purchase of this Book. If Wiley receives notification within the warranty period of defects in materials or workmanship, Wiley will replace the defective Software Media.

   (b) WILEY AND THE AUTHOR(S) OF THE BOOK DISCLAIM ALL OTHER WARRANTIES, EXPRESS OR IMPLIED, INCLUDING WITHOUT LIMITATION IMPLIED WARRANTIES OF MERCHANTABILITY AND FITNESS FOR A PARTICULAR PURPOSE, WITH RESPECT TO THE SOFTWARE, THE PROGRAMS, THE SOURCE CODE CONTAINED THEREIN, AND/OR THE TECHNIQUES DESCRIBED IN THIS BOOK. WILEY DOES NOT WARRANT THAT THE FUNCTIONS CONTAINED IN THE SOFTWARE WILL MEET YOUR REQUIREMENTS OR THAT THE OPERATION OF THE SOFTWARE WILL BE ERROR FREE.

   (c) This limited warranty gives you specific legal rights, and you may have other rights that vary from jurisdiction to jurisdiction.

## 6. Remedies.

**(a)** Wiley's entire liability and your exclusive remedy for defects in materials and workmanship shall be limited to replacement of the Software Media, which may be returned to Wiley with a copy of your receipt at the following address: Software Media Fulfillment Department, Attn.: *CliffsNotes® Praxis II® Elementary Education (0011/5011, 0012, 0014/5014) with CD-ROM,* Second Edition, John Wiley & Sons, Inc., 10475 Crosspoint Blvd., Indianapolis, IN 46256, or call 1-877-762-2974. Please allow four to six weeks for delivery. This Limited Warranty is void if failure of the Software Media has resulted from accident, abuse, or misapplication. Any replacement Software Media will be warranted for the remainder of the original warranty period or thirty (30) days, whichever is longer.

**(b)** In no event shall Wiley or the author be liable for any damages whatsoever (including without limitation damages for loss of business profits, business interruption, loss of business information, or any other pecuniary loss) arising from the use of or inability to use the Book or the Software, even if Wiley has been advised of the possibility of such damages.

**(c)** Because some jurisdictions do not allow the exclusion or limitation of liability for consequential or incidental damages, the above limitation or exclusion may not apply to you.

## 7. U.S. Government Restricted Rights.
Use, duplication, or disclosure of the Software for or on behalf of the United States of America, its agencies and/or instrumentalities "U.S. Government" is subject to restrictions as stated in paragraph (c)(1)(ii) of the Rights in Technical Data and Computer Software clause of DFARS 252.227-7013, or subparagraphs (c) (1) and (2) of the Commercial Computer Software - Restricted Rights clause at FAR 52.227-19, and in similar clauses in the NASA FAR supplement, as applicable.

## 8. General.
This Agreement constitutes the entire understanding of the parties and revokes and supersedes all prior agreements, oral or written, between them and may not be modified or amended except in a writing signed by both parties hereto that specifically refers to this Agreement. This Agreement shall take precedence over any other documents that may be in conflict herewith. If any one or more provisions contained in this Agreement are held by any court or tribunal to be invalid, illegal, or otherwise unenforceable, each and every other provision shall remain in full force and effect.